Macroeconomics

Macroeconomics

an open economy approach

Eric J. Pentecost

Department of Economics
Loughborough University

First published 2000 by
MACMILLAN PRESS LTD
Houndmills, Basingstoke, Hampshire RG21 6XS
and London
Companies and representatives
throughout the world

ISBN 0–333–57329–3 hardcover
ISBN 0–333–57330–7 paperback

A catalogue record for this book is available
from the British Library.

This book is printed on paper suitable for recycling and made from
fully managed and sustained forest sources.

10   9   8   7   6   5   4   3   2   1
09 08 07 06 05 04 03 02 01 00

Printed in Great Britain by
Antony Rowe Ltd
Chippenham, Wiltshire

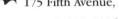
Published in the United States of America by
ST. MARTIN'S PRESS, INC.,
Scholarly and Reference Division
175 Fifth Avenue, New York, N.Y. 10010

ISBN 0–312–23368–X

For Gillian

Contents

Preface

This macroeconomics textbook is aimed at intermediate-level students who have previously completed an introductory economics course and most probably a course in elemantary quantitative methods. There are four main justifications for yet another intermediate-level macroeconomics text.

The first is that none of the current crop of largely US texts deal adequately with the open economy. Rather than including two or three chapters only on the open economy, this book introduces the open economy from the outset. Thus this book is a text on open economy macroeconomics with the more traditional closed economy results derived as special cases. This reflects my concern to teach a macroeconomic principles course that is revelant to the small, open economies of western Europe and especially for the UK. There are a number of features of closed economy macroeconomic models that are especially unappealing in the open economy context. For example, in an open economy the money supply can not be realistically taken as exogenously given when exchange rates are fixed since, except in the unlikely event of complete sterilisation, it will fluctuate with the balance of payments position. Conversely, the implications of a fiscal or monetary policy expansion cannot be considered in isolation from their impact on the external sector and the balance of payments. On the supply side, the aggregate supply curve is not in general vertical in the open economy context unless purchasing power parity (PPP) holds continuously, which implies that international product markets are fully integrated. Since the emprical evidence is strongly aganist short-run PPP it seems reasonable to postulate a positively-sloping aggregate supply curve in the short run.

The second justification for this text is a frustration that the existing stock often present students with a puzzling array of models which seem largely unrelated. This text attempts to provide a more unified treatment of macroeconomics than other modern texts, while at the same time incorporating the latest research findings and a good number of real world issues. The approach is to fully develop the three principal macroeconomics models – the income–expenditure model, the *IS–LM* model and the *AD–AS* model – in ascending order of complexity, demonstrating at each stage the relationship between each model and the next. Recent theoretical developments are added within this three-model framework whenever possible, and the limitations of the specific models are addressed as part of this model continuity.

The third justification for this text is a strong belief that at the intermediate level students should be encouraged to think like economists and be familiar with the use of models as problem-solving devices and not as diagrams to be memorized for examinations! To facilitate this learning process there are clear benefits from starting with the simplest model and building up to the more complex. In this text therefore, and very much against the recent trend, the inherently dynamic issues such as economic growth, business cycles, inflation and expectations adjustment are largely left until the final part of the book when students are hopefully familiar with the basic models. In practice this means starting with comparative static methods and models that examine the goods market (Part II), the financial sector (Part III) and the labour market (Part IV), before finally, in Part V, dynamic methods are used to study the causes of economic growth, business cycles and inflation. In each part of the book the core model is developed to its fullest extent before moving on to the next addition. Thus the most complex models come in Part V, but they are built up gradually, sector by sector, through the rest of the book.

The final motivation for this textbook is that macroeconomics is primarily an empirical science. The use of UK and European data and the application of the models to the UK and western European economic problems are essential if students are to understand and appreciate the subject. Without exception, US texts do not make widespread use of UK or European Union (EU) country data or address European problems. The examples used in this text are based largely, although not exclusively, on the UK economy, but many EU economies have suffered similar problems and have similar economic structures to the UK and so the problems and the models translate to a considerable extent.

While I have tried to keep the analysis as simple as possible, the usual amounts of mathematics are assumed (essentially basic calculus) although these results in most cases can be omitted without impairing the reader's understanding. The analysis is perhaps a little harder in the open economy context and therefore to help keep the analysis as simple as possible assumptions such as perfect capital mobility and perfect foresight are frequently used in the early parts of the text.

The structure of the text allows the book to be used in several different ways. It has been conceived to support a two-semester intermediate macroeconomics course for students majoring in Economics, although not all the chapters are covered. Generally, for this cohort of students, Chapters 2 and 3 are omitted since these topics are covered in the preliminary year. They are included in the book for revision purposes and for other groups of students who have not taken such classes. The book could, however, also be used on various one-semester programmes on macroeconomic models or applied macroeconomics courses. The following are some of the possible ways that the text could be used:

- **A two-semester course in intermediate macroeconomics**
  Chapters 1, 4–19.
- **A one-semester course in applied macroeconomics**
  Chapters 2, 6, 7, 11 plus parts of Chapters 12, 13 and 15 that appertain to unemployment, and part of Chapter 16 on growth-accounting and growth policy.
- **A one-semester course in macroeconomic models**
  Chapters 3–5, 8–10 and 12–14.
- **A one-semester traditional demand-oriented course**
  Chapters 4–11 plus early sections of Chapter 19.

- **A one-semester course on the supply side**
  Chapters 12–18 with a review of the demand side from Chapter 9.

The instructor's guide that goes with the text includes suggested solutions to the end of chapter problems. These are a selection of the exercises that I have used in tutorials for several years; they are a mixture of problem-solving questions and conceptual questions designed to help students familiarise themselves with how the models work. There is no substitute for practicing with the models to enhance understanding. I have also reproduced essay questions which I have used either as examination or term-paper questions.

This book has been derived from my lectures to second-year undergradutates in Economics at Loughborough University since 1990, although only recent cohorts of students will recognise them, as they have developed extensively over recent years. The course was initially based on Mike Artis's *Macroeconomics* (Oxford University Press, 1984), but then moved on to Dornbusch and Fischer, *Macroeconomics* (McGraw-Hill, various editions) when the former became unavailable. William Branson's classic textbook, *Macroeconomic Theory and Policy* has greatly influenced the way I think about macroeconomics and so there may be more than a hint of Branson in this text.

ERIC J. PENTECOST

Acknowledgements

I am grateful to David Greeenaway for initially getting me involved in this project and Stephen Rutt for his extreme patience when the manuscript was delayed and delayed and delayed. Several colleagues at Loughborough have read various parts of the text and noted many errors, most of which I hope have been eliminated. In particular, and without implication, I am grateful to John Presley and Brian Tew, who both provided detailed comments on several different drafts of Chapter 1; to Leigh Drake and Max Hall both of whom spotted a number of errors in my tutorial exercises and corresponding chapters in their tutoring of the course; to Graham Smith (School of Oriental and African Studies, University of London) who provided detailed comments on Chapters 4–11; and to John Sessions (Brunel University) who undertook the same task for Chapters 12–14.

Throughout this project I have enjoyed the support of my family, especially my wife Gillian, who shows patience without bounds. John and Anne, whose rowdiness also knows no bounds, have provided light-hearted moments and without whose love and understanding this book could not have been written.

ERIC. J. PENTECOST

PART I

The Background to the Study of Macroeconomics

CHAPTER 1
The Origins and Development of Macroeconomics

Aims and objectives

- To gain a perspective on modern debates by examining the historical development of Macroeconomics.
- To examine the context and contribution of Keynes's General Theory which was the first formal attempt at a unified treatment of monetary and real analysis to produce macroeconomics.
- To assess recent interpretations of Keynes' work and provide an overview of subsequent schools of thought that form the analytical core of the text.

Introduction

Macroeconomics is concerned with the study of the economy as a whole. That is, it is concerned to explain the determinants of the level of aggregate output, the rate of growth of aggregate output, the general level of prices and the rate of growth of prices (inflation). Macroeconomics as we know it today stems from *The General Theory of Employment, Interest and Money*, by John Maynard Keynes, whose publication in 1936 set out the agenda for macroeconomics. Keynes wrote:

> The division of economics between the theory of value and distribution on the one hand and the theory of money on the other is, I think, a false division. The right dichotomy is, I suggest, between the theory of the individual industry or firm and of the rewards and distribution between different uses of a given quantity of resources on the one hand, and the theory of output and employment as a whole on the other. (Ch. 21, p. 293)

Keynes's distinction between 'the theory of output and employment as a whole' (macroeconomics) and 'the theory of the individual industry or firm', which is now called microeconomics, is primarily to do with whether or not the level of resources should be regarded as variable or taken as given. In microeconomics, the full employment of resources is assumed given, so that microeconomics is concerned with the optimal allocation of resources between alternative uses and the distribution of total product. On the other hand, macroeconomics is concerned with how best to achieve the full utilisation of resources, so that the level of effective demand achieved is commensurate with the fullest possible employment of labour consistent with price level stability.

Macroeconomics is the branch of economics that is policy-orientated, with much of the analysis focused on the way in which macroeconomic variables are affected by government policies. Typical macroeconomic questions are, for example: To what extent can government policies affect the level of output and employment in the economy? To what extent is inflation the result of government policies? Should the government attempt to achieve a target level for the exchange rate or allow the exchange rate between domestic and foreign currencies to be determined largely by market forces? Although macroeconomics has always been policy-orientated, Keynes' influence as an advisor on economic policy reinforced the existing long-standing link between aggregate analysis and statistical data. Thus, more than any other branch of economics, macroeconomics is an empirical science in that the major objectives are to devise theoretical explanations for similar data patterns and to offer guidance to policy-makers.

Although Keynes is the founder of modern macroeconomics, he was by no means the first economist to hypothesise about the determinants of the level of effective demand and rate of growth of employment, output and prices. It is therefore useful in appreciating modern policy debates to understand the origins of some of the concepts and issues in macroeconomics and the methods of analysis used to elucidate these policy problems. Moreover, this historical analysis will demonstrate how the important issues of the day have usually preceded, and to a very large extent determined, the development of macroeconomic theories. To this end, the next section examines the origins of macroeconomics analysis in the seventeenth and eighteenth centuries, up to the early twentieth century, and Keynes' *General Theory*. Sections following then consider the nature of the Keynesian revolution and briefly outline the developments in macroeconomics since the Second World War, that form the basis of the discussion which will be developed in greater detail in the rest of this book.

The development of macroeconomics before Keynes

In studying the development of macroeconomics it is not sufficient just to understand the different policy issues, it is necessary also to appreciate that the social relations that make up society change over time. The subject's development is therefore not only related to the economic issues of the day, but also to the particular social and institutional arrangements. Since the end of the seventeenth century social change has given rise to different models of analysis which reflect both the changing mode of economic organisation and the changing economic issues of the day. Adam Smith (1723–90), writing in the last quarter of the eighteenth century, noted 'The different progress of opulence in different ages and nations has given occasion to two different systems of political economy with regard to enriching the people.' These two systems are 'the system of commerce' or 'mercantile system' and the 'system of agriculture'. It is in these systems where the origins of macroeconomic analysis are to be found.

The origins of macroeconomics

In the seventeenth and eighteenth centuries Britain prospered due to the growth of overseas trade and commerce. This mercantile system spawned a group of diverse pamphleteers that had one clear economic doctrine – an export surplus adds to the wealth of the nation. The Mercantilists, as they became known, advocated and supported policies by which the government could secure and maintain a surplus on the balance of trade. In an era before the system of international finance was highly developed, a country running a balance of payments deficit with the rest of the world – that is, paying more abroad on imports than it had received from the sales of exports – had to make good the shortfall in cash. Thus if the aggregate value of imports exceeded the total value of exports for a country over a period of time, say a year, then gold and silver flowed abroad as payment for the excess of goods and services imported. Thus a trade deficit gave rise to a 'drain of treasure'. This was of concern to the Mercantilists, since they appreciated that a trade deficit reduced the effective demand for domestic output, because the money that flowed abroad boosted foreign incomes while reducing the amount of money to be spent on domestic production. On the other hand, a trade surplus led to an inflow of gold and silver that could be spent on domestically produced goods and services. This analysis led the Mercantilists to advocate protectionist policies to keep out imports.

In a simple economy where money is used only for transactions, it follows that the value of transactions involving goods and services in any one year must be exactly equal to the stock of money multiplied by the number of transactions that each unit of money finances during the year. In symbols: $M^sV = PT$, where M^s is the stock of money, V is the velocity of circulation of each unit of currency, P is the average price level and T is the volume of transactions. Mercantilists, such as Locke (1632–1704), emphasised the effect of M on T; that is, an increase in the money supply from a trade surplus stimulates economic activity by raising the volume of transactions. On the other hand the Mercantilists, while keen to advocate the view that trade surpluses were 'good' because they gave rise to an inflow of gold and silver, were also aware of the notion that more 'money makes goods dearer' (Mun, 1664). Indeed William Petty (1662) – perhaps the first macroeconomist – opposed the indefinite accumulation of bullion, arguing that 'There is a certain measure and due proportion requisite to drive the trade of a Nation, more or less than which would prejudice the same.' Thus Petty seems to acknowledge the point that too much money may reduce trade, presumably by generating inflation which in turn makes domestic goods less competitive on world markets, so reducing the exports of the nation. Richard Cantillon (1680–1734) – the most sophisticated of the Mercantilists – integrated the views of Locke (1694) and Petty by arguing that the effect of an increase in the money supply depended upon the source of the increase. Cantillon (1733) maintained that trade was stimulated if the inflow of gold and silver was derived from a trade surplus, but that prices rise directly without promoting an expansion of output if the source of the increase is due to increased production of gold. This view is not too far removed from modern day monetarist thinking on the cause of inflation, which is attributed to the money supply growing at a faster rate than real output.[1]

The second of Adam Smith's systems of political economy – the system of agriculture – was the system that enriched the French nation in the eighteenth century, and which also led to a major analytical advance in economic analysis. Although the British philosophers offered some insights into the importance of trade and public works in sustaining the level of effective demand for domestic output, they did not develop a coherent body of logical economic analysis. This task was taken up by the Physiocrats who were the first to present a model of the circular flow of income in terms of a system of social classes. France in the eighteenth century was essentially a feudal economy, with the rent of land together with the taxes levied on farmers being the source of funds to support the court, the army and all the arts of civilisation. Rent was taken from the peasants as a share of the crop, and the peasants had to provide their own subsistence and the necessary investment in seed corn and equipment out of the remainder. This gives rise to the Physiocratic view that the land, which yields rent, is the only source of net output.

The leading Physiocrat was François Quesnay (1694–1774) who set out his analysis of the economic system in terms of an abstract system, illustrating the flows of commodities in the process of production and consumption. This *Tableau Economique*, first printed in 1758, was based on the circulation of the blood and resembles the modern input–output table, based on three social classes: landlords, peasants and artisans. At the beginning of each year the peasants own a stock of seed corn from last year's harvest. This feeds them and provides them with input of seed for a year; they cultivate the land and produce a crop which in Quesnay's example is twice the stock they started with. With this they replace the stock that was used up in the process of production, and the surplus or net output they pay to the landlords as rent. The landlord consumes part directly and the rest he uses to buy products from the artisans, such as

---

[1] Not only did the Mercantilists instigate the modern quantity theory of inflation, but it is interesting that the last Mercantilist, Sir James Steuart (1712–80), in his *An Inquiry into the Principles of Political Economy* (1767) argued the case for public expenditure to create employment. Steuart argues, 'The more a work is useful after it is done, so much the better; because it may then have the effect of giving bread to those who have built it … Expensive public works, are therefore a mean of giving bread to the poor, and of advancing industry, without hurting the simplicity of manners (p. 387).

clothes, tools and so on. The artisans are assumed to own their productive equipment – looms, forges and so forth, and the revenues they receive for their manufactures are used to buy raw materials, replace worn-out machinery and to feed themselves. What they receive is just equal to the value of their output. They do not contribute to the surplus. Therefore the surplus comes only from the land and accrues to the peasants.

Two policy prescriptions were derived from this analysis. First, it was wrong for the government to tax the peasants, as this would deplete the stock that is necessary for them to consume in the course of reproducing the surplus. Secondly, that it was desirable to improve methods of cultivation to raise the ratio of surplus to stock, since by raising the net product, the demand for the output of the artisans and the wealth of the nation in general would be increased. The importance of the analysis here is that it was the first attempt at the development of the circulation flow of income in modern macroeconomics.

Classical political economy

The growing importance of manufacturing industry soon made the Physiocratic vision obsolete, but their successors the Classical School, took over the idea of an economic mechanism based on three social classes to provide an analysis of the dynamics of the new industrialising society. Adam Smith and David Ricardo (1772–1823) transformed Quesnay's original social classes into landlords, capitalists and workers. The consumption of the workers was mere subsistence level, the function of the capitalist was to accumulate, and the consumption of the landlords was a deduction from the surplus available for accumulation. The distribution of the annual product between these three social classes is most important since it is this that determines whether

> its ordinary or average value ... annually increase, or decrease or continue the same from one year to another. (Smith [1961], *Wealth of Nations*, ch. 11, p. 270)

Adam Smith (1776) argued very much in favour of the capitalist who by pursuing his own self- interest would secure a larger share of income and lead a drive towards economic growth. Smith in a much cited phrase says that:

> It is not from the benevolence of the butcher, the brewer or the baker that we expect our dinner, but from their regard to their own self-interest. We address ourselves, not to their humanity but to their self-love and never talk to them of our necessities but of their advantages. (Smith [1961], Book 1, ch. 11, p. 18)

The 'self interest' of Smith was that of the traders and the employers of labour. The self-interest of the workers was not considered. For Smith, wages were part of the cost of production; the wealth of the nation did not include the consumption of workers, only the surplus of production over costs, for the surplus could be reinvested to expand output in the future. It was, however, Ricardo who developed the most sophisticated dynamic theory of distribution and economic growth based on Quesnay's transformed three classes.

Ricardo (1817) argued that workers were paid subsistence wages that could not be reduced. Therefore, as society grew, capitalist farmers would take more land into cultivation. As the extra land brought into production would be less fertile than the previous land, it would not be so profitable. At the same time the landlords would be able to demand higher rents as land became more scarce. Thus the capitalists would suffer a falling rate of profit, squeezed on the one side by the ever-more demanding landlords and by the rising level of wages for the workers who were also in increased demand, or, at the very best, whose subsistence wages could not be reduced. The falling rate of profit would lead to stagnation and an end to economic growth. In this view of the growth process one class loses out (the capitalists) at the expense of another (the landowners), despite the capitalist class being the principal generators of wealth. This analysis of the emerging capitalist system led Ricardo to attack the Corn Laws that were protecting the interests of the landlords by preventing the import of cheap grain from continental Europe. Ricardo argued that if imports of corn were allowed, then the price of corn would be reduced. The less fertile land would then go out of cultivation, rents would fall and the rate of profit would rise as a consequence. A rise in the rate of profit would encourage the capitalist farmers to the detriment of the landlords, but since farmers were the only source of surplus and accumulation economic growth would be enhanced.

Malthus (1766–1834), on the other hand, in an attempt to justify the unproductive labour of landlords, suggested that continual accumulation by the capitalist farmers may prove to be self-defeating, in that it would lead to excess production which could not be sold due to a lack of demand. Malthus argued that unproductive labour – that is the landlord class – is necessary if demand in the economy was to be sufficient to buy back all the output produced. For Malthus, the attempt of the capitalist to accumulate results in a reduction in the landlord's unproductive consumption. A fall in consumption implies a fall in the price of output such that capitalists find their profits reduced with increased pressure to curtail production. In short, a reduction in unproductive consumption could result in a lack of effective demand. Only by slowing down the rate of capital accumulation could the trend towards economic stagnation be avoided.

Ricardo dismissed Malthus's argument by invoking Say's Law of markets. Say's Law can be crudely expressed as 'supply creates its own demand'. Say (1767–1832) argued that:

> In reality we do not buy articles of consumption with money, the circulating medium with which we pay for them. We must in the first instance have bought this money itself by the sale of our produce. (Letters to Malthus, p. 2)

Say believed that in the long run there is a tendency toward equality of aggregate supply and aggregate demand, and thus a general over-supply or glut of commodities is impossible. That is to say, there could be no lack of effective demand.

The reason for this is that the act of production itself creates incomes for the factors of production that these same factors then spend on other production. Say had in mind a general equilibrium setting where the demand for each producer's output depends upon the supply (where incomes are created) of every other producer. The 'correct' output of any producer makes no sense until it is related to what every other producer is doing. A general glut has no meaning since aggregate supply and aggregate demand depend upon each other. Although an oversupply of goods in the aggregate is not possible, it is still possible, however, that a glut could occur in any single market. An over-supply in one market simply leads to a fall in the price of the commodity, but this is the signal by which market economies reallocate resources to the production of another good. Thus an over-supply in one market is just an under-supply in another and is eliminated by a fall in the relative price of the commodity in excess supply.

In the early nineteenth century, when the predominant industrial structure was the cottage industry, where the owner, producer and consumer were essentially the same person, Say's Law had intuitive appeal. The capitalist has no income to buy the output of his neighbour until he had first sold some of his output. The outcome of the debate between Malthus and Ricardo was a victory for Ricardo and the almost universal adoption of Say's Law by economists working in the classical liberal tradition, including John Stuart Mill (1806–1873) whose *Principles of Political Economy* (1848) became the undisputed bible for economists up until 1900.

At the same time as J.S. Mill, Karl Marx (1818–83) challenged the liberal interpretation of classical political economy. Marx accepted the class basis of Ricardo's analysis, but argued that capitalism contained the seeds of its own destruction. For Marx, like Ricardo, it was the capitalist class who received the profits from investment and who by continual accumulation generated economic growth. Marx, however, argued that although the capitalists received the profits it was the industrial workers – the proletariat – who produced it. Whereas the Physiocrats saw the land as the only factor of production capable of producing a surplus, Marx saw labour as the only source of surplus. Because the final value of output is greater than the raw material cost and the only addition to the raw material inputs is the time and effort of the labourers, then the extra value produced must be due to labour. The labourers may use machines to facilitate production, but since the machines are man-made then they too are due to the skills and effort of labour in a previous period, and hence their contribution to final output is also really a payment due to labour. Thus for Marx the origin of profit is labour and the proletariat are exploited by the capitalists.

In Marx's dynamic system competition forces the capitalists to invest profits in labour-saving machinery for if they do not do this, then their efficiency falls and they are forced out of business. If labour-saving machines are installed, there will be a fall in employment and a rise in unemployment. As unemployment rises, wages (if not at subsistence level) will fall, or else the workers will be threatened with redundancy to be replaced by some of the 'reserve army' of the unemployed. Marx, however, also believed that a fall in employment meant a fall in profits, because the value of what is produced depends on the skill and the man-hours involved in production. The falling rate of profit leads some capitalists to go bankrupt and join the ranks of the workers. The fewer capitalists who remain become richer, while the workers become more numerous and poorer. This process continues until most of the economy's wealth is concentrated in but a few hands. At this point, claims Marx, the workers, who are the overwhelming majority of the population, revolt and overthrow the political and economic structure called capitalism, which is replaced with the next social structure – socialism. In the colourful language of Marx (1867):

> Centralisation of the means of production and socialisation of labour at last reach a point where they become incompatible with their capitalist integument. Thus integument is burst asunder. The knell of capital private property sounds. The expropriators are expropriated. (*Capital*, Vol. 1, p. 763)

The novelty in Marx was perhaps not so much in his economic thinking, but in his political and social extension of the classical model of economic growth.

In Marx's reinterpretation of the classical system, however, it is clear that he rejected Say's Law that dominated the orthodox literature until Keynes. Once Say's Law is rejected then the case for gluts or a lack of effective demand is reopened. Marx's rejection of Say's Law is clear:

> Nothing can be more childish than the dogma, that because every sale is a purchase, and every purchase a sale, therefore the circulation of commodities necessarily implies an equilibrium of sales and purchases ... No one can sell unless some one else purchases. But no one is forthwith bound to purchase, because he has just sold. (*Capital*, Vol. 1, p. 87)

Whether Marx had an underconsumption theory of the economy's dynamics is less clear. In his analysis the capitalist's drive for accumulation means that more and more surplus value is diverted to investment spending while the proportion devoted to consumption diminishes. Thus over time the growth of consumption falls relative to the growth of the capital goods industries. The output of the capital goods industries is not needed in the consumption goods industries because consumption is declining. Clearly this situation cannot continue and a crisis results. The lack of demand is caused by the distribution of income between capitalists and workers and the consequent overproduction of goods. Workers are needed as consumers but their wages are held down and unemployment allowed to rise; the realisation of surplus value is thwarted by the limited resources of the very groups who are required to purchase the output. Marx writes:

> The ultimate reason for all real crises always remains the poverty and restricted-consumption of the masses as opposed to the drive of capitalist production to develop the productive forces as though only the absolute consuming power of society constituted their limit. (*Capital*, Vol. 3, p. 484)

These comments on the failure of consumption to keep pace with growing productive capacity – a lack of effective demand – help identify Marx as a forerunner of Keynes.

The continental and neo-classical economists

Despite the contributions of Malthus and Marx, for nearly a hundred years the notion of supply creating its demand dominated economic thinking. With the neo-classical revolution of the 1870s the issues of accumulation, class conflict and growth were largely displaced by static supply and demand analysis for individual factors of production or products, and the subject area of macroeconomics largely disappeared from the forefront of mainstream economic theory in England. There was, however, growing evidence by the mid-nineteenth century, as Marx noted, that the capitalist system exhibited cycles in economic activity that became known as trade or business cycles. These cycles seemed to be a feature of an industrial society and had the effect of making the distinction between being unemployed and employed more important. Prior to the mid-nineteenth century Britain was a semi-agricultural society where everyone who wanted to work did work and widespread underemployment, rather than unemployment, was a characteristic feature of the economy.

This observed cyclical phenomenon stimulated a new branch of macroeconomics, which developed wholly independently of the debate on gluts between Malthus and Ricardo and did not challenge Say's Law, because it was concerned with the existence of short-run, cyclical fluctuations and not the automatic re-attainment of long-run equilibrium. Clement Jugular (1819–1905) was first to establish the existence of business cycles by collecting time-series data on prices, interest rates and central bank balances. Having discovered a ten-year cycle from his data he developed a morphology of the cycle in terms of phases: upgrade, explosion and liquidation.

The early theories of the causes of business cycles emphasised the role of money. Lord Overstone (1857) argued that credit expansions lead to rises in prices, which in turn lead to a rise in interest rates in order to contract bank lending. For J.S. Mill the chief cause of depression was a lack of confidence, largely the aftermath of reckless inflation of credit. Marshall (1923) and Pigou (1927) argued that the start of an upswing is usually due to some factor that changes business expectations of profit. As new projects are taken on they may be financed by an expansion of monetary policy. The banking system in this model partly determines the stock of money by varying the level of lending with the state of profit expectations. The process of a transfer of income to entrepreneurs occurs and some fixed income earners may even reduce their money holdings as prices start to rise, in an effort to maintain their levels of consumption. As the upswing progresses, speculators determine the pace by buying goods on credit to resell quickly. Eventually, the inevitable downturn begins. There are a number of possible causes, but the cessation of the monetary expansion is usually top of the list, as banks become nervous about further extending credit.

On the continent, around the turn of the century, systematic work on business cycles began to appear in which a fundamental maladjustment between savings and investment is responsible for the business cycle, rather than an overexpansion of bank credit. Tugan-Baranowsky (1901), Spiethoff (1925) and Aftalion (1927) all made valuable contributions to this literature, but the most sophisticated example of this strand of the literature was due to Hayek (1931), who drew on Bohm-Bawerk's theory of the length of the production process and Wicksell's concept of the natural rate of interest.

Hayek argues that interest rates below the natural rate encourage investment in capital goods production forcing up the prices of capital goods. Production is moved away from consumption goods to capital goods to meet this higher demand. Since labour is a complementary factor of production, employment and wages also rise as the boom phase of the cycle takes hold. Higher wages, of course, generate a rising demand for consumption goods and prices of consumption goods also begin to rise. The rise in consumption goods prices, however, begins a reversal of the direction of resources away from capital goods to consumption goods production. Generally higher levels of investment put upward pressure on interest rates, and as interest rates rise the demand for capital goods – with a long production period – decline in favour of consumption goods that have a much shorter production period. This is the start of the slump, which is intensified by the fact that some of the capital goods are industry-specific, and hence become useless and workers are made redundant. The critical element in the movement from boom to slump is the switch from capital goods to consumption goods production.

For continental economists, business cycle theory was no longer a matter of mere disturbances to credit and confidence, but something much more fundamental relating to the dynamic role of investment, the relation between savings and investment, the innovation process, the time lags involved in the use of fixed capital, and the principle of effective demand. Keynes, however, does not directly refer to this line of analysis in the *General Theory*, although he is critical of Hayek's view of the cycle which proposed an automatic adjustment mechanism by which the economy automatically reverted from recession to expansion. Instead, the focus of Keynes attack on neo-classical economics was his attack on Pigou, who discounted the idea of autonomous investment affecting demand and on whom the continental investment analysis had made no impact at all. Pigou viewed the macroeconomic system as smoothly adjusting and tending automatically to full employment. He viewed the recurring short-run fluctuations to aggregate demand as amplified because wage rates were not sufficiently plastic. The more rigid wages are, the more employment will fluctuate. Pigou says: 'if the wage rate is perfectly plastic, the alteration in the quantity of labour at work will be nil' (Pigou, 1927, *Industrial Fluctuations*, p. 176). This view was repeated in his *Theory of Unemployment* (1933). Frictional maladjustments alone account for the failure to fully utilise the available productive power. Pigou entertained no inadequacy of neo-classical theory.

Pigou does not, however, refer explicitly to Say's Law. The reason, as suggested by Hansen (1953), is simply that Say's Law was cast in terms of a society that had largely passed away – a society in which most producers were typically self-employed individual proprietors, whether peasant farmers or master craftsmen. In such a society the producer sold his product, not his labour. The greater the number of producers the greater the size of the market. Products were exchanged against products; supply created its own demand. This statement did not fit with the economy of the 1920s or 1930s, any more than it does with today's society. The ownership of the means of production had become divorced from control as joint- stock companies emerged as the principal form of industrial organisation. For Pigou the problem related to the aggregate demand for labour. Pigou's version of Say's Law therefore ran in terms of the tendency for the economy, under free competition, to provide full employment in the labour market. Pigou concluded that:

> …the state of demand for labour, as distinguished from changes in that state, is irrelevant to employment, because wage rates adjust themselves in such a manner that different states of demand, once established, tend to be associated with similar average rates of unemployment. This implies that, from a long-period point of view, the real wage-rates for which people stipulate, so far from being independent of the demand function, are a function of that function in a very special way… The implication is that such unemployment as exists at any time is due wholly to the fact that changes in demand conditions are continually taking place and that frictional resistances prevent the appropriate wages adjustment from being made instantaneously. (*Theory of Unemployment*, 1933, p. 252)

Thus whatever the level of demand there will always be, via wage adjustment, a tendency towards full employment. It was this theory of automatic adjustment, dominant in the current orthodoxy in the 1930s, that Keynes attacked in his *General Theory*.

The Keynesian revolution

In his *General Theory of Employment, Interest and Money*, Keynes set out to attack the notion that the economy had an automatic tendency towards full employment. The motivation for this assault was based on empirical observation – the observation being that of persistent mass unemployment during the great depression of the interwar period. This was due, according to Keynes, to a lack of effective demand; that is, an excess supply of commodities or a glut – in the words of Malthus – with no automatic tendency for full employment to be re-established.

Keynes' analysis stemmed from the point that savings and investment decisions were divorced in practice. Production and investment decisions were made by managers, whose decisions were based on what they perceived to be the future prospects for their business. If they were pessimistic in the case of a slump they would hold back new investment which would lead to a further decline in demand as the capital goods firms supplying industries saw their orders decline. Although higher investment demand would bring about greater prosperity, no individual businessman would be prepared to risk investment because of the uncertainty of the future level of demand. Hence the slump would persist as pessimistic business expectations become self-fulfilling.

Moreover, Keynes also denied that the rate of interest would move to equate savings and investment. Because interest rates were less than half of 1 per cent in the 1930s, Keynes believed they were unable to fall any further, and hence unable to clear the market for savings and investment. Hence there prevailed an excess supply of savings. Businessmen would, however, rather seek to hold idle money balances than invest in potentially loss-making extra capacity. Thus Keynes developed a new motive for holding money – the asset demand for money – because of the uncertainty attached to physical investment.

The theory of the price level is another area of difference between Keynes and his predecessors. Keynes believed that prices were determined by marginal prime costs, but that the main constituent of marginal prime costs were money wages. Real wages were determined in the short run by diminishing marginal productivity, since as demand rises (falls) prices rise (falls) which has the effect of reducing (raising) real wage rates. In some respects this was an acknowledgement that in a modern industrial economy the general level of prices depends in part on the level of money wage rates. At the time it also showed that cutting wages is not a remedy for unemployment because it would cause demand to fall and hence prices to fall more or less in proportion to the reduction in costs.

The change brought about by the Keynesian revolution was to focus on the short-run problems and not the long run when, to quote Keynes' famous dictum, 'we are all dead'. Secondly, the old dichotomy between 'money' and the real economy was broken down. The monetary system is seen as part of the operation of the economy as a whole, which has an important influence on interest rates, but a more indirect link to the level of prices. Finally, and most important, there is no mechanism to guarantee continuous full employment when the private sector is left to its own devices, but it is possible by means of government policy to control, or at least to mitigate, fluctuations in economic activity. This was the most important message of the *General Theory*. Keynes was, however, perfectly willing to let the price mechanism determine the efficient allocation of resources once full employment had been achieved, and did not wish to see or advocate a complex system of microeconomic controls.

In the last fifty years this Keynesian orthodoxy has itself come under threat and reasserted itself, as the problem of persistent unemployment first disappeared and then reappeared. These developments make up the most part of this book, but before turning to a detailed examination of these ideas an overview of the participating schools of thought will be useful. **Figure 1.1** shows a schematic outline of these schools of thought, which will serve as a route map through the next section.

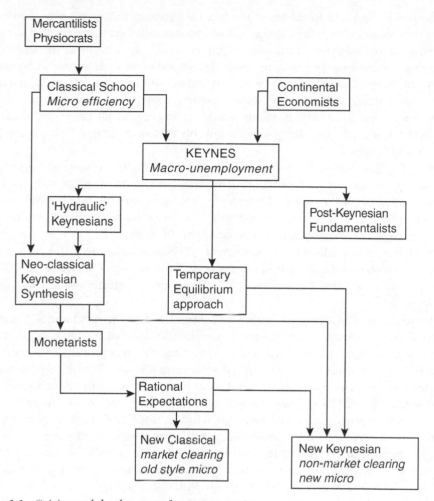

Figure 1.1 *Origins and development of macroeconomics*

Developments since Keynes

In the early postwar years the *General Theory* set out the direction for macroeconomics. Much of the essence was in the Beveridge Report on *Full Employment in a Free Society* (1944), which argued for macroeconomic policy to be geared towards maintaining the level of effective demand to give a level of output consistent with full employment. Advances in technology that transformed the nature of economics helped such policies. National income accounting methods meant that after the Second World War, for the first time economists could obtain access to macroeconomic data on output, employment and prices, in addition to the traditional data on interest rates and measures of the money supply. Moreover, the methods devised to compute national income were based on the aggregate quantities of consumption, investment and government spending suggested by Keynes. In addition to data there soon followed an expansion in computer power that enabled economists to formally test some of the hypotheses suggested by Keynes, in a more rigorous and robust fashion unavailable to previous generations by applying newly-developed econometric methods. Finally, the wars themselves had led to a rise in public spending which legitimised the role of the state, and gave the state a greater role in the economy and hence greater leverage to affect aggregate demand. Yet despite all these technical and political advantages, the Keynesian revolution was soon under threat from both within and without.

Like all great books, the *General Theory* was in parts ambiguous which gave rise to questions of interpretation. The standard interpretation due to Hicks (1937), encapsulated in the *IS–LM* model, although overwhelmingly predominant and examined at length in this text, was not universally accepted. There were two principal contending interpretations. The first, from within Cambridge and dubbed 'fundamentalist' by Coddington (1976), emphasised the importance Keynes attached to the role of uncertainty, and the second – the general disequilibrium theorists – emphasised the role of quantity constraints and non-clearing markets.

The fundamentalist or post-Keynesian school disliked the mechanistic nature of Hicks' *IS–LM* interpretation because it ignores the issue of unstable expectations and uncertainty. The post-Keynesians argue that the recognition of uncertainty undermines the traditional concept of static equilibrium. This interpretation of Keynes has developed along two lines. The first stems directly from Keynes and argues that unstable expectations which lead to fluctuations in business confidence and impinge on investment demand render the market economy an extremely imperfect tool for maintaining full employment, and suggest a reason for government intervention. In a world of uncertainty, which follows as a consequence of unstable expectations, time takes on a new importance in that it is non-reversible such that decisions taken today cannot be reversed tomorrow. This implies that the focus on neo-classical static equilibrium situations, as in Hicks' interpretation, is both misleading and irrelevant. The existence of uncertainty also leads to the demand for liquidity and gives rise to the role of hoarding as a means of generating deficient demand conditions.

The second strand of post-Keynesian thought is derived from the work of Robinson (1933) on imperfect competition, and Kalecki (1939) on mark-up pricing and the degree of monopoly power, rather than from Keynes. This branch of post-Keynesian theory can therefore deal with multinational corporations' pricing policies in product markets and trade-union wage-bargaining behaviour in the labour market. To a very large extent the acceptance of imperfectly competitive behaviour was simply an acknowledgement that the world had changed, based on empirical evidence. Indeed, Tew (1999) argues that by the time of his 1937 paper in the *Economic Journal*, Keynes had already moved his position significantly towards Kalecki's theory of pricing. This second strand of post-Keynesian thought, although a long time in the background, has reemerged in the 1980s as one of the key elements in the so-called New Keynesian economics.

The second challenge from within came in the late 1960s with the work of Clower (1965) and Leijonhufvud (1968). Clower argued that the principal difference between the *General Theory* and neo-classical general equilibrium theory was about non-clearing markets; that is, about the analysis of markets in disequilibrium. In general equilibrium analysis all markets clear and no trades take place at disequilibrium prices. It is as if there is a fictional auctioneer who calls out various prices, to which agents respond by offering to buy or sell, and who then changes prices taking into account the various *ex ante* excess demands, until a price vector is established at which all markets are cleared. Then, and only then, are agents allow to trade. All markets are in equilibrium and hence all decisions to buy and sell can be affected. Clower argued that Keynes effectively removed the auctioneer. In this situation agents trade at false prices – that is non-market clearing prices. In the short run disequilibrium prices may prevail with adjustment being thrown onto quantity changes. Such false trading will effect the income of some of the market participants and in turn generate feedback effects upon other markets. Some traders will experience a fall in income from what they would have expected to have earned had no false trading taken place, and hence they will react by reducing their demands in alternative markets. The existence of false trading in one market may so constrain income as to impose income constraints in alternative markets, which generate further income constraints. The problem with this school of thought is that it had no theory of how prices are determined or, more importantly how prices change. This made it particularly vulnerable when global inflation emerged as the most pressing macroeconomic problem in the early 1970s.

The challenges from within both questioned the role of markets due to uncertainty or imperfect competition on the one hand, or to the lack of information on the other. The challenge from without came from both theory and from facts. The *General Theory* did not have a fully developed theory of the price level, with prices based on marginal prime costs which were essentially driven money wages. This made it particularly vulnerable to attack when inflation rose in all the major economies in the late 1960s. Despite the seminal work of Phillips (1958), who had attempted to graft onto the *General Theory* a theory of wage inflation, the notion of demand management fell into disrepute as government demand management came to be blamed for rising inflation. The rise of inflation spurred a theoretical reaction to the Keynesian orthodoxy that became known as *monetarism*. Monetarism was based on a restatement of the classical quantity theory of money by Friedman (1956) and his supporters at the University of Chicago, who argued that an excess growth of the money supply was the only cause of inflation. Moreover since the money supply was assumed to be under the control of the authorities, the government, and in particular the Keynesian-inspired demand-management policies pursued by the government, were to blame for the rise in inflation. Although these arguments were hotly disputed, see for example the debate between Friedman (1972) and Tobin (1972b) in the *Journal of Political Economy* of the same year, the monetarist message dented Keynesian confidence in demand-management policies.

A second and even larger theoretical challenge emerged in the mid-1970s. Whereas the monetarists conceded that Keynes' view might be valid in the short run, but would lead to inflation in the longer run, the introduction of the *rational expectations hypothesis* into macroeconomics denied even the short-run effectiveness of demand-management policy and led to strongly anti-interventionist policies being advocated. There were two aspects to the rational expectations revolution. First, it was based on a microeconomic analysis of markets; it sought to reconcile macroeconomic analysis with the microeconomic foundations. This led to a microeconomic analysis of markets which, it was assumed, could be aggregated to give a macroeconomic market. Although it is far from clear that such an aggregation procedure is robust, this led to the presumption that prices move freely to clear all markets – an assumption in complete contrast to Keynes and the post-Keynesians. The second aspect of the rational expectations hypothesis is that agents are assumed to have complete information about the structural model and to use it to forecast the future level of prices and output. In this case policy is wholly ineffective even in the short run, since agents are able to second guess the policy-making authorities' actions and devise their optimal response which may work to offset these actions.

Thus this view of economic policy is even more strongly anti-interventionist than the *laissez-faire* philosophy of the classical school. This school was dubbed the *New Classical School*. The New Classical School while adopting Friedman's long-run monetary framework grafted on the assumption of rational expectations. This essentially means that as agents knew the structural model underlying the decision-making process and used this model to make predictions, which were on average correct, then the authorities could not use a short-run stabilisation policy, since agents with full information would act so as to anticipate and frustrate such actions. Thus Friedman's idea that in the long run any attempt to expand demand would only result in higher prices became transformed into the notion that any action announced by the authorities would be completely offset in the short run by the actions of the private sector.

In this environment, government policy can only work if private sector agents are in some way deceived or surprised. This can happen if the government has an informational advantage over the private sector or, more sinisterly, if the government lies about its intentions. In either case, however, the notion of a systematic, discretionary macroeconomic policy is ruled out. The response to this policy-ineffectiveness result was slow to come about. Eventually, however, the so-called New Keynesians emerged and effectively restored short-run policy effectiveness by the introduction of microeconomic rigidities into the macroeconomic system. This emergence of the New Keynesian school was prompted by the casual observation that the New Classical model was not predicting observed phenomena. The late 1970s and early 1980s saw an unprecedented rise in unemployment, partly as a result of the fight against inflation using essentially classical remedies. Thus once again real world events gave an additional impetus to the development of macroeconomic analysis. The New Keynesian school of thought is, however, very diverse and many kinds of rigidities have been suggested, especially in the context of the labour market. Some commonly used examples are wage contracts, which lock workers into contracts which have to be honoured despite changing economic circumstances, or imperfect competition in product markets which mean that suppliers are slow to adjust prices in the presence of price shocks.

It is interesting to note that at the beginning of the twenty-first century Keynesian economists are still concerned with price rigidities and market failure, and the Classicists and neo-Classicals continue to focus their analysis on fully-flexible prices and clearing markets. Although this point of difference seems to have moved little, the types of models and methods of analysis are virtually unrecognisable from those at the start of the nineteenth century.

Summary

- Macroeconomics has always been concerned with the quantity of money in circulation, the flow of income around the economy and the distribution of this income between different social groups.
- Keynes attempted to bring together monetary analysis and real analysis in an attempt to build an integrated system in which money was not neutral in its effect on the real economy.
- The Keynesian revolution has been variously interpreted as the economics of disequilibrium, the economics of uncertainty and imperfect competition, and as a general equilibrium system.
- Recent work in macroeconomics has emphasised the importance of expectations, the need for rigorous microeconomic foundations, but also, increasingly, of the role of imperfect competition.

Suggested further reading

Schumpeter (1952) and Blaug (1968) are two seminal texts on the history of economic thought, while Backhouse (1985) provides an excellent overview of economic analysis from Adam Smith. Readers interested in the more recent debates should consult Coddington (1982) and Hoover (1985), both of which include review articles previously published in the *Journal of Economic Literature*. Hansen (1952) contains an excellent account of the context of the *General Theory* and Shaw (1988) provides an excellent discussion of the more recent debates in macroeconomics. The disequilibrium approach is reviewed succinctly in Hines (1971), whereas Stoneman (1979) and Malinvaud (1977) offer formal models. The Post-Keynesian interpretation is reviewed in Shapiro (1977). The New Classical approach to macroeconomics is found in Minford and Peel (1983) and Attfield *et al*. (1991). Two good surveys of the New Keynesian Economics are Gordon (1990) and Greenwald and Stiglitz (1993).

Essay titles

1. What is the importance of the Physiocrats in the development of macroeconomic analysis?
2. 'Classical Economics was built upon Say's Law of Markets. Therefore to question the notion of automatic full employment Keynes had to destroy Say's Law.' Discuss.
3. Explain the origin and meaning of surplus value in Marx's model. In what sense might the notion of surplus value be considered a theory of exploitation?
4. Examine the role of the underconsumption theories in the development of macroeconomic thinking.
5. To what extent have the objectives and method of analysis of macroeconomics changed over the past 200 years?

CHAPTER 2
The Social Accounting Framework for Macroeconomic Analysis

Aims and objectives

- To review the circular flow of income and the implied income accounting framework which underlies macroeconomics, and to consider the interdependence between the three principal macroeconomic markets – those for goods and services, labour and financial assets.
- To review the methodology of the measurement of the level of national income, consumption, investment, net exports, the price level, rates of unemployment and the components of the money supply and balance of payments.
- To undertake a preliminary analysis of the foreign exchange market and balance of payments.

Introduction

One area of macroeconomics where Keynes has had a permanent effect is with the development of the system of national income accounting. Indeed Hicks (1992) has argued that '... the Keynesian *method* ... depends on the table of "social accounts", or of "National Income and Expenditure"' (p. 3). Although Hicks never fully develops this point there are several plausible interpretations. The first is that by aggregating 'like' variables together and separating 'unlike' variables the infinitely large number of transactions that take place in the economy as a whole can be reduced to a small number of aggregate variables. This approach underlies Keynes' *General Theory* and has formed the basis of macroeconomic analysis ever since. On the product side of the accounts, for example, this means that aggregation is undertaken by that sector of the economy which does the spending. Thus households' spending is aggregated together and called consumption, because it is primarily determined by the aggregate levels of income and wealth. Expenditure by businesses is called investment and is related to the cost of capital, profits and expectations about future demand. On the other hand, expenditure by the government sector is largely determined by political factors and only distantly related to consumer and business decisions.

A second point about the importance of social accounting to the Keynesian method is that Hicks perceives the Keynesian method to be dynamic. Thinking about how to measure goods and services produced, over a particular interval of time, helps to bring an appreciation of the inherent dynamics of the economy. At the simplest level many currently produced goods and services are not consumed, but are used to produce goods in many *future* periods. Therefore to an extent current production is influenced both by the inherited capital stock and by expectations about future levels of demand. Thus the dynamics of the production process are also an essential part of the Keynesian method.

The system of social accounts, although a vital part of the method of macroeconomics, is also an indispensable source of data. These accounts measure a large number of important aggregate macroeconomic variables, such as the level of output, the general level of prices, private consumption, investment and public expenditure. The subtleties involved in the measurement of these variables are numerous and inherently difficult to explain in detail. In this chapter, therefore, only a brief sketch of the basic framework will be given with specific emphasis on the variables and linkages between variables that will be frequently referred to in later chapters of this book. The next section develops a schematic framework based on the circular flow of income, which can be used to develop a few basic principles that underlie the accounts. In the following sections the methods of computing gross domestic product (GDP) and aggregate price level deflators are discussed, and the principal flows in the labour market including the measurement of participation and unemployment rates are examined. Finally, the statistical relationship between the financial side of the economy is introduced by considering the linkage between the goods market and the financial sector, including the balance of payments, the money supply and the government financing constraint.

The social framework for national income accounts

As the Physiocrats demonstrated 250 years ago, in order to understand the flows of income around the economy it is necessary to divide the economy into broad groups. Whereas the Physiocrats used social classes – landlords, peasants and artisans – the postwar development of national income accounting is based on two functional groupings – households and firms. Households and firms interact in two sets of markets: the factor markets, where the factors of production, land, labour and capital are exchanged; and the goods markets where final products are bought and sold.

To begin to understand the basic structure of the national income accounts assume that the economy is closed to foreign trade and that there is no government sector. The private sector is then divided into two sectors called households and firms, as shown schematically in **Figure 2.1.** In this circular flow of income and expenditure all the firms' outputs are purchased by households and all household factor services are purchased by firms. In the absence of any external force the same equilibrium level of income would continue indefinitely.

In more detail, on the right-hand side of the diagram the broken line represents the flow of factor services; that is land, labour and capital used in the production

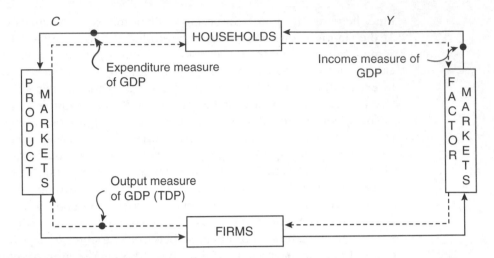

Figure 2.1   *The circular flow of income*

process. The solid line flowing in the opposite direction, from firms to households, is the monetary payments received by these factors of production for their services provided in the production process. This is called income, Y. The right-hand side of **Figure 2.1** therefore measures the income accruing to the factors of production as a result of the numerous transactions in the *factor markets*. On the left-hand side the broken line represents the flow of final goods and services produced by firms over the period of the accounts; this is called output or total domestic product, TDP. The solid line denotes households' expenditure on the output produced which we can call consumption, C. The left-hand side of the figure therefore measures the total output of the economy by the expenditure on production as a result of exchanges in the *product markets*. By definition, the flows on each side of the diagram must be equal. Therefore the incomes received by households from providing factor services equals the expenditure by households on final output, that is: total output=total income=total expenditure, or in this simple model $TDP=Y=C$.

To complicate the model suppose that households do not spend all of their income. That is, they save some of their income. Savings, S, are therefore defined to equal $Y-C$. Furthermore, assume that some of the goods and services produced by the firms are not purchased by households, but by other firms. These expenditures by firms are likely to be on capital goods, required to extend or enhance production facilities in the future. These expenditures by firms are called investment, I. The total value of expenditure in the economy is now expenditure by households plus expenditures by firms; that is $C+I$. For there to be equality between output and income requires that $C+S=C+I$ or $S=I$. The method of income accounting ensures that savings always equals investment *ex post*, because any unsold goods are classed as additions to stock which are included as part of firms' investment. Thus all income is attributable to $C+I$ and so it follows that $S=I$.

It is straightforward to add further sectors to this model of the circular of income. In addition to the demands from households and firms, there will be a demand from the government and a demand from overseas firms and households for the output of the domestic economy. Thus the total demand for domestic output (called total final expenditure, *TFE*) can be represented as $C+I+G+X$, where G is the demand from government for both consumption and capital goods and X is the demand from foreign companies, households and government for a part of the domestic output. There will, of course, also be some goods produced in foreign markets that domestic resident households and firms may wish to buy. Expenditure by domestic residents on foreign production is called imports, and denoted as M. Since these imports represent expenditure by domestic residents that is not on domestic production they must be subtracted from *TFE* to get the gross domestic product (*GDP*) of the domestic economy; that is:

$$GDP = Y = C + I + G + X - M \qquad (2.1)$$

Equation 2.1 is the national income identity for an open economy that holds in every period of time.

Alternative measures of GDP in practice

Equation (2.1) gives a schematic definition of GDP. It also shows that GDP can be measured in three alternative but equivalent ways, because by definition national income (Y) is equal to output (*GDP*) which is equal to expenditure on output $(C+I+G+X-M)$. Moreover since these equalities hold for each period of time, the period of time over which GDP is to be measured must also be defined. In fact the national accounts usually measure national income over a particular year. Because the accounts are only concerned with output in a particular year, it follows that transactions in second-hand goods, such as cars or houses, do not count as part of current production since they were produced in a previous year. Hence only goods and services produced during the relevant year can count as part of gross domestic product.

The first approach to measuring GDP is to measure the country's output of goods and services produced within a year. There are two problems to be overcome from the outset. The first is how to value the output. This could be valued at 'factory gate' prices or at market prices. The difference between these two sets of prices is basically that market prices include indirect taxes (less subsidies) such as value added tax (VAT), imposed on the product at the point of final sale, and so are generally higher than 'factory gate' prices. Since the value of output should not include tax-additions to product prices basic prices[1] should be used.

---

[1] Until 1998 referred to as factor cost prices. Basic prices replaced factor cost in national accounts from 1998. The difference between the two concepts is that the factor cost measure stripped out all taxes, whereas basic prices include indirect taxes on production, although not taxes levied on the final products.

The second problem would be that of double counting. If the output of all firms is simply added together, some goods which are final products to one industry, but inputs in another, would be counted twice in total output. For example, consider the output of the car industry. The final output will be motor cars, but in producing these vehicles the industry uses the outputs of other industries, such as the steel and rubber industries, as inputs in the production process. Thus simply to add up the value of steel output, rubber output and car output would be to double count both rubber and steel output that have been used up in the production of cars. In practice this is avoided by using the notion of *value added*. In this case the value of each industry's inputs are deducted from the value of output to give the notion of value added. Suppose the value of the motor car is £15 000. The rubber tyres purchased by the car producer cost £200 and the steel inputs cost some £5000. Then the value added by the car producer to the total inputs cost is £15 000 − £5200 = £9800. Assuming that the steel and rubber industries used no other inputs, then the value added by these industries is the value of their output, which is £5200, so the total value of output is £9800 plus £5200 which is £15 000. Thus the sum of the value added is equal to the value of the car, but if all outputs are added the value is £20 500 due to double counting of both steel and rubber inputs. If the value added for each industry is summed up across all industries then a measure of gross domestic product (GDP) valued at current basic prices, is obtained. This is labelled as $GDP_{bp}^{\pounds}$.

The second approach to measuring GDP is to measure the value of expenditure on domestic output. These expenditures can come from domestic households, firms, government or foreign agencies. In this case, since expenditures on goods and services take place at market prices which include indirect taxes (less subsidies), the value of expenditure on final goods and services will be different from that measured by value added, because it is valued at a different set of prices. A more serious problem, however, is that not all expenditure will be used to buy goods and services from domestic firms. Some expenditure will be used in buying goods produced abroad by foreign firms, but since this demand is not part of domestic production it must be subtracted from households' expenditure to give a measure of the value of domestic output. Therefore GDP at current market prices is defined as:

$$GDP_{mp}^{\pounds} = C + I + G + X - M \tag{2.2}$$

To reconcile GDP at basic prices with the measure of GDP at market prices, the basic price adjustment (*BPA*), corresponding to the value of indirect taxes (less subsidies) imposed on the final products needs to be added onto the $GDP_{bp}^{\pounds}$ measure. Therefore the relationship between these measures is simply:

$$GDP_{mp}^{\pounds} = GDP_{bp}^{\pounds} + BPA \tag{2.3}$$

Tables 2.1 and **2.2** show these two measures of GDP for the UK in 1997. $GDP_{bp}^{\pounds}$ was valued at £711.3 billion and $GDP_{mp}^{\pounds}$ at £802 billion, after adding in the basic cost adjustment of some £90 billion. **Table 2.2** shows that consumption

Table 2.1 *GDP (output approach), current market prices*

GDP (output approach)	£ million
1. Output of goods and services	1 517 112
2. (less) Intermediate consumption	−805 842
3. Final value of output of goods & services (1 + 2)	711 270
4. VAT on products	55 686
5. Other taxes	43 051
6. (less) Subsidies	−8 035
7. *GDP at current market prices*	*801 972*

Source: United Kingdom National Accounts, The Blue Book, 1998 edition, ONS.

Table 2.2 *GDP (expenditure approach), current market prices*

GDP (expenditure approach)	£ million
1. Household consumption	500 616
2. NPISH consumption	18 484
3. Government consumption	157 406
4. *Total final consumption*	*666 506*
5. Gross fixed capital formation	133 710
6. Changes in inventories	3 101
7. Acquisition less disposals of valuables	−219
8. *Total gross capital formation*	*136 592*
9. Exports of goods and services	228 702
10. (less) Imports of goods & services	−229 334
11. *External balance of goods & services*	*−632*
12. Statistical discrepancy between expenditure components and GDP	−494
13. *Gross domestic product at current market prices* (4 + 8 + 11 + 12)	*801 972*

Source: United Kingdom National Accounts, The Blue Book, 1998 edition, ONS.

is by far the biggest single category of expenditure, which amounted to £509.1 billion in 1997 or 64 per cent of GDP at market prices, while investment, including stock-building, amounted to £136.6 billion or 17 per cent of GDP. It is important to note that these measures of GDP are not measured entirely without error: hence the statistical discrepancy in row 12 of **Table 2.2**.

The third measure of GDP is concerned with measuring GDP not as an output, but as the value of inputs to the production process. From **Figure 2.1** the value of income received should be equal to the value of output produced. On the income side there are two adjustments that are required. The first is that to attain a measure of 'national' rather than 'domestic' income, the income earned by British nationals abroad needs to be added and income due to foreign national earned in the UK needs to be deducted. This adjustment is particularly important for businesses. For example, a Toyota car plant in England will produce output that is part of England's domestic product (that is, it is produced in England). Some of the income earned, however, will be remitted to Japan in the form of dividends or profits and so is not part of English income, but rather part of Japanese income. These flows, of course, are two-way as British firms' operations abroad produce goods and services which are part of foreign GDP, but which generate income for British nationals. The difference between these income flows is called net income from abroad (NIA) and must be added to GDP to give gross national income (GNI). That is:

$$GDP^{\pounds}_{mp} + NIA^{\pounds} = GNI^{\pounds}_{mp} \tag{2.4}$$

The second adjustment needed to obtain a measure of national income is to acknowledge that during the production process some capital wears out. Therefore if the stock of capital is to be maintained every year some machines have to be replaced. Thus some of the national income has to be used up to purchase new machines. With this deduction, called capital consumption or depreciation (Dep), from GNI the measure of net national income (NNI) at current market prices or simply national income (NI) is obtained. In symbols:

$$NI^{\pounds} = GNI^{\pounds}_{mp} - Dep \tag{2.5}$$

Table 2.3 shows that national income was £725.2 billion in 1997. Note that net income from abroad (line 16) includes both net property and entrepreneurial income, worth £12.1 billion in 1997 that accrues to businesses and the much smaller, net compensation of employees, of £0.08 billion. Note also that these three alternative measures of GDP for the UK economy in 1997 do not turn out to be the same in practice, due to statistical discrepancy between the income measure and expenditure measures of GDP as indicated in line 12 of **Table 2.3**. There is no economic significance in this purely statistical discrepancy.

Price deflators

The preferred measure of the value of output is GDP at current market prices. More important for macroeconomics is a measure of real GDP, or GDP at constant prices, since this measure does not rise with inflation as do the current price measures. Constant price GDP gives a measure of the *volume* of output, rather than the *value* of output. The same point applies to all the components of GDP: what macroeconomists need are measures of these components at constant

Table 2.3 *GDP (income approach), current market prices*

	£ million
1. Public, non-financial corporations gross operating surplus	4 070
2. Private, non-financial corporations gross operating surplus	166 500
3. Financial corporations, gross operating surplus	17 661
4. Adjustment for financial services	−26 564
5. General government	12 434
6. Households & NPISH	44 438
7. Total gross operating surplus $(1+2+3+4+5+6)$	218 539
8. Mixed income	42 623
9. Compensation of employees	432 280
10. Taxes on production and imports	115 572
11. (less) Subsidies	−8 035
12. Statistical discrepancy between income components & GDP	993
13. *GDP at market prices* $(7+8+9+10-11+12)$	*801 972*
14. Net compensation of employees from the rest of the world	83
15. (less) Taxes (plus) Subsidies on production from rest of the world	−2 605
16. Net property and entrepreneurial income from the rest of the world	12 085
17. *Gross national income at market prices* $(13+14+15+16)$	*811 535*
18. (less) Capital consumption (depreciation)	−86 343
19. *Net national income at market prices* $(17+18)$	*725 192*

Source: *United Kingdom National Accounts, The Blue Book*, 1998 edition, ONS.

prices. In order to obtain constant price estimates the current price estimates must be divided into a volume and a price component. To illustrate how this is done by statisticians consider aggregate consumption.

Aggregate consumption at current market prices consists of the expenditure by households on all consumption goods that can be written as:

$$C_{it} = \sum_{i=1}^{n} q_{it} p_{it} \tag{2.6}$$

where the index i refers to the product of which there are n in total and the subscript t refers to the time period. Thus $p_j q_j$ is the amount of expenditure (price × quantity) on good j. Consumption in the base period, period zero, is therefore given as:

$$C_{i_0} = \sum_{i=1}^{n} q_{i_0} p_{i_0} \tag{2.7}$$

The ratio of consumption at current market prices to consumption at base year prices can be expressed as follows:

$$\frac{C_{it}}{C_{i_0}} = \frac{\sum_{i=1}^{n} p_{it}q_{it}}{\sum_{i=1}^{n} p_{i_0}q_{i_0}} = \frac{\sum_{i=1}^{n} p_{it}q_{it}}{\sum_{i=1}^{n} p_{i_0}q_{it}} \times \frac{\sum_{i=1}^{n} p_{i_0}q_{it}}{\sum_{i=1}^{n} p_{i_0}q_{i_0}}$$

(2.8)

Equation (2.8) shows that the ratio of the current and base period expenditures on consumption can be disaggregated to give two indices: a Paasche price index and a Laspeyres quantity index. The Paasche price index is a current quantity-weighted index and is the implied price deflator for consumption. On the other hand, the Laspeyres quantity index is a base price-weighted index of the quantity of consumption goods purchased and is used to derive the constant price consumption series. Thus providing the current quantity bundle at base period prices can be measured, that is $\sum_{i=1}^{n} p_{i0}q_{it}$, in addition to consumption at current and base period prices, then a series for the implicit consumption price deflator can be derived.

It is worth noting that all implied price deflators are Paasche price indices. In contrast, the retail price index is a Laspeyres price index. Therefore, even if the bundles of goods included in these two indices were identical and were consumed in identical proportions, the two indices would give a slightly different measure as to the price change over any specific period of time. It follows from this discussion of implicit deflators that each of the components of final expenditure has their own specific implied deflator. It also follows that GDP has an implied price deflator. Since this particular deflator includes all the goods and services produced in the economy over the period it is a broad price index and is often used to compute the rate of inflation in the economy. The GDP deflator is not, however, directly affected by any rise in import prices, because imports are deducted from final expenditure. Therefore the GDP deflator rises with import prices only to the extent that the rise in import prices is reflected in rises in money wages and profits.

Table 2.4 shows three different UK price deflators and the implied measures of price inflation for each index. The trend in the measures is broadly the same, although there are some slight differences year on year. For example in 1995,

Table 2.4 *Price deflators*

	Retail price index		Producer price index		GDP$_{mp}$ deflator	
	1987 = 100	%Δ	1995 = 100	%Δ	1995 = 100	%Δ
1994	144.1	2.5	96.1	1.9	97.5	2.9
1995	149.1	3.5	100.0	4.0	100	2.6
1996	152.7	2.4	102.6	2.6	103.3	3.3
1997	157.5	3.1	103.6	1.0	106.1	2.7
1998	160.6	3.4	104.2	0.6	108.0	1.8

Source: *Economic Trends*, March 1999, ONS.

the retail price index (RPI) showed a 3.5 per cent rise on 1994, whereas the GDP deflator showed a rise of only 2.6 per cent. The PPI is the producer price index that shows the price of manufactured products in the home market. Although the rate of increase in the PPI exceeded both the GDP deflator and the RPI in 1995 – rising at 4 per cent per annum – in 1997 it showed the lowest rate of increase – just 1 per cent – compared to 3.1 and 2.7 per cent on the RPI and GDP deflators, respectively.

Labour market indicators

In addition to the measures of GDP and various price deflators that emerge from the product market of national accounts, the factor markets where the factors of production are hired, purchased or rented for an income stream also generate useful statistics for a macroeconomist.

The most important of all these statistics is that for the rate of unemployment. This is the key to much of macroeconomic policy but, like all economic statistics, it is only imperfectly measured. **Table 2.5** shows two alternative definitions that differ on account of their coverage. The standard measure used in the UK until recently is simply the ratio of those claiming benefit – the claimant count – to the workforce plus the claimant count on a specific day in each month. That is, the rate of unemployment, u, is measured as:

$$u - \frac{Claimant\ count}{Workforce + Claimant\ count} \times 100 \tag{2.9}$$

The claimant count excludes students who claim benefit during a vacation who intend to return to full-time education and the workforce, shown in the first column of **Table 2.5,** includes employees, the self employed, members of HM forces and participants in work-related government training. Thus increasing the numbers on government training programmes actually reduces the rate of unemployment on this measure. On the other hand, the International Labour Office (ILO) data is based on the Labour Force Survey and is defined as the percentage of

Table 2.5 *Labour market statistics*

	Workforce 000s	Unit labour costs index (Δ%)	Unemployment rate (ILO) (%)	Unemployment rate (CC) (Δ%)	Productivity index (Δ%)
1995	260 48	112.4 (1.8)	8.7	8.0	100.0 (1.7)
1996	263 25	114.6 (2.0)	8.2	7.3	101.3 (1.3)
1997	267 70	118.4 (3.3)	7.0	5.5	103.1 (1.8)
1998	270 25		6.4	4.7	

Source: Economic Trends, December 1998, ONS.

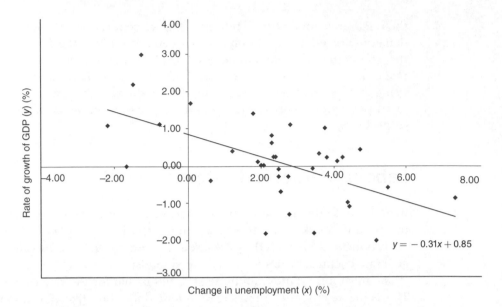

Figure 2.2 *Okun's Law*

economically active people who are unemployed. It is interesting to note that the ILO data gives a higher rate of unemployment than the traditional UK measure. For example, in both 1997 and 1998 the ILO measured unemployment in the UK as about 1.5 per cent higher than the claimant count measure, at 7 per cent compared to 5.5 per cent in 1997 and 6.4 per cent compared with 4.7 per cent in 1998.

What relationship should be expected between unemployment and real GDP? Since employed workers help to produce goods and services and the unemployed do not, increases in the unemployment rate should be associated with decreases in GDP. The negative relationship between unemployment and GDP is called Okun's Law, after Okun (1962). For the UK, **Figure 2.2** shows the scatter plot between GDP growth and the change in the rate of unemployment, over the period 1961–97, which confirms an inverse relationship. This relationship shows that the average trend rate of economic growth is 0.85 per cent per annum. In addition, for every percentage point the unemployment rate rises, real GDP growth typically falls by 0.3 per cent. Thus if the unemployment rate falls from 8 to 6 per cent then the rate of growth of GDP will rise by 0.6 per cent.

An alternative measure of the relationship between output and the labour market is to measure the ratio between GDP and employment. This is the average productivity of labour and is shown in **Table 2.5** to have been growing in the UK at an average annual rate of about 1.6 per cent since 1995. Productivity, or output per head, is believed to be a key element in the forces that determine economic growth, which will be considered in chapter 16.

Sectoral balances, the flow of funds and the balance of payments

The introduction of sector balances at this juncture is to highlight the connection between the flows of income and expenditure, discussed so far, and changes in the stocks of financial assets in the economy. These linkages between the real and financial sectors of the economy will become important in Part III of this text. In order to highlight these connections in as simple a fashion as possible, assume that there is no indirect taxation, no income from abroad, no depreciation of the capital stock, no price changes and no rental incomes.

From equation (2.1) GDP at current market prices can be written as the sum of factor incomes or the sum of final expenditures:

$$GDP = C + I + G + X - M = C + S + T \tag{2.10}$$

where S is private sector savings and T stands for total government tax revenue. This identity can be rearranged to highlight the sectoral elements in GDP. Subtracting the right-hand side from the left gives:

$$(I - S) + (G - T) + (X - M) = 0 \tag{2.11}$$

Identity (2.11) enables three sectors of the economy to be distinguished: the non-bank private sector (nbps), which includes the personal and corporate sectors, the public sector and the overseas sector. Each of the expressions in brackets indicates that particular sector's net acquisition of financial assets. For example, if $I > S$ then the private sector as a whole will be spending more than its income and will need to borrow from the other sectors of the economy. This borrowing implies that its net acquisition of financial assets ($NAFA_p$) will be negative. Similarly, if the government spends more than its income, so that $G > T$, then it will have to finance this excess of expenditure over income by borrowing from other sectors in the economy, and so $NAFA_g < 0$. For the overseas sector $(X - M)$ represents payments less receipts of income so if $X > M$ the overseas sector is borrowing from the domestic sectors and $NAFA_o < 0$. Therefore equation (2.11) can also be written in terms of the net acquisition of financial balances, which because (2.11) is an identity must satisfy:

$$NAFA_p + NAFA_g = NAFA_o \tag{2.12}$$

The borrowing referred to in the previous paragraph can be undertaken through the financial system and, in particular, through the banking sector. The banking sector plays only a passive role in macroeconomics analysis, although the sector as a whole plays an important intermediary function in bringing net lenders and net borrowers together. The financial imbalances that emerge are essentially financed by transactions in the financial markets which pass through the banking sector, although the banking sector itself is not able to directly influence the spending decisions of agents and so influence the variables in equation (2.11). This implies that the consolidated balance sheet of the banking sector always balances.

Assume, for simplicity, that the banking sector has only one liability, namely the deposits of its customers, denoted D. The banking sector's assets are of three kinds: advances to customers, A, holdings of government bonds, B_b, and holdings of foreign government bonds, F_b, that are part of the banks foreign currency reserves. Therefore the banks' balance sheet is given by:

$$D = A + B_b + F_b \tag{2.13}$$

A second identity that is closely associated with the banking sector is that for the money supply. The money supply, M^s, is defined as the sum of deposit liabilities, D and notes and coin in circulation, N, such that:

$$M^s = N + D \tag{2.14}$$

Combining (2.13) and (2.14) and writing in first differences gives:

$$\Delta M^s = \Delta N + \Delta A + \Delta B_b + \Delta F_b \tag{2.15}$$

The public sector deficit, given as $G - T$, must be financed by borrowing from other sectors in the economy. The authorities can arrange this by selling government debt instruments to all the other sectors. These instruments are liabilities to the government but assets to all other sectors. Therefore:

$$G - T = \Delta B^s = \Delta N + \Delta B_b + \Delta B_p + \Delta B_o \tag{2.16}$$

This says that the public sector deficit is financed by printing notes and coin (ΔN) or by selling debt to the banking sector, the private sector, or the overseas sector. Using (2.16) to replace ΔN in (2.15) gives:

$$\Delta M^s = (G - T) - \Delta B_p - \Delta B_0 + \Delta A + \Delta F_b \tag{2.17}$$

The final identity is that for the overseas sector. If the domestic country runs a current account surplus, that is domestic export receipts, X, exceed domestic import payments, M, then the overseas sector is in deficit and will have to borrow to finance its deficit. This is the same as saying that the domestic economy will be accumulating foreign assets as payment for the deficit that the rest of the world is running with the domestic economy. That is:

$$X - M = \Delta F_b + \Delta F_p \tag{2.18}$$

Equation (2.18) shows that the current balance surplus is equal to the net domestic accumulation of foreign assets by the banks, F_b, and by the non-bank private sector, F_p. The net accumulation of assets by the banking sector can be regarded as official financing, whereas that undertaken by the private sector is done so voluntarily for risk management or profit purposes. This can be used to substitute for ΔF_b in (2.17) to give:

$$\Delta M^s = (X - M) + (G - T) - \Delta B_p + \Delta A + \Delta K_o \qquad (2.19)$$

such that $\Delta K_o = \Delta B_o + \Delta F_p$, which is the net capital inflow to the domestic economy. Equation (2.19) shows that the government budget deficit does not have to be associated with an increase in the money supply. It can be financed by the government borrowing from the non-bank private sector or from the overseas sector. The overseas sector may help to fund the budget deficit either by the foreign private sector investing in the home economy thereby generating a capital inflow or, by running a current balance deficit against the domestic economy, which will increase domestic official reserves. In an open economy it is clear that the money supply is not under the control of the domestic authorities, unless the balance of payments position is unchanging. The current balance surplus will lead to an increase in the money supply unless it is 'sterilised' by the authorities undertaking offsetting actions, by selling domestic bonds to the domestic private sector. Thus as $(X - M)$ increases, ΔB_p is increased by the same amount leaving the money supply unchanged. The crucial point to note at this stage, however, is the interdependence between the product market and the financial market flows.

Equation (2.17) has a statistical counterpart called the counterparts to the change in the money stock. This is reproduced in simplified form as **Table 2.6** for the years 1994–98. The table is presented in identical fashion to (2.17), with one exception. Because in the real world banks do have liabilities which are not

Table 2.6 *Counterparts to changes in money stock M4*

£ billion	$G-T$	ΔB_p	ΔF_b	ΔB_o	ΔA	NDL	$\Delta M4$
	1	2	3	4	5	6	7
1994	39.3	−22.9	−7.5	4.0	31.6	−15.0	25.3
1995	35.4	−21.9	−3.4	3.4	57.7	−8.3	56.1
1996	24.8	−19.1	17.9	8.9	59.1	−12.1	59.4
1997	11.8	−13.0	25.3	5.1	68.5	−6.6	80.5
1998	−6.6	3.9	11.1	4.3	63.4	−6.2	58.5

Note: Figures may not add exactly due to the inclusion of public sector net cash requirement information on a ESA95 basis.

1. Public sector net cash requirement (formerly the PSBR).
2. Purchases of government debt by non-bank private sector.
3. External and foreign currency transactions of UK banks and building societies.
4. Purchase of UK government stocks by the overseas sector.
5. Banks' and building societies' sterling lending to the non-bank private sector.
6. Net non-deposit sterling liabilities of UK banks and building societies.
7. Money supply, M4 $(1+2+3+4+5+6)$.

Source: *Economic Trends*, ONS, March 1999.

part of the money supply, these must be subtracted from the specification given as (2.17). The components of the money supply, measured as M4, do vary substantially over time. For example, the government's cash requirement in the UK was negative in 1998 – that is, the government sector was in surplus rather than in deficit – whereas only a few years earlier the government cash requirement was a significant factor raising the money supply. In 1998 the government also repurchased debt from the nbps, as evidenced by a positive sign on ΔB_p, rather than sold debt as in the previous years. One common feature in **Table 2.6** is that bank lending to the non-bank private sector, ΔA, is large and positive, adding to the increment in the money supply each year.

Equations (2.18) and (2.19) are of some importance for open economies. Equation (2.18) is the balance of payments. It shows that the balance of payments must always balance, because it is an accounting identity. Therefore to refer to a balance of payments problem or a balance of payments deficit is strictly incorrect, since overall the balance of payments always balances. Reference to a deficit of surplus in the context of the balance of payments usually refers to some sub-account within the balance of payments. The most important of these accounts is the current account balance, since a current account deficit means that the domestic economy is spending more than it is producing and borrowing from abroad to finance the difference. The current account balance is made up of the trade balance and the invisibles balance. The trade balance is simply the balance between exports and imports of goods. The invisibles balance consists of three sub-balances: the balance of trade in services, net income from abroad and net transfers. The largest of these balances is the balance on interest, profits and dividends. **Table 2.7** shows the UK balance of payments position between 1995 and 1997, indicating the various sub-balances, and shows that the UK is usually in deficit on the trade balance, but in surplus on the income and services balances which sometimes results in a current account surplus as in 1997. The financial account is the result of transactions by both domestic and foreign residents in international capital markets. The net capital inflow is the outcome of foreign residents' purchases and sales of domestic assets, while the capital outflow is the result of domestic residents' purchases and sales of foreign assets. Part of the net capital outflow is the net purchase of foreign currency assets by the domestic authorities – that is, the change in official reserves which is a result of the authorities' actions in the foreign exchange market.

The foreign exchange market is shown in **Figure 2.3**. On the vertical axis is the exchange rate, measured as the domestic price of foreign currency and on the horizontal axis is the quantity of foreign currency. The demand curve for foreign currency slopes down reflecting the fact that purchases of foreign currency will buy more as it becomes cheaper. The agents who demand foreign currency are domestic residents who have bought goods (imports) or assets (capital outflow) from abroad and now need to purchase the currency to pay for them. Similarly the supply curve for foreign currency slopes up, since more will be supplied if the price is higher. Underlying the supply curve for foreign currency are domestic residents who have sold home produced goods (exports) or domestic assets

Table 2.7 *The UK balance of payments accounts*

£ billions	1995	1996	1997
1. Exports of goods	153.7	167.4	171.8
2. Imports of goods	−165.4	−180.5	−183.7
3. *The trade balance*(1+2)	−11.7	−13.1	−11.9
4. Services balance	8.9	8.9	11.9
5. Income balance	6.0	8.1	11.0
6. Transfers	−6.9	−4.5	−4.8
7. *The current account balance* (3+4+5+6)	−3.7	−0.6	6.1
8. *The capital account*	0.5	0.7	0.3
9. Net capital inflow	116.2	220.9	248.1
10. Net capital outflow of which [change in reserves]	−115.3 [0.2]	−219.2 [0.5]	−256.2 [2.4]
11. *Financial account balance* (9+10)	0.9	1.8	−8.1
12. Errors and omissions (7+8+11)	2.3	−1.9	−0.2

Source: *Economic Trends*, Annual Supplement, ONS, 1998.

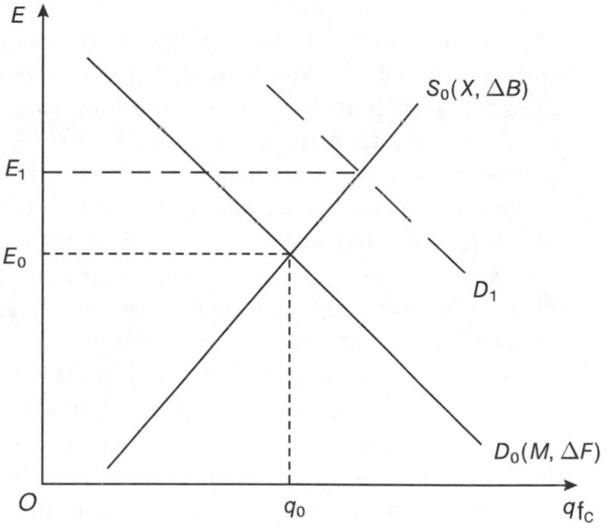

Figure 2.3 *The foreign exchange market*

(capital inflows) abroad and are converting their foreign currency receipts into sterling. If the exchange rate is freely floating the equilibrium exchange rate will be at E_0 in **Figure 2.3**. To understand why the authorities need to purchase or sell foreign currency – that is, why official reserves rise or fall – suppose the authorities wish to maintain the exchange rate at E_1. At E_1 there is an excess supply of foreign currency so in order to hold the price of foreign currency at E_1 the authorities have to buy up the excess supply using sterling. Thus demand for foreign currency rises, shifting the demand curve out to D_1 and the exchange rate is held at E_1. In this intervention the authorities have purchased foreign currency which they add to the official reserves to prevent the exchange rate from appreciating from E_1 to E_0. From **Table 2.7** the change in reserves is small, because the UK is operating a floating exchange rate policy so that there is little intervention in the markets by the authorities. What little net intervention there was between 1995–97 seems to have involved the sale of reserves (hence the positive sign on reserves in **Table 2.7**) which would have tended to depress the price of foreign currency and raise the price of sterling.

The balance of payments accounts, the government financing identity and the money supply formation table show explicitly how the real economy and the financial sector are connected statistically. Other interdependencies must wait until later chapters, but it should be clear that macroeconomics is about aggregate market interrelationships.

Conclusion and the limitations of GDP as a measure of economic welfare

This chapter has examined the principles underlying the national income accounting procedures used by most developed countries. It has focused on the concept of GDP at constant market prices, because this is the measure that most closely corresponds to output in the following chapters of this book. It has, however, also tried to illustrate the statistical connections between the flows of goods and services, the labour market and net transactions in financial assets. Like all economic statistics, however, these statistics are less than perfect. This means that care is needed when interpreting statistics for policy purposes. For example, it is very common in both economics and politics to regard the level and growth of real GDP as a symbol of increasing welfare and affluence, but there are several serious limitations with this use of GDP.

First, the measures of GDP discussed in this chapter exclude non-market transactions; the most obvious of which is that of housewives services, although it also includes the other parts of the informal economy such as child minding, window cleaning and newspaper delivery. Although these exclusions mean that the level of GDP is underrecorded, provided the ratio of market to non-market services is roughly constant a change in GDP will reflect a change in both market and non-market services. A shift, however, from non-market to market services will bring about an increase in measured GDP due simply to the increase in the size of the market sector of the economy. Thus, if housewives were to undertake paid employment in the market sector and to employ professional child minders to look after their children then GDP would rise.

A second problem involved with using real GDP as a measure of welfare concerns the possibility that market prices do not reflect the social costs of production; that is, there are externalities in the economy. In the case of air pollution, greater output will be associated with greater pollution that means GDP will overstate the increase in welfare. Indeed, deducting the full cost of the externality may even lead to a fall in welfare, although GDP will have risen. There is a potential further difficulty in comparing GDPs between countries, since it is not clear what exchange rate should be used to make the conversion into a common currency. Should this be the average exchange rate over the accounting period, or the exchange rate at the end of the period. Furthermore if local price changes are not fully reflected in the exchange rate changes then the relative GDP growth may be under or overvalued.

A third limitation of GDP as a measure of welfare is that it does not deal with distribution issues. A rise in GDP may be associated with a much greater inequality of incomes between the very rich and the very poor. Such inequalities, however distasteful or divisive to society as a whole, are completely disregarded by measures of welfare which focus on the level of GDP. This notion of inequality is also a problem when making international comparisons of GDP. GDP per capita may be much larger in country Y than in country X, but this is not to say that social welfare is also greater in country Y than in country X.

Statistics by themselves, however, are unable to speak for themselves; without a framework for reference they are meaningless. In the next chapter the tools required for economic model-building are briefly reviewed to facilitate the development of such a framework.

Summary

- The key measure of economic activity is gross domestic product (GDP) at constant market prices.
- The average level of prices can be measured by the consumer price index (CPI) or by the producer price index (PPI).
- The measurement of unemployment is very important for macroeconomics although there is considerable debate as to the appropriate measure. The ILO provides a consistent cross-country measure.
- The money supply is not an exogenous variable that can be controlled by the authorities, but a variable dependent in part upon the balance of payments position of the economy and the monetary and exchange rate policy pursued by the authorities.
- Although GDP at constant prices is frequently used as a measure of economic welfare, it not only excludes some important activities, such as housework, but is not able to capture changes in the distribution of income which may be welfare-enhancing, or the effects of polllution or overcrowding that may serve to reduce welfare.

Suggested further reading

There are a number of texts dealing exclusively with national income accounting principles. For example, see Stone and Stone (1977), Hicks (1971) and Beckerman (1968). King (1984) provides a more modern view of the national accounts. Feature articles in the *Bank of England Quarterly Bulletin* and the Office of National Statistics monthly *Economic Trends* or the annual *Blue Book* provide most of the statistical updates needed for the UK. The OECD and the IMF both maintain macroeconomic databases with national income accounts data, labour market statistics and the main financial indicators.

Essay titles

1. To what extent do the national income accounts measure the wealth of a nation?
2. 'Since the money supply can not be wholly controlled by the government it is an inappropriate variable to serve as a policy instrument.' Discuss.
3. Can there ever be a balance of payments deficit?

Questions

1. Explain why the national income accounts do not measure all the economic activity that takes place.
2. Distinguish between (a) GDP, GNI and national income; (b) current prices, constant prices and basic prices; (c) trade balance and the current account balance.
3. 'Since a Laspeyres index undervalues the price change and the Paasch index overvalues the price change, economists have little idea as to actual rate of change of prices.' Discuss.
4. If society chooses more leisure time and a reduction in its material wants, its decisions may eventually lead us to conclude that it is worse off; if it decides to work more in order to acquire more things, the opposite conclusion would result. Explain.
5. Explain why the money supply is not an exogenous variable in an open economy. What actions may the authorities undertake to try to limit the effect of the balance of payments on the money supply?
6. Explain Okun's Law.

CHAPTER 3

Basic Concepts and Methods of Macroeconomics

Aims and objectives

- To review some of the key concepts in economic modelling, such as the distinction between stocks and flows and real and nominal values.
- To introduce the notion of an economic model and to stress the role of such models in helping to explain economic data.
- To introduce the methodology of macroeconomic analysis – comparative static equilibrium and simple dynamic analysis – without the use of formal mathematics.

Introduction

This chapter serves as a bridge between the accounting background of macroeconomics discussed in Chapter 2 and the rest of the text, which is primarily concerned with the principles of macroeconomic analysis. Macroeconomic analysis is conceptually distinct from that of measuring macroeconomic variables. For example, from Chapter 2, UK GDP at constant 1995 market prices in 1997 was £802 billion. This statistic does not say why GDP was at this level rather than some other higher or lower level. To explain why GDP is at one level and not another requires a theoretical model. These models are, by definition, simplifications of the real world that are designed to help understand the real world. This point is absolutely vital. Models should not be confused with reality. Moreover, this implies that it is wholly tautological to dismiss a model as 'unrealistic', when, of course, if the model was realistic it would not only cease to be a model, but likely also to cease to be useful! That said, however, some model assumptions are more realistic than others or, perhaps more accurately, more appropriate to specific circumstances than others and this must also be acknowledged. To be able to understand any branch of economics requires us to understand how models work and how they can be used to analyse policy issues. Prior to this, however, students must be well-versed in some of the key terms and concepts that are frequently used in the model-building process.

The purpose of this chapter, therefore, is to introduce and review some of the key ideas and concepts used in macroeconomic model-building. These terms are not necessarily mathematical, although some can be thought of in mathematical terms, but all are conceptual and essential for understanding the modelling process. The modelling method used in this book is largely diagrammatic, although some basic mathematics will be used from time to time to further elucidate or develop particular concepts.

The chapter is structured as follows. The next section examines the principal elements of an economic model, and the sections following consider the difference between stocks and flows; review the standard concept of equilibrium; and consider the analytical methods of statics, comparative statics and dynamics and the relationship between these methods.

Economic models

A model is a system of structural equations or relationships. These relationships are called 'structural' because they represent the basic structure of the economic system being studied. In general, structural relationships can be classified into two types: *definitional* and *behaviourial* equations.

Definitional equations or *identities* are truisms that must hold in all instances by definition of terms. These equations contain neither causal statements nor descriptions of decision processes. The national income accounting relationships reviewed in Chapter 2, for instance, are examples of definitional equations. They do not provide an answer to the question of what determines the economy's level of output in any period. The GDP identity might say that UK GDP at market prices and constant prices in 1997 was £802 billion, but it does not say whether this is the most that could have been produced or what determines that level of output. This is a definitional equation that is true by definition. These identities hold at all points in time and give no indication as to the direction of causality between the variables.

To discover what factors determine the level of output of the economy a model is needed to link economic variables in a causal manner. That is to say, behavioural relationships between economic variables have to be identified and specified so that changes in one variable are related to changes in another. These *behavioural* equations represent predictions about how individuals or groups of individuals behave in response to particular stimuli. These behavioural relationships are sometimes called *functional* relationships, since one variable is said to be a function of, that is depends upon, another. A particular structural equation like the consumption function consists of a single *dependent* variable, that is consumption, and any number of *independent* or *explanatory* variables, such as disposable income, interest rates and so on. The direction of causality for a particular structural equation is from the independent variable or variables to the dependent variable; that is, in the case of the consumption function, a change in disposable income causes a change in consumption.

These behavioural or functional relations represent how agents are *expected* or *plan* to behave. That is they deal with agents *desired*, *planned* or *ex ante* consumption behaviour and not with *actual*, *realised* or *ex post* consumption patterns. For example, the simple consumption hypothesis is that given a rise in disposable income agents would *plan* to increase their consumption. Whether or not they do actually succeed in increasing their consumption depends on a large number of other factors remaining unchanged. Suppose, for instance, that the rise in disposable income was accompanied by an unanticipated large rise in interest rates. Although households may have expected to increase their consumption, the sharp rise in interest rates may have led then to actually reduce consumption to take advantage of the current high rate of interest on savings. In this case, clearly, agents did not behave as they planned because of a change in a factor not captured in this simple model of the consumption function. Actual consumption would therefore record no change despite the rise in disposable income. It is therefore important to distinguish between planned and actual values in macroeconomics, since these will only be equal in equilibrium. In general all functional or behavioural relationships refer to planned or desired behaviour.

In a behavioural equation the explanatory variables may be *endogenous* or *exogenous* to the model as a whole. *Endogenous variables* are those variables that are explained by the model. They help to determine the other endogenous variables in the model and are, in turn, determined partly by the other endogenous variables. Mathematically this means the model is simultaneous, with one equation for each endogenous variable. In simultaneous systems a change in one endogenous variable will lead to a change in at least one other endogenous variable. Note, from a graphical point of view, that the variables on the axes are endogenous variables. They may or may not be the only endogenous variables, but they are most certainly endogenous. Changes in the variables measured on the axes always lead to *movements along the schedules* and not to shifts of the schedules. Thus, in the case of the consumption function with consumption on the vertical axis and disposable income on the horizontal axis a rise in disposable income will lead to a movement along the consumption function. *Exogenous variables* are not explained by the model, but are determined outside the model. In any particular model the exogenous variables are chosen *a priori*. The exogenous variables determine the endogenous variables but are not affected by them. From a graphical point of view exogenous variables are assumed to be held constant when the figure is drawn, but when they change they cause the entire schedule to *shift*.

The simple, linear consumption function in **Figure 3.1**, can be used to illustrate this point. Suppose the level of income is initially at Y_0^D and consumption at C_0. A rise in the level of disposable income to Y_1^D will give rise to an increase in consumption to C_1, by moving the initial point at A on the consumption function up to point B. This is a movement along the consumption function. On the other hand, suppose now there is a rise in the rate of interest. Since this is an exogenous variable in the consumption function, the whole consumption function will shift down to the right. That is consumption will be lower at all levels of

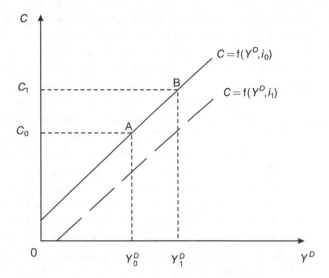

Figure 3.1 *Shifts and movements along a line*

disposable income as consumption is reduced in favour of saving. In **Figure 3.1** this shift is represented by the dotted line below the initial consumption relation.

It is only by hypothesising about functional relationships that any progress can be made towards explaining the observed facts. Moreover, devising theories however indispensable in the process of explanation is only a step in the process, for the theories postulated may not be consistent with the data. In order to decide which theories are to be rejected, and hence which theories are to be retained, the theories must be tested against the 'facts'. Furthermore, even a theory that is supported by the facts is not proof of the theory, since theories can never be proved. The theory is merely not rejected by, or inconsistent with, the observed data. Sometimes conflicting theories are consistent with the same set of data in which case it is not possible to reject either theory, both being said to be 'observationally equivalent'.

Stock and flow variables

The concepts of stocks and flows are not difficult to understand but they are very easily confused. Stocks and flows are both variables, measuring quantities that may rise or fall over time. The distinction between them is that a *stock* is a quantity measurable at a *specific point in time* whereas a *flow* is a quantity that can only be measured *over an interval of time*. To take a specific example, consider the level of water in a bath tub. Suppose that there are 25 gallons of water in the bath. This is a measure of the stock of water in the bath at some specific point in time. If, however, the flow of water into the bath from the running tap is 2 gallons a minute, then this is a flow variable and the stock of water will be rising as the new flow adds to the existing stock.

To use an economic example, the number of persons employed in the UK is a stock variable, referring to the number of persons employed at a specific point in time, whereas the number of new employees over a particular time period is the flow of persons into employment. Thus at the end of 1997 there were some 26 982 000 people in employment in the UK. In the first quarter of 1998 this number in employment had risen to 27 020 000. The stock increased, because there was a flow into employment of 38 000 during the quarter. Another example is afforded by the relationship between the stock of capital and the flow of investment. If $K(t)$ is the stock of capital at the beginning of time period t and $I(t)$ and is the flow of new investment goods over the period t, then it follows that the capital stock at the start of the next period, $t+1$, is given as $K(t+1)=K(t)+I(t)$. These examples show that stock variables cannot be negative: they are either positive or zero. Flow variables, on the other hand, can be either positive or negative, since flows may rise of fall. In the case where $K(t+1)<K(t)$ it must be true that the depreciation of the existing capital stock exceeded the flow of replacement capital goods.

Equilibrium and disequilibrium

The notions of equilibrium and disequilibrium are to an extent familiar to all students from their study of social or physical sciences. The definition of equilibrium in the physical sciences is a position of rest from which the system under study does not depart. Disequilibrium, on the other hand, is simply when the balance of forces are not equal and the system is changing.

In social science the relevant variables are continuously changing over time, and therefore the state of balance that defines equilibrium may perhaps be expressed as a state of no change over time. This is not to say that nothing ever changes, but rather that the actions are repetitive in nature so that each time period exactly duplicates the preceding period. Consider, for example, the standard microeconomic model of demand and supply. In **Figure 3.2** the planned quantity demanded per period of time (Q_t^d) and the planned quantity supplied per period of time (Q_t^s) are in equilibrium at price P_0. At a higher price there is disequilibrium since there is excess supply, while at a lower price there is excess demand. In this model, in the event of disequilibrium the forces are such as to move the price back to its equilibrium position, at P_0, and the quantity back to its equilibrium level at Q_0. The price–output combination of P_0Q_0 will continue indefinitely for all future periods of time unless the system is disturbed in some way by an exogenous shock.

Even in this simple analysis, however, the concept of equilibrium is an inherently dynamic notion. In saying that if the price was above the equilibrium price the price would fall to clear the market assumes a specific dynamic adjustment process; that is, that prices fall when there is an excess of supply. It is necessary therefore to introduce dynamics.

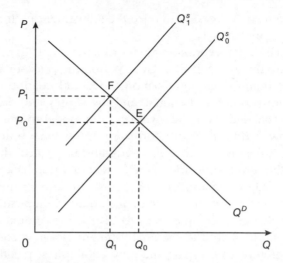

Figure 3.2   *A comparative static shift*

Statics and dynamics

The essential difference between statics and dynamics is that in *static analysis* only positions of equilibrium are considered, whereas in *dynamic analysis* the movement between one equilibrium position and another is made explicit. Therefore the role of time in the model is also made explicit.

In constructing economic models time may be incorporated by splitting it up into periods and examining how what happens in one period is related to what happened in preceding periods, and to what is expected to happen in succeeding periods. In other words, the variables in dynamic models are 'dated' whereas in static analysis the variables all refer to the same time period. Because static analysis ignores the passage of time it is not able to explain the process of change in a model. It can indicate the position of the model for a given period but it cannot, except in special circumstances, reveal what the position will be in any other period. In the special case where the model is not changing, but simply repeating the same motion period after period, static analysis can reveal both where the system is in the present period and where it will be in all future periods. This special case is referred to as the 'stationary-state equilibrium' because the equilibrium remains unchanged from one period to the next.

Static analysis, on its own, can only be applied to a model in which a single, non-shifting equilibrium position is established by the relationships among the variables. Applying the method of static analysis to a model in a period when it is in disequilibrium can only show that for that particular period the values of the variables will be changing from that period to the next. Static analysis can explain why this is a disequilibrium, what relationship among the variables is necessary for equilibrium and in what direction the system will move next. It cannot, however, explain the actual process of adjustment from one equilibrium position to the next. To be able to trace the adjustment path through time requires explicitly dynamic analysis.

The microeconomic model of supply and demand can again be used to illustrate this point. If for a given period the price–quantity combination is other than the equilibrium combination, price and quantity must change. Since an equilibrium position is assumed, and the supply and demand curves do not shift, then the changes over time will lead the model to this equilibrium position. There is, however, insufficient information to say what time path price and quantity follow in adjusting to this new equilibrium, since that requires explicit dynamics, although the position of the final equilibrium is known. Static analysis is meaningful only when applied to models with equilibrium positions. Moreover, the economic forces that determine the equilibrium position of a model may be expected to change over time so as to displace the initial equilibrium and, under certain conditions, lead to the establishment of a new equilibrium position. It is possible therefore to compare the new equilibrium position with the initial equilibrium position. This is in fact the method of *comparative statics*. Note that it does not help to explain the actual time path of the variables followed between the two equilibrium positions, but it does enable a comparison of the two positions. Comparative statics will be the most popular type of analysis used in this book.

Consider once again the model of supply and demand. In **Figure 3.2** the original equilibrium is defined by the intersection of the supply and the demand curves at E. Suppose that there is now a shock to the model, such as a rise in production costs. This will cause the supply curve to shift up to the left, from Q_0^s to Q_1^s. From comparative statics it is clear that the new equilibrium will be at F and that the equilibrium price will be higher and the equilibrium quantity supplied and demanded will be lower than in the initial equilibrium. Thus a rise in production costs this period has the effect of raising prices and reducing quantity at some future period. Comparative static analysis *assumes* that the model is dynamically stable, in that the model will return to a stable equilibrium position following the shock. If the model is inherently unstable then comparative static analysis ceases to be a very useful approach to the problem. Furthermore, comparative statics says nothing about the speed of adjustment to the new equilibrium, or the direction of change of the variables between the two comparative static equilibria. For these types of questions dynamic analysis is required.

Dynamic analysis requires that some form of adjustment mechanism be specified. In the demand and supply example above it can be postulated that the price will rise if there is excess demand, and that the price will fall if there is excess supply. Additionally, it can be assumed that the rate of rise or fall in price is proportional to the size of the excess demand or supply on the market. This can be expressed mathematically as:

$$\Delta P = \theta(Q^d - Q^s) \tag{3.1}$$

The left-hand side of equation (3.1) denotes the change of prices and the right-hand side the excess demand on the market. Hence the price will rise if demand exceeds supply. The speed of the adjustment is given by the parameter θ. If $\theta = 0$

there will be no change in the price of the good. On the other hand if $\theta \to \infty$, prices will adjust so quickly that there will never be any disequilibrium between the quantities demanded and supplied. For values of θ between zero and infinity the speed of adjustment is finite. In addition to (3.1) suppose also that quantity demanded and supplied are both linear functions of the price level so that:

$$Q^d = \delta_0 - \delta_1 P$$
$$Q^s = \sigma_0 + \sigma_1 P \tag{3.2}$$

which says simply that demand varies inversely with price (that is the demand curve has a negative slope) and that supply varies directly with price (that is the supply curve slopes up). Substituting for Q^d and Q^s in (3.1) using equations (3.2) gives:

$$\Delta P = \theta(\delta_0 - \sigma_0) - \theta(\delta_1 + \sigma_1)P \tag{3.3}$$

This says that a rise in P will lower the rate of change of P. Therefore, the price level is converging towards the equilibrium price level. To understand this rewrite (3.3) as:

$$\Delta P_t = P_{t+1} - P_t = \lambda_0 - \lambda P_t \quad \text{or} \quad P_{t+1} = (1-\lambda)P_t + \lambda_0 \tag{3.4}$$

where

$$\lambda_0 = \theta(\delta_0 - \sigma_0), \quad \lambda = \theta(\delta_1 + \sigma_1).$$

This simplest model gives six potential time paths for prices, as shown in **Figure 3.3**, depending on the sign and size of λ. If, for example, $\lambda = 1$ then $P_{t+1} = \lambda_0$. That is, prices are constant. In panel (a) of **Figure 3.3** the price line is horizontal at λ_0. On the other hand if $0 < \lambda < 1$, then $1 > (1-\lambda) > 0$ and the time path of prices is convergent and monotonic, as shown in panel (b) of **Figure 3.3**. Similarly in panel (c) prices are non-convergent or unstable as $(1-\lambda) > 1$. This says that the price is larger in each period than it was the period before. Panels (d), (e) and (f) show the case where the time path of price is oscillatory, rather than monotonic. Note that prices may still be convergent, unstable or constant as in the upper panels. In general if $(1-\lambda)$ lies 'inside the unit circle' that is $-1 < (1-\lambda) < 1$ then stability is guaranteed.

The interesting thing about all this as far as economic modelling is concerned is that the value of $(1-\lambda)$ is determined by the structural parameters of the economic model. Suppose in the market under consideration that quantities are believed to be relatively unresponsive to prices. In this case δ_1 and σ_1 will be small numbers, say 0.2 and 0.3. If the speed of adjustment is 0.5 then the value of $(1-\lambda)$ is $0.5 \times 0.5 = 0.25$ and the price stable, adjusting monotonically back to equilibrium. On the other hand if the quantities are highly responsive to price then the possibility of instability is increased. For the sake of argument suppose that δ_1 and σ_1 are 5 and 2 respectively, with the speed of adjustment at 0.5 as

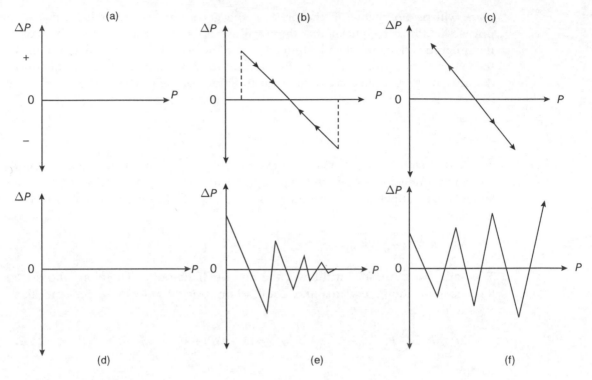

Figure 3.3 *Stability analysis*

before then the model is unstable or non-convergent as $(1-\lambda) = -5$, which lies outside the unit circle. The point to be emphasised here is that although the mathematics of difference equations is necessary to understand the possible alternative time paths and what they look like, it is the economic behaviour that determines whether or not the model is stable, not the mathematics.

The problem with dynamic analysis of the kind discussed in this section is that the 'time' referred to is not 'calendar time' but 'model time'. That is to say there is no means of translating from a particular adjustment speed of the model to a specific number of months or quarters in calendar time. The only way to gain knowledge about real world adjustment speeds is through statistical estimation. As equation (3.3) shows the rate of change of prices depends not only upon the speed of adjustment of the model but also on the structural parameters of the supply and demand equations, thus making such statistical estimation a non-trivial and frequently difficult exercise.

Conclusions

This chapter has provided a brief review of some of the principal modelling terminology that will be used in this book, although it has not reviewed differential calculus. Although this is a mathematical technique used in the book none of the arguments in the following chapters depend upon it. It is now time to apply the terminology and tools developed in this chapter to the simplest macroeconomic model – the income–expenditure model.

Summary

- Economic models are a deliberate abstraction from reality in order to facilitate our understanding of the real world, and thus by enabling economists to make predictions about policy changes enhance policy-making.
- Economic models have a common framework consisting of behavioural relations and identities that can be solved diagrammatically for equilibrium prices and quantities, for a given set of exogenous variables.
- Models are a central feature of economic analysis since without them no sense can be made of economic statistics.

Suggested further reading

There are a number of excellent texts that deal with models in economics and most especially the mathematical techniques frequently employed to solve these models. The classic text on mathematical methods in economics with numerous economics examples is Chiang (1985), *Fundamental Methods of Mathematical Economics*, 3rd edn, McGraw-Hill. Texts which are perhaps more user-friendly for undergraduates are Thomas (1991) and Wisniewski (1991).

Essay title

1. 'Since models are an abstraction from reality they are very unlikely to be able to explain it.' Discuss.

Questions

1. Distinguish between the following pairs of terms: (a) stocks and flows; (b) identities and behavioural relations; (c) exogenous and endogenous variables.
2. Which of the following economic variables are flows and which are stocks: consumption, employment, investment, the rate of unemployment, the workforce, bank lending, budget deficit?
3. Write down a simple consumption function.

   (a) State which of the variables is the dependent variable and comment on the direction of causality implied.
   (b) In view of this comment on the direction of causality between income and consumption in the context of the national income identity.

4. Consider the two-equation model of consumption and income where the consumption function is $C_t = a + bY_{t-1}$ and the national income identity is $Y_t = C_t + I_t$.

   (a) By substituting the consumption into the income identity derive a dynamic equation for Y_t.
   (b) What is the condition for convergence, following disturbance to autonomous spending, I_t? Provide an economic interpretation of this condition.
   (c) Compute an expression for the equilibrium level of income. (Hint – in equilibrium $Y_t = Y_{t-1} = \overline{Y}$ where $\overline{Y}$, is the equilibrium level of income.)

5. Use the supply and demand model developed in the text to examine the stability of the market, given the alternative values of (a) $\lambda = 0.5$; (b) $\lambda = -0.5$; (c) $\lambda = 1.8$; and (d) $\lambda = 2.5$.

PART II
The Income–Expenditure Framework

CHAPTER 4
The Income–Expenditure Model and Goods Market Equilibrium

Aims and objectives

- To consider the primary determinants of the principal macroeconomic aggregates such as consumption, investment and net exports.
- To examine the determinants of the level of equilibrium income.
- To show that rises in autonomous spending increase output by more than the initial increase in spending; that is, there is a multiplier effect.

Introduction

One of the key questions in macroeconomics is what are the determinants of effective demand and how can the level of effective demand be maintained so that the economy produces at its fullest potential? This is in fact the question that underlies the simplest macroeconomic model that will be developed in this chapter: the income–expenditure model. This is the model that many elementary texts begin with and which was derived from Keynes' *General Theory of Employment, Interest and Money*, although it is, of course, a gross simplification of the ideas in that book. The key idea is that output is demand-determined, such that if the level of aggregate demand can be explained then so too can the level of output. An alternative way of saying the same thing is to make the assumption that prices are fixed, so that more output can be produced at the same unit cost if demand rises. Such characteristics are unlikely to prevail in the real world, except in cases of severe recession or depression such as that of the 1930s. Unfortunately such circumstances seem to reoccur all too often throughout the history of the industrial world thus giving this very simple model a continued *raison d'etre*.

In addition to being the simplest macroeconomic model another reason for starting with it is that it is the model most closely linked to the national income accounting framework developed in Chapter 2. The model is developed in several stages. The next section makes explicit the connection between the model and the system of national income accounting used in Chapter 2. The determinants of the various components of aggregate expenditure are then identified, solving the model for the equilibrium level of national income. Following this, the concept of the multiplier is examined and the effects of changes in exogenous parameters and variables considered. In the final section the construction of the good market equilibrium schedule – the IS curve – will be developed.

The national income identity and model equilibrium

This simple model begins from the national income accounts. In the national income accounts GDP can be viewed as a flow of income or output. In either case the total value (at market prices) of goods and services produced in the economy is the same so that the basic GDP identity is:

$$PC+PI+PG+PX-EP*M=GDP_\$=PC+PS+PT+PR_f \qquad (4.1)$$

where P is the general level of prices; C is real consumption expenditures; I is real investment expenditures; G is real government purchases of goods and services; X is volume exports of goods and services; E is the exchange rate (measured as the domestic price of foreign currency); $P*$ is the foreign level of prices (measured in foreign currency); M is volume of imports of goods and services; S is gross real private sector saving; T is net real tax revenues; and R_f is total private transfer payments to overseas residents.

Equation (4.1) is an identity; that is, it is true by definition. If I is defined as gross investment and S includes depreciation, to be gross private sector savings then Y is equal to GDP. If, on the other hand, I is defined as net investment, then S must also be defined as net private saving (by deducting depreciation allowances) and then equation (4.1) is an identity for national income or net national product. Ignoring the very small term in R_f and replacing money GDP by its equivalent, PY, then the identity becomes:

$$PY=PC+PI+PG+PX-EP*M=PC+PS+PT \qquad (4.2)$$

National income, PY, is measured at current prices and is frequently referred to as nominal or money GDP. For macroeconomics it is real GDP rather than money GDP that matters, so dividing (4.2) through by domestic output prices, P, gives GDP at constant prices:

$$Y=C+I+G+X-\left(\frac{EP*}{P}\right)M=C+S+T \qquad (4.3)$$

This identity says that real output is equal to real expenditure, which in turn is made up of domestic consumption, domestic investment, government expenditure and real net exports. If prices are assumed to be constant, then setting $P=P^*=1$, and assuming that initially the exchange rate, E is also equal to unity gives:

$$Y=AE=C+I+G+X-M \tag{4.4}$$

This identity defines GDP at constant prices, Y, as being equal to real aggregate expenditure (AE) given by $C+I+G+X-M$.

In terms of a diagram, with AE on the vertical axis and Y on the horizontal axis, equation (4.4) can be represented by a straight line passing through the origin, as in **Figure 4.1**. If the axes have the same scale then the line will make an angle of 45 degrees, or, more technically, a slope of plus unity.[1] Less technically as demand rises aggregate output rises in direct and exact proportion. It follows from this that all points to the right of the $Y=AE$ line are points of excess supply and points to the left of the $Y=AE$ line are points of excess demand. To see this consider point F in **Figure 4.1**. Aggregate expenditure is the same at F as it is at E, but output is higher at F than at E, that is at Y_1, rather than at Y_0. Hence point F is a point of excess supply of output. For the model to be in equilibrium we must be at some point on the $Y=AE$ line. Whereabouts we are on this line depends upon the level of the aggregate expenditure function.

The determinants of aggregate expenditure

The determinants of aggregate expenditure (AE) depend upon the specific behavioural hypotheses for each of the components, C, I, G, X and M. It is the determinants of these aggregates that form the basis of this section.

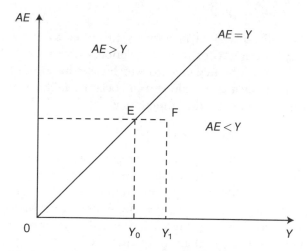

Figure 4.1 *Equilibrium in between expenditure and output*

---

[1] To see this result simply differentiate equation (4.4) with respect to AE. This gives the trivial result that $\partial Y = \partial AE$ and hence $(\partial AE/\partial Y)=1$.

Let us begin with the principal influences on real consumption, C. The principal determinant of consumption expenditures is real, personal disposable income. Following Keynes' (1936) dictum, that:

> The fundamental psychological law, upon which we are entitled to depend with great confidence both *a priori* from our knowledge of human nature and from the detailed facts of experience, is that men are disposed, as a rule and on the average, to increase their consumption as their income increases, but not by as much as the increase in their income. (ch. 8, p. 96)

Although Keynes went on to argue that a greater proportion of income is saved as real income increases, implying that the consumption function should be non-linear, for simplicity the consumption function is written as a linear function of real personal disposable income. That is:

$$C = \alpha_0 + \alpha_1(Y - T) \tag{4.5}$$

where T is total tax revenue, so that $Y - T$ is national income less tax revenue, that is disposable income. The α's are the constant parameters of the equation. α_1 is the marginal propensity to consume, which gives the addition to consumption from any increase in disposable income. Since it is expected that any rise in disposable income will be partly spent and partly saved, α_1 should be strictly less than one and greater than zero. α_0 represents autonomous consumption, that is, consumption expenditures which are independent of disposable income.

Total tax revenue, T, is assumed to be a simple positive function of income, so that as incomes rise so does the tax take. Thus the tax function is specified as:

$$T = \tau_0 + \tau_1 Y \tag{4.6}$$

where the marginal propensity to tax is given by τ_1 which is strictly less than unity. The intercept term, τ_0, denotes tax raised independently of income. This could in fact be negative, in which case this could be interpreted as 'negative tax revenue' such as is paid out in social benefits. Thus substituting (4.6) into (4.5) gives the consumption function as:

$$C = (\alpha_0 - \alpha_1 \tau_0) + \alpha_1(1 - \tau_1)Y \tag{4.7}$$

Equation (4.7) says that the marginal propensity to consume out of gross income is $\alpha_1(1 - \tau_1)$, which is the marginal propensity to consume out of disposable income multiplied by one minus the marginal propensity to tax. Since $1 > (1 - \tau_1) > 0$ it follows that the marginal propensity to consume out of disposable income is larger than that out of gross income and that $\alpha_1(1 - \tau_1)$ is greater than zero but less than unity; that is $0 < \alpha_1(1 - \tau_1) < 1$.

The second element of aggregate demand is that of private investment expenditures, I. It is assumed that these expenditures depend inversely upon the rate of interest, i. Investment is the demand for capital goods that are wanted because they will produce additional goods and services in the future. Thus expectations about the future are an important determinant of investment demand. When a firm buys a capital good the costs are incurred in the present but the revenues the firm expects to gain from the sale of goods produced using the capital good will occur in the future. The firm must therefore compare costs and revenues that occur at different time periods. The way of doing this is to bring all the future costs and revenues to their value in the current period. This is called their present value.

The net present value (NPV) of an investment project is the discounted value of all revenues minus the discounted value of all costs and is given as:

$$NPV = -Q_0 + \frac{R_1}{(1+i)} + \frac{R_2}{(1+i)^2} + \cdots + \frac{R_n}{(1+i)^n} \qquad (4.8)$$

where i is the market rate of interest, Q_0 is the initial cost of the capital good and R_t represents the net revenue expected in the t'th year. Given that firms wish to maximise their NPV, which is equivalent to maximising the present value of their future profits, they will adopt all investment projects which have a positive NPV. If the market rate of interest falls, expectations about future business conditions improve, or the price of capital goods declines the NPV of any investment project will rise. There will therefore be more projects with NPV>0 and hence greater demand for investment goods. With expectations and capital goods prices held fixed we can write the demand for investment as a negative (linear) function of the rate of interest:

$$I = \beta_0 - \beta_1 i \qquad (4.9)$$

Strictly, investment depends upon the real rate of interest, r, which is the difference between the nominal rate of interest, i, and the expected rate of inflation, $\hat{P}^e$, that is, $r = i - \hat{P}^e$. In this simple model, however, it is assumed that the expected rate of inflation is zero so that the nominal and real rates of interest are equal. It will also be assumed for the time being that i is itself determined exogenously by the government, denoted as i although the determination of the interest rate will be reconsidered in Chapter 8.

The government sector's demand for goods and services, G, is assumed to be determined by the government independently of the state of the macroeconomy. Although this assumption is to some extent incorrect, as G generally rises in recession and declines in booms, it is not important in the context of this model. Exogenous variables are indicated with bar on top so that exogenous G is denoted as $\bar{G}$.

The final components of aggregate demand stem from the economy's net trade with the rest of the world. The home country will sell goods to foreign residents which are called exports, denoted X, for the home country. On the other hand, some of domestic expenditures rather than being spent on domestic output will be spent on foreign-produced goods. These goods are called imports, denoted M, into the home country.

Let us begin with exports. The demand for domestic goods by foreign residents will depend on two factors: the level of consumer's income (that is foreign income) and the price competitiveness of domestic goods in foreign markets. With all other things held constant, the higher the level of foreign incomes the greater will be the demand for domestically produced goods. Thus there will be a positive relationship between domestic exports and foreign real income, Y^*. The second influence on the demand for domestic exports is their price competitiveness. If home goods are to be competitive in the foreign market then their prices must be compared with locally produced substitutes. Thus the price ratio, EP^*/P is referred to as the real exchange rate, e, or competitiveness, where E is the nominal exchange rate, defined as the domestic price of foreign currency and P^*/P is the ratio of foreign prices to domestic output prices. A rise in e means that domestic goods are relatively cheaper compared with locally produced goods and therefore, assuming these goods have some price elasticity, demand for domestic exports is expected to rise. Similarly a rise in domestic output prices will make domestic goods more expensive in foreign markets and so will, other things held constant, reduce the demand for domestic exports. Hence there is a positive relationship between X and e. The export function can be written as:

$$X = \delta_0 + \delta_1 \bar{Y}^* + \delta_2 \bar{e} \tag{4.10}$$

Note that the competitiveness term is equal to unity and does not change in this simple model. Note also that both foreign income and the real exchange rate are exogenous in (4.10). Since both explanatory variables are exogenously given in the context of this model exports can also assumed to be exogenously determined.

The model for imports has the same basic structure. The domestic demand for foreign goods and services depends upon the relative price of foreign goods relative to domestic goods and on the level of expenditure in the home economy. Imports are usually assumed to depend positively upon domestic income; this, however, ignores the fact that for most industrialised countries imports often consist of raw materials which are used up in the manufacture of domestic goods for export. So a rise in the demand for exports often necessitates a rise in imports. It is therefore preferable to express imports as a positive function of total final expenditure, TFE, which is defined as: $TFE = Y + M = C + I + G + X$, so that imports are able to rise with exports. A rise in the domestic price of foreign currency, that is a devaluation of the domestic currency, will result in higher domestic prices for imports and so imports will also be inversely related to the real exchange rate, e. This gives:

$$M = m_0 + m_1 TFE - m_2 e = m_0 + m_1 (Y + M) - m_2 e$$

Grouping terms in M together gives:

$$M = \mu_0 + \mu_1 Y - \mu_2 e \tag{4.11}$$

where $\mu_0 = m_0/(1 - m_1), \mu_1 = m_1/(1 - m_1), \mu_2 = m_2/(1 - m_1)$.

μ_1 is the marginal propensity to import out of income and will therefore lie between unity and zero, which means that m_1, the marginal propensity to import out of expenditure, is less than 0.5. Domestic and foreign price levels are assumed to be constant and equal to unity, so that the real and nominal exchange rates are identical.

Combining these behavioural relationships for consumption, investment, exports and imports together and combining terms gives the following equation for *planned* aggregate expenditure:

$$AE = \delta + [\alpha_1(1-\tau_1) - \mu_1]Y - \beta_1\bar{i} + \bar{G} + \delta_1\bar{Y}^* + (\delta_2 + \mu_2)\bar{e} \tag{4.12}$$

where $\delta = \alpha_0 - \alpha_1\tau_0 + \beta_0 + \delta_0 - \mu_0$.

This expression shows that the aggregate expenditure function is directly related to domestic and foreign levels of income, government spending and the real exchange rate, and inversely related to the rate of interest. This function can, of course, be shown on a graph. **Figure 4.2** shows this function plotted in (AE, Y) space. Because the coefficient on Y in equation (4.12) is expected to be positive,[2] but less than one, then the AE function has a positive slope in (AE, Y) space. The intercept denoted by Z is made up of all the other terms in (4.12), that is:

$$Z = \delta - \beta_1\bar{i} + \bar{G} + \delta_1\bar{Y}^* + (\delta_2 + \mu_2)\bar{e}.$$

The same exogenous variables are given in the brackets beside the AE function in **Figure 4.2** indicate the variables that are constant along the AE line. A change in any of these variables will cause the line to shift and the signs above these variables indicate the direction of the shift in the line following an increase in the respective variable.

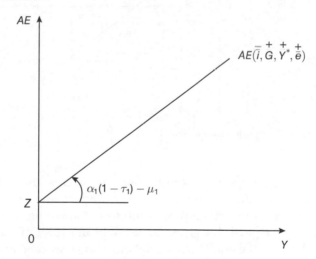

Figure 4.2 *Aggregate expenditure function*

---

[2] The first term is unambiguously positive, since $\tau_1 < 1$, so for the expression to be positive requires that $\alpha_1(1-\tau_1) > \mu_1$; i.e. that the marginal propensity to consume out of gross income exceeds the marginal propensity to import. Although strictly an empirical question it seems unlikely that this restriction will not hold in practice.

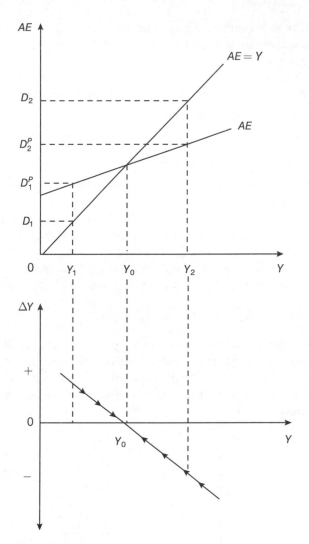

Figure 4.3 *Equilibrium income*

The aggregate expenditure line represents the total planned expenditure schedule for the economy. When *planned* expenditure equals actual expenditure the model is in equilibrium. Therefore combining the lines in **Figures 4.1** and **4.2** onto **Figure 4.3** gives the equilibrium level of national income at Y_0. The point about the equilibrium level of national income in **Figure 4.3** is the fact that this level of income is reached automatically and the model will not deviate from this level of income once it is reached unless the model is subject to an exogenous shock. To understand this, consider the situation at income level Y_1. At Y_1 the actual demand for domestic output is given by D_1, whereas agents plan to purchase D_1^P. Thus there is a potential excess demand for output. This will cause firms to increase their output since, as prices are fixed, more profit can be made by selling more goods. Indeed firms will expand output up to Y_0 where once again planned aggregate expenditure and aggregate supply are in balance. Similarly, at Y_2, there exists an excess supply of output, with planned expenditure falling short of actual expenditure. This results in firms accumulating stock, which ultimately leads them to cut back production to Y_0, where again planned expenditure equals output. Thus at all levels of output below Y_0 there is a situation of excess expenditure and output is rising, whereas at all points to the right of Y_0 output is falling as supply exceeds planned expenditure. The phase diagram below **Figure 4.3** shows that output rises in proportion to the excess expenditure over output (and falls in proportion to excess supply of output) and that a stable equilibrium is automatically established at Y_0.

The multiplier

The process described above implies that if the model is stable, as assumed, then it will tend automatically towards the equilibrium level of income at Y_0. However, in this model the equilibrium level of income will be affected by changes in the marginal propensities to consume, tax or import, by changes in the exogenous variables, i, G, Y^* and e and by changes in the shift parameters, α_0, β_0, δ_0, τ_0 and μ_0. In this section we see how changes in these some of these parameters and variables affect the equilibrium level of income.

Consider, for example, the effect of an exogenous increase in investment expenditures by private sector firms; that is a rise in β_0. This could be due, for example, to a change in businessmen's expectations about the future. If they become more optimistic about future demand for their products they will want to increase their capacity to produce. This will immediately raise aggregate demand, as δ rises, thereby shifting the AE line up to the left, to AE_1, as in **Figure 4.4**. This in turn will lead to a higher equilibrium level of output (and employment), at Y_1. The same qualitative effect will take place if either G, Y^* or e increases (or i falls). An important point to note here is that the level of income increases by more than the increase in the level of investment. This is due to the multiplier effect.

The size of the multiplier effect can be calculated by setting aggregate expenditure (AE) equal to income (Y) and then totally differentiating with respect to the relevant variable. Hence setting AE equal to Y gives:

$$Y = \delta + [\alpha_1(1-\tau_1) - \mu_1]Y - \beta_1\bar{i} + \bar{G} + \delta_1\bar{Y}^* + (\delta_2 + \mu_2)\bar{e} \tag{4.13}$$

Collecting terms in Y together and expressing Y as a function of the exogenous variables and parameters gives:

$$Y = \frac{\delta - \beta_1\bar{i} + \bar{G} + \delta_1\bar{Y}^* + (\delta_2 + \mu_2)\bar{e}}{1 - \alpha_1(1-\tau_1) + \mu_1} \tag{4.14}$$

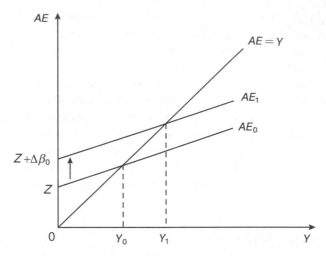

Figure 4.4   *Autonomous rise in investment*

The multiplier effect of the exogenous rise in investment is given by differentiating Y in equation (4.14) with respect to β_0. This is simply:

$$\frac{\partial Y}{\partial \beta_0} = \frac{1}{1 - \alpha_1(1 - \tau_1) + \mu_1} \qquad (4.15)$$

This multiplier is also relevant for autonomous changes in consumption, α_0, exports, δ_0, imports, $-\mu_0$ and also for a change in the level of government expenditure, G. The size of the multiplier clearly depends upon the size of the marginal propensities to consume, tax and import. Moreover, since the denominator is 1 minus the slope of the aggregate expenditure line it follows that the steeper the aggregate expenditure line the greater the multiplier effect. This is demonstrated in **Figure 4.5**, where the lines AE_1 and AE_2 both pass through point A, but with different slopes. An identical rise in autonomous investment will give rise to a higher equilibrium level of income in the case of AE_2 than with AE_1, because AE_2 has the steeper slope: that is, *ceteris paribus*, it has a larger marginal propensity to consume or lower marginal propensity to import, or both. Thus income rises to Y_2 in the case of the AE_2 line but only to Y_1 for AE_1 in **Figure 4.5**.

   This version of the multiplier is the most general. There are several special cases that can be usefully identified. First, in the case of a closed economy the marginal propensity to import would be zero ($\mu_1 = 0$) and therefore the multiplier would be larger, as the denominator in (4.15) becomes smaller. Second, if there are no income taxes, in addition to no imports, then the multiplier becomes larger still, as the denominator reduces to just $1 - \alpha_1$, which is the marginal propensity to save from disposable income. This is the simplest multiplier common in introductory textbooks. A third intermediate case presents itself as

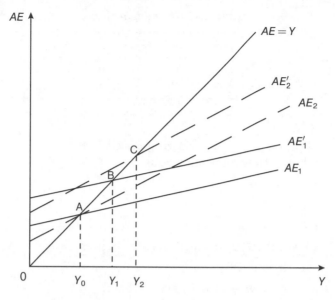

Figure 4.5 *The multiplier size effect*

when there is an open economy, but no income taxes, so that $\tau_1 = 0$ but $\mu_1 > 0$. In this case the multiplier becomes: $1/(1 - \alpha_1 + \mu_1)$. This exercise serves to illustrate that the multiplier is not a constant but depends on the type of model economy under consideration. The multiplier is largest in a no-tax closed economy case and smallest in the open economy with income tax case.

The derivation of the multiplier as in equations (4.14) and (4.15) obscures the fact that the multiplier is an inherently dynamic process. To see this aspect of the multiplier process refer to **Table 4.1**. Equation (4.13) can be written more simply as $Y = Z + aY$, such that $a = \alpha_1(1 - \tau_1) - \mu_1$ and where a rise in β_0 is equivalent to a rise in Z. A unit rise in β_0 will cause a unit rise in Y in period one. In the second period, although there is no further change in β_0, the rise in income from the first period now induces a further rise of a in Y. In the third period the rise in income of a in period two induces a further rise in income of a_2 and so on. The total effect upon Y of the unit change in β_0 is therefore the sum of all of these increments, that is: $1 + a + a^2 + a^3 + \ldots + a^{n-1}$ as shown in **Table 4.1**. This is simply the sum of a geometric progression (see **Box 4.1**) which is given by $1/(1-a)$, where $a = \alpha_1(1 - \tau_1) - \mu_1$, is the slope of the *AD* line. Simply substituting for a with its equal gives the equation for the multiplier previously derived as equation (4.14).

The key idea of the multiplier is that particular autonomous changes in expenditure will have much larger effects upon output. This means that small changes in investment, perhaps as a result of changes in business expectations about the future, will have a magnified effect upon domestic output. It is also true, of course, that discretionary fiscal policy changes, say through changes in government expenditure, will also have a multiple effect upon output. Such fiscal policy

Table 4.1 *The mulplier process*

Time	0	1	2	3	4 .....n	
$\Delta\delta$	0	1	0	0	0	0
ΔY	0	1	a	a^2	a^3	a^{n-1}

Box 4.1

The sum of a geometric progression is as follows. Define the sum, S, as:

$$S = 1 + a + a^2 + a^3 + \cdots + a^{n-1} \qquad \text{(B4.1)}$$

multiply by a:

$$aS = a + a^2 + a^3 + \cdots + a^n \qquad \text{(B4.2)}$$

substract (B4.2) from (B4.1) which gives:

$$S(1-a) = 1 - a^n \qquad \text{(B4.3)}$$

As $a < 1$ as $n \to \infty$ $a^n \to 0$ so we have:

$$S(1-a) = 1 \text{ or } S = 1/(1-a) \qquad \text{(B4.4)}$$

which is given in the text.

---

changes are considered in Chapter 5. To conclude this chapter an alternative way of representing goods market equilibrium is demonstrated.

The *IS* curve

An alternative way to present the results in this chapter is to use the so-called *IS* curve.[3] This plots goods market equilibrium, the locus of points along which output equals planned aggregate expenditure, in interest rate–output space. This line can be derived from equation (4.14) above, which also represents goods market equilibrium. As i falls the right-hand side of (4.14) rises, and so to maintain equilibrium Y must also increase. In other words the fall in i raises aggregate expenditure by an extent that must be matched by a rise in output if goods market equilibrium is to be maintained.

Figure 4.6 shows the relationship between the *IS* curve and the income–expenditure model. In the upper panel, equilibrium national income is given at Y_0 with the rate of interest at i_0. In the lower panel the combination of income at Y_0 and interest rate at i_0 gives point E. Next consider a fall in the rate of interest to i_1. In the upper panel of **Figure 4.6** the AE schedule moves up to the left, since

---

[3] This was the name given to the goods market equilibrium schedule by Hicks (1937), in the context of a closed economy without government, in which case goods market equilibrium requires only that investment (I) equals savings (S).

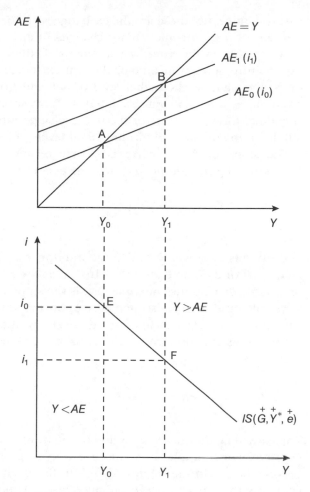

Figure 4.6 *Derivation of the* IS *curve*

planned investment and aggregate expenditure will be higher due to the fall in the rate of interest, and a new equilibrium level of income will be established at Y_1. In the lower panel the lower rate of interest, as represented by the line from i_1, will intersect with a line extrapolated downwards from the level of income at point F. This is also an equilibrium point like point E. Joining points E and F gives a downward-sloping line for goods market equilibrium, called the *IS* curve.

All points above and to the right of the *IS* curve are points of excess supply of goods ($Y > AE$) and correspond with those points to the right of the $Y = AE$ equilibrium in **Figure 4.3**. To return to equilibrium at given rates of interest requires a fall in output. All points below and to the left of the *IS* curve are positions of excess demand for goods ($Y < AE$); again for given rates of interest, a rise in Y is required to return the model to equilibrium. Note that the endogenous variables are now i and Y and changes in these variables result in movements along the *IS* schedule. All other variables, other than i and Y, are held constant in the upper part of **Figure 4.6**, these are the exchange rate, the level of government expenditure and foreign income. Hence changes in any of these variables cause the *IS* curve to shift in the same way as they shift the *AE*. Thus a rise in government expenditure, foreign income or the real exchange rate, will all shift the *IS* curve up to the right, as the higher level of demand brings forth higher output for a given price level and rate of interest. Correspondingly, a fall in government spending, foreign income or the real exchange rate will shift the *IS* down to the left, lowering the level of income for all levels of interest rates.

The slope of the *IS* curve is closely related to the slope of the *AE* line. Differentiating equation (4.14), with respect to i and Y gives:

$$\frac{\partial i}{\partial Y} = -\frac{1 - \alpha_1(1 - \tau_1) + \mu_1}{\beta_1} < 0 \tag{4.16}$$

The slope is negative. Note that the multiplier as given in equation (4.15) is the reciprocal of the numerator of (4.16), so as the slope of the *AE* line is related to the simple expenditure multiplier, so is the slope of the *IS* curve. In addition, the slope of the *IS* curve also depends upon the responsiveness of investment to changes in the rate of interest, as given by the parameter, β_1. Defining the autonomous expenditure multiplier as k then the slope of the *IS* curve can be written as:

$$\frac{\partial i}{\partial Y} = -\frac{1}{k\beta_1} < 0 \tag{4.17}$$

Thus anything that raises the value of the multiplier will reduce the slope of the *IS* curve. For example, in a closed economy $\mu_1 = 0$, so that the multiplier will become larger. In this context therefore the *IS* curve will be 'flatter' in a closed economy than in an open economy. This is demonstrated in **Figure 4.7**. From point A a fall in the rate of interest from i_0 to i_1, will lead to a rise in output from

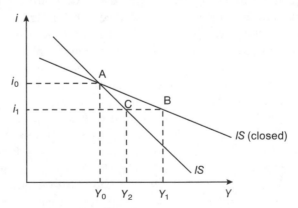

Figure 4.7 *The slope of the* IS *curve in closed and open economies*

Y_0 to Y_1 in the case of the closed economy, but to only Y_2 for the open economy *IS* curve. The reason is that the fall in the rate of interest raises expenditure, which in the open economy case raises imports, Therefore increasing the demand for foreign output rather than domestic output. Hence the open economy *IS* curve will have a steeper slope than the closed economy version.

Conclusions

This chapter has reviewed and extended the basic income–expenditure model of the demand for goods and services. In particular, the model has been developed in the context of an open economy where the demand for domestic output from foreign residents has been assumed to be exogenous. In the next chapter the problems of economic policy-making in an open economy with fixed exchange rates and in the absence of international capital flows will be considered in greater detail.

Summary

- The largest component of aggregate expenditure is consumption, which accounts for about 65 per cent of GDP in the UK, although investment is the most volatile.
- Consumption is largely determined by income through the marginal propensity to consume. Net exports are related to income (through the marginal propensity to import) but also to the real exchange rate. A rise in the real exchange rate denotes a rise in the price competitiveness of domestic production relative to foreign production.
- The open economy multiplier is smaller than the closed economy multiplier, because in an open economy some proportion of any rise in spending by domestic agent will be spent on imported goods and services.
- The *IS* schedule denotes goods market equilibrium. In an open economy this schedule has a steeper slope than in the closed economy, reflecting the smaller size of the open economy multiplier.
- Fluctuations in foreign income can generate fluctuations in aggregate expenditure due to the fact that domestic exports depend directlly on foreign demand and thus there is the potential for a global business cycle.

Suggested further reading

The principle statement of the multiplier is Keynes (1936) – Chapter 10 – on the Marginal Propensity to Consume and the Multiplier, although Kahn (1931) is usually attributed with the first formal statement of this concept; but see also Goodwin (1947). The commentary on Keynes's chapter 10 in Hansen (1953) is highly instructive. The more technically minded would also benefit from reading Samuelson (1948). The notion of the *IS* curve comes from Hicks' (1937) classic interpretation of the *General Theory*. All of these contributions, however, focus on closed economies and thus are not identical to what has been set out in this chapter. One of the first expositions of the foreign trade multiplier is Robinson (1952).

Essay titles

1. 'Savings always equal investment.' Discuss.
2. What forces at work in the real world might act to constrain the long-run effect of the multiplier?
3. Critically evaluate the simple income–expenditure model as a theory of the determination of the level of output, the balance of trade and interest rates.

Questions

1. Use the income–expenditure model to predict the effect of:

   (a) An increase in the rate of interest;
   (b) An increase in the level of foreign income;
   (c) A cut in the marginal rate of income tax.

2. The following model represents the income– expenditure system, where the variable symbols are defined in the text:

   $$Y = C + I + G + X - M$$
   $$C = 50 + 0.9(Y - T)$$
   $$T = 0.5Y$$
   $$M = 50 + 0.5(Y - T)$$
   $$I = G = 300 \text{ and } X = 400$$

   (a) compute the equilibrium level of national income;
   (b) what is the value of the government expenditure multiplier?
   (c) what is the value of the balance of payments?
   (d) is the government's budget in surplus or deficit?

3. Suppose the government wishes to raise the level of national income by 300. Using the model of question 2 above compute:

   (a) the increase in government spending that would be necessary to bring this about;
   (b) the increase in the rate of income tax necessary to bring this about;
   (c) the effect on the budget balance of (a) and (b).

4. Why does the *IS* curve slope downwards? Explain how from any position off the *IS* curve the model automatically adjusts back to a position on the *IS* line.

5. Suppose the domestic authorities fix the interest rate at i. Show the effect of devaluation on the level of national income, using the *IS* curve. Using the model given in the text write down an expression for the magnitude of the multiplier.

6. What are the limitations of the income–expenditure model as a model of the macroeconomy?

CHAPTER 5

Fiscal Policy and Devaluation Analysis

Aims and objectives

- To investigate relative sizes of alternative fiscal policy multipliers in the open economy income–expenditure model.
- To consider the problems of measuring the stance of fiscal policy and to develop the concept of the high employment budget surplus (HEBS).
- To examine the role of devaluation in raising output and in alleviating the current balance constraint on fiscal expansions.

Introduction

In this chapter the effects of economic policy on the fixed-price, income–expenditure model are considered. Two kinds of economic policy are considered: fiscal policy and devaluation analysis. Fiscal policy, defined as a discretionary change in government expenditure or taxation, will be shown to have potentially powerful effects on domestic income, subject to the balance of payments constraint that prevents ever-expanding output even in a world of fixed prices. An alternative policy instrument, which can be shown to both raise income and improve the trade balance, is a devaluation, although to attain this result requires some particular conditions to be satisfied. In the final part of this chapter the effects of a simultaneous fiscal expansion and devaluation, are considered in recognition of the Tinbergen principle (Tinbergen, 1952) that with two targets, domestic output and the trade balance, two independent instruments are needed to simultaneously achieve both objectives. It is shown that although it is possible to reconcile the two policy objectives such a policy may be subject to serious limitations in practice.

Fiscal policy

There are basically three types of discretionary fiscal policy that can be employed in this model: a change in government spending, a change in lump-sum taxes or a change in income taxes. Each of these types of fiscal policy change will have a different sized multiplier. These multipliers can be obtained from the goods market equilibrium equation derived in Chapter 4, as equation (4.14) and repeated here as equation (5.1):

$$Y = \frac{\delta - \beta_1 \bar{i} + \bar{G} + \delta_1 \bar{Y}^* + (\delta_2 + \mu_2)\bar{e}}{1 - \alpha_1(1 - \tau_1) + \mu_1} \tag{5.1}$$

Differentiating equation (5.1) with respect to G, τ_0 and τ_1 respectively, gives the three multipliers as follows:

$$\frac{\partial Y}{\partial G} = \frac{1}{1 - \alpha_1(1 - \tau_1) + \mu_1} = k_G$$

$$\frac{\partial Y}{\partial \tau_0} = \frac{-\alpha_1}{1 - \alpha_1(1 - \tau_1) + \mu_1} = k_{\tau_0} \tag{5.2}$$

$$\frac{\partial Y}{\partial \tau_1} = \frac{-\alpha_1 Y}{1 - \alpha_1(1 - \tau_1) + \mu_1} = k_{\tau_1}$$

Thus an increase in government expenditure is associated with a multiplier of k_G. This is identical to the autonomous investment spending multiplier discussed in Chapter 4. An increase in lump sum taxation, on the other hand, leads to a reduction in income of $-\alpha_1 k_G$. It is important to note that the latter multiplier effect is smaller than the former, since the marginal propensity to consume, α_1, is strictly less than one. This implies that a simultaneous and equal increase in G and τ_0 will have a net expansionary effect. A 'balanced budget' expansion of government spending therefore will lead to an increase in output.

To see this note the difference between the expansionary effect due to the rise in G and the contractionary effect of a rise in τ_0. That is, from (5.2) above:

$$\partial Y = \frac{\partial G}{1 - \alpha_1(1 - \tau_1) + \mu_1} - \frac{\alpha_1 \partial \tau_0}{1 - \alpha_1(1 - \tau_1) + \mu_1} \tag{5.3}$$

with $\partial G = \partial \tau_0$ we get that:

$$\partial Y = \frac{1 - \alpha_1}{1 - \alpha_1(1 - \tau_1) + \mu_1} \partial \bar{G} = \frac{1 - \alpha_1}{1 - \alpha_1 + (\alpha_1 \tau_1 + \mu_1)} \partial \bar{G} \tag{5.4}$$

which is strictly greater than zero. In the special case of the balanced budget multiplier where $\tau_1 = 0$, all taxes are lump-sum taxes and hence unrelated to income, and where the economy is closed to foreign trade so that $\mu_1 = 0$, the expression (5.4) reduces to unity. Thus the balanced budget multiplier is only unity in this special case. In the general case the balanced budget multiplier is less than unity since $\alpha_1 \tau_1 + \mu_1 > 0$. **Figure 5.1** shows this case. From the initial position at A an increase in government spending shifts AE_0 up to AE_1 and income from Y_0 to Y_1. The rise in lump sum taxation equal to $\partial \tau_0 = \partial G$ has the effect of shifting AE_1 down

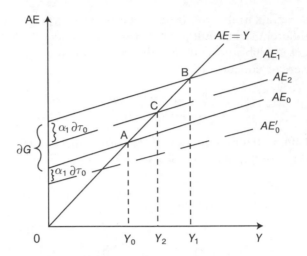

Figure 5.1 *The balanced budget multiplier*

to AE_2 (that is by $\alpha_1 \partial\tau_0$) and income falls back to Y_2. Thus the balanced budget multiplier has a positive net effect on income.

The size of the income tax multiplier, given by $k\tau_1$, depends on the initial level of income in addition to the marginal propensity to consume. This implies that a cut in the income tax rate will have a greater effect when the level of income is high than when the level of income is low. Thus, when a cut in income tax is most necessary, that is in a recession, the income tax cut will be less effective. On the other hand, a rise in the marginal tax rate in a boom will have more potency in reducing income than in a recession, when, of course, it is likely to be less important. **Figure 5.2** shows the effect of a cut in the rate of income tax at different levels of income. At point A, with income at Y_0, a cut in the rate of tax causes the AE_0 line to swivel upwards to AE_1, leading to a rise in income from Y_0 to Y_1. A further cut in the marginal tax rate of the same magnitude at point B causes the AE_1 line to swivel up again to AE_2. This increase in income is given by $Y_2 - Y_1$ which is greater than $Y_1 - Y_0$, although the cut in income tax is identical. This is simply because the cut in income tax has more effect the higher is the initial level of national income.

There are three principal points to note about these results. Firstly, that the open economy fiscal policy multipliers are all smaller than their closed economy counterparts since each contains μ_1 in the denominator. The reason is simply that in an open economy part of any increase in domestic income goes to purchase imports; that is, foreign goods rather than domestic goods. Such purchases raise foreign demand rather than domestic demand and generate foreign rather than domestic income. The second point to note about the multipliers is that the largest multiplier possible is the government expenditure multiplier, which is the same as the exogenous investment demand multiplier outlined in Chapter 4. The assumption underlying this result is that the government purchases all of its extra demand from domestic producers. It does not purchase any of the extra goods and services demanded from overseas suppliers. How realistic this result is

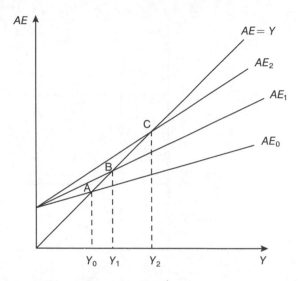

Figure 5.2 *The income tax multiplier*

will depend upon the structure of the domestic economy and the specific demands made by the government. A third result that follows from this is that the government expenditure multiplier will always be larger than the tax multiplier. So to raise income by a specific amount will require a much bigger tax cut than an increase in government expenditure. The reason is again simply because any rise in disposable income, resulting from a tax cut, will not all find its way to domestic demand. Some of the rise in income may be saved and some will be spent on foreign goods. Therefore the government expenditure multiplier will be larger than both of the tax multipliers.

The effectiveness of the three fiscal instruments used in this simple model show that domestic output can be influenced by discretionary fiscal actions. The problem in practice is to be able to measure the effectiveness of such discretionary changes in raising output. This is a problem because the most obvious measure of the change in fiscal stance, the change in the budget deficit, is not a reliable indicator of discretionary actions because it may fluctuate in the absence of any fiscal policy change. For example, **Figure 5.3** shows the budget deficit naturally increases as income falls, and falls as income rises. In the figure the T line slopes up reflecting the positive marginal propensity tax and has a slope of τ_1, while the G line is drawn horizontal reflecting the fact that government spending is assumed to be exogenous of income. Thus, although changes in the G or T lines will alter the budget balance, changes in income occurring for other reasons will also alter the budget balance even in the absence of a fiscal change. Hence the budget is balanced at Y_0, but in deficit at Y_1, given by distance 0A in **Figure 5.3**, although there has been no change in fiscal stance.

The high employment budget surplus (HEBS) employs a simple dodge to overcome this problem by evaluating the budget balance at a given level of income.

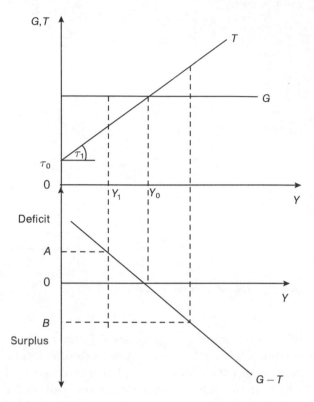

Figure 5.3 *The budget balance*

In this way any changes that are registered must be due to changes in fiscal policy since the effect of changes in income has been neutralised. **Figure 5.4** shows that if we choose Y_0 to be the level of income consistent with high employment, then an increase in taxes from T_0 to T_1 would, at Y_0, generate a HEBS, given by AB in the top section and 0S in the lower section of the figure. Matching this increase in taxes with a rise in G from G_0 to G_1 would give a deficit equal to BC in the upper quadrant and 0D in the lower quadrant. Thus the change in HEBS should be interpreted as suggesting that an increase is a contractionary fiscal action and a decrease is an expansionary one. Note that the HEBS line in the lower quadrant of **Figure 5.4** is horizontal, indicating that HEBS is independent of the level of income.

Although this measure of discretionary fiscal policy is superior to the budget deficit or public sector borrowing requirement (PSBR) there are still a number of problems associated with it. The first is that from our analysis of the multiplier effects the output generating effects of a rise in government expenditure are greater then those of a cut in tax rates, since part of the tax cut falls on savings. These differential effects on output need to be allowed for in computing the HEBS, by attributing weights to both government expenditure and tax changes. If a weight of unity is given to G and a weight of α_1 to T then in a closed economy an adequate measure of the fiscal stance can be derived. In an open economy,

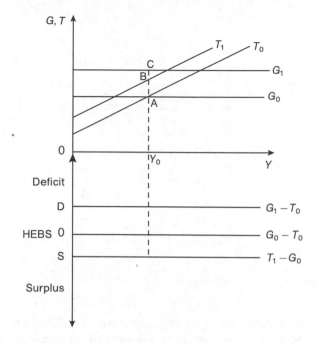

Figure 5.4 *The high employment budget surplus (HEBS)*

however, the import content of both tax and spending changes have to be included as well, so the weights become $(1 - \mu_G)$ on G and a weight of $[\alpha_1(1 - \mu_G)]$ on T, where μ_G and μ_C are the marginal propensities to import from government expenditure and consumption respectively.[1] Use of these weights will give a measure of the weighted high employment budget surplus (WHEBS) which is preferable to the unweighted measure. One problem with the WHEBS, however, is that it may give misleading signals if the actual level of income is a long way from the chosen level of income as shown by **Figure 5.5**. Suppose we chose to measure WHEBS at Y_0. The marginal change in the tax function from T_0 to T_1, records a change in WHEBS of AB at Y_1 according to the tax schedule, T_0. On the other hand, according to tax schedule T_1 at Y_1, the budget deficit is much larger denoted by AC and hence fiscal policy more expansionary.

The nature of the current balance constraint

The analysis of discretionary fiscal policy as described above may imply that there is no limit to the extent to which income can be increased in the absence of a capacity constraint. In an open economy context this is not the case since changes

---

[1] To the extent that the government sector does not buy from abroad, then $\mu_G = 0$ and the weight of unity is appropriate.

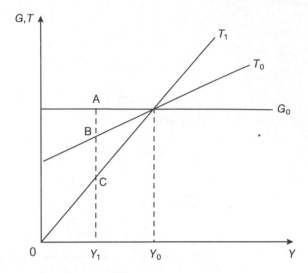

Figure 5.5 *The WHEBS problem*

in income effect the current account balance. Therefore the balance of payments on current account may act as a constraint on domestic fiscal policy expansion. In this section the nature of this constraint on fiscal actions is examined.

The balance of payments on current account is defined as the difference between exports and imports. From Chapter 4 the current account was specified in real terms as:

$$B = X - M \tag{5.5}$$

where it was implicitly assumed that domestic and foreign prices and the exchange rate are held constant and normalised to unity. Substituting the specified functions for export and import volumes from Chapter 4 the balance on current account is given by:

$$B = (\delta_0 - \mu_0) + \delta_1 Y^* - \mu_1 Y + (\delta_2 + \mu_2)e \tag{5.6}$$

This equation is very important, because it shows that as domestic demand (income) rises so the current account of the balance of payments deteriorates, as more imports are sucked into the economy. That is:

$$\frac{\partial B}{\partial Y} = -\mu_1 < 0 \tag{5.7}$$

This current balance relationship is shown in **Figure 5.6** together with the aggregate expenditure and *IS* schedules showing goods market equilibrium. The current balance line slopes down since for given levels of foreign income, Y^*, and the real exchange rate, e, the current balance worsens as domestic demand increases. Hence a fiscal expansion, which shifts out the *IS* and *AE* lines from IS_0 to IS_1 and from AE_0 to AE_1 respectively, also causes the current balance to move from initial balance into deficit, given by the vertical distance OD. This diagram shows the conflict between external balance, as measured by the current account

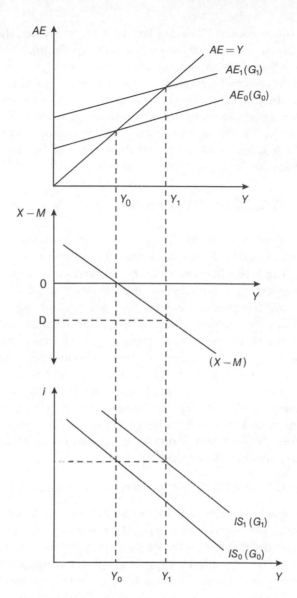

Figure 5.6 *The balance of payments constraint*

balance and internal balance, as measured by the level of domestic income. Unless the government reverses the fiscal expansion the balance of payments will continue to deteriorate leading to a loss of foreign currency reserves and perhaps eventually to a run on the currency.

To avoid such damaging events the authorities have to find a way of alleviating the current balance constraint. There are in fact a number of options available, although not all of them will be considered here. The first is for the authorities to borrow money from foreign banks or from international organisations such as the International Monetary Fund (IMF), to finance the deficit. Such borrowing is usually short-term, allowing the authorities more time to undertake the necessary adjustment. A second alternative would be to allow the exchange rate to float freely on the foreign exchange market, so as to give continual external balance. In practice such freely floating exchange rates are often implausible and hence some intervention (and financing) is likely to be needed. A third option would be to find an additional policy instrument to fiscal policy to influence the trade balance. One such instrument could be the exchange rate. This is the option considered in the next section.

Devaluation analysis

To evaluate the effects of devaluation on domestic income is not straightforward for two reasons. Firstly, the effect of devaluation on the balance of trade ambiguous. The arises because devaluation raises the domestic price of imports relative to exports, that is the terms of trade decline, which means that the home economy has to sell more exports for each unit of imports. Thus the terms of trade effect has a negative effect on the trade balance and domestic income. On the other hand, because devaluation makes exports cheaper in foreign currency and imports more expensive in domestic currency, exports are encouraged and imports discouraged, thereby improving the balance, of trade. Secondly, a devaluation even it is does initially improve the trade balance, will generate a rise in income which will raise the demand for imports thereby worsening the balance of trade and reducing the level of income. In this section these two effects: the relative price effect (or direct effect) and the induced income effect (or indirect effect) are considered in some detail.

The direct effect – the elasticity approach

The elasticity approach to devaluation was pioneered by Marshall (1923) and Lerner (1944) and later extended by Robinson (1937) and Machlup (1939, 1955). The model focuses on the demand conditions and assumes therefore that supply elasticities for domestic exports and foreign imports are perfectly elastic, so that changes in demand volumes have no effect on prices. This assumption means that domestic and foreign prices are fixed so that changes in relative prices are caused solely by changes in the nominal exchange rate.

In order to investigate the effect of devaluation on the current account balance consider the nominal trade balance identity, which is written as:

$$B_\pounds = PX - EP^*M \qquad (5.8)$$

This says that the nominal current balance, $B_\pounds$, is equal to the value of exports less the value of imports, both expressed in terms of the home currency. Since P and P^* are taken to be fixed they can be normalised to unity so that in real terms the trade balance, B, is:

$$B = X - EM \qquad (5.9)$$

Substituting for X and M from equations (4.10) and (4.11) in Chapter 4 gives:

$$B = \delta_0 + \delta_1 Y^* + \delta_2 E - E(\mu_0 + \mu_1 Y - \mu_2 E) \tag{5.10}$$

where, because $P = P^* = 1$, the real and nominal exchange rates are equivalent so that $E = e$. To find the effect of a change in the exchange rate on the balance of trade equation (5.10) is totally differentiated to give:

$$\partial B = (\delta_2 + E\mu_2 - M)\partial E + \delta_1 \partial Y^* - E\mu_1 \partial Y \tag{5.11}$$

Defining the price elasticity of demand for exports, η_x, as the percentage change in exports over the percentage change in price (represented by the exchange rate), and the price elasticity of the demand for imports, η_m, as the percentage change in imports over the percentage change in price (again represented by the exchange rate), gives:

$$\eta_x = \frac{\partial X}{\partial E}\frac{E}{X} = \delta_2\frac{E}{X} > 0, \quad \eta_m = \frac{\partial M}{\partial E}\frac{E}{M} = \mu_2\frac{E}{M} > 0 \tag{5.12}$$

using the fact that $(\partial X/\partial E) = \delta_2$ and $(\partial M/\partial E) = \mu_2$ from equations (4.10) and (4.11). Substituting these expressions into equation (5.10) gives:

$$\partial B = \left(\eta_x\frac{X}{E} + E\eta_m\frac{M}{E} - M \right)\partial E + \delta_1 \partial Y^* - \mu_1 \partial Y \tag{5.13}$$

In trade balance equilibrium, $B = 0$, so from equation (5.9) $X = EM$ so that $X/E = M$. From this it follows that M can be taken outside the term in brackets and dividing through by the change in the exchange rate, ∂E the final expression is:

$$\frac{\partial B}{\partial E} = (\eta_x + \eta_m - 1)M + \delta_1\frac{\partial Y^*}{\partial E} - E\mu_1\frac{\partial Y}{\partial E} \tag{5.14}$$

If this expression turns out to be positive then a devaluation of the domestic currency, that is a rise in E, will improve the current account of the balance of payments. This expression shows that a change in the exchange rate has two kinds of effects on the balance of trade: a direct effect, through changes in relative prices and an indirect effect due to the effect of the devaluation on foreign and domestic incomes.

To begin with consider only the direct effects of devaluation on the trade balance. The direct effects will improve the trade balance if the first term in equation (5.14) is positive. This will be positive if the sum of the price elasticities of demand for exports and the demand imports are greater than one; that is if $\eta_x + \eta_m - 1 > 0$, or alternatively, $\eta_x + \eta_m > 1$. This is known as the *Marshall–Lerner* condition. If this condition holds then devaluation is likely to improve the trade balance, although this condition is only a necessary and not a sufficient condition.[2]

If the Marshall–Lerner condition holds then the price effects of devaluation are smaller than the quantity effects. To see this consider **Figure 5.7** which shows

---

[2] It is not a sufficient condition because we have ignored the induced income effects coming from the last two terms in equation (5.14).

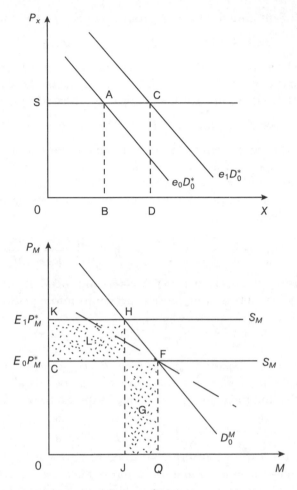

Figure 5.7 *Exchange rate change on exports and imports*

the market for domestic exports and imports. The supply prices are fixed in local currency, but the demand schedules vary in foreign currency. Initially export receipts are 0SAB. After a devaluation the foreign currency price falls so the demand line shifts to the right, raising export receipts to 0SCD, which improves the trade balance. On the import side however, the effects of devaluation are less clear cut. The devaluation raises the supply curve so that import prices rise in terms of domestic currency and import payments change from 0CFQ to 0KHJ. Thus domestic residents save area G but lose area L. If $G > L$ then imports payments fall and the trade balance improves, but if $G < L$ the import payments increase which tends to worsen the balance of trade. **Figure 5.7** can be used to illustrate that the more price elastic the demand for imports schedule the more likely is $G > L$. To do this imagine a flatter import demand function passing through point F, this will show that area G becomes larger and L smaller. The

Marshall–Lerner condition derived above is a formalisation of this argument. Hence if the sum of the demand elasticities exceeds unity the relative price effect will operate to improve the trade balance, but in practice the effect of devaluation on the trade balance is an empirical question and may be country-specific.

Although there are enormous technical problems involved in estimating the elasticity of demand for imports and exports the empirical evidence suggests that for the fifteen major industrial countries the Marshall–Lerner condition holds, with an average value for $\eta_x + \eta_m$ of about 2.0. These results are based on estimates of the elasticities over a two-to-three year time horizon, so do not preclude an initial worsening of the trade balance immediately following devaluation. Indeed there is a general consensus that elasticities are lower in the short run than in the medium to longer run. Goldstein and Kahn (1985) conclude that the medium run elasticities (greater than two years) are about twice as large as the short run elasticities (less than six months). Furthermore, the short run elasticities almost always fail to sum to unity while the long-run elasticities almost always sum to greater than unity.

The possibility that in the short run the Marshall–Lerner condition may not be fulfilled although it generally holds in the longer run, leads to the so-called J-curve effect. Suppose following devaluation that domestic import prices rise immediately but that import volumes do not fall immediately, due to previously agreed contracts, the sluggish nature of chang in consumer tastes, firms' 'pricing to market,' or whatever. Then clearly the impact effect of devaluation will be to worsen the trade balance as import payments rise sharply. It is not until import volumes begin to fall and export production rises to meet the higher demand that the trade balance starts to recover. Hence in **Figure 5.8** the trade balance is assumed to be in balance when the devaluation takes place at time t_1. Following the devaluation the trade balance immediately deteriorates until t_2, after which it begins to improve as import volumes decline and export volumes rise, reaching a surplus position by time t_3. How long the surplus can be maintained is also open to doubt since eventually the domestic economy must come up against a supply

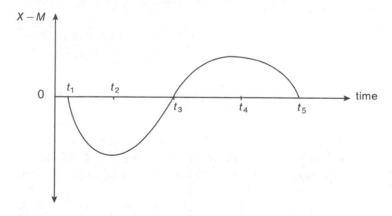

Figure 5.8   *The J-curve effect*

constraint, which will trigger a rise in the general level of prices, which will tend to reverse, at least partially, the trade balance gains from the devaluation. Hence by time t_4 in **Figure 5.8** the surplus is declining. Indeed if the decline continues until time t_5, the gains from the devaluation will have been entirely temporary and the J-curve will have become an S-curve.

The direct effects of devaluation on the trade balance according to this approach are doubtful in both the short run and the long run, but quite hopeful in the medium term if the Marshall–Lerner condition holds. This approach, however, is only a partial equilibrium approach because the effect of the devaluation on income and the subsequent effects of rising income on the trade balance have been ignored until now.

The indirect effect – the absorption approach

The elasticities model is incomplete because it ignores the income terms in equation (5.14). The first term, $\partial Y^*/\partial E$, can legitimately be ignored because it is likely to be very small for most countries. That is, a domestic devaluation is unlikely to have a very large effect on world income. Ignoring the effects on world income leaves only the induced effect of devaluation on domestic income.

Alexander (1952) proposed that the national income identity be written as:

$$B = Y - A \tag{5.15}$$

where Y is income and A is absorption (domestic expenditure) which is equal to $C + I + G$. The important thing about this equation is that it emphasises the point that if the balance of trade is to improve then output, Y, must rise by more than expenditure, A. Alexander specified the absorption function as

$$A = a_1 Y + a_d \tag{5.16}$$

where a_1 is the marginal propensity to absorb and a_d represents direct effects on absorption. Substituting this into (5.15) gives:

$$B = (1 - a_1) Y - a_d \tag{5.17}$$

To see the effect of devaluation on this model totally differentiate (5.17) and divide through by the change in the exchange rate, ∂E, which gives:

$$\frac{\partial B}{\partial E} = (1 - a_1) \frac{\partial Y}{\partial E} - \frac{\partial a_d}{\partial E} \tag{5.18}$$

This equation can now be rearranged in terms of the change in the exchange rate on income, that is: $\partial Y/\partial E = (\partial B/\partial E + \partial a_d/\partial E)/(1 - a_1)$. Substituting for $\partial Y/\partial E$ in equation (5.14), rearranging and normalising E to unity, gives:

$$\frac{\partial B}{\partial E} = \frac{(1 - a_1)(\eta_m + \eta_x - 1)M}{1 - a_1 + \mu_1} - \left(\frac{\mu_1}{1 - a_1 + \mu_1} \right) \frac{\partial a_d}{\partial E} \tag{5.19}$$

This equation measures the total effect of devaluation on the trade balance. As the first term shows, the Marshall–Lerner condition is a part of the overall condition. In what follows it will be assumed that this condition is satisfied so that $\eta_m + \eta_x - 1 > 0$.

In addition to the Marshall–Lerner condition being valid it is also assumed that $a_1 < 1$. Alexander argued that as a devaluation would give rise to a greater demand for domestic output this would in turn lead to a sharp rise in investment expenditures so making the marginal propensity to absorb greater than unity. Thus devaluation would worsen the trade balance even if the Marshall–Lerner condition were satisfied. In the context of the model developed so far, however, the marginal propensity to invest out of income is zero, since the investment function does not depend upon income. Therefore the marginal propensity to absorb is the same as the marginal propensity to consume out of disposable income; that is $a_1 = \alpha_1(1 - \tau_1)$, which is defined to be less than unity.

There is however, a second factor working against a successful devaluation – the terms of trade effect of devaluation. The terms of trade is simply the price of exports divided by the price of imports. Since devaluation tends to make imports more expensive in domestic currency terms, which is not matched by a rise in domestic export prices, a devaluation means that the terms of trade will deteriorate. The deterioration in the terms of trade represents a loss of real income because more units of exports have to be given up to obtain a unit of imports. Hence the terms of trade effect lowers income so making it less likely that a rise in E will improve the balance of payments. This effect however, is likely to be empirically small so it is highly likely that the first term in (5.19) will be positive as required.

The only possibility therefore of devaluation worsening the trade balance is if the devaluation has strong, positive direct effects through the second term in (5.19). This seems unlikely. The principal direct effect of devaluation on absorption identified by Alexander was the cash balance effect. The argument was that any devaluation would serve to raise prices, especially as full employment was approached, in which case the value of individuals real cash balances would decline. In order to rebuild these balances to their desired levels individuals would therefore cut back their spending and so reduce absorption. In this case the direct effect on absorption reinforces the effect of the devaluation. To the contrary, however, Laursen and Metzler (1950) argued that devaluation by raising the price of foreign goods relative to domestic goods would lead to substitution towards domestic goods away from imported goods that would raise absorption. If this effect were to predominate then the trade balance could deteriorate as a result of devaluation.

This discussion has shown that ultimately the effect of devaluation on the trade balance is an empirical issue. On balance, however, if the marginal propensity to consume is less than unity (as it must be), the Marshall–Lerner condition holds (as it probably does for most industrial countries) and there is spare capacity in the devaluing economy, then devaluation is likely to improve the trade balance, especially in the medium term. Furthermore the effectiveness of devaluation may be enhanced if it is used in combination with another policy instrument. This case is considered in the next section.

The Swan model of internal and external balance

The idea behind this model is to combine fiscal policy and exchange rate policy in such a way as to maintain simultaneous external and internal balance. We have seen that while an expansionary fiscal policy raises output it causes the balance of payments to deteriorate. On the other hand, devaluation may raise domestic output and generates an external surplus. Combining both policies together it should be possible to influence both policy targets in a favourable manner. This is best illustrated in a simple diagram, due to Swan (1955).

Figure 5.9 shows the line of external or current account balance, labelled *EB*. This line has a positive slope in (E, G) space. This can be proved by differentiating equation (5.10) above with respect to E and G, where $\partial Y = k_G \partial G$ and k_G is the government expenditure multiplier:

$$\frac{\partial E}{\partial G} = \frac{k_G \mu_1}{(\eta_x + \eta_m - 1)M} > 0 \tag{5.20}$$

In terms of economics, the *EB* line slopes up because any fiscal expansion will worsen the balance of payments, so requiring a devaluation of the exchange rate, that is a rise in E, to restore external balance. Hence a rise in G must be offset by a rise in E for the external account to remain in balance. Thus for a given exchange rate, such as E_0, a point like A, to the left of the *EB* line, is a position of external surplus. Similarly point C, to the right of *EB* is a position of external deficit, since G is too high to give external balance at E_0.

The locus of internal balance, denoted *IB* in **Figure 5.10**, has a negative slope. This can be deduced from equation (4.13) in Chapter 4. Differentiating with respect to E and G, bearing in mind that income is held constant gives:

$$\frac{\partial E}{\partial G} = -\frac{1}{\delta_2 + \mu_2} < 0 \tag{5.21}$$

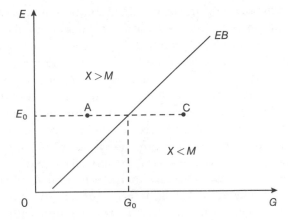

Figure 5.9   *External balance line*

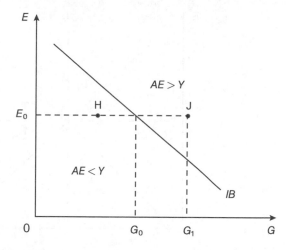

Figure 5.10 *Internal balance line*

The economic rationale behind this relationship is as follows. A rise in G will raise income, but to prevent income from rising above its equilibrium level the exchange rate must appreciate (a fall in E) to reduce aggregate demand for domestic goods and services. Therefore points to the right of IB in **Figure 5.9** are points of excess demand or boom while points such as H, to the left of IB are points of excess domestic supply or slump.

Where the IB and EB schedules cross (at A) is the position of both internal and external balance, as shown in **Figure 5.11**. This figure divides up into four zones of economic misery, which are labelled I to IV. Zone I is that of external surplus and internal boom; zone II is consistent with external deficit and internal boom; zone III exhibits external deficit and internal slump and finally zone IV shows external surplus and internal slump. It follows from any of these positions of misery that a combination of exchange rate and fiscal policy is required to return the model to equilibrium at A. To illustrate this point consider a point like C, which is in zone II. If just fiscal policy is used to restore internal balance, then G is reduced until point D is reached. At D although there is now internal balance there is an external surplus. Returning to point C, if just exchange rate policy is used to correct the internal boom, the exchange rate will appreciate until point F is reached, in which case the external deficit is now larger than before. Only if both fiscal policy and exchange rate policy are used can both internal and external balance be achieved simultaneously.

Unfortunately this turns out to be more complicated than it at first appears. The policy combinations required depend crucially upon not only which zone the policy-makers thinks they are in, but exactly whereabouts in the zone! Consider point C again. In terms of reaching A, fiscal policy needs to be contracted and the exchange rate revalued, as shown by the direction arrows through C. On the other hand, at point H rather than at C, although still in the same zone,

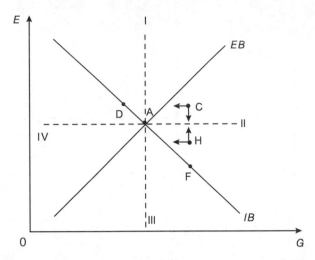

Figure 5.11 *The Swan model*

devaluation of the exchange rate needs to be combined with fiscal contraction to reach point A. Thus although fiscal policy needs to be contracted it is not clear, unless it is known what part of the zone the economy is in, as to whether the exchange rate should be revalued or devalued. Moreover this problem exists in all zones: whereas one policy instrument is always unambiguous with regards to its direction of change the other instrument is always ambiguous, depending as to what part of the zone you are in. This clearly makes the model less useful for policy formation purposes than at first was apparent.

This is, however, not the only limitation of this simple model. A second problem is that it assumes that foreign and domestic income levels are unchanged. Any shocks to income levels will cause the *IB* and *EB* lines to shift which makes it very difficult for the authorities to establish in which zone the economy is likely to be, and hence to undertake the appropriate combination of policies. Indeed, misjudgment on this matter could be very important since the economy may be driven away from the new equilibrium rather than towards it, in which case macroeconomic policy would be deemed destabilising.

Another problem is that governments may not be prepared to use the exchange rate in the way this model requires. For example, during the 1960s governments were frequently reluctant to change the value of the exchange rate regarding its value as a matter of prestige. The ability of the authorities to control the exchange rate, however, is not so great as it once was with the enormous sums of internationally mobile capital in the world economy. This huge stock of capital can be used for speculative purposes against an individual currency, about which the national authorities can do very little. The question of international capital mobility will be considered in later chapters, but the omission of international capital flows from this model, makes it less useful as a guide to economic policy.

Conclusions

This chapter has shown that economic policy formulation in an open economy is more complex than in a simple closed economy model. The complication comes about because the authorities have to operate within a balance of payments constraint in the medium term. This means that fiscal policy can not be used to stimulate domestic demand indefinitely unless there is a great deal of spare capacity in the domestic economy or unless the authorities are prepared to use devaluation as a supporting policy instrument. The problem with this is that the effects of devaluation on the trade balance are complex and uncertain. Moreover, governments may be unwilling or unable to use the exchange rate in the manner required, especially if they believe that devaluation may have potential consequences for future inflation.

Summary

- The government expenditure multiplier is the largest of the fiscal policy multipliers. In an open economy the balanced budget multiplier is always greater than unity, even if the marginal propensity to tax is zero.
- The budget deficit is not a good measure of the stance of fiscal policy because it varies endogenously with the level of income. The use of the high employment budget surplus (HEBS) helps to alleviate this problem, although this is not entirely without problems.
- Fiscal policy expansions are constrained in the open economy context by the current account balance.
- A necessary, but not sufficient condition, for a successful devaluation is that the Marshall–Lerner condition holds, such that the sum of the demand elasticities of exports and imports exceed unity.
- The Swan model of economic policy in an open economy without capital flows, suggests that two independent instruments are needed to simultaneously achieve two targets. Thus internal and external balance can be simultaneously achieved using a combination of fiscal and exchange rate policies.

Suggested further reading

The best source of information on UK fiscal policy and measuring the fiscal stance is the *National Institute Economic Review*. Although it is now a little dated the analysis by Savage (1982) is interesting in this regard, but see also Miller (1985). Classic works on open economy economic policy include those by Laursen and Metzler (1950), Swan (1955), Corden (1960) and Johnson (1958), the latter of which emphasises the need for expenditure switching and expenditure reducing policies. Haberler (1949) gives a detailed account of the Elasticities Approach while Alexander (1952) is the original source of the Absorption Approach to devaluation. Alexander (1959) attempts a rather technical synthesis of the two approaches. For a historical review of balance of payments theory, which ties this analysis to that in Chapter 1, see Frenkel and Johnson (1976).

Essay titles

1. Explain the concept of a discretionary fiscal policy. What are the problems that the authorities may face in trying to pursue an expansionary discretionary fiscal policy?
2. Does devaluation always improve the trade balance?
3. With international interdependence comes the consequence that a business cycle originating in one country can spread to all economies. Explain how this can happen and assess the empirical importance of this for the UK economy.

Questions

1. (a) Define the concept of a balanced budget.
   (b) Under what circumstances is the balanced budget multiplier equal to unity?
   (c) To what extent are these circumstances relevant to modern industrial economy?

2. Is the PSBR (public sector borrowing requirement) a good measure of the fiscal stance? If not, why not?

3. Use an income–expenditure diagram in conjunction with a panel to show the budget position, to show the effect of an exogenous fall in investment on the government's attempt to pursue a balanced budget.

4. Explain why devaluation does not necessarily improve the trade balance of an economy with spare capacity. Relate this to a Marshall–Lerner condition.

5. (a) Draw the Swan diagram indicating the nature of the disequilibrium in each of the four zones.
   (b) What policy advice would you offer a government faced with an external deficit and an internal boom?
   (c) How might your advice differ if the government insisted on maintaining a fixed exchange rate?

CHAPTER 6
Consumption

Aims and objectives

- To examine alternative theories of consumption, including the current, relative and normal income theories.
- To examine the intertemporal microeconomic foundations of the normal income theories of aggregate consumption behaviour.
- To examine the empirical evidence for the modern theories of consumption and the implications for macroeconmic policy.

Introduction

Aggregate consumption is the largest component of aggregate expenditure accounting for about 65 per cent of GDP in the UK in 1997. It is therefore important for the implementation of macroeconomic policy to be able to predict consumption reasonably well. The term 'consumption', however, is not straightforward to define. Consumption means the using up of services yielded by a good, such as the consumption of a meal in a restaurant or the pleasure gained from a concert. This is different from 'consumer's expenditure' which is the act of purchasing a good or service, which may last for more than one period. For example, the purchase of a car is part of consumer's expenditure, but it will not all be consumed in the current period. Indeed if the car is used for three years the flow of consumption services from it will last for three years. This distinction between the purchase of a meal in a restaurant and the purchase of a car is the distinction between a non-durable good and a durable good, because the latter yields consumption services over several periods, whereas the non-durable good is wholly consumed in the current period. In this regard durable goods are like investment goods, in that they provide a flow of services over several periods, but they are classed as part of consumption because they are purchased by households, rather than by firms. The reason for this is that whereas an investment good purchased by a firm is used to produce other goods and services for sale in the market place, households do not use their motor cars or washing machines for producing other goods for sale.

In this chapter the determinants of aggregate consumption and the savings ratio are examined. The approach is largely an historical one, beginning with Keynes' theory and ending with a consideration of the random-walk models of consumption from the 1980s. The next section considers the current income theories of consumption and the early empirical studies which attempted to test them. This is followed by an examination of the microeconomic foundations of the intertemporal choice models of consumption; the normal income theories of consumption, due to Ando and Modigliani (1963) and Friedman (1957); a review of the recent empirical evidence; and finally a discussion of the importance of these theories in the context of the standard income–expenditure model and their implications for the efficacy of monetary and fiscal policy.

Current income hypotheses

The notion of the consumption function stems from Keynes' *General Theory of Employment Interest and Money* (1936) and so it is the natural starting point for a discussion of alternative theories of consumption.

The absolute income hypothesis

Keynes set out three complementary assumptions regarding consumption:

1. Consumption will rise as disposable income rises.
2. An increase in consumption will be smaller than the increase in disposable income. That is to say the marginal propensity to consume (MPC) is greater than zero but less than unity. In terms of the model set out in Chapter 4, $0 < \alpha_1 < 1$.
3. The average propensity to consume (C/Y) is greater than the marginal propensity to consume, but is assumed to fall as income rises, since, on average, the rich spend less of their income than the poor.

These propositions can be expressed in terms of a linear consumption function, as in Chapter 4, where:

$$C = \alpha_0 + \alpha_1(Y - T) = (\alpha_0 - \alpha_1\tau_0) + \alpha_1(1 - \tau_1)Y \tag{6.1}$$

The first point to notice is that the marginal propensity to consume out of disposable income, α_1, is larger than the marginal propensity to consume out of gross income, $\alpha_1(1 - \tau_1)$ since a proportion of any rise in gross income will be used to pay taxes. Because the function is linear, it is assumed that both marginal propensities to consume are constant, although the average propensities to consume fall as income rises. To see this divide equation (6.1) by Y to get:

$$\frac{C}{Y^D} = \frac{\alpha_0}{Y^D} + \alpha_1 \quad \text{or} \quad \frac{C}{Y} = \frac{\alpha_0 - \alpha_1\tau_0}{Y} + \alpha_1(1 - \tau_1) \tag{6.2}$$

where Y^D is disposable income and the first term in both expressions falls as income rises, thus confirming the assumption that the average propensity to consume (APC) falls as income rises. This is the *absolute income hypothesis* (AIH) and it is illustrated in **Figure 6.1**. The line 0E is the 45-degree line along which all disposable income is consumed. The linear consumption function above is drawn so that at low levels of disposable income consumption exceeds income. At income level Y_1, consumption is given as the distance $0C_1$, while savings are given by S_1 and represent that amount of disposable income not spent. The average propensity to consume is given by the level of consumption divided by the level of income, which is C_1/Y_1, and can be represented by the slope of line 0B. This picture can also be used to show that the APC declines as income rises. Suppose now that income is Y_2, which is greater than Y_1. The APC is now given by the slope of the line 0D, which is less than the slope of the line 0B so the APC has declined.

The early empirical evidence, from cross-section and time-series data, found support for the linear version of Keynes' absolute income hypothesis, with $\alpha_0 > 0$ and statistically significantly different from zero, whilst the marginal propensity to consume, α_1, took a value between zero and one. Forecasts for the USA in the late 1940s, however, predicted a level of aggregate consumption that was far lower than the actual levels observed. This is consistent with the view that the simple consumption function had shifted upwards. Kuznets (1946) published the first long-run time-series data for the USA for the period 1869–1929, which showed that the ratio of aggregate consumption to national income – that is the APC – had remained constant at about 0.84–0.89 for the entire period. This data set implies that the $APC = MPC = k$ and that the consumption function passes through the origin. This kind of proportional consumption function is written as:

$$C = kY \tag{6.3}$$

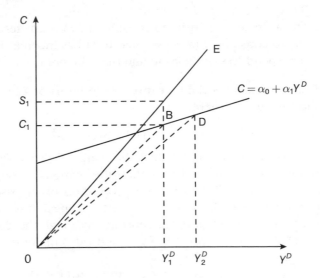

Figure 6.1 *Absolute income hypothesis*

So although the early empirical work showed that budget data and short-run time-series data supported the AIH, Keynes' proposition that the APC falls as income rises was in conflict with the long-run data. By the end of the 1940s the picture appeared to be that while long-run time-series data suggested a consumption function with no intercept and a constant APC, both the short-run time-series and cross-section data suggested a function with an intercept and for which MPC<APC. Although this difference could easily be reconciled by arguing that the short-run consumption function was shifting over time, there was no good theoretical reason as to why this should happen.

The relative income hypothesis

The first attempts to provide a theoretical reconciliation of the short-run and long-run findings was undertaken by Duesenberry (1949) and Modigliani (1949) who independently developed the **relative income hypothesis** (RIH) of consumption. Duesenberry's hypothesis was based on two propositions: (1) the demonstration effect and (2) the ratchet effect.

The cross-section data suggested that higher income groups save a much higher propor- tion of their income than low-income groups. Consumption there-fore not only depends on a household's absolute income, but also on its relative income. Those earning higher incomes can maintain the same, or slightly better, standards of living than their neighbours, and still save a larger proportion of their incomes. On the other hand those with relatively low incomes, in an attempt to 'keep up with the Jones's' spend most of their income and in some cases even dis-save. The effect of the richer groups demonstrating a high standard of living, which the relatively poor try to copy, is the *demonstration effect*. Over time, however, the average income per head increases which allows the lower-income groups to catch up with the Jones's, while simultaneously the Jones's can increase their spending to stay ahead. Therefore as absolute income rises over time, so the consumption of all groups rises and the cross-section consumption function shifts upwards.

The second hypothesis – the *ratchet effect* – is based on the idea that it is harder for a household to reduce than to increase its expenditures. Once a family has embarked on a high level of consumption, it will be difficult for them to reduce consumption if income falls. The long-run consumption pattern of spending the same proportion of income is not reversed. A fall in income causes the APC to rise because consumption falls by a smaller absolute amount than income. Thus the APC depends upon the level of peak disposable income $\tilde{Y}^D$ relative to current disposable income. This can be expressed by the following consumption function:

$$\frac{C}{Y^D} = \alpha_0 + \alpha_1\left(\frac{\tilde{Y}^D}{Y^D}\right) \tag{6.4}$$

Multiplying through by current disposable income Y_t^D, (6.4) becomes:

$$C_t = \alpha_0 Y_t^D + \alpha_1 \tilde{Y}^D \tag{6.5}$$

If income were to grow at a constant rate of g then $Y_t^D = (1+g)Y_{t-1}$ and moreover if $\tilde{Y}^D = Y_{t-1}$, (6.5) can be written as:

$$C_t = \left(\alpha_0 + \frac{\alpha_1}{1+g} \right) Y_t^D \tag{6.6}$$

Since for most economies income can be regarded as having grown at a roughly constant rate with only relatively minor cyclical fluctuations, (6.6) suggests that long-run time-series data will give a consumption function possessing no intercept and with a constant APC and MPC both equal to the coefficient on Y_t^D. A short-run cyclical fall in income, however, leads to $Y_t^D < \tilde{Y}^D$ with $\tilde{Y}^D$ remaining constant until Y^D rises again to this level. Under these circumstances equation (6.6) can be written as (6.5) where the intercept is a constant equal to $\alpha_1 \tilde{Y}^D$ and the MPC $= \alpha_0$. Thus the consumption function obtained from the short-run time-series data is of the Keynesian type with an MPC smaller than that obtained from the long-run consumption given by equation (6.6).

This combination of short-run and long-run behaviour gives the ratchet effect that is shown in **Figure 6.2**. Suppose the initial level of income is at Y_0 and that income rises over time, moving up the long-run function, until it reaches Y_1. At Y_1 income begins to decline cyclically, whereupon consumption falls back along the shallower curve given by BD, as consumers try to maintain their previous levels of spending when income was at its peak level. Consumption remains on this curve until incomes rise to Y_1, when consumption then continues to grow up the long-run function towards point F. If the next cyclical income peak is at Y_2, then once income declines from this peak consumption falls back along the new (higher) short-run function, labelled GF. Since the intercept of this function is higher than the previous intercept there is a ratchet effect, with the short-run function gradually shifting upwards.

An interesting further implication of equation (6.6) is economies that experience relatively high economic growth should have relatively lower APCs. This

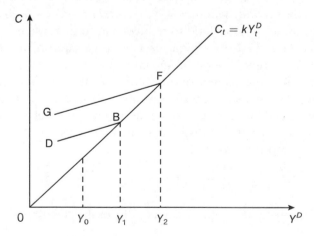

Figure 6.2   *The ratchet effect*

implication is in fact in accordance with observation that countries with the highest growth rates tend to have the largest saving–income ratios.

Intertemporal choice

Although Duesenberry's model introduces some dynamics into consumption behaviour, it does have rather unusual microeconomic foundations assuming, for example, that individuals' utility from consumption depends in part on the consumption of other individuals. A more traditional way of introducing dynamics is through the notion of intertemporal choice. It is this microtheoretic framework which underlies the modern normal income theories of consumption, to be discussed in the next section.

Consumption is assumed to be the purpose of all economic activity. Therefore household utility is taken to depend upon its lifetime profile of consumption. To keep the analysis as simple as possible it is assumed that the individual lives for only two periods: today, period 1, and tomorrow, period 2. Lifetime utility for the household will therefore depend positively upon consumption in both periods, that is:

$$U = U(c_1, c_2) \tag{6.7}$$

The household is assumed to maximise lifetime utility subject to the constraint imposed by the household's wealth, where wealth is defined as the present value of all future income. In a two-period model this is simply:

$$A_1 = y_1 + \frac{y_2}{1+i} \tag{6.8}$$

where A_1 represents the households expected lifetime's real wealth measured in terms of period 1, y_1 is this period's real income and y_2 is next periods income discounted by the (real) rate of interest, i. It is also assumed that agents know with certainty the expected future rate of interest and that the capital market is perfectly competitive, so that the household can lend or borrow as much as it wants, at the going rate of interest without affecting that rate. Transactions costs are also assumed to be zero.

Figure 6.3 shows the structure of this model. The vertical axis measures income and consumption in period 2 and the horizontal axis measures income and consumption in the current period. Because this is a two-period model and consumption is the sole aim of economic activity, it follows that lifetime wealth will be the constraint on lifetime consumption, that is:

$$c_1 + \frac{c_2}{1+i} = y_1 + \frac{y_2}{1+i} \tag{6.9}$$

The budget constraint, BC, indicates the maximum amount of lifetime consumption. If the household wants to consume all of its lifetime income stream in period 1, by borrowing against period 2 income, then the maximum amount that can be consumed in period 1 is $y_1 + y_2/(1+i)$ which is the intercept of the budget line on the period 1 axis. Conversely, if the household decides to consume nothing in period 1, delaying all consumption until period 2, the maximum it can consume in period 2 will be $y_1(1+i) + y_2$ which is given by point B on the period 2 axis. The slope of the budget constraint is given by differentiating the wealth constraint, for a given level of the interest rate, which gives:

$$\frac{\partial y_2}{\partial y_1} = -(1+i) \tag{6.10}$$

Assume the household receives income of y_1 in period 1 and y_2 in period 2, which defines point A, on BC. Also assume that the household has an indifference map, representing preferences for consumption in periods 1 and 2, as given in **Figure 6.3** by the lines, U_1, U_2 and U_3, and where the subscripts on U denote increasing levels of utility. In order to maximise utility, the optimal consumption position for the household, given the budget constraint and the preference map, is at point E, where utility is given by the indifference curve labelled U_2. From point E it is clear that the individual household saves in period 1, since $c_1 < y_1$, and then dis-saves in period 2 as $c_2 < y_2$. At point E the slope of the indifference curves are exactly equal to the slope of the budget constraint, so the ratio of the marginal utility of consumption in period 1, $\partial U/\partial c_1$ to that in period 2, $\partial U/\partial c_2$ is exactly equal to $-(1+i)$. That is, the marginal rate of substitution between consumption in period 1 and consumption in period 2 is $-(1+i)$.

Furthermore, if the indifference curves are homogenous of degree zero, then the slopes of all indifference curves are identical along a straight line passing through the origin. This implies that the marginal rate of substitution of c_1 for c_2 depends

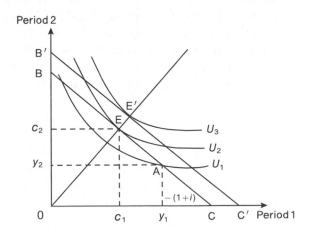

Figure 6.3   *The intertemporal model*

only on the ratio c_1/c_2 and not on the absolute sizes of c_1 and c_2. This assumption has the economic implication that if a consumer received an extra pound's worth of resources he would allocate it between c_1 and c_2 in exactly the same proportion as he allocated his original resources. That is, as wealth rises, with a constant rate of interest, the budget lines shift out parallel, leaving the optimal c_1/c_2 ratio unchanged no matter what the size of wealth. The c_1/c_2 ratio will, however, still depend on the interest rate and on the shape of the indifference map. The constancy of c_1/c_2 for a given rate of interest means that c_1 and c_2 are in fact constant proportions of total wealth, A, that is $c_1 = \alpha_1 A_1$ and $c_2 = \alpha_2 A_2$ where the α's are independent of A.

Figure 6.4 shows the effect of a change in the rate of interest on the level of consumption in each period. Suppose the rate of interest rises from i_0 to i_1. The higher level of interest will cause the budget constraint to swivel around through the initial endowment point at A. The higher rate of interest will increase the potential income available in period 2, and so point B moves up to B'. The same rise in the interest rate means that in period 1 income in period 2 is discounted more heavily, so point C moves inwards to C'. Given the individual's indifference map the new equilibrium position will be at point F, where the movement from E to F is made up of the familiar income and substitution effects. The income effect, represented by the movement form point E to G, is the increase in consumption in period 1 due to the rise in income available in period 1. The substitution effect, represented by the movement from G to F, is the reduction in consumption in period 1, due to the higher rate of interest on saving in period 1. It is important to note that these two effects work in the opposite direction and so the overall effect on consumption of a rise in the rate of interest is strictly ambiguous. In **Figure 6.4**, however, the substitution effect dominates the income effect and consumption falls in period 1, but rises in period 2.

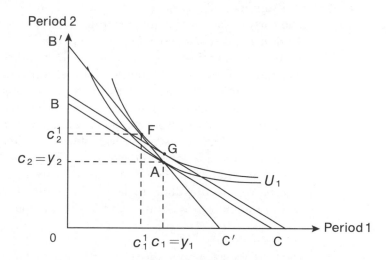

Figure 6.4 *A rise in the rate of interest*

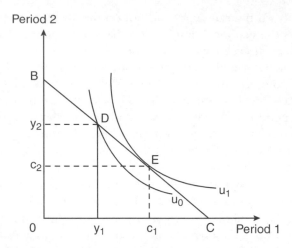

Figure.6.5 *Liquidity constraint*

This simple two-period framework provides a number of important insights into the determinants of consumption. The position of the budget constraint is determined by three variables – income in each period and the rate of interest. If the consumer's income should rise in any period, the present value of his wealth will increase as the budget line moves out to the right nearly parallel to BC^1 in **Figure 6.3**. Thus, the household can reach a higher level of utility than that at E, such as that at E'. One implication of this analysis is that current-period consumption will vary less than income, since any a rise in income in any one period will be spread across consumption in all periods. A second implication of the analysis is that the effect of changes in the real rate of interest will serve to alter the allocation of income to consumption in any one period. Thus a rise in the interest rate in period 1 will cause a fall in consumption in period 1 and a rise in consumption in period 2 if the substitution effect dominates the income effect. Similarly, a fall in the interest rate in period 1 will increase consumption in period 1 and reduce consumption in period 2.

This inter-temporal model assumes that individuals are able to spread their consumption across time because of their capacity to borrow and lend at market rates of interest. Because of this consumption is related to lifetime income or wealth, rather than current income. This analysis, however, ignores the fact that individuals may face borrowing constraints, particularly in the early part of their lives. **Figure 6.5** shows an individual with an initial income endowment of y_1 but with consumption expenditures of c_1. Thus in period 1 this individual is borrowing against future income to finance his current consumption. Suppose now that the banks are unwilling to lend to this individual because they are uncertain about the individual's future ability to repay the loan and hence fear that he may

---

[1] The shift will not be strictly parallel since the effect of a rise in income in period 1 will shift the point B further out than the point C, since B moves out by $(1+i)\,\Delta y_1$ whereas C moves out by only Δy_1.

default. In this case the individual will face a liquidity constraint and will have to reduce current consumption, c_1, to match his current income. In this case the individual's budget constraint in Figure 6.5 is given not by BDC, but by BDy_1, and his utility is reduced to u_0 from u_1. Thus in both periods the individual's expenditure is tied closely to current income. If such liquidity constraints are a common feature of the real world then it should be expected the consumption will still depend largely on current income, rather than on wealth, although wealth effects could still have some effect on consumption.

Normal income theories of consumption

There are two principal models that fall into this category, both which are based on the microeconomic foundations of intertemporal choice: Modigliani's **life-cycle hypothesis** (LCH) and Friedman's **permanent income hypothesis** (PIH).

The life-cycle hypothesis

Modigliani and Brumberg (1954) in their life-cycle hypothesis of consumption generalised the two-period model, by assuming that households planned their lifetime consumption patterns so as to maximise their total utility during their lifetime. Thus a household of age T maximises a utility function of the form:

$$U = U(C_T, C_{T+1}, \ldots, C_L) \tag{6.11}$$

where C_j is planned consumption at age j and L is the household's expected age at death. Providing the household intends to just exhaust its total resources by the time of its death, this utility function has to be maximised subject to the lifetime budget constant:

$$A_{T-1} + Y_T + \sum_{j=T+1}^{N} \frac{Y_j^e}{(1+i)^{j-T}} = \sum_{j=T}^{L} \frac{C_j}{(1+i)^{j-T}} \tag{6.12}$$

where A_{T-1} represents physical and financial assets at the beginning of the household's T'th year, Y_T is the household's earned income at age T, Y_j^e its expected earned income at age j and N is the expected age at retirement. Assuming that the marginal rate of substitution of consumption in any one year for consumption in any other year depends only on the ratio of consumption in these two years, then by analogy with the two-period case, planned consumption at age T becomes a constant proportion of total lifetime resources at age T, A_T, that is:

$$C_T = \alpha_T A_T \tag{6.13}$$

where A_T is equal to the sum of the three terms on the left-hand side of equation (6.12). Similarly for future years planned consumption is given by $C_j = \alpha_j A_j$, for

$j = T+1, T+2 \ldots L$. As in the two-period case, the α's are dependent on the rate of interest and on the household's preferences, but in the lifetime case they also depend upon on the age of the household. The age of the household is important because it is assumed to wish to totally exhaust all its resources during its lifetime. Thus the nearer a household gets to the end of its life the greater the proportion of its resources it will plan to consume in any given year.

The most important implication of the LCH is that a change in current income, Y_T, will affect current consumption, C_T, only to the extent that it affects household wealth, A_T. This is an important difference between this model and the absolute and relative income hypotheses. The implication is that changes in current income will not have much effect on consumption, unless the household is towards the end of its life.

Combining equations (6.12) and (6.13) gives consumption at age T of:

$$C_T = c_T A_{T-1} + c_T Y_T + c_T \sum_{j=T+1}^{N} \frac{Y_j^e}{(1+i)^{j-T}} \tag{6.14}$$

Since expected future incomes, Y^e, are likely to be closely related to current income, Y_t, equation (6.14) can be regarded as relating current consumption to current income at age T and to financial and physical assets at the beginning of the household's T'th year. For the economy as a whole, therefore, an aggregate relationship of the form:

$$C_t = \alpha_0 Y_t + \alpha_1 A_{t-1} \tag{6.15}$$

is expected. With this form, since A_{t-1} rises over time, the short-run relationship between consumption and income will have a non-zero intercept and moreover this intercept will shift upwards over time as A_{t-1} increases.

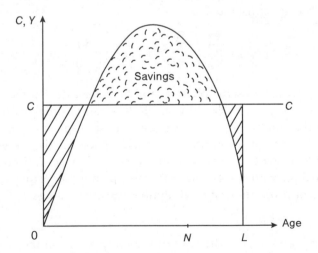

Figure 6.6   *The life-cycle model of consumption*

Finally, consider the case where the interest rate is zero, so that there is no rate of time preference. The household now plans to consume at a constant rate throughout its lifetime. For such a household income is likely to rise steadily at first until somewhere near the expected age of retirement, N, and decline, possibly quite sharply, afterwards, as shown in **Figure 6.6**. Consumption on the other hand proceeds at a constant rate. It is clear from **Figure 6.6** that even with a zero rate of interest and an absence of time preference, a typical household will still borrow and save. Without saving during its 'middle age' and dis-saving during its retirement a household would be restricted to consuming no more and no less than its current income during each year of its life. An important motive for saving in the LCH is therefore the desire to flatten out the lifetime profile of consumption expenditures and to avoid the restrictions that might be imposed by a varying level of income.

The permanent income hypothesis

The permanent income hypothesis (PIH), like the LCH, has its roots in the intertemporal model of consumer behaviour, although there are a few subtle differences between the two models. For example, Friedman (1957), generalises the two-period model into a model with an 'indefinitely long horizon' rather than to a current life-span, and defines wealth as the discounted sum of all future receipts, including income from non-human assets. However, in a competitive world of complete certainty the value of non-human assets would exactly reflect the discounted sum of future earnings on them and hence, under these conditions, the Friedman and Modigliani measures of wealth would be the same.

Friedman defines current planned or *permanent consumption*, C^p, as depending, as in the two-period model, on current wealth, A. Wealth is defined as the discounted sum of all future income receipts, which in period t is given as:

$$A_t = Y_t + \frac{Y_{t+1}}{(1+i)} + \frac{Y_{t+2}}{(1+i)^2} + \cdots \qquad (6.16)$$

where Y_t represents total expected receipts in year t and i is the rate of interest. Also, like the LCH, Friedman makes the simplifying assumption that the utility function is homogenous in all its arguments so that planned or permanent consumption is directly proportional to A, so:

$$C^p = qA \qquad (6.17)$$

where q is the factor of proportionality, dependent on the consumer's tastes, τ.

The crucial new feature of Friedman's PIH is the concept of permanent income, Y^p, itself. Theoretically, Y^p is the maximum amount a consumer can spend while maintaining total wealth intact. It is therefore the rate of return on wealth. Consider again the two-period model described earlier. Since initial wealth is A_1, and the rate of interest is i, then at the end of the first period wealth will be equal to $(1+i)A_1=A_2$. If consumption during period 1 is equal to iA_1, then wealth at the start of period 2 will be exactly equal to A_1, and hence wealth will have been maintained intact, thus $iA_1=Y^p$. This argument, naturally follows for the multi-period model. Equation (6.17) can now be written as:

$$C^p=qA=q\left(\frac{Y^p}{i}\right)=kY^p \tag{6.18}$$

where $k=(q/i)$.

What Friedman has done is to replace the stock concept of wealth with a flow concept of permanent income. This is achieved by annualising the concept of wealth. This procedure raises an awkward inconsistency since if an individual consumes an amount equal to his permanent income, then by definition his wealth remains unchanged. Equation (6.18), however, implies that a consumer will normally consume less than his permanent income (since k tends to be less than unity) and hence permanent wealth will be increasing. It is not clear why an individual should wish to plan for ever increasing wealth. The factor of proportionality, k, depends upon the rate of interest, i and tastes, τ. That is:

$$C^p=k(i,\tau)Y^p \tag{6.19}$$

The problem with the PIH is that neither permanent income nor permanent consumption can be observed. To get around this problem Friedman considers that measured income and measured consumption are both made up of a permanent and a transitory component, so that:

$$Y=Y^p+Y^t \quad \text{and} \quad C=C^p+C^t \tag{6.20}$$

where Y and C are measured income and consumption and the superscript, t, denotes the transitory component. Permanent income is therefore that part of income which the household regards as normal or expected, while transitory income is the difference between measured and permanent income which arises from unforeseen occurrences or chance (such as a win on the lottery). Since permanent consumption depends upon permanent income, in practice permanent income must be whatever quantity the consumer sees as determining his planned consumption: that is permanent income can be whatever the consumer believes it to be!

In order to give the model some predictable power Friedman makes two further assumptions:

1. the transitory components of income and consumption are uncorrelated with their respective permanent counterparts; and

2. the transitory component of consumption is uncorrelated with the transitory component of income.

Although the first of these assumptions is non-controversial and follows from the definition of a transitory component, the second proposition is much more debatable, suggesting that a lottery win does not increase transitory consumption. Friedman justifies this by arguing that in the face of a transitory rise in income individuals usually stick to the consumption plan and just opt to increase their savings. An alternative explanation is that his definition of consumption includes only the flow of services from durable goods and not the expenditure on durable goods. If transitory income is spent on durable goods, then this can be classified as unplanned saving, rather than unplanned consumption, and the assumption looks much more credible. This view, however, is at odds with macroeconomic policy since such policies are more concerned with total consumer's expenditure.

The assumptions that transitory consumption is not correlated with either permanent consumption or transitory income means that when the sample population is classified by income levels for each income class the transitory variations in consumption will cancel out. Therefore for each income class $\overline{C}^t_j = 0$, and the average permanent consumption is the population average:

$$\overline{C} = \overline{C}^p_j \tag{6.21}$$

Friedman's model can also be used to test the cross-section data result that APC > MPC, even though the basic postulate of the theory is that the ratio of permanent consumption to permanent income is a constant, k. Consider a randomly selected sample of the population classified by income levels. A group j, with average observed income $\overline{Y}_j$, above average population income, will have a positive average transitory income component, such that $\overline{Y}^t_j > 0$. For this above average group the observed average income will be greater than permanent income, so that $\overline{Y}_j > \overline{Y}^p_j$. All income groups will have the same average permanent consumption given by equation (6.19) so that $\overline{C}^p_j = \overline{k}\overline{Y}^p_j$, but since transitory income is not related to either transitory income or permanent consumption, all groups, including the above average income group, will have a zero average transitory-consumption component, so that $\overline{C}_j = \overline{C}^p_j$. Linking these two elements gives:

$$\overline{C}_j = \overline{C}^p_j = \overline{k}\overline{Y}^p_j \tag{6.22}$$

Thus, the above average group will have average measured consumption equal to permanent consumption, but average measured income greater than permanent income, so that its measured average consumption to income ratio will be less than $\overline{k}$. Similarly, a below average income group h will have a measured consumption to income ratio greater than $\overline{k}$.

These results are shown in **Figure 6.7**. The line from the origin represents the relationship between permanent income and permanent consumption. The

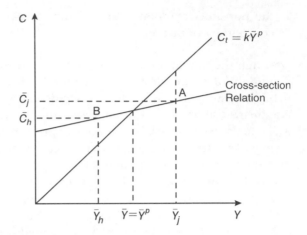

Figure 6.7 *The permanent income hypothesis*

point $\bar{Y}$ is the population average measured income and if the sample is taken in a normal year when measured average income is on trend, average transitory income will be zero, so that $\bar{Y}=\bar{Y}^p$. Consider now sample group j with incomes above the population average. This group has a positive transitory income so that measured income is greater than permanent income, so that $\bar{Y}_j^p<\bar{Y}_j$ as shown in the figure. Average consumption, both measured and permanent for group j is given by multiplying permanent income by k to obtain permanent consumption along the solid line. Thus for an above average income group, j, the point A is below the permanent consumption line in **Figure 6.7**. A similar story follows for the below average income group, h. For this group the average observed income is below the average so that the average transitory income is negative. Therefore measured and permanent consumption for group h is at $\bar{C}_h$. The position of $\bar{C}_h$ and $\bar{Y}_h$ gives the point B, which lies above the solid k-line. Joining the points A and B gives the cross-section consumption function. This function has a smaller slope than the underlying permanent consumption function, so that in cross sectional studies it is expected that MPC < APC if the PIH is correct.

The PIH can also be used to explain the time-series data. In **Figure 6.8** the long-run permanent consumption function is again given by $\bar{k}$. In a boom year when income is above the trend, individual households will experience a positive transitory income, while maintaining the same level of permanent consumption. This is shown in the figure as the distance $\bar{Y}_1-\bar{Y}^p$. On the other hand in times of slump, households will attempt to maintain their long-run levels of consumption, thus transitory income will be negative as given by the distance $\bar{Y}_2-\bar{Y}^p$. Again joining the points A and B gives the short-run time series consumption function, where again the short-run MPC is less than the long-run MPC and MPC < APC, but in the long run APC = MPC.

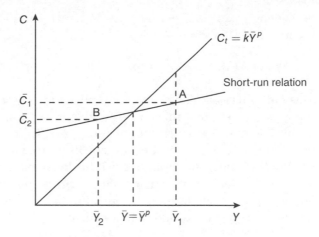

Figure 6.8 *Time-series version of the permanent income hypothesis*

Expectations formation and measuring permanent income

One of the problems with testing the permanent income hypothesis is that permanent income is unobservable: it depends on people's expectations of future income. Therefore any testable model of the PIH has to include a model of expectations formation. In this section two alternative hypotheses about expectations formation are considered: the *adaptive* and the *rational* expectations hypotheses.

Friedman assumed that expectations were adaptive, so that future income expected is based on current and past levels of income. The adaptive expectations hypothesis can be represented as:

$$Y_t^p - Y_{t-1}^p = \theta(Y_t - Y_{t-1}^p) \tag{6.23}$$

This equation says that permanent income is changed according to the gap between this period's measured income and the last periods' permanent income. The extent of the adjustment is given by the adjustment parameter, θ, which always lies between 0 and 1. If $\theta = 0$, then there is no change in permanent income, so that $Y_t^p = Y_{t-1}^p$, whereas if $\theta = 1$, permanent income is immediately revised to match current measured income, so that $Y_t^p = Y_t$. Typically, with θ less than one, permanent income is adjusted by some fraction of the gap between $Y_t^p = Y_{t-1}^p$. Rearranging equation (6.23) to group permanent income terms together gives:

$$Y_t^p = (1 - \theta)Y_{t-1}^p + \theta Y_t \tag{6.24}$$

The problem with this expression is that it still contains the term in Y^p which is unobservable. However, if equation (6.24) is lagged one period to give an expression for Y_{t-1}^p, this can then be used to substitute for Y_{t-1}^p in equation (6.24).

So lagging (6.24) one period gives $Y^p_{t-1} = (1-\theta)Y^p_{t-2} + \theta Y_{t-1}$ and then substituting into (6.24) gives:

$$Y^p_t = (1-\theta)[(1-\theta)Y^p_{t-2} + \theta Y_{t-1}] + \theta Y_t = (1-\theta)^2 Y^p_{t-2} + \theta \sum_{i=0}^{1} (1-\theta)^i Y_{t-i} \qquad (6.25)$$

This rather nasty-looking expression unfortunately still contains a term in Y^p, but the good news is that this term is of decreasing importance, since its coefficient in this equation is smaller than that in (6.24). To see this, if $\theta = 0.5$ the coefficient on Y^p in (6.24) is 0.5, but in equation (6.25) the coefficient on Y^p_{t-1} is $(0.5)^2 = 0.25$. It follows from this that further substitutions for Y^p_{t-2}, Y^p_{t-3} etc., will lead to the final coefficient on the term being so small as to be negligible. Suppose rather than lagging the equation one period we had lagged it N periods. The final expression would then look like:

$$Y^p_t = (1-\theta)^{N+1} Y^P_{t-N-1} + \theta \sum_{i=0}^{N} (1-\theta)^i Y_{t-i} \qquad (6.26)$$

The next step is to assume that $N \to \infty$, since Friedman assumes an infinitely-lived individual, whence the first term in (6.26) goes to zero leaving only the final term. Substituting for permanent income in Friedman's model, given by (6.19), we get:

$$C^p_t = kY^p = k\theta \sum_{i=0}^{\infty} (1-\theta)^i Y_{t-i} \qquad (6.27)$$

This says that permanent consumption is equal to current and previous levels of measured income, where the weights attached to previous levels of income decline as we move further back in time.

The final step is to employ the Koyck transformation to equation (6.27). This transformation is needed because, although equation (6.27) does not include unobservable permanent income, it does include *all* past levels of measured income, which effectively prevents empirical estimation due to multicollinearity. The Koyck transformation is a simple way of simplifying geometrically declining distributed lag functions, like equation (6.27). This transformation involves two steps: the first is to multiply equation (6.27) through by $(1-\theta)$ and lag one period; and the second is to then subtract the lagged equation from the initial equation. The first lag of (6.27) multiplied by $(1-\theta)$ is:

$$(1-\theta)C_{t-1} = k\theta \sum_{i=0}^{\infty} (1-\theta)^{i+1} Y_{t-i-1} \qquad (6.28)$$

Subtracting (6.28) from (6.27) gives:

$$C_t - (1-\theta)C_{t-1} = k\theta \sum_{i=0}^{\infty} (1-\theta)^i Y_{t-i} - k\theta \sum_{i=0}^{\infty} (1-\theta)^{i+1} Y_{t-i-1} = k\theta Y_t \qquad (6.29)$$

since the right hand side terms all cancel out apart from the term in $k\theta Yt$, leaving a consumption function of the form:

$$C_t = k\theta Y_t + (1-\theta)C_{t-1} \qquad (6.30)$$

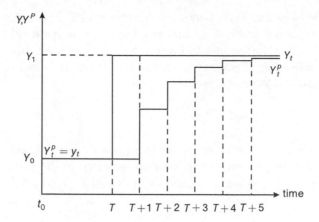

Figure 6.9 *Adaptive expectations*

Thus to test the PIH using time-series data and assuming adaptive expectations, requires the level of real consumption to be regressed upon the level of real income and the lagged level of consumption. The short-run MPC is simply $k\theta$, whereas the long-run MPC is equal to k and in the long run the APC = MPC = k. Since, by assumption $0 < \theta < 1$, it follows that the short-run MPC is less than the long-run MPC. This result has similar policy implications to the LCH.

The problem with the adaptive expectations hypothesis is that it assumes that agents make systematic errors when computing their forecasts, and that such behaviour is inconsistent with rational economic behaviour at the microeconomic level. In this context the notion of systematic errors implies that when income is continually rising agents will continually under-predict their permanent income, because the adaptive expectations hypothesis posits only partial adjustment. Thus when income is rising they will underpredict permanent income in each period and when income is falling they will overpredict permanent income in each period. To see this consider **Figure 6.9**, where income is initially at Y_0 at time t_0. A rise in income to Y_1 at T then leads to agents to adjust upwards their measure of permanent income. If we assume that $\theta = 0.5$, then half the adjustment will be complete in the next period. Hence permanent (or expected) income will rise by half as much as the actual income in period 1. In period 2 permanent income will again be adjusted upwards, by half of the gap between actual and permanent income. This process will continue until permanent income becomes imperceptibly different from actual income. Note, however, that throughout the adjustment period, agents continually under predict the expected level of income, although the actual level of income is observed to have risen to Y_1 by period 2. Because agents do not adjust their behaviour they are said to make 'systematic' errors. Not to adjust the level of permanent income once the new actual level of income is observed is irrational.

Rational agents on the other hand, use all available information to predict the future and will not make systematic forecast errors. Hence immediately the rise in actual income is observed, in period $T+1$, they will immediately adjust their expected level of permanent income upward by the full extent (shown by the vertical dotted line in **Figure 6.9**). To see how this works formally, consider the definition of permanent income at the start of period t, invoking rational expectations. We can write:

$$Y_t^p = E_{t-1}Y_t^p + \varepsilon_t \tag{6.31}$$

where E is the expectations operator. Equation (6.31) says that the level of permanent income in period t is that expected in the previous period plus any random error, ε_t. Taking expectations at period $t-1$, throughout equation (6.31) we get:

$$E_{t-1}Y_t^p = E_{t-1}Y_t^p + E_{t-1}\varepsilon_t = Y_{t-1}^p \tag{6.32}$$

since $E_{t-1}\varepsilon_t = 0$, because the mean of a random variable is zero, and in the absence of shocks the expected value of permanent income is expected to be the same in this period as last period. Combining (6.31) and (6.32), the forecast error in permanent income is given as:

$$Y_t^p - E_{t-1}Y_t^p = Y_t^p - Y_{t-1}^p = \varepsilon_t \tag{6.33}$$

The change in consumption is proportional to the change in permanent income according to equation (6.18) so:

$$C_t - C_{t-1} = k(Y_t^p - Y_{t-1}^p) = k\varepsilon_t \tag{6.34}$$

or $C_t = C_{t-1} + k\varepsilon_t$ where $E_{t-1}(k\varepsilon_t) = 0$. This says that consumption follows a random walk, or alternatively, that the best guess about next period's consumption is this period's consumption, because it embodies the latest assessment of permanent income which in turn includes all knowable information at the current date. The implication of this is that adding lagged values of income to (6.34) should not improve our ability to predict consumption at period t, given variables known at $t-1$.

The policy implications of this result, due to Hall (1978), are interesting, since they provide a contrast to those obtained using adaptive expectations. In this case with rational expectations, the path of permanent income may undergo a complete revaluation following a small piece of new information. The short-run MPC and hence the multiplier may then be quite large.

Recent empirical studies of consumption

Because of the importance of consumption in total expenditure there have been an enormous number of studies of the consumption function. As noted earlier, the study of Kuznets (1946) found that although the data were broadly consistent with Keynes' AIH, there was some suggestion that the consumption function might shift upwards over time.

This finding gave rise to a whole battery of tests which tried to explain the upwards shift in the consumption function as due to increasing wealth – a factor also mentioned by Keynes as potentially important for consumption. These tests were invariability based on the LCH and PIH of consumption. Ando and Modigliani (1963) estimated the MPC in the life-cycle model to be about 0.68–0.71, for the USA, while the coefficient on wealth is in the region of 0.07–0.1. It is expected that the life-cycle model would exhibit a smaller MPC than the PIH, because the former also includes a wealth variable whereas in the latter the wealth effect is included in permanent income. In terms of the PIH, Friedman reports a value of the long-run MPC of 0.9 for the USA, with the adjustment coefficient $\theta = 0.33$, which gives a short-run MPC of around 0.3.

During the 1970s a great deal of attention was given to the possibility that inflation rates may go some way to explaining consumption behaviour. This assumes that consumers suffer from some form of money illusion, in that they somehow confuse real and monetary values. Juster and Wachtel (1972), for example, argued that high rates of inflation are associated with high variability of inflation rates and this variability generates uncertainty about the real values for future incomes, which in turn leads to higher savings on precautionary grounds. Although Juster and Wachtel found evidence to support this hypothesis on US data, Townend (1976) using UK data failed to find evidence for the precautionary saving hypothesis. Deaton (1977) also looked at the role of inflation in the consumption function, but he looked at the rate at which inflation accelerates. In Deaton's model a divergence between the actual and expected rate of inflation lead to general price rises being mistaken for relative price rises by consumers and this leads to decline in the APC. Deaton finds evidence for this effect in the UK.

One of the most comprehensive studies of UK consumption was that by Davidson *et al.* (1978). They found a model that explained the annual change in consumption by the annual change in real income and a disequilibrium effect from the previous year, but that this equation was not adequate for forecasting purposes for the period 1971–75. To enhance the equation's performance the annual rate of inflation and the change in the annual rate of inflation are added to the equation. Although the model now forecasts satisfactorily there are reasons for concern. Firstly, the inflation effects are clearly an add-on to the initial model and are presented without adequate theoretical motivation. Second, if inflation effects are important for the mid-1970s why is the model not run again for the whole sample period 1958–70 with inflation effects? Bean (1978) in fact shows that the inclusion of the rate of inflation can be justified as a wealth effect. As inflation rises the real value of wealth falls and so does consumption. Thus the high saving–income ratios of the 1970s are probably the result of wealth effects rather than Deaton-type inflation effects.

With the 1980s and the incorporation of the rational expectations hypothesis in macroeconomics most tests of consumption took the form of the rational expectations permanent income hypothesis (REPIH), following Hall (1978). Hall found that lagged consumption had a coefficient of close to unity for the USA and this finding was supported by Daley and Hadjimatheou (1981) for the

UK. These tests are, however, weak tests since they are compatible with a number of alternative models of consumption. A stronger test is therefore the orthogonality test which involves the regression of the change in consumption on the changes in other variables, such as income, higher-order lags of consumption, stock prices and so on. If the REPIH is correct then none of these additional variables should be significant. However, Hall found stock prices significant for the USA and Daley and Hadjimatheou found lagged income and higher orders of lagged consumption significant for the UK. Thus on the basis of these tests the REPIH model seems to be rejected by the data.

Conclusions for economic policy

From the normal income theories of the consumption function, it appears that household real wealth or net assets have a significant effect on the consumption

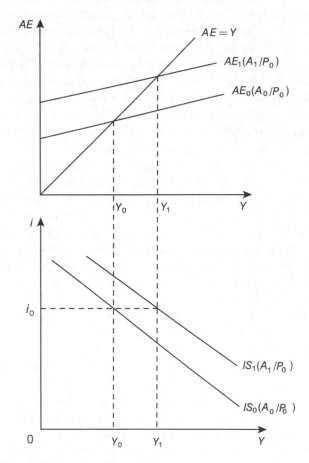

Figure 6.10 *The effect of a rise in wealth*

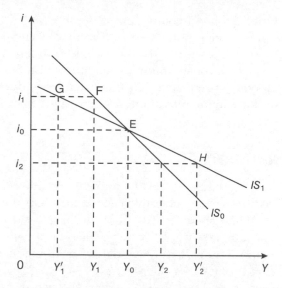

Figure 6.11 *Effect of wealth on the slope of the* IS *curve*

function. Indeed Keynes mentioned these effects in the *General Theory*, but he played down their importance. If household real assets are an important determinant of consumption what are the implications of this for the income–expenditure model and the *IS* curve of goods market equilibrium? The consumption function of Chapter 4 can be amended to include a new argument in real net assets of households, A/P, so that the function is now:

$$C = \alpha_0 + \alpha_1(1 - \tau_1)Y + \alpha_2(A/P) \tag{6.35}$$

where α_2 gives the impact effect of the change in real wealth on consumption, which is expected to be positive, but less than one.

The real net assets of households are made up of three elements: the real capital stock K; the real stock of outside money M/P and the real stock of public sector bonds held by the private sector $(B/i)/P$; that is: $(A/P) = K + (M + B/i)/P$, where P is the general level of prices, and B/i is the nominal value of the bond stock outstanding. The effect of including net assets in the consumption function gives an extra exogenous (shift) variable in the equation for aggregate expenditure, and in addition, also leads to the *IS* curve having a flatter slope. These effects are shown in **Figures 6.10** and **6.11**. **Figure 6.10** shows the effect of a rise in net assets on the position of both the *AE* line and the *IS* curve. The *AE* line shifts up from AE_0 to AE_1, as the rise in assets leads to a rise in consumption and hence in aggregate expenditure. The *IS* curve in the lower quadrant also shifts up from IS_0 to IS_1, as consumption expenditures rise for each level of the rate of interest.

In **Figure 6.11** the initial *IS* curve is given by IS_0. A rise in the rate of interest to i_1 will not only lower the rate of investment, up the curve to F; but also lower the value of the bond component of wealth, which in turn will serve to lower consumption taking point F to G. The new *IS* curve will be IS_1, which is the flatter curve, GEH, since the rise in the rate of interest reduces income by more than $Y_0 - Y_1$, since consumption expenditures also fall. Thus the effectiveness of monetary policy is enhanced in this extended model of the consumption function, as changes in the rate of interest have a greater effect on income.

Summary

- The absolute and relative income hypotheses of consumption do not have rigorous microeconomic foundations. On the other hand the modern, normal theories of consumption do have such foundations and postulate that consumption depends upon life-time income or wealth. This is consistent with the view that individuals want to maintain relatively smooth consumption profiles over their lifetimes.

- The life-cycle hypothesis suggests that the propensities to consume out of disposable income and wealth depend on a person's age. Saving is believed to be low when income is relatively low (such as when the individual is young or old), and high when the individual is middle-aged and income is relatively high. Saving also depends on the age distribution of the population and the growth of the economy.

- The permanent income hypothesis argues that consumption depends upon permanent or expected average income and that short-run or transitory income shocks only affect current consumption to the extent that they change the expected average lifetime income.

- If consumption is smoothed as the normal income theories suggest then tax rate changes, even if permanent, have less effect on consumption than the current income theories suggest. Therefore fiscal policy changes are likely to have little impact on the level of current aggregate expenditure.

- The empirical evidence suggests that the rate of interest does not have a major effect on consumption. Although wealth is generally found to be a significant determinant of consumption, current income has by far the largest effect, which is inconsistent with the normal income theories.

- The evidence that income is the most important determinant of consumption is consistent with the view that households have little wealth or face liquidity constraints so their consumption tracks their income, butthey have small levels of savings that they draw on in the event of sharp falls in income or emergency spending needs. This is called buffer stock saving. Periods of relatively high inflation also seem to be associated with an increase in the savings ratio which may also be linked to the buffer stock notion, as households attempt to rebuild their savings which are being eroded by inflation.

Suggested further reading

The absolute income hypothesis is well documented in Keynes (1936), Chapters 6–9 and Duesenberry (1952) is the original statement of the relative income hypothesis. The life–cycle hypothesis is due to Modigliani and Brumberg (1954) and Ando and Modigliani (1963). Friedman (1957) is the original exposition of the permanent income hypothesis. Useful surveys of the consumption function are Farrell (1959) and Ferber (1973) and, more recently, Deaton (1992). The extensive empirical evidence is reviewed in Thomas (1984) and in Surrey (1989), which are written for students. The classic study of the UK consumption function was Davidson, Hendry, Srba and Yeo (1978). Hall (1978), and Daly and Hadjimatheou (1981) reexamine the permanent income hypothesis with rational expectations.

Essay titles

1. Compare and contrast the permanent income hypothesis with the current income theory of consumption behaviour. What do these models predict will happen to consumption if there is a cut in the rate of income tax?
2. Explain the permanent income hypothesis of consumption. What extra assumptions did Friedman have to invoke to make the hypothesis testable?
3. Evaluate the usefulness of the microeconomic foundations of the modern theory of the consumption function. What importance does this theory give to real personal disposable income in determining consumption?

Questions

1. Distinguish between consumption of durable goods and consumer purchases of durable goods. Why is this distinction important?
2. Use the two-period intertemporal model of consumption to show the effect of the following:
   (a) an increase in income in period 2;
   (b) a fall in the rate of interest on consumption in both period 1 and period 2;
   (c) supposing the individual faces a borrowing constraint in period 1, how does this affect his consumption in both periods?
3. In the context of the permanent income hypothesis what happens to consumption when:
   (a) there is a Christmas bonus?
   (b) there is a temporary tax increase?
   (c) there is a major house repair required?
4. Using the life-cycle hypothesis of consumption what are the implications of:

   (a) households facing a liquidity constraint;
   (b) the effectiveness of a tax cut.

5. Write down a formal model for the adaptive expectations hypothesis and give a verbal interpretation of this equation. Why does Friedman use this hypothesis in his PIH and what are the implications?
6. Assume that you have established an empirical consumption function of:

$$C_t = 0.40Y_t + 0.20Y_{t-1} + 0.006A_t$$

where C, Y and A are real consumption, real income and real wealth, respectively. What would you estimate to be:
(a) the short-run MPC?
(b) the long-run MPC?
(c) the long-run APC?

CHAPTER 7
Investment

Aims and objectives

- To examine alternative theories of investment since Keynes.
- To examine the microeconomic production technologies that underpin the alternative models of investment.
- To evaluate the empirical evidence for these theories of physical investment and the responsiveness of investment to changes in monetary policy.

Introduction

Investment is the accumulation over time by firms of physical capital goods. There are three different types of real capital goods, although two of these types are the most important in this chapter. The three types are: *fixed capital*, items such as plant, machinery and buildings; *working capital*, which consists of stocks of raw materials, manufactured inputs and final goods awaiting sale; and *residential investment*, which includes new houses for purchase or rent. This chapter will be largely concerned with investment in fixed capital, commonly referred to as gross domestic fixed capital formation.

Investment is very much smaller than consumption, but it is the most volatile component of aggregate demand. Despite its size investment is very important for the macroeconomy, since it is only by investing in plant and machinery that the economy can produce goods for consumption in the future. Thus investment is an inherently dynamic process, whereby consumption is sacrificed today in order to enhance production and consumption in the future. Investment is therefore an element of economic growth, to which we will return later. From a theoretical point of view a stationary economy is one where the capital stock is constant and the level of investment is exactly equal to the rate of depreciation of the existing capital stock. So although existing machines are replaced as they wear out, there are no new additions to the capital stock, thus *net investment*, I_N, is zero. In this case *gross investment*, I_G, is exactly equal to *replacement investment*, I_R. This can be represented by a simple I_G identity:

$$I_G = I_R + I_N \qquad\qquad (7.1)$$

Table 7.1 records the share of gross investment in GDP in several OECD countries since the 1960s. It shows that Britain has invested a lower share of GDP than Japan, Germany, France, Italy and the USA. The UK also ranks second lowest over this longer period when housing investment is excluded. Japan is clearly an outlier, investing a substantially higher fraction of GDP than any of the other countries, with the continental European countries next, consistently allocating a higher share of national income to investment than either the USA or the UK. Indeed, Kitson and Michie (1996) argue that the 'the key reason why British industry has been doing relatively poorly has been the under-investment in manufacturing' (p. 196). It is therefore important to examine the determinants of investment.

In the following sections four principal alternative theories of investment will be considered: Keynes' theory of the marginal efficiency of investment; accelerator models; Jorgenson's neo-classical theory of investment; and financial theories of real investment which attempt to link physical investment to stockmarket valuation. In the final sections recent empirical evidence is reviewed and the implications of these modern theories for the aggregate demand function and the *IS* curve of goods market equilibrium are considered.

Keynes' theory of investment

Keynes' theory of investment is to be found in Chapter 11 of the *General Theory* (Keynes, 1936). There are two distinctive components: first, Keynes emphasises the role of expectations in driving investment demand, and, second, in contrast to much of the postwar literature on investment, he explicitly refers to the supply price of capital goods which is related to the marginal efficiency of capital (MEC).

For Keynes the value to the owner of a unit of capital equipment was the flow of income, Q_j, it would yield over its life in excess of the purchase cost. This flow can be thought of as the net present value of income (NPV), or the demand price, V^D, of the machine. Thus the discounted net lifetime income of the

Table 7.1 *Investment as a share of GDP (%)*

1960–93	Japan	Italy	Germany	France	USA	UK
Gross fixed capital formation	31.3	22.8	22.4	22.4	18.4	18.1
Gross fixed capital formation (excl. residential construction)	25.1	15.9	15.9	15.5	13.8	14.4
Gross fixed capital formation: machinery and equipment	12.4	9.8	8.7	8.9	7.6	8.4

Source: Bond and Jenkinson (1996) *Oxford Review of Economic Policy*.

machine is given as:

$$NPV = Q_0 + \frac{Q_1}{(1+i)} + \frac{Q_2}{(1+i)^2} + \cdots + \frac{Q_j}{(1+i)^j} = \sum_{j=0}^{N} \left(\frac{Q_{t+j}}{(1+i)^j} \right) = V_t^D \qquad (7.2)$$

where i is the rate of interest and N is the life of the asset. Thus if the NPV, or the demand price, is greater than zero the investment project is profitable, in that expected future revenues exceed costs. As progressively more marginal projects are added the demand price of new capital declines until NPV = 0, after which additional projects yield negative returns (losses). **Figure 7.1** shows this demand schedule for capital goods, which falls as the demand price falls, for a given market rate of interest and the stream of expected returns.

In addition to the concept of the demand price of capital goods Keynes also introduced the concept of the marginal efficiency of capital (MEC). The marginal efficiency of capital is defined as the rate of discount, ρ, which would make the present value of the series of annuities given by the expected returns from the capital asset during its life to just equal the supply price, V^s; that is:

$$\sum_{j=0}^{N} \frac{Q_{t+j}}{(1+\rho)^j} = V_t^s \qquad (7.3)$$

where the supply price of a capital asset is the price which would just induce a manufacturer to newly produce an additional unit of such assets. That is the supply price is the replacement cost of a new machine and not the cost of the purchase of a second-hand machine, which of course, does not add to the stock of capital in the economy as a whole. Thus the MEC or ρ, is drawn for a given stream of expected returns and the supply price of capital. Note that is does not depend upon the market rate of interest. Indeed, only if $\rho > i$, will new capital equipment be profitable to acquire, since only then will the MEC exceed the market rate of interest, which denotes the return on alternative assets. In equilibrium Keynes argued that 'The rate of investment will be pushed to the point on the investment demand schedule where the marginal efficiency of capital in general is equal to the rate of interest' (p. 137). That is to say, where $\rho = i$.

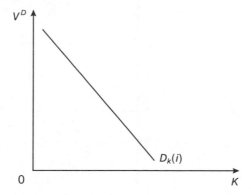

Figure 7.1 *The demand price of capital*

Figure 7.2 shows the derivation of the MEC schedule. The top section shows the negatively-sloped demand for capital schedule as $D_K(i)$, exactly as in **Figure 7.1**. In addition the top section also includes the supply price of capital goods, V^s, which for the moment is assumed to be constant. The market for capital goods is in equilibrium at point A, where the rate of interest, i_0 is equal to the marginal efficiency of capital, ρ_0. In the lower section the MEC schedule is derived. A fall in the rate of interest from i_0 to i_1 has the effect of shifting the demand for capital goods line to the right in the upper section, as the lower rate of interest raises the demand price. Since $\rho > i$ more capital goods are demanded which reduce the marginal efficiency of capital until it again is exactly equal to the market rate of interest. So at point B the capital goods market is again in equilibrium. The MEC schedule therefore has a negative slope and denotes the points of capital goods market equilibrium, given the supply price of capital and expected returns.

There are two problems with the story so far. The first is that the supply price of capital has been assumed to be constant, whereas Keynes argues that marginal efficiency of capital will diminish as the investment in it increases because the pressure on the facilities producing that type of capital will cause its supply price to rise. Thus the supply price can only be regarded as constant while the capital goods industry is simply replacing worn out machines, such that net investment is zero. A rise in the supply price of capital will shift the MEC schedule of **Figure 7.2** inwards, and will serve to reduce the optimal size of the capital stock. The second problem is that the determinants of the flow of new investment have not been considered, only the determinants of the optimal capital stock.

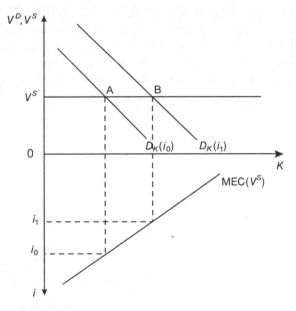

Figure 7.2 *The derivation of the MEC schedule*

Figure 7.3 shows the MEC schedule in the left-hand panel and the flow of new investment, the marginal efficiency of investment (MEI) locus in the right-hand panel. At the initial rate of interest, i_0, which equals the MEC, the optimal capital stock is given by K_0. In the right-hand panel there is no net investment. Suppose there is now a fall in the rate of interest, which will lead to an increase in the demand for capital goods since, $\rho > i$. The increase in the demand for capital goods, however, is likely to cause a rise in the price of these capital goods, at least in the short run. As the supply price of capital increases the MEC schedule shifts inwards, to MEC_1, from MEC_0 in **Figure** 7.3. This fall in the MEC schedule results in a lower optimal capital stock at $0K_2$ than there would have been if there had been no increase in the supply price of capital, when it would have reached $0K_1$. Because the increase in the optimal capital stock is lower, so the flow of new investment is correspondingly lower. The flow of new investment is determined by the MEI schedule and given by $0I_2$ in the right-hand panel of **Figure** 7.3, which is equal to the distance $K_2 - K_0$. It is the MEI schedule that is the investment schedule. The difference between the marginal efficiency of capital and the marginal efficiency of investment is that the latter takes into account the fact that as the market rate of interest falls the supply price of capital goods rises. As the supply price of capital goods rises the MEI schedule becomes steeper.

Once the capital stock has increased to K_2 net investment is again zero and the MEI_1 schedule will have shifted inwards to MEC_2, to intersect the vertical axis at i_1. This process will take time, hence the flow of net investment will last for several periods before the capital stock reaches its new optimal level. This also suggests that an expansionary monetary policy will have a somewhat uncertain effect on the level of investment expenditure, since to the extent that the supply price of capital rises, the effect on the demand for investment will be curtailed.

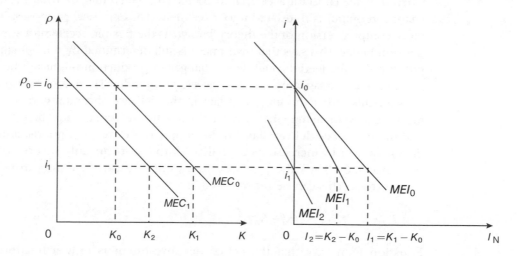

Figure 7.3   *The MEC and MEI schedules*

The second aspect of Keynes theory of investment is that regarding expectations about the future. Expectations enter through the demand price of capital goods. Changes in expectations of future returns will change the demand price of capital assets and the MEC schedule, and hence the equilibrium rate of investment at any given interest rate. Thus a rise in optimism will result in a rightward shift in both the MEC and MEI lines thereby stimulating the level of investment. Similarly a bout of business pessimism will result in these schedules shifting to the left and the level of new investment falling.

The Keynesian aggregate investment function can be summarised as:

$$I = \beta_0 - \beta_1 i \tag{7.4}$$

This is a duplication of the investment function of Chapter 4, but where exogenous shifts in expectations are captured by the term β_0.

The accelerator theory of investment

Although Keynes' theory of investment included both demand-side and supply-side elements, much of investment theory since the Second World War has focused almost exclusively on the demand for investment, at the expense of the supply side. It has, however, attempted to endogenise the treatment of expectations which Keynes believed to be so important and to provide a more obviously dynamic theory. The first postwar theories were the accelerator theories.

The naive accelerator model states that net investment is determined by the current change in output; that is:

$$I_{Nt} = K_t - K_{t-1} = v(Y_t - Y_{t-1}) \tag{7.5}$$

where v is the constant acceleration coefficient, which tells us what fraction of the change in output is translated into investment. For empirical purposes, however, a more complex version of the theory, known as the flexible accelerator was found to perform better. This says that investment is still determined by the demand for output, but that the feed-through from changes in production might not be as simple and direct as envisaged by the naive accelerator model. There are two potential reasons for this: either the firm faces lags in the delivery of capital goods, or because firms are slow to change their expectations of future demand for their products.

If the firm faces delivery lags in the supply of new capital goods, although the firm may wish to increase its capital stock today, it can only secure some of the new machines. Thus the firm's desired capital stock, K_t^d, differs from its actual capital stock. This can be represented as:

$$I_{Nt} = K_t - K_{t-1} = \lambda(K_t^d - K_{t-1}) \tag{7.6}$$

Equation (7.6) says that the actual net investment is only a fraction λ of the desired investment, measured as the difference between the firm's capital stock at the end of the previous period and the desired capital stock for this period. If it is also assumed that the desired capital stock is proportional to output, such that $K_t^d = vY_t$, then, substituting into (7.6) gives:

$$I_{Nt} = K_t - K_{t-1} = \lambda(vY_t - K_{t-1}) = \lambda vY_t - \lambda K_{t-1} \tag{7.7}$$

or, gathering terms in K_{t-1},

$$K_t = v\lambda Y_t - (1-\lambda)K_{t-1} \tag{7.8}$$

Lagging (7.8) one period gives $K_{t-1} = v\lambda Y_{t-1} - (1-\lambda)K_{t-2}$, and so on by simple substitution gives

$$K_t = \lambda vY_t - (1-\lambda)v\lambda Y_{t-1} + (1-\lambda)^2 v\lambda Y_{t-2} + \cdots \tag{7.9}$$

and so,

$$I_{Nt} = \Delta K_t = \lambda v\Delta Y_t + (1-\lambda)v\lambda\Delta Y_{t-1} + (1-\lambda)^2 v\lambda\Delta Y_{t-2} + \cdots \tag{7.10}$$

or, more compactly, using the summation operator:

$$\Delta K_t = \lambda v \sum_{j=0}^{N} (1-\lambda)^j \Delta Y_{t-j} \tag{7.11}$$

Equation (7.11) says that investment is a weighted average of past changes in output, where since λ and $(1-\lambda)$ are fractions the importance of any given change in output on current investment declines through time.

From an empirical point of view the problem with this formulation is that the lagged values of changes in output are likely to be highly correlated so precluding estimation. Therefore, as in Chapter 6, the Koyck transformation is used to simplify the dynamics. This involves multiplying (7.11) through by $(1-\lambda)$ and lagging one period and then subtracting the resulting equation from (7.11). The result is:

$$I_{Nt} = \Delta K_t = v\lambda\Delta Y_t + (1-\lambda)\Delta K_{t-1} \tag{7.12}$$

The second explanation of the flexible accelerator focuses on expectations. Suppose firms base their expectations of future demand, on which their investment decisions depend, by looking at past levels of demand. Current investment will then be a weighted average of current and past changes in output. Assume that the firm is fully adjusted so that the desired capital stock is equal to the actual capital stock, but that the desired stock of capital depends upon expected output at time t. That is,

$$K_t = K_t^d = vY_t^e \tag{7.13}$$

Therefore

$$\Delta K_t = \Delta K_t^d = v\Delta Y_t^e = v(Y_t^e - Y_{t-1}^e) \tag{7.14}$$

If entrepreneurs have adaptive expectations, then their expectations will change by some fraction, λ, of last period's error. That is:

$$Y_t^e - Y_{t-1}^e = \lambda(Y_{t-1} - Y_{t-1}^e) \tag{7.15}$$

where, as before $0 < \lambda < 1$. Simple manipulation of (7.15) shows that:

$$Y_t^e = \lambda Y_{t-1} + \lambda(1-\lambda)Y_{t-2} + \lambda(1-\lambda)^2 Y_{t-3} + \cdots \tag{7.16}$$

and substituting into (7.14) we get the flexible accelerator formulation once again.

$$\Delta K_t = v\Delta Y_t^e = \lambda v \sum_{j=0}^{N} (1-\lambda)^j \Delta Y_{t-1-j} \tag{7.17}$$

Applying the Koyck transformation the empirical version of this model becomes:

$$I_{Nt} = v\lambda \Delta Y_{t-1} + (1-\lambda)\Delta K_{t-1} \tag{7.18}$$

Equation (7.18) is very similar to (7.12), the only difference being the lagged response of investment to changes in output.

The accelerator investment models are based on specific assumptions about the underlying technology of the firm. The crucial determinant of investment is the level of demand or output. Relative prices, such as interest rates, wages and capital goods prices seem to play no role in this model. The reason for this is that there are further assumptions regarding the technology faced by the firm and the substitutability between capital and labour. Consider a firm facing a fixed-coefficients technology. The firm would then produce the desired level of output that minimised cost. In **Figure 7.4** quantities of capital, K, and labour, N, are plotted on the axes and the fixed-coefficients technology is given by the right-angled isoquants, labelled Y_0 and Y_1. The dash lines passing through point A denote various relative prices between capital and labour. It should also be apparent that these relative prices are irrelevant to the firm. The minimum cost of production is at A regardless of relative factor prices. Thus increasing the stock of capital up say, to K_2, does not yield higher output. Hence there is a unique optimum level of capital and labour needed to produce each level of output, these are (K_0, N_0) for Y_0 and (K_1, N_1) for Y_1.

An alternative explanation allows capital and labour to be substitutes in the production process. In this case relative prices are important, but they are assumed to remain constant. Thus in this case the output isoquants need to homogenous of degree zero, such that a ray from the origin cuts each point of tangency between the cost constraint and the curved isoquants. This is shown in **Figure 7.5** and implies that the marginal rate of substitution between capital

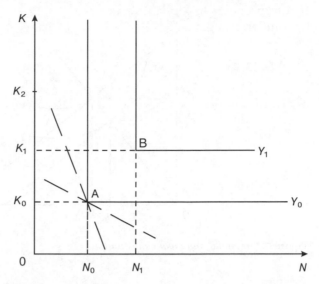

Figure 7.4   *Fixed coefficients technology*

and labour is the same at all levels of output. Thus the capital–labour ratio is constant along the ray OY.

The neo-classical theory of investment

Jorgenson (1963) developed the neo-classical theory of investment in response to the limited factor-substitution permitted in the accelerator-type models. This neo-classical theory assumes that the firm operates in perfectly competitive markets such that firms have perfect foresight and face given current and future prices. Thus the marginal product of capital is equal to the real rental price of capital.

More formally, Jorgenson specifies a production, $Y = F(K, N)$ where N is the labour input and where there are decreasing returns to scale. In conditions of perfect competition the marginal product of capital, MPK, must equal the real rental price of capital, R/P so that:

$$\frac{\partial Y}{\partial K} = F_{K(K,N)} = MPK = R/P \tag{7.19}$$

The concept of the user cost of capital (or the rental cost of capital services) is not a measurable input price like the wage rate, since typically capital goods are bought in one period and used over a number of subsequent periods, rather than rented, as are labour services. This is the major difference between the labour and capital markets and the thing that makes capital theory so complex and the measurement of capital inputs difficult. For this theory to have any practical use a way of measuring the user cost of capital is needed.

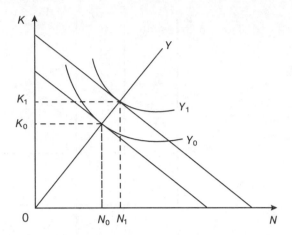

Figure 7.5 *Capital and labour substitution*

There are in fact three components that make up the user cost of the good to its owner in each period of its life.

1. *The opportunity cost.* This is the interest foregone on buying the machine rather than investing the money in an alternative asset, such as a bank deposit. If the firm buys a machine for £100 000 and the rate of interest at which it could lend that sum is 5 per cent per annum, then the firm is giving up £5000 per annum that it could have earned as interest. That is, iq per annum where q is the purchase price of the capital good.
2. *Depreciation cost.* The capital good, once purchased, depreciates in value each year. If the rate of depreciation is δ and the cost of the machine is £q, then the machine falls in value by δq per annum. If the rate of depreciation is 10 per cent per annum and the machine costs £100 000 then the depreciation cost is £10 000 in the first year.
3. *Capital cost.* Any change in the market price of the machine once purchased enters into the user cost. If the market price of a new machine of similar vintage and style is rising through time, this will pull up the price of used machines. If the price rises above the original purchase price (less depreciation), this causes a capital gain to the firm (that is a negative cost) equal to $\partial q/\partial t$ – the time rate of change of q.

Adding these three components together gives the user cost, R, as:

$$R = q(i + \delta) - \frac{\partial q}{\partial t} \tag{7.20}$$

The real user cost is computed by deflating each of the variables in (7.20) by q. This has the advantage that the final term in equation (7.20) becomes the rate of change of the price of capital goods. Since capital goods prices are likely to rise in line with the general level of prices, it is frequently assumed that

$(\partial q/\partial t)(1/q) = (\partial P/\partial t)(1/P) = \hat{P}$, which is the rate of inflation as measured by the GDP deflator. Rearranging (7.20) gives:

$$\frac{R}{P} = (i - \hat{P} + \delta) \tag{7.21}$$

This equation serves to bring out the notion that the real user cost of capital depends upon the real rate of interest, $i - \hat{P} = r$, and not the nominal rate. If lenders and borrowers are concerned about the real or purchasing power value of their assets and liabilities they should discount nominal rates of interest, i, for the expected rate of inflation, $\hat{P}$. If both i and $\hat{P}$ go up by the same amount the real rate will not change and neither will investment decisions or the equilibrium capital stock.

Armed with the notion of the user cost of capital, let us return to the interpretation of equation (7.19), which is now written as:

$$PMPK = q(i + \delta) - q \tag{7.22}$$

In discrete time this dynamic equation becomes:

$$P_{t+1}MPK_{t+1} = q_t i + q_{t+1}\delta - (q_{t+1} - q_t)$$
$$= (1+i)q_t - (1-\delta)q_{t+1} \tag{7.23}$$

which can be rearranged as:

$$q_t = \frac{P_{t+1}MPK_{t+1}}{(1+i)} + \frac{(1-\delta)q_{t+1}}{(1+i)} \tag{7.24}$$

This relationship says that the supply price of capital goods, q, equals the discounted future revenue stream plus the part of the capital stock still in use. This is therefore identical to the NPV concept noted earlier.

In the neo-classical world with perfect competition, perfect foresight and no adjustment costs the firm adjusts instantaneously to changes in its environment. It is therefore always optimally adjusted, so that $K = K^d$. This, however, presents a problem in deriving an investment function; since investment is the change in the capital stock, a firm that responds instantaneously to a disturbance has an infinite rate of investment and hence an investment function cannot be identified. This problem is avoided by ruling out instantaneous changes to the capital stock in response to a change in the real user cost.

Jorgenson is able to do this by assuming that forward prices or discounted future prices of both capital goods and capital services are left *unchanged* by variations in the rate of interest. To understand this look again at the equation for the user cost of capital. With R and q constant any change in i must be matched by a change in q. Therefore a fall in i must be matched by a fall in q. Since future capital goods prices are lower, firms will desire higher capital stocks, implying a higher rate of investment. Thus investment is inversely related to the rate of interest. This argument is illustrated in **Figure 7.6**, which shows the time path of the

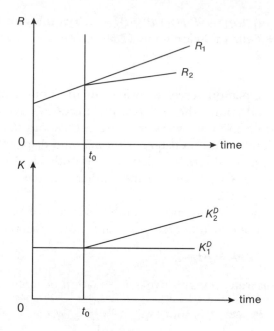

Figure 7.6 *The neo-classical investment model*

user cost and the capital stock. R_1 is the path of the user cost before the fall in the rate of interest at time t_0, and R_2 is the path after the change, but $R(t_0)$ is constant. Assuming other prices are given, the desired path of the capital stock, if the rate of interest had remained unchanged, is given by K_1^D while K_2^D is the path after the fall in i. Thus from t_0, $K_2^D > K_1^D$, that is a fall in the rate of interest increases investment.

Jorgenson's model is important for a number of reasons. Firstly, because it was the first investment model to be derived from an optimisation model of the firm. Secondly, because a firm's behaviour is myopic; that is, despite the fact that the model is fully dynamic with firms looking ahead at future variables, equation (7.22) contains only current variables. This is because the model has no adjustment costs and because the technology allows continuous substitution between factors of production. Thirdly, in contrast to the accelerator theories the neo-classical theory emphasises relative prices, interest rates and tax variables as important influences upon firm's investment.

Although Jorgenson's theoretical approach has much to commend it, his empirical tests of the model were deficient. In the empirical version of the model Jorgenson assumes a standard Cobb–Douglas production function, which is written as:

$$Y = AK^\alpha N^\beta \tag{7.25}$$

where A is a constant representing technical progress, the subscripts α and β denote the marginal products of capital and labour and $\alpha + \beta < 1$ implying that there are decreasing returns to scale. Thus if all inputs double then output will less than double. The marginal product of capital in the Cobb–Douglas function is obtained by partially differentiating (7.25) with respect to K, and is given as:

$$\frac{\partial Y}{\partial K} = \alpha A K^{\alpha-1} N^\beta = \alpha \frac{Y}{K} \tag{7.26}$$

If it is assumed that the market for capital is perfectly competitive, such that all factors of production are paid their marginal product, then the marginal product of capital must equal the real user cost of capital goods, R/P, where P is the aggregate price level, so that:

$$MPK = \alpha \frac{Y}{K} = \frac{R}{P} \tag{7.27}$$

Solving (7.27) for the desired, equilibrium capital stock, K^D, gives:

$$K^D = \alpha \frac{Y}{R/P} \tag{7.28}$$

Therefore, the equilibrium capital stock rises with output and falls with an increase in the real user cost of capital. Using (7.28) and assuming that $K = K^d$ we have:

$$\Delta K_t^d = \alpha \Delta \left(\frac{PY}{R}\right)_t \tag{7.29}$$

Jorgenson then adds the *ad hoc* assumption of adjustment or delivery lags, so that only a part, λ, of the goods ordered this period are actually delivered. Thus

$$I_t = \Delta K_t = \lambda_0 \Delta K_t^D + \lambda_1 \Delta K_{t-1}^D + \cdots + \tag{7.30}$$

Therefore, by substitution we have:

$$I_t = \alpha \sum_{j=0}^N \lambda_j \Delta \left(\frac{PY}{R}\right)_{t-j} \tag{7.31}$$

This is the basic form of the model tested by Jorgenson. Unfortunately there are major problems with it, in that it does not reflect the theoretical model. Because relative prices and output enter the equation in a composite term Jorgenson is unable to demonstrate what he really wants to show, that relative prices matter. Secondly, it is inconsistent with the theory because an optimally adjusted firm would not face any delivery lags and because output is an endogenous variable to the perfectly competitive firm.

Tobin's Q-theory of investment

Tobin (1969) devised a way of relating investment demand to financial variables which is more amenable to empirical treatment than other investment models, while still having a firm theoretical basis. In fact the crucial variable, Tobin's Q, has already been defined as equation (7.24). Let us reconsider this equation, but first divide through by q_t, the price of new capital goods, to give:

$$1 = \frac{[1/(1+i)][P_{t+1}MKP_{t+1} + (1-\delta)q_{t+1}]}{q_t} \tag{7.32}$$

This is in fact the expression for Tobin's marginal Q. The denominator is the price of new capital goods. The numerator has three components: the term in the first set of square brackets is simply the discount rate; inside the second set of brackets, the first term is the additional revenue from sales of output and the second term is simply the increase in the value of the firm's capital in period $t+1$, that is the value of capital in the next period, less any depreciation. The numerator is therefore the increment to the value of the firm in the next period, from the purchase of one more machine, discounted back to the current period. So Tobin's marginal Q is the rate of change in the value of the firm to the added cost of acquiring new capital. If the firm is in equilibrium, then $Q=1$, as in (7.32).

Under constant returns to scale, from elementary theory of the firm, the marginal cost is proportional to average cost and thus with constant returns to scale marginal Q is proportional to average Q. That is, marginal Q can be expressed as the ratio of the firm's total valuation, PV, to the total cost of its capital, qK, which is known as average Q:

$$Q = \frac{PV}{qK} \tag{7.33}$$

Average Q has the advantage of being directly measurable, unlike the user cost or the expected marginal revenue product of capital. If the replacement cost of capital is known, then given the stock market value of the firm, average Q can be calculated directly. The observable value of the firm already contains the market's expectations about returns over all future periods and it is also adjusted for risk. Thus the analyst does not have to develop a theory of expectations formation, since the market does it for them. To give additional intuition about the role of Q consider a firm which has the choice between investing in new plant and machinery or taking over another firm. If the Q of the target firm is less than unity (its equilibrium level) then it is cheaper for the firm to buy the target firm and to use its capital than to purchase the equivalent capital goods. Similarly, if $Q>1$ then it is cheaper for the firm to purchase new capital goods rather than take over the firm.

This emphasis on financial markets in Q-theory is appealing because the firm or individual has a choice between investment in real or financial assets. This is an example of the interdependence between different markets which is an important feature of macroeconomics as future chapters will confirm.

Empirical studies of investment demand

Empirical studies of the investment demand function have yielded conflicting results. This is most likely due to the strong dependence of investment on expectations of variables, which are not directly measurable, and to the complex lag structure between changes in the determining variables and the consequent change in investment. Assessment of the empirical literature on investment is also difficult because of the lack of comparability between the studies. For the USA investment functions have been estimated at the firm, industry and macro-economic level for cross-sections of firms and for time-series data. The UK empirical literature is rather sparse but focused more on the macroeconomic level, either for manufacturing investment or private sector investment.

There is broad agreement in both the UK and the US studies that output, output growth or sales is an important determinant of investment. Estimates of the elasticity of the demand for the capital stock with respect to output cluster around unity, which are consistent with constant returns to scale. This formal evidence is confirmed by the CBI *Quarterly Industrial Trends Survey*, which reported over the period 1985–96 that 'uncertainty about demand' was the most common factor inhibiting investment. Although the CBI surveys also indicate that the required rate of return is an important factor limiting investment, this is much harder to identify in econometric studies. This is not surprising, for even if interest rates were the only consideration, the required rate of return would depend on the *ex ante* real interest rate, which itself depends on unobservable expectations of inflation. That said, since the 1960s a number of US studies have reported interest rates to be a significant determinant of investment, so giving support to Keynes' theory and the neo-classical approach. Until relatively recently UK studies have, with some exceptions, failed to show that the cost of capital is a significant determinant of investment. Savage (1978) in a survey of British studies concluded that no satisfactory relationship had been found between investment in plant and machinery and cost of capital variables. More recently, however, Oulton (1981) and Jenkinson (1981) using Tobin's Q ratio, have found Q to be significantly related to investment and to offer a slightly better explanation of investment than a pure accelerator model.

The lag structure of investment equations is another contentious issue. A principal finding is that a change in an exogenous variable leads to a change in investment over a long period. The average lag, that is the time between the change in an exogenous variable and the time when 50 per cent of the long-run effect on investment has taken place, both for the USA and the UK seems to be of the order of 1.5–2 years. Another result that seems to be fairly wellsubstantiated is the shorter lag for output changes than for relative prices (see Bean, 1981).

Conclusions and implications for economic policy

The implications of these theories needs to be integrated into the theory of aggregate expenditure developed so far in this book. One of the principal implications is that the aggregate expenditure (*AE*) schedule and the *IS* curve will become flatter, since investment depends directly upon the level of real income, through the accelerator hypothesis discussed earlier (pp. 124ff). The other theories of investment discussed in this chapter clarify a number of other forces on the investment demand function which may cause it to shift. For example, changes in the price of capital goods or changes in the expected rate of inflation will both cause the demand for investment goods to be shifted.

To explicitly include the 'accelerator effect' in the static investment equation developed in Chapter 4, and to explicitly specify the elements of the real rate of interest in line with the user cost of capital model, the new investment

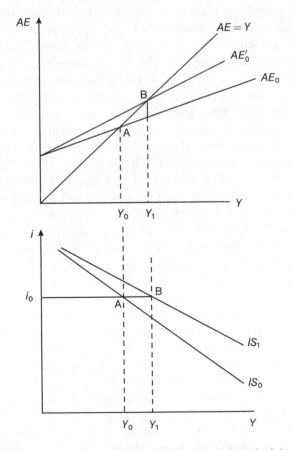

Figure 7.7   *Effect of the accelerator on the slopes of the* AE *and* IS *schedules*

equation becomes:

$$I = \beta_0 - \beta_1(i - \hat{P}) + \beta_2 Y \tag{7.34}$$

The denominator of the expenditure multiplier of Chapter 4 will now be smaller, since it will include the deduction of a positive parameter, β_2. Therefore the new multiplier will be larger and the slope of the AE line steeper. The slope of the AE line is now:

$$\frac{\partial AE}{\partial Y} = [\alpha_1(1 - \tau_1) - \mu_1] + \beta_2 \tag{7.35}$$

where the term in square brackets is the slope of the planned expenditure schedule given in Chapter 4. Since the multiplier is just the reciprocal of one minus this expression it follows that the multiplier must be greater than in the simple model

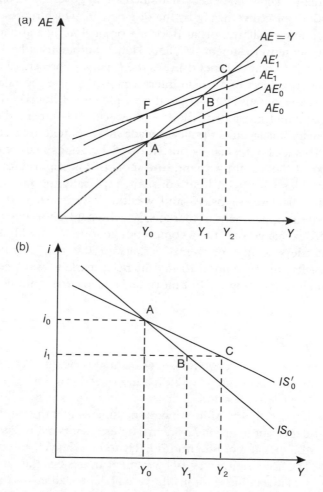

Figure 7.8 *Fiscal and monetary policy with an income elastic investment function*

of Chapter 4, that is:

$$\frac{\partial Y}{\partial \beta_0} = \frac{1}{1 - \alpha_1(1 - \tau_1) - \beta_2 + \mu_1} \tag{7.36}$$

where β_2 is the responsiveness of investment to a rise in the level of income. It then follows that the *IS* slope must be smaller than before, so the curve is flatter. These modifications are represented in **Figure 7.7**, where the upper panel denotes the goods market equilibrium in (*AE, Y*) space and in the lower panel in (*i, Y*) space. The initial equilibrium is given at A in both quadrants, with the standard *AE* and *IS* schedules passing through points A. The inclusion of the income term in the investment equation leads to both schedules swivelling up, to give a new equilibrium level of income at points B.

Since the multiplier is larger than in the simple income–expenditure model both monetary and fiscal policy will be more potent in this extended model. **Figure 7.8**, panel (a) shows the effect of an increase in government spending. The *AE* lines are both displaced vertically, by the distance *AF*, which represents the rise in spending. The new equilibrium is at B for the original *AE* line and at C for the new, income-augmented investment *AE'* line. Hence output rises by $Y_1 - Y_0$ at B compared to $Y_2 - Y_0$ at point C. Panel (b) uses the *IS* curve representation of the goods market to show the effect of a cut in interest rates. A cut in the rate of interest from i_0 to i_1 increases output by $Y_1 - Y_0$ in the simple model compared to $Y_0 - Y_2$ in the income-augmented investment model. Thus with investment directly related to income demand management policy is made more potent in its effect on output.

This is about as far as our study of the goods market can be taken in the context of the income–expenditure model. It is important to note that a number of variables have been held constant; especially the rate of interest, the exchange rate, the level of prices and wealth. In the next part of this text attention is turned to the financial markets, which enables variables such as the interest rate and exchange rate to become endogenous. This will also help to illustrate the interdependence between markets in the macroeconomy, as goods markets shocks are transmitted to the financial markets and vice versa. This makes for a much more complex, but more realistic macroeconomic model.

Summary

- Investment is expenditure on capital goods that adds to the capital stock. In the UK investment spending has been between 15–22 per cent of GDP in the postwar period.
- Keynes' theory of investment postulates that the rate of interest and business expectations are the principal determinants of investment spending, although the investment function is likely to be relatively interest inelastic.
- The neo-classical view of investment argues that the real user cost of capital – the real rate of interest plus the rate of depreciation – is the principal determinant

of investment. In Tobin's Q-theory the firm will undertake new investment if the valuation of the firm is greater than the replacement cost of capital.

- In the accelerator model, investment responds to the adjustment of the capital stock to its new desired level, and is of particular empirical appeal being the only really dynamic theory of investment. To the extent that investment can be explained by the accelerator hypothesis, then investment spending also epends upon the level of income, which by making the IS curve more interest-elastic enhances the potency of fiscal and monetary policy.
- The empirical evidence suggests that investment is very difficult to forecast being subject to long and variable lags and until recently, at least in the UK, only small changes in the rate of interest. To the extent that capital markets are imperfect, internal funds are cheaper than external funds, then profit and profit expectations are likely to be important determinants of investment. The recent evidence seems to be consistent with this view which is broadly consistent with the accelerator models.

Suggested further reading

The literature on investment is technical; however, a good and easy to read review of the policy issues from a UK perspective in to be found in Bond and Jenkinson(1996). Keynes (1936) Chapter 11 presents the marginal efficiency of capital and Chapter 12 the somewhat controversial chapter on the state of long-term expectations, which Keynes (1937) re-emphasised. The neo-classical theory is given by Jorgenson (1963) and Tobin (1969), while Eckaus (1953) and Knox (1952) review the accelerator theory. Surveys of the literature are found in Junankar (1972), Jorgenson (1971), Baily (1978) and, more recently, Chirinko (1993). The US empirical evidence is reviewed in Bischoff (1971) and Clark (1979). Oulton (1981) and Summers (1981) investigate the role of taxation on investment incentives in the context of rational expectations and Tobin's Q-theory approach, and Fazzari *et al*. (1988) consider US evidence that financial market imperfections are important for investment.

Essay titles

1. Explain the relationship between output and investment that is implied by the accelerator theory. How do costs of adjustment affect the model?
2. 'Since investment decisions are undertaken with a particular view of the future, expectations must be the centre of all plausible theories of modern investment.' Discuss.
3. Compare and contrast the accelerator theory of investment demand with the neo-classical theory of Jorgenson, commenting on the degree of empirical support for each theory.
4. How do modern theories of the investment function incorporate business-men's expectations about the future?

Questions

1. (a) Carefully explain the terms net present value and marginal efficiency of capital.
   (b) What is the importance of these terms for Keynes' theory of investment?
   (c) How does uncertainty about the future enter Keynes' theory of investment and what are its implications?
2. Distinguish between the naïve and flexible accelerator models of investment. Are there any problems created for the policy-maker in the recognition of the accelerator effect on investment?
3. Compare the assumed underlying production technologies in the accelerator and neo-classical models of investment. Which might be the most appropriate in the real world?
4. (a) Explain the elements of, and the underlying rationale for, the real user cost ocapital.
   (b) Derive from the Cobb–Douglas production function given as $Y = AK^{\beta}N^{(1-\beta)}$, an expression for the marginal product of capital.
   (c) Set the marginal product of capital from (b) equal to the real user cost of capital, from (a), to derive an expression for the optimal capital stock. To what extent does your result encapsulate both accelerator and neo-classical views of investment?
5. Carefully explain Tobin's average Q. What are the limitations of average Q as a determinant of real net investment?
6. Why might it be empirically difficult to estimate plausible models of investment expenditures?

PART III
THE *IS–LM* Framework

CHAPTER 8

Financial Assets, Asset Market Equilibrium and Monetary Policy

Aims and objectives

- To identify the principal classes of financial asset and asset markets.
- To develop the portfolio balance approach to the financial sector with a view to explaining the determinants of interest rates, exchange rates and international capital movements.
- To explain how alternative monetary policy actions have different quantitative effects on interest rates and exchange rates, and hence different effects on the real side of the economy.

Introduction

The macroeconomic framework developed in Part II concentrated on the aggregate expenditure on goods and services and the principal determinants of those expenditures. Some potentially important variables, such as interest rates, the exchange rate, the money supply and the stock of financial wealth were assumed to be exogenous to the model. In this part of the book the determinants of these financial variables are considered using a portfolio-balance framework, that will lead on to an examination of the operation of monetary policy that works through the financial markets by way of a portfolio-balance mechanism. The interactions between the financial markets and the goods market are the subject of Chapters 9 and 10, and a more detailed analysis of the demand for money than is possible here follows in Chapter 11.

This chapter begins with an overview of the various types of financial assets that may be considered in macroeconomics, followed by a brief discussion of the determinants of the demands for these assets. We then consider the supply of the various financial assets, with particular reference to the supply of money, and examine the asset market equilibrium conditions and hence the determinants of the domestic nominal interest rate, the exchange rate and, under fixed exchange rates, the net capital outflow. The net capital outflow is the *ex ante* balance of payments on capital account under fixed exchange rates. The final sections use this portfolio-balance framework to help understand the operation of monetary policy under both fixed and floating exchange rates, and consider the special case when domestic and foreign bonds are perfect substitutes.

The characteristics and types of financial assets

In the macroeconomy there are a very large number of potentially different financial assets; for example, money, bonds, equity, insurance schemes and property bonds would all count as financial assets. To make any analysis of the financial sector tractable a number of simplifying assumptions are required regarding the number of assets that can be explicitly treated. In general terms the asset choice is restricted to just three: domestic money, domestic bonds and foreign bonds, which will be introduced in turn.

Money is defined as any asset that is generally acceptable in the final settlement for purchases, and the supply of money can be thought of as the stock of such assets outstanding at a point in time. In this book it is assumed that money is non-traded; that is to say, only domestic residents hold domestic money. The essential characteristic of money is that it is a perfectly liquid asset. It therefore carries no (or at least only a low) rate of interest, which may be regarded as a reward for illiquidity, and is a riskless asset in the absence of inflation. In addition to being a store of value it is also a medium of exchange and a unit of account. Money, therefore, efficiently facilitates exchange in the economy.

A bond is an imperfectly liquid asset since in order to convert it into cash it has to be sold on a market with the risk of making a capital loss if the selling price is below the price at which the bond was purchased. The alternative of waiting until the bond matures and the principal repaid, involves time which is included in the cost of illiquidity. Hence a financial asset is regarded as more illiquid the longer its time to maturity. The price of a bond on the market is the present value of the income stream to which the bond is a claim. This can be written as:

$$p_b = \frac{Q_n}{(1+i)} + \frac{Q_n}{(1+i)^2} + \cdots + \frac{Q_n + PR}{(1+i)^n} \tag{8.1}$$

where Q_n is the nominally fixed annual income, i is the nominal rate of interest and PR is the principal which is repaid after n years. If the bond is a perpetuity, such that it is not redeemable, the price P_b, is given by:

$$p_b = \frac{Q_n}{1+i} \sum_{t=0}^{n} \left(\frac{1}{1+i} \right)^t \tag{8.2}$$

By using the rules of geometric progression (see **Box 4.1** in Chapter 4) this can be written as:

$$p_b = \left(\frac{Q_n}{1+i} \right) \left(\frac{1}{1-(1+i)^{-1}} \right) = \frac{Q_n}{i} \tag{8.3}$$

which shows that if the rate of interest rises the price of existing bonds must fall. This happens in order to equalise the rates of return on bonds issued at different dates with different coupon rates. Therefore bond yields are inversely related to bond prices.

In practice there are two types of bonds, those that are redeemable at a fixed future date and those which are perpetuities. To keep the analysis as simple as possible it is assumed that all bonds are perpetuities. In an open economy context and in the absence of exchange controls domestic residents may choose to hold either domestic bonds, denoted B, issued by the domestic government, or foreign currency bonds issued by the foreign government, denoted B^*, which are held by both foreign and domestic residents.

There are two important differences between the way in which domestic bonds and foreign bonds are treated in this book. The first is that domestic bonds are assumed to be non-traded while foreign bonds are traded. Hence the domestic bond stock is all held by domestic residents while the stock of foreign-currency-denominated bonds, B^*, are held partly by domestic residents, B_d^*, and partly by foreign residents, B_f^*. The second difference between domestic and foreign bonds is that foreign bonds are denominated in foreign currency. Hence exchange rate movements will affect the domestic value of foreign currency bonds. Specifically, a depreciation of the domestic currency will raise the domestic currency value of foreign-currency-denominated bonds, while an appreciation will lower the domestic currency value of the foreign bonds. Therefore, in addition to the risk associated with illiquidity, there is also the additional risk associated with exchange rate movements for domestic residents holding foreign currency denominated assets.

All other financial assets are excluded from the analysis, or are assumed to move in proportion with the included assets. Therefore, in aggregate the financial wealth constraint for the domestic non-bank private sector is given by:

$$\frac{A}{P} = \frac{M^s}{P} + \frac{B^s}{P} + \frac{EB_d^*}{P} \quad \text{or} \quad 1 = \frac{M^s}{A} + \frac{B^s}{A} + \frac{EB_d^*}{A} \tag{8.4}$$

where A denotes the total stock of nominal non-bank private sector wealth measured in home currency units, M^s is the money stock held by the domestic non-bank private sector, B^s is the total stock of domestic government debt held by the domestic private sector, B_d^* is the stock of foreign currency debt held by the domestic non-bank private sector, and E is the exchange rate measured as the domestic price of foreign currency used to convert the foreign-currency-denominated bond stock into domestic currency units. P is the domestic price level, used to convert nominal values into real values. For the time being, as in Part II, the price level is assumed to be constant and exogenous to the model, although it is included here since it will be needed to understand the effect of exogenous changes in the price level in Chapter 9. The basic choice confronting domestic residents is how to allocate their financial wealth between these competing assets. To understand this process the specific demand functions for each of these assets must be considered.

Demand functions for financial assets

The demand functions for money and for domestic and foreign-currency bonds are all rather similar, and strictly interdependent, although for clarity to begin with they are examined separately.

Money is a unique asset in that money is demanded in order to buy goods and services; that is, to facilitate transactions. More precisely, money is held to smooth out the time difference between monthly pay cheques and daily payments made for food and other items. As incomes rise, both income and expenditure streams grow and these money balances held to smooth out the cash flow must also grow. This is the *transactions motive* for demanding money and this increases with the level of real income. Money is also demanded as an asset because it serves as riskless asset and store of value. Although money earns a low or zero yield, it also offers zero risk, which makes it fundamentally different to other assets. Thus if individuals believe that bond prices are going to fall, they will hold their wealth in cash, because in that way they can protect the value of their wealth. High bond prices are associated with low interest rates; thus as bond prices rise and the expectations of future falls dominate, agents will switch out of bonds into cash. Hence a fall in interest rates increases the demand for money as an asset. This is the *asset motive* for holding money.

Both of the components of the demand for money, the asset and the transactions demand, should be expressed as a demand for real money balances, $M^d/P = m^d$. This is self-evident in the case of the transactions demand. Suppose the price level doubles overnight so that with a given level of real income, money income and money expenditures double. In this case the demand for transactions balances would also be expected to double, since the money transactions which these balances are financing have doubled. Thus the transactions demand is a demand for real money balances. The asset or precautionary demand for money is also a demand for real money balances. Suppose we go to bed holding a given amount of money based on current interest rates and expectations about bond prices. Overnight, the authorities change the currency from sterling to euros, with two euros to one pound. When we wake in the morning, we find that our salary is 40 000 euros, rather than 20 000 euros, and all prices have doubled. There is no reason for us to change our demand for money since all prices and incomes have changed proportionately. Nothing has altered in real terms. Thus the asset demand for real money balances would also be unchanged.

According to these arguments the demand for real money balances may be summarised as:

$$\frac{M^d}{P} = \lambda_0 + \lambda_1 Y - \lambda_2 i - \lambda_3 (\bar{i}^* + x) + \lambda_4 \frac{\bar{A}}{P} \tag{8.5}$$

Equation (8.5) says that the demand for money depends positively on both the level of real income, reflecting the transactions demand for money, and on the stock of financial wealth, reflecting portfolio size. The returns on domestic bonds and foreign bonds, are i and $i^* + x$, respectively, are negatively related to the demand for real money balances, where x denotes the expected depreciation of the domestic currency. To understand why the return on the foreign currency bond depends on the expected depreciation of the domestic currency as well as the foreign rate of interest, consider a foreign bond offering a yield of 5 per cent per annum. If the domestic holder of the foreign currency bond expects the domestic currency to appreciate by 5 per cent over the year, that is for x to fall by 5 per cent, then the total return on the bond will be zero, since any potential gains in foreign currency are wiped out by the appreciation. On the other hand, if the domestic currency is expected to depreciate by 5 per cent then the total gain from holding the foreign bond will be 10 per cent. For the time being, however, the expected change in the exchange rate is assumed to be constant. This avoids the need to specify how agent's expectations are formed and enables the analysis to remain comparatively static in nature.

The demands for foreign and domestic bonds, like the demand for money, also depend upon the level of real income, although the direction of the effect is counter-intuitive. The crucial point is that if the stock of non-bank private sector wealth is assumed to be given, then a rise in income that raises the demand for money through the transactions motive must necessitate a fall in the demand for other assets. Therefore a rise in income will reduce the joint demand for foreign and domestic bonds. For simplicity it is assumed that the demand for both domestic and foreign bonds fall as income rises, although this need not be the case. If, for example, the rise in the demand for money was exactly offset by a fall in the demand for foreign bonds, then there need be no change in the demand for domestic bonds.

The demands for bonds are also assumed to depend positively on their own returns and negatively on the returns of the competing asset. This is to assume that the assets are *gross substitutes*. Suppose we are holding both domestic and foreign bonds and the rate of interest suddenly rises on domestic bonds. There are two effects: the income effect and the substitution effect. According to the *substitution effect* we will sell some of the foreign bonds in exchange for domestic bonds which now offer a higher return. On the other hand, the *income effect* says that because we now earn a higher return on each domestic bond that we hold, we can sell some of the bonds, while still earning the same level of income from the portfolio. If it is assumed that more income is preferred to the same income, then we would substitute domestic bonds for foreign bonds in our asset portfolio and the substitution effect is dominant. On this argument the demand for domestic bonds depends positively on the domestic rate of interest and negatively upon the expected foreign rate of return. Similarly, the demand for foreign bonds by domestic residents depends positively on the foreign rate of return and negatively on the domestic rate of interest. The real demand for domestic and foreign bonds can be summarised as:

$$\frac{B^d}{P} = \phi_0 - \phi_1 Y + \phi_2 i - \phi_3(\bar{i}^* + \bar{x}) + \phi_4 \frac{\bar{A}}{P} \tag{8.6}$$

$$\frac{F^d}{P} = \zeta_0 - \zeta_1 Y - \zeta_2 i + \zeta_3(\bar{i}^* + \bar{x}) + \zeta_4 \frac{\bar{A}}{P} \tag{8.7}$$

In these demand relations it is important to remember that the foreign rate of interest, the expected depreciation of the exchange rate, the stock of financial wealth and the price level are all given.

Asset supplies

To move from the demand for each of the assets to the respective asset market equilibria some assumptions need to be made about the supply of each of the three assets, subject to the wealth constraint, given as equation (8.4).

Domestic bonds are a liability of the domestic government and are issued to finance the budget deficit. By purchasing government bonds (or securities) the banking sector or private sector effectively lends to the government. In this context the supply of domestic bonds is wholly under the control of the authorities and hence can be regarded as an exogenous variable. The supply of foreign currency bonds, on the other hand, are most easily thought of as issued by a foreign government and hence a policy variable for that government. Since the home country is assumed to be small relative to the rest of the world, the supply of foreign bonds for domestic residents to buy can be assumed to be infinite at a given rate of interest, $\bar{i}*$.

The supply of money, however, is more complicated, the quantity being determined by the banking system as shown schematically in **Table 8.1.** A central bank's first function is to act as banker to the government, to whom it is compelled to provide the main banking services, especially that of providing credit. The second function of the central bank is to hold the nations foreign currency and gold reserves. Suppose the government needs to raise £500 million without raising taxation. The government simply approaches the central bank, which prints £500 million of money in exchange for government IOUs (government bonds). Thus in **Table 8.1** the central bank's assets have increased by £500 million as have its liabilities, through the issuing of notes and coin. These notes and coin are referred to as high-powered money or base money.

The government sometimes borrows in order to buy assets. Typically the government may use the loan to buy back its own liabilities from their holders in the non-bank private sector (nbps). This is known as an open-market purchase. The effect will be an expansion of the money base just as before, since the government simply gives the central bank assets (government debt) which it has acquired from the nbps. This action raises the stock of high-powered money; that is the money supply has been increased. Conversely, the government could decide to reverse the process by issuing debt so as to raise cash from the nbps – this is an open-market sale. If the government subsequently spends the proceeds from this sale there is no effect on the money base. If, on the other hand, the central bank decides to use the proceeds so as to repurchase some of its debt from the central bank (thereby reducing L_G) it effectively reduces the supply of base money.

Table 8.1 *The banking system balance sheet*

Central bank			
Assets		*Liabilities*	
Gold and foreign exchange reserves	R	Currency – high-powered money	H
Lending to government	L_G		
Commercial banks			
Assets		*Liabilities*	
Currency and deposits with the central bank	H_b	Deposits from the public	Dep
Lending to the personal and corporate sectors	L		
Consolidated banking sector			
Assets		*Liabilities*	
Gold and foreign exchange reserves	R	Currency in circulation $H - H_b =$	H_p
Domestic credit: $L + L_G =$	D	Deposits from the public	Dep
Money supply: $R + D =$	M^s	Money supply: $H_p + Dep =$	M^s

The commercial banks' principal function is to take deposits from the nbps and lend these funds on to other members of the personal and corporate sectors. Thus to the commercial bank deposits are a liability, since they may have to be repaid if requested. On the other hand the funds lent on to firms are assets to the bank, since they can recall these loans if necessary. The commercial banks are also required for prudential reasons to maintain a stock of cash and deposits at the central bank to settle interbank debts and to act as a reserve should there be a rush for repayment by depositors. These items are shown in the centre panel of Table 8.1.

The consolidated balance sheet shows the combined positions of the banking system as a whole, which ultimately gives two identical measures of the quantity of money. From the right-hand side of the balance sheet the monetary liabilities of the banking sector are given as: $M^s = H_p + Dep$; that is cash in circulation plus the deposits of the nbps. By definition this sum must also equal the monetary assets of the banking system that are: $M^s = D + R$. That is to say, domestic credit extended to the government and the nbps plus the stock of foreign exchange reserves. These two elements of the money supply are very different. The domestic credit component of the money supply is almost wholly due to bank lending either to the government or to the private customers. Bank lending to the government is under the direct control of the authorities. Commercial bank lending to the private sector, however, is not so easy for the authorities to control, although of course the authorities can determine the amount of reserves the commercial banks must hold at the central bank. Since the authorities can in principle regulate the H_b/Dep ratio, it assumed that they can closely regulate domestic credit. In other words domestic credit, D, is an exogenous policy variable. The stock of international reserves, however, represent a buffer stock of international currencies and other short-term assets, with which to purchase the domestic currency so as to support the exchange rate. Their size is determined by the accumulation of foreign currency bought by the central bank on previous occasions to support other countries currencies, relative to the home currency. Changes in the reserves therefore come about as a result of central bank intervention in the foreign exchange markets. For example, if there is an excess supply of domestic currency a fall in the price of domestic currency – a depreciation – can only be prevented by the central bank using some reserves to purchase the domestic currency. Since the excess supply or demand on the foreign exchange markets is determined by the *ex ante* balance of payments position, then it follows that changes in reserves are not under the control of the authorities. In particular, a balance of payments deficit results in a fall in reserves as they are sold to prevent a depreciation of the home currency, and a surplus leads to an accumulation of reserves as domestic currency is sold to purchase foreign currency to prevent the price of domestic currency rising. In other words the change in reserves is determined by the balance of payments and is an endogenous variable. It follows, therefore, that the money supply is also endogenous with a fixed exchange rate policy.

Suppose the authorities choose not to intervene in the foreign exchange markets to support the currency. In this case $\Delta R = 0$ and therefore $\Delta M^s = \Delta \overline{D}$. This will be the case under a freely floating exchange rate regime when the balance of payments for official financing is identically equal to zero. Under a floating exchange rate system the money supply is an instrument of policy and exogenously determined. By contrast, as noted above, a fixed exchange rate system is one such that the balance of payments for official financing is not zero, with the surplus or deficit being covered by the central bank accumulation or sale of foreign exchange reserves. This distinction between fixed and floating exchange rate scenarios is crucial to understanding how monetary policy operates in an open economy and will be used extensively throughout the remainder of this book.

Asset market equilibrium

Combining the supply assumptions with the three aggregate asset demand functions the market equilibrium relations can be written as:

$$\left(\frac{\overline{D}+R}{P}\right) = \lambda_0 + \lambda_1 Y - \lambda_2 i - \lambda_3(\bar{i}^* + \bar{x}) + \lambda_4(\overline{A/P}) \tag{a}$$

$$\left(\frac{\overline{B}^s}{\overline{P}}\right) = \phi_0 - \phi_1 Y + \phi_2 i - \phi_3(\bar{i}^* + \bar{x}) + \phi_4(\overline{A/P}) \tag{b} \quad (8.8)$$

$$\left(\frac{E.B^*_d}{\overline{P}}\right) = \zeta_0 - \zeta_1 Y - \zeta_2 i + \zeta_3(\bar{i}^* + \bar{x}) + \zeta_4(\overline{A/P}) \tag{c}$$

These equations say that the real supply of money is equal to the real demand for money; the real supply of domestic bonds is equal to the real demand; and the supply of domestically held foreign bonds is also equal to demand. Because of the wealth constraint only two of the asset market equilibrium equations in (8.8) are independent. In this context if the domestic and foreign bond markets are in equilibrium at current rates of interest and income then it follows that the domestic money market must also be in equilibrium. This is known as *Walras' Law*. For this reason the model is overdetermined and it is possible to drop one of these equations from the analysis. Before using this simplification, however, a diagrammatic treatment of the asset market equilibrium relations will be presented.

Any diagrammatic treatment suffers from the problem that there are alternative ways of representing these asset equilibrium relations because there are in principle four endogenous variables to represent on just two axes! The endogenous variables are the domestic interest rate, domestic income, the exchange rate and the domestic demand for foreign bonds. If it is assumed that the level of income is determined in the goods market, from the point of view of the financial sector this can be taken as given, which reduces the number of potential endogenous variables from four to three. To further reduce the dimension of the system an assumption has to be made about the exchange rate regime in operation. If the exchange rate is allowed to float then B_d^* becomes exogenous and the nominal exchange rate, E, becomes the second endogenous variable with i. On the other hand, if the exchange rate is fixed by the domestic authorities, then E becomes exogenous and the number of endogenous variables is reduced to two: i and B_d^*. Because changes in both E and B_d^* have the same impact on the asset market demand functions the asset market equilibrium schedules are identical in both cases.

Figure 8.1 shows the construction of the money market equilibrium line, or *MM* curve. The left-hand panel depicts the money market, with interest rates on the vertical axis and money demand and supply on the horizontal. In the right-hand panel the domestic nominal interest rate, i, is again on the vertical axis, but on the horizontal axis is plotted the home currency value of foreign bond holdings, EB_d^*. Under floating exchange rates B_d^* is given and the axis represents the exchange rate. On the other hand when fixed rates are assumed, E is given and the horizontal axis measures the capital outflow.

In the left-hand panel the demand for money line is drawn negatively sloped with respect to the domestic rate of interest, for given levels of domestic income, prices, wealth, the foreign rate of interest and exchange rate expectations. This demand for money line slopes down because of the negative relationship between domestic money demand and the nominal rate of interest. The money supply line is drawn vertically, since it does not depend upon the domestic rate of interest. The money market clears at point A, where the money demand and supply schedules intersect. At rates of interest, above i_0 there is an excess supply of money and at lower rates of interest there is an excess demand for money. In the right-hand panel of **Figure 8.1** the money market equilibrium schedule is drawn in (i, EB_d^*) space. The point A in the left-hand panel corresponds to the point A in the right-hand panel, both being points of money market equilibrium.

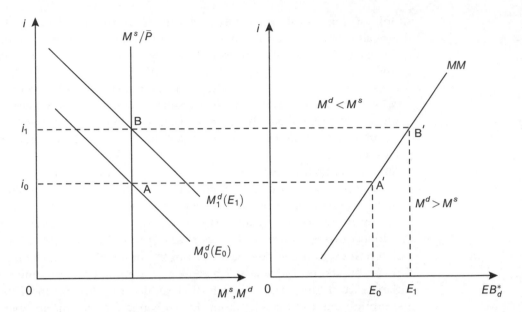

Figure 8.1 *Money market equilibrium*

To derive the *MM* line, assume there is a rise in the domestic currency value of foreign currency bond holdings by domestic residents that raises wealth and causes the demand for money function to shift up to the right in the left-hand panel. When combined with a given money supply, money market equilibrium is established at B where the interest rate is higher than at A, at i_1. In the right-hand panel the point B′ must lie above and to the right of point A′, because both the interest rate and the level of wealth (represented by the rise in E) have risen. This is also a point of money market equilibrium and so the money market equilibrium schedule in (i, EB_d^*) space exhibits an upward (positive) slope.

At all points to the right of the *MM* line there is an excess demand for money, and at all points above and to the left of the line there is an excess supply of money. The line slopes up because a rise in the level of wealth leads to a higher demand for money, which for a given supply must be offset by a higher rate of interest to maintain money market equilibrium. More formally, differentiating (8.8a), with respect to i and EB_d^*, assuming that the level of income and the price level are constant gives: $\partial i / \partial EB_d^* = \lambda_2 / \lambda_4 > 0$. In this context, a rise in the money supply, a rise in the foreign rate of interest or an expected depreciation of the exchange rate will shift the *MM* line to the right. On the other hand, a rise in the price level or a rise in income, Y, will shift the *MM* line to the left.

The equilibrium structure of the bond markets is similar to that of the money market. In **Figure 8.2** the left-hand panel shows the demand function for bonds to be positively sloped since the demand for bonds rises with the rate of interest. The supply of bonds is exogenously given, as indicated by the vertical line labelled $\underline{B}^s$. The domestic bond market clears where the supply and demand are

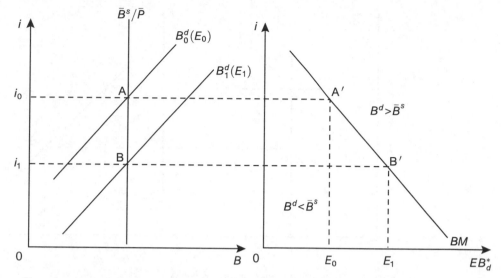

Figure 8.2   *Bond market equilibrium*

equal at point A. Consider now a rise in EB_d^* on the bond demand schedule. Since bond demand is directly related to wealth the demand curve shifts down to the right, to give a new equilibrium position at B, with a lower interest rate of i_1. In the right-hand panel, point A′ corresponds to the point A in the left-hand panel. The rise in EB_d^* and the associated fall in the rate of interest means that point B′ in the right-hand panel must lie below and to the right of A′. The bond market equilibrium schedule, BM, therefore has a negative slope in (i, EB_d^*) space. The BM line slopes down because a rise in wealth increases the demand for bonds, which for a given supply of bonds, necessitates a fall in the rate of interest to restore equilibrium in the bond market. All points to the right of BM are points of excess demand for bonds and all points below BM are points of excess supply.

More formally, the slope is given by differentiating equation (8.8b) with respect to i and EB_d^*, (for a given level of P) which gives: $\partial i/\partial(EB_d^*) = -\phi_2/\phi_4 < 0$. The BM line is drawn for a given price level, foreign interest rate, state of exchange rate expectations, level of income and the domestic bond supply. A rise in the foreign interest rate, the expected rate of depreciation or the level of domestic income will lower the demand for domestic bonds, shifting the BM line to the left. A rise in the supply of bonds or a fall in the price level will shift BM to the right.

The final equilibrium locus to consider in this theory of portfolio equilibrium is that of the domestic demand for foreign bonds. Because the home country is assumed to be small relative to the foreign country, domestic residents are unable to affect the supply of foreign assets, which to domestic residents is perfectly elastic, such that the foreign rate of interest is given. This is shown in the left-hand panel of **Figure 8.3**, where the supply of foreign bonds is given by the B^{*s} line and the real domestic demand for foreign bonds shown as B_d^* slopes up in (i, i^*) space. The domestic demand for foreign bonds slopes up since a rise in

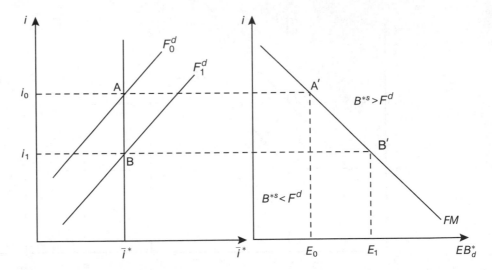

Figure 8.3 *Domestic demand for foreign bonds*

the domestic rate of interest curtails the demand for foreign bonds which has to be offset by a rise in i^* if demand is to remain unchanged. The equilibrium is given where the supply and demand lines intersect at A. This point corresponds to point A′ in the right-hand panel. Now assume that EB_d^* rises for all rates of interest. In the left-hand panel the demand for bonds line shifts down to the right, since a higher level of domestic wealth means a higher demand for foreign bonds, which to maintain bond-market equilibrium requires a fall in the domestic rate of interest. In the right-hand panel the new equilibrium position B′ must lie to the right and below point A′, so that the *FM* line has a negative slope in (i, EB_d^*) space. At all points above *FM*, there is an excess supply of foreign currency bonds to domestic residents, resulting in domestic residents selling these bonds, leading to a net capital inflow (or an appreciation of the exchange rate). Below *FM* there is an excess demand for foreign bonds and a capital outflow from the home country (or a depreciation of the exchange rate).

More technically, differentiating equation (8.8c) with respect to i and EB_d^* gives the formal slope of the *FM* line as $\partial i / \partial (EB_d^*) = -\zeta_2/\zeta_4 < 0$. As with the other asset market equilibrium lines in this section the *FM* line is drawn for a given price level, real wealth, real income and the foreign interest rate. A rise in the foreign rate of interest or expected domestic currency depreciation will raise the demand for foreign bonds and hence shift the *FM* locus up to the right, while a fall in the foreign interest rate will shift *FM* down to the left.

Figure 8.4 combines the three equilibrium asset market schedules on to a single set of axes. There are several points of interest. First, the relative slopes of the *BM* and the *FM* lines are ambiguous, depending upon the relative responses of the demands to interest rate and wealth changes. Since the rate of interest reflects the own price of bonds, it is assumed that the *BM* line is more interest-elastic than the *FM* line. Therefore the *BM* line is drawn flatter then the *FM* line,

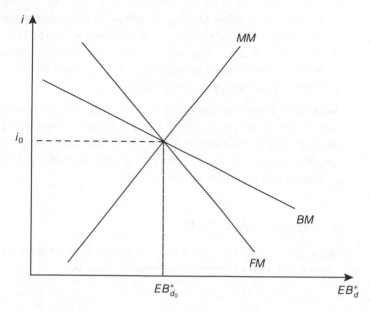

Figure 8.4 *Financial markets equilibrium*

although strictly this is an empirical issue. Secondly, with three asset market equilibrium schedules linked by the wealth constraint, if two markets in equilibrium then the third market will also be in equilibrium, via Walras' Law. This means that only two of the equilibrium loci need to be drawn to locate the position of equilibrium. Which locus is dropped does not matter, so in practice the locus omitted will be which ever is the most convenient for the analysis at hand. A third reason for putting all the equilibrium loci together is that it is useful to demonstrate the substitutability between the assets. In the case where both domestic bonds and foreign bonds are perfect substitutes the two assets must have a common price and so the two bond market equilibrium equations reduce to $i = \bar{i}^* + \bar{x}$. This special case is known as perfect capital mobility and is a useful result because it allows the model to be greatly simplified. This, and another special case, is considered later, after studying the most general model.

Monetary policy

Now that the financial sector is in place, the role of monetary policy in this model can be examined. The advantage of developing the financial sector in this way is that it avoids the unrealistic 'helicopter money' of most textbooks, whereby the money supply is assumed to increase by a drop of notes from some kind of UFO. In practice an increase or reduction in money supply only happens because agents are encouraged to alter their portfolio of assets. This can be done in three ways:

1. By the authorities buying or selling domestic government bonds to the non-bank private sector – an open market operation (OMO);

2. By the authorities buying or selling foreign currency bonds to the non-bank private sector – a foreign exchange operation (FXO);
3. By the authorities buying or selling domestic government bonds to the non-bank private sector in exchange for foreign currency bonds – a sterilised foreign exchange operation (SFXO).

Moreover from our earlier discussion (pp. 150ff), it is clear the nature of monetary policy is different under fixed than under floating exchange rates, since the money supply is endogenous in the former and exogenous in the latter. To avoid any confusion on this issue this section is sub-divided into a fixed rate and a floating exchange rate section.

Fixed exchange rates

With fixed exchange rates the change in foreign currency reserves is dependent on the balance of payments position. That is:

$$\Delta R = (X - M) - \Delta B_d^* \tag{8.9}$$

where the exchange rate is normalised to unity. For the stock of nbps real wealth to be maintained constant, as assumed so far, it is important that the current account balance is assumed to be in continuous balance (this assumption is relaxed in Chapter 10). Therefore $X - M = 0$ which implies that $\Delta R = -\Delta B_d^*$. This enables the asset market equilibrium equations to be rewritten in terms of changes as follows (with $P = E = 1$):

$$(\Delta \overline{D} + \Delta R) = \lambda_0 + \lambda_1 \Delta Y - \lambda_2 \Delta i - \lambda_3 \Delta \overline{i}^* + \lambda_4 (\Delta \overline{D} + \Delta \overline{B}^s)$$

$$\Delta \overline{B}^s = \phi_0 - \phi_1 \Delta Y + \phi_2 \Delta i - \phi_3 \Delta \overline{i}^* + \phi_4 (\Delta \overline{D} + \Delta \overline{B}^s) \tag{8.10}$$

$$\Delta B_d^* = \zeta_0 - \zeta_1 \Delta Y - \zeta_2 \Delta i + \zeta_3 \Delta \overline{i}^* + \zeta_4 (\Delta \overline{D} + \Delta \overline{B}^s)$$

The only way in which this affects the diagram, (**Figure 8.4**) is that the domestic bond market is now independent of ΔB_d^* and so can be drawn as horizontal in the fixed exchange rate case.

Consider an open market purchase by the authorities in order to increase the money supply. The authorities effectively buy back some of the outstanding stock of debt from the non-bank private sector in exchange for cash (or bank deposits). The authorities encourage this portfolio shift by offering 'good terms'; that is, higher than current market clearing prices for the debt. This in turn lowers interest rates and makes the non-bank private sector willing to hold the additional cash. Thus the authorities have increased the money supply outstanding by simply exchanging bonds for cash in non-bank private sector portfolios. In terms of symbols, the effect of this open market operation is to increase $\overline{D}$ and reduce $\overline{B}^s$, that is $\Delta \overline{D} = -\Delta B^s$. This operation is shown in **Figure 8.5**.

Figure 8.5 gives the initial position at point A. The increase in domestic credit, $\Delta \overline{D}$, causes the *MM* line to shift to the right, to MM_1, since for a higher money supply a lower rate of interest is needed to encourage the nbps to hold the cash.

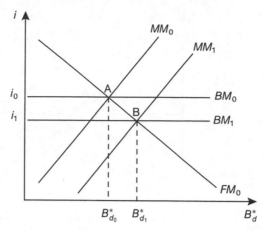

Figure 8.5 *Open market purchase*

The fall in the bond supply, $-\Delta \bar{B}^s$, implies that a lower rate of interest is needed to reduce the demand for bonds, so the *BM* line shifts down to BM_1. The *FM*-line is unaffected by this OMO since the effect of the rise in $\Delta \bar{D}$ is exactly offset by the fall in $\Delta \bar{B}^s$ as can be seen from (8.10). Thus from the initial equilibrium at A the effect of the open market purchase of domestic bonds by the domestic authorities is to take the model to the equilibrium at B. At B all asset markets are in equilibrium with all outstanding asset supplies willingly held. The effect of this change has been to cause a capital outflow from the domestic economy as domestic residents, who have sold domestic bonds to the government, have attempted to purchase foreign bonds with the proceeds.

Figure 8.6 shows the effect of a foreign exchange operation to increase the money supply. In symbols this can be written as: $\Delta \underline{D} = -\Delta B_d^*$. As before, the *MM* line moves to the right to MM_1 as $\Delta \underline{D}$ increases. This increase in domestic credit has the effect of shifting both of the other schedules. The *BM* line shifts down to BM_1, as before, since the rise in domestic credit raises the demand for bonds, which to maintain bond market equilibrium, must be offset by a fall in the rate of interest. In this case the *FM* line also shifts up, as domestic residents try to purchase foreign currency assets. The fall in the rate of interest will therefore be smaller in this case than in the case of an OMO, because the *FM* line also shifts up, to FM_1. The increase in domestic credit raises the demand for foreign currency bonds, which is partly met by a rise in the domestic interest and partly by a capital outflow as residents attempt to acquire the bonds to balance their portfolios. Thus the difference between and OMO and a FXO is that in the former case the fall in the interest rate is larger and the capital outflow smaller; that is the equilibrium is at B, rather than at C, as in this case.

The third kind of monetary policy is a sterilised intervention in the bond markets (SFXO). The purpose of this operation is to influence interest rates without changing the money supply. To ensure this it is necessary that there are no capital outflows or inflows, since these flows directly change reserves that lower or raise

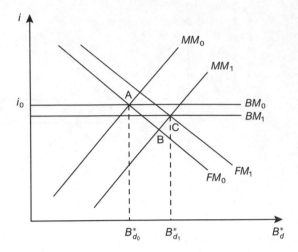

Figure 8.6 *Foreign exchange operation*

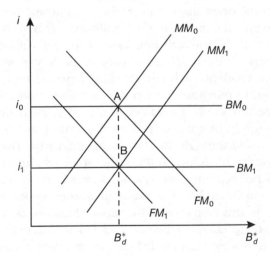

Figure 8.7 *Sterilised bond market intervention*

the money supply. Thus it is important that any changes in ΔB_d^* are offset by equal and opposite changes in $\Delta \overline{B}^s$. Thus a SFXO is defined as: $-\Delta \overline{B}^s = \Delta B_d^*$. In **Figure 8.7** the effect of the fall in the domestic bond stock is to shift all lines down to MM_1, BM_1 and FM_1, since a fall in the bond stock requires a lower rate of interest to maintain money market, bond market and foreign bond market equilibrium. In the money market because reserves must not change, the fall in the domestic bond stock lowers the demand for money that must be offset by a fall in the rate of interest. In this case, because, there is no capital outflow, the fall in the rate of interest is larger than in the other two cases.

Floating exchange rates

Under floating exchange rates, $\Delta R = 0$, by definition, and so the asset market equilibrium equations now become:

$$\Delta \overline{D} = \lambda_0 + \lambda_1 \Delta Y - \lambda_2 \Delta i - \lambda_3 \Delta (\overline{i^*} + \overline{x}) + \lambda_4 \Delta (\Delta \overline{D} + \Delta \overline{B}^s + B_d^* \Delta E)$$

$$\Delta \overline{B}^s = \phi_0 - \phi \Delta_1 Y + \phi_2 \Delta i - \phi_3 \Delta (\overline{i^*} + \overline{x}) + \phi_4 (\Delta \overline{D} + \Delta \overline{B}^s + B_d^* \Delta E) \qquad (8.11)$$

$$B_d^* \Delta E = \zeta_0 - \zeta \Delta_1 Y - \zeta_2 \Delta i + \zeta_3 \Delta (\overline{i^*} + \overline{x}) + \zeta_4 (\Delta \overline{D} + \Delta \overline{B}^s + B_d^* \Delta E)$$

where again prices are assumed to be fixed, together with exchange rate expectations and the quantity of foreign currency assets held by domestic residents. Since the analysis is essentially the same as for the fixed exchange rate case the treatment can be brief. An important point to note, though, is that in this context the portfolio balance model of the financial sector becomes a theory of exchange rate determination. Under floating exchange rates the exchange rate is determined together with the interest rate in the financial sector. This reflects the importance of international financial capital flows relative to flows in goods and services, which in the modern world are very small in comparison. Thus the most important factors determining exchange rates are not the competitiveness of goods and services, but the stock of money and the stock of bonds outstanding and the level of income. In the following analysis an increase (fall) in the money supply leads to a depreciation (appreciation) of the exchange rate and and an increase (decrease) in the supply of domestic bonds to an appreciation (depreciation) of the exchange rate.

An open market sale in which $\Delta \overline{D} = -\Delta B^s$ leaves the *FM* line unaffected. The *MM* and *BM* lines both shift downwards, to MM_1 and BM_1 respectively, as a lower rate of interest is needed to clear the money and bond markets. In **Figure 8.8** therefore the equilibrium shifts from point A to point B and the exchange rate depreciates from E_0 to E_1. Thus an expansion in the money supply leads to depreciation of the exchange rate. The reason is that with a lower return on domestic bonds domestic residents try to purchase foreign bonds that have a higher yield. This increased demand for foreign currency pushes up the price of foreign currency and lowers the price of domestic currency.

A foreign exchange operation has the same effect on the exchange rate as an open market operation, but the exchange rate depreciation is greater, as the authorities are dealing directly with foreign currency securities. In this case $\Delta \overline{D} = -\Delta E B_d^*$ and so the efforts of the authorities to buy foreign currency bonds from the nbps will increase the supply of home currency so leading to a depreciation of the home currency. In **Figure 8.9**, from the initial equilibrium at A, the

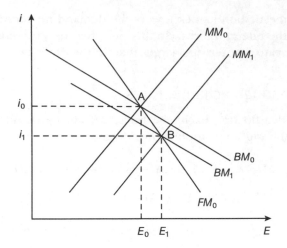

Figure 8.8 *Open market purchase with floating exchange rate*

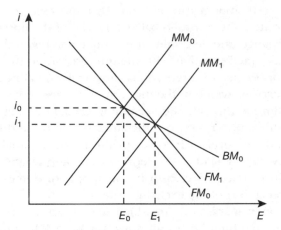

Figure 8.9 *FXO with a floating exchange rate*

domestic bond market is unaffected by the foreign exchange purchase and so the final equilibrium must lie on BM_0. The *MM* line shifts to the right to MM_1, as the higher level of domestic credit requires a fall in the rate of interest to equate the money market, and the *FM* line shifts up to FM_1, as the fall in EB_d^* means that a rise in the interest rate is needed to re-equilibrate the foreign bond market. Again the exchange rate depreciates following an expansion in the money supply.

In the case of a sterilised intervention in the foreign exchange market, the money supply does not change, but the composition of private portfolios is altered. In this case, illustrated in **Figure 8.10**, the domestic bond purchase

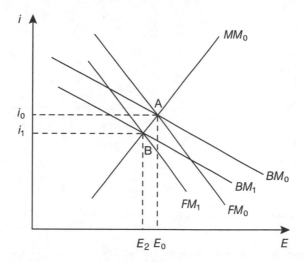

Figure 8.10 *FXO with a floating exchange rate*

shifts the *BM* line to the left, as the interest rate must fall for every level of the exchange rate to maintain domestic bond market equilibrium. The *FM* line also shifts down to the left, since the exchange rate must be lower for each interest rate to maintain foreign bond market equilibrium. The final equilibrium is therefore at B where the domestic interest rate is lower and the exchange rate has appreciated from E_0 to E_2. This case demonstrates not only that the exchange rate need not depreciate when interest rate fall, but how the type of monetary policy is important for the level of the exchange rate.

Special cases

While the portfolio balance model developed in this chapter provides a general framework for understanding the operation of monetary policy and its influence on the exchange rate, when combined with the goods market the complete model becomes complicated, frequently involving shifts in all three asset market equilibrium lines. Therefore two special cases of this model that will frequently be used in subsequent chapters are introduced in this section.

Suppose that the domestic monetary authorities decided that rather than attempt to control the money supply they would instead fix the nominal rate of interest. This would make the money supply an endogenous variable and the domestic rate of interest exogenous. The effect of this policy would be to make domestic bonds and domestic money perfect substitutes and hence the *MM* and *BM* schedules would be horizontal at the predetermined rate of interest. This case is shown in **Figure 8.11**. Changes in domestic monetary policy are reflected in the upward or downward movement of the *MM* line. A tightening of monetary policy being associated with a rise in the rate of interest as the domestic authorities sell

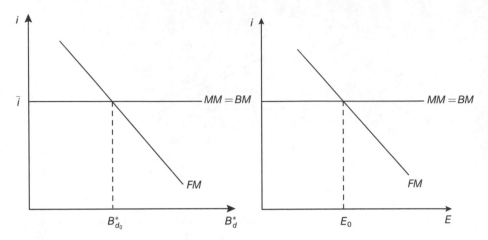

Figure 8.11 *Endogenous money supply case*

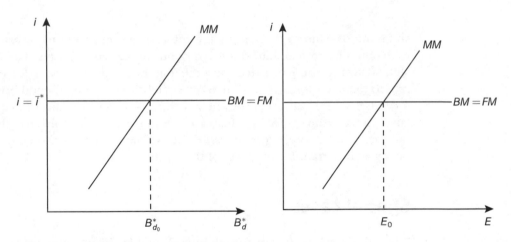

Figure 8.12 *Perfect capital mobility case*

bonds to the nbps so taking cash out of circulation, and a slacking of monetary policy being associated with a fall in the rate of interest. Indeed this is how monetary policy has been characterised in Part II of this text, before the portfolio balance framework was in place. This special case, however, assumes that domestic interest rates can be set independently of foreign interest rates. In the modern world the developed economies do not operate with significant capital controls and therefore domestic and foreign government debt prices tend to be equalised internationally subject to a small risk premium. Thus because domestic and foreign government debt instruments are close substitutes then their prices and yields will be very similar, as market-makers arbitrage between the markets. This leads on to a second, more realistic special case, when domestic and foreign bonds are perfect substitutes.

In this case, as shown in **Figure 8.12**, it is the *FM* and *BM* lines that become horizontal at the predetermined foreign rate of interest. This effectively means that the domestic authorities have very little influence over monetary policy which is dominated by the foreign country. Any attempt to hold domestic interest rates below the foreign rate will lead to infinitely large capital outflows from the domestic country and, if floating, to exchange rate depreciation. In this case when domestic and foreign bonds are perfect substitues the exchange rate is determined by the money supply. This special case is known as the monetary approach to the exchange rate. With the large stock of internationally mobile capital in the international economy this type of special case is perhaps more realistic than that of the home country fixing its interest rate independently of the foreign rate.

Conclusions

In this chapter a general model has been developed to explain the stock equilibrium in financial markets and the market adjustments following monetary policy disturbances. These markets can be regarded as determining the level of domestic interest rates, the exchange rate and the stock of foreign assets held by domestic residents for a given levels of prices, foreign interest rates, output and wealth. In particular, it has been demonstrated that monetary policy actions by domestic authorities in general affect all financial markets and the specific policy combination is important for the magnitude of interest rate changes and capital inflows and also for the direction of the exchange rate change. Chapter 9 will integrate the discussion of the financial markets and interest rates of this chapter with the determination of income and goods market equilibrium discussed in Chapters 4 and 5, to provide a theory of the determination of income and interest rates with fixed prices and real wealth.

Summary

- There are three principal asset markets – the markets for domestic money, domestic bonds and foreign assets. Asset demands are assumed to vary directly with the stock of financial wealth and their own yield, and inversely with the yields on other assets.
- The financial system with three asset markets and only two prices to determine – the interest rate and the exchange rate – is overdetermined. By invoking Walras' Law one market can be dropped because all markets are linked by the wealth constraint.
- Under floating exchange rates the money supply is independent of the balance of payments and the asset markets determine the equilibrium interest rate and exchange rate. With a fixed rate system the exchange rate is exogenously set by the authorities and the money supply is endogenous along with the rate of interest and the net capital outflow.

- Monetary policy can take one of three forms – an open market operation, a foreign exchange market operation or a sterilised foreign exchange market operation. In the former case the exchange rate depreciates and the interest rate falls thereby transmitting a positive shock to the goods market where investment and net exports would be expected to rise.
- An exogenous rise (fall) in income will lead to an appreciation (depreciation) of the exchange rate.
- If domestic and foreign assets are perfect substitutes, then sterilisation policy – whereby the balance of payments effects on the money supply are neutralised – is impossible and the two bond markets collapse to a single market. The domestic interest rate is now equal to the (exogenous) world rate of interest plus the expected depreciation of the exchange rate.

Suggested further reading

There is little elementary reading for this topic although Pilbeam (1998) does give an excellent account of the portfolio balance model of the exchange rate. Argy (1994) and Taylor (1990) give a more advanced treatment. The theory of portfolio balance as it relates to the demand for money in a closed economy is due to Tobin (1958) and is superbly reviewed in Laidler (1993). The general equilibrium approach to the financial sector stems from Tobin (1969) and is extended to the open economy by McKinnon (1969). The balance of payments aspects of portfolio adjustment are emphasised by Allen (1973), Kouri and Porter (1974) and Dornbusch (1975). The portfolio balance model of the exchange rate is due to Branson (1977) and Allen and Kenen (1978) and summarised in Pentecost (1993). Niehans (1984) reviews alternative monetary policy strategies in a floating exchange rate context.

Essay titles

1. What are the characteristics which economists use to distinguish between the principal financial markets in a macroeconomics?
2. Explain the relationship between the balance of payments and the money supply. How does the adoption of floating exchange rates affect this relationship?
3. 'The equilibrium exchange rate is primarily determined in the financial markets by the level of the money supply.' Discuss.

Questions

1. Explain why the money demand depends directly on income, but the demand for bonds varies inversely with income.
2. Why is the money supply endogenous under fixed exchange rates, but exogenous under floating exchange rates? Examine the implications for the money supply if the authorities follow a 'dirty' or a 'managed' float.
3. Explain how the domestic monetary authorities can tighten domestic monetary policy using (a) open market operations and (b) sterilised foreign exchange operations, under fixed exchange rates.
4. Analyse the effect on the exchange rate and the domestic rate of interest of an open market purchase of domestic bonds. How might your answer differ if the authorities sterilised the effects of the open market operation?
5. Show the effect of (i) a rise in the foreign rate of interest and (ii) a use in output, on the exchange rate and the level of domestic interest rates when domestic and foreign assets are perfect substitutes.
6. To check that you understand how to derive the asset market equilibrium schedules, try to derive all three schedules in (i, Y) space, by keeping the capital flow and the exchange rate constant along each schedule.

CHAPTER 9

The Short-run *IS–LM* Model of Economic Policy

Aims and objectives

- To integrate the goods market model of income determination with the asset market model of interest rate and exchange rate determination in order to build a complete model of aggregate demand.
- To examine the effectiveness of monetary and fiscal policies under both fixed and floating exchange rates in the integrated *IS–LM–FF* model of the open economy.
- To examine the effect of foreign real and monetary shocks on the level of domestic income and to determine the optimal exchange rate policy for a small, open economy.
- To derive the aggregate demand schedule (*AD* schedule) relating equilibrium income to the aggregate price level.

Introduction

The principal aim of this chapter is to provide an integrated treatment of the goods market (examined in Chapters 4 and 5) and the financial markets (considered in Chapter 8) in order to examine the simultaneous determination of output, interest rates and exchange rates. The model developed in this chapter is an extended version of the seminal *IS–LM* model, due to Hicks (1937). The principal difference between the model developed here and that of Hicks, is the explicit treatment of the public and overseas sectors of the economy, whereas Hicks used a closed economy version of the model.

In order to be able to combine asset market equilibrium with goods market equilibrium it is crucial to be able to understand the difference between a stock equilibrium and a flow equilibrium (see Chapter 3 for a review of these terms). The model can only be in full equilibrium when assets stocks are unchanging – that is when the quantity of money and the stock of bonds outstanding are willingly held by the non-bank private sector (nbps). The asset markets, however, will only be in equilibrium when the goods market is in equilibrium – that, is when the expenditure on goods matches the supply of goods, such that there are no additions to stock or stock decumulation by firms. In other words, goods market equilibrium is a necessary but not sufficient condition for general equilibrium. From this it follows that general equilibrium will only be reached at the point where the *IS*, *BM*, *MM* and *FM* loci, of Chapters 4 and 8, intersect.

The combination of stock and flow equilibrium means that the financing of the government budget deficit or the effect of a current balance surplus or deficit on the money supply and the stock of financial wealth cannot strictly be ignored. To simplify things in this chapter, however, a fiscal policy expansion refers to a 'balanced budget' expansion, which from Chapter 4 is known to have a multiplier of greater than unity. By only considering balanced-budget expansions, the question of how the fiscal deficit is financed can be deferred until Chapter 10. The other possible linkage between the asset market stocks and goods markets flows is through the effect of changes in foreign exchange reserves, reflecting balance of payments imbalances, on the domestic money supply and hence on to the stock of wealth. As explained in Chapter 8, under a floating exchange rate system this link is broken and the money supply is independent of the balance of payments position. Under fixed exchange rates, however, the stock of financial assets will be increasing with a balance of payments surplus and contracting with a balance of payments deficit. To prevent a balance of payments surplus (deficit) from increasing domestic financial wealth, it is assumed in this chapter that such inflows (outflows) which add (subtract) to the money supply are fully sterilised by an automatic contraction (increase) in the stock of government bonds outstanding. Hence, although the money supply may rise due to a balance of payments surplus, the total stock of financial wealth, $\bar{A}$, remains unchanged since $\Delta R = -\Delta \bar{B}^s$.

The plan of the chapter is as follows. The next section recasts the model of the financial sector to be fully consistent with goods market equilibrium as represented by the *IS* curve. We then examine the effectiveness of fiscal and monetary policy in the full *IS–LM* model of aggregate demand under fixed exchange rates, and then extend the model to the floating exchange rate case with both static and regressive exchange rate expectations. The optimality of various exchange rate regimes is then considered and the case for a managed float is developed. The final sections show how the *IS–LM* model can be further reduced to an aggregate demand (*AD*) curve, and offer a brief critical appraisal of the usefulness of the fixed-price *IS–LM* in the formation of macroeconomic policy.

The short-run *IS–LM* model

By holding the stock of financial wealth constant the model of this chapter is a short-run model without asset accumulation. The principal task of this section is to re-cast the *MM–BM–FM* model of the financial sector so that the asset equilibrium schedules can be drawn in (i, Y) space, leaving the capital flow and the exchange rate implicit. A re-examination of equations (8.8), reproduced here as equations (9.1), shows that this is fairly straightforward.

$$\left(\frac{D+R}{\bar{P}}\right) = \lambda_0 + \lambda_1 Y - \lambda_2 i - \lambda_3 (\bar{i}^* + \bar{x}) + \lambda_4 (\bar{A}/\bar{P}) \qquad \text{(a)}$$

$$\left(\frac{\overline{B}^s}{P}\right) = \phi_0 - \phi_1 Y + \phi_2 i - \phi_3 (\overline{i}^* + \overline{x}) + \phi_4 (\overline{A}/\overline{P}) \qquad \text{(b)} \qquad \text{(9.1)}$$

$$\left(\frac{E.B_d^*}{P}\right) = \zeta_0 - \zeta_1 Y - \zeta_2 i + \zeta_3 (\overline{i}^* + \overline{x}) + \zeta_4 (\overline{A}/\overline{P}) \qquad \text{(c)}$$

The money market equilibrium schedule will have a positive slope in (i, Y) space, since for a given money stock a rise in income will increase the demand for money, necessitating a rise in the rate of interest to restore money market equilibrium. More formally this can be shown by differentiating equation (9.1a) with respect to income and the rate of interest, that is: $\partial i/\partial Y = \lambda_1/\lambda_2 > 0$. This is shown in **Figure 9.1**, where the money market equilibrium locus, now relabelled *LM*, is drawn upward-sloping, where all points above the *LM*-curve are positions of excess supply of money and points like C, below the *LM* curve, are points of excess demand for money.

The domestic bond market locus is given in **Figure 9.1** and now re-labelled as *BB* in (i, Y) space. Formally the slope of *BB* is given as: $\partial i/\partial Y = \phi_1/\phi_2 > 0$, which is obtained by differentiating equation (9.1b) with respect to income and the rate of interest. In terms of economics, the *BB* linc has a positive slope, since for a given supply of bonds, a rise in the rate of interest increases demand, so necessitating a rise in income to reduce demand in order to restore equilibrium. It is assumed that the *BB* line is less steep than the *LM* line since the interest elasticity of domestic bonds is likely to be greater than the interest rate elasticity of the demand for money, given that the rate of interest is the own yield on bonds.

The foreign bond market equilibrium locus in **Figure 9.1** is shown to be negatively sloped, since for a given stock of foreign bonds a rise in the domestic rate

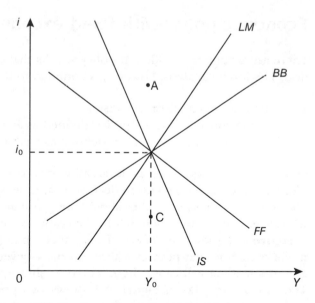

Figure 9.1 *General equilibrium in goods and financial markets*

of interest reduces the demand for foreign bonds so requiring a fall in income to restore the balance between supply and demand. Formally this is shown as: $\partial i/\partial Y = -\zeta_1/\zeta_2 < 0$, which is obtained by differentiating equation (9.1c) with respect to income and the rate of interest. Because the *FF* line represents the external asset position of the domestic economy, points away from *FF* correspond to capital flows, under fixed exchange rates and exchange rate changes under a floating exchange rate system. Thus at a point such as A, above the *FF* line, there is a capital inflow as domestic residents sell foreign currency assets and try to purchase domestic securities. Under a floating exchange rate regime point A would be associated with an exchange rate appreciation. At point C, therefore, there is either a capital outflow or exchange rate depreciation depending on the exchange rate regime in operation.

As noted at the end of Chapter 8, if domestic and foreign bonds are perfect substitutes then their yields will be the same. In this case equations (9.1a) and (9.1b) collapse to: $i = i^* + \bar{x}$ as the cross-interest elasticities of demand become infinite, that is as $\phi_3 = \zeta_2 \rightarrow \infty$. This condition is also known as perfect capital mobility. Moreover, with a fixed exchange rate system the expected rate of depreciation is zero, so $\bar{x} = 0$, which has the effect of making the *BB* and *FF* lines horizontal at the predetermined rate of interest, such that $i = i^*$.

The final line on **Figure 9.1** is that of the *IS* curve. This is exactly as derived in Chapter 4, with the negative slope indicative of the fact that as interest rates fall investment demand is stimulated, which gives rise to an increase in output. The *IS* curve is assumed to have a steeper slope than the *FM* line since it is expected that the demand for financial assets is more responsive to interest rate changes than the demand for investment in physical assets (see Chapter 7).

Economic policy with fixed exchange rates

There are a number of different policy shocks that can be considered in this section. The formal analysis, however, is confined to three kinds of policy change:

1. A balanced budget fiscal expansion;
2. An expansionary monetary policy, defined as an open market purchase;
3. A foreign monetary expansion, defined as a fall in the foreign rate of interest.

Other policy changes such as devaluation or a rise in foreign income, for example, have the same qualitative effect on output as a fiscal expansion. The multiplier effects of these and other shocks are given in the Appendix to this chapter, with diagrammatic treatment left to the reader as an exercise.

Figure 9.2 shows the effect of a balanced budget fiscal expansion from the initial equilibrium at point A where income is given at Y_0. The balanced budget rise in spending will cause the *IS* curve to shift up to the right from IS_0 to IS_1. The upper panel (a) of **Figure 9.2** shows two possible outcomes. In a closed economy context, income would rise to Y_1 and a new equilibrium would be

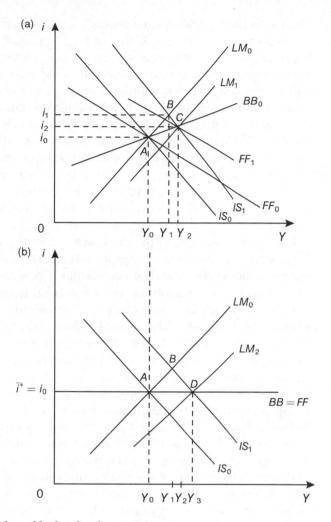

Figure 9.2 *A balanced budget fiscal expansion*

established at point B. The higher rate of interest at point B implies that private
sector investment is lower at B than at A. Thus although the balanced budget rise
in spending has raised income, there has been some crowding-out of private
investment expenditures. In the open economy case, however, point B is not an
equilibrium position unless the capital inflow, as a result of higher domestic rate
of interest, is sterilised so as not to increase the money supply.

To sterilise the capital inflow the authorities will effectively exchange non-bank
private sector foreign currency assets for domestic currency bonds (rather
than cash), since the latter would increase the money stock. Thus in terms of
Figure 9.2 the fiscal expansion would be simultaneously undertaken with a sale
of domestic bonds to the nbps which would shift the *BB* line to the left, and the
purchase of foreign currency bonds from the nbps which would shift the *FF* line
to the right, so that both *BB* and *FF* lines intersect the *IS* and *LM* lines at point B.

Thus at point B private sector agents' portfolios are in balance and interest rates are higher at i_1 and output higher at Y_1. The complete sterilisation of the money supply, however, is not necessary in this case. Although the stock of real financial wealth must not change, its composition can change. Hence, the capital inflow will be reducing B_d^*, but simultaneously the authority's reserves of foreign currency will be rising, as residents sell foreign currency and purchase domestic currency bonds. If these two flows are identical then the nbps will hold more cash in its portfolios and less foreign currency bonds and there will be no change in the stock of outstanding domestic bonds. In this case the equilibrium is at point C in the upper panel of **Figure 9.2**. At point C the income level is higher at Y_2, and the interest rate rise smaller. In this context the open economy multiplier is larger than the closed economy multiplier because the degree of crowding out is lower.

Finally the lower panel (b) of **Figure 9.2** shows an identical balanced budget expansion, but with perfect capital mobility. The initial equilibrium is at point A exactly as before, but the final equilibrium is now at point D, with income higher than Y_2 and Y_3. The reason for this is that because domestic and foreign assets are perfect substitutes the authorities are unable to sterilise any reserve changes. Hence, the (infinitely) large capital inflow at point B results in an increase in reserves and the money supply, shifting the *LM* curve to LM_2. The rise in income from Y_0 to Y_3 is equivalent to the government expenditure multiplier derived in Chapter 5. There is no crowding-out of private investment because the rate of interest is constant. This analysis suggests that the potency of fiscal policy is enhanced in an open economy with a fixed exchange rate and a high degree of capital mobility, compared with both the closed economy and low capital mobility cases.

Figure 9.3 shows the effect of an increase in the domestic monetary base due to an open market operation. The rise in the money supply shifts the LM_0 line to LM_1 and the purchase of domestic bonds from the nbps shifts the BM_0 line to BM_1. At the intersection with the *IS* curve, at point B, there is a net capital outflow as domestic nbps residents sell their domestic bonds in exchange for foreign currency bonds, which now carry the relatively higher rate of interest. This portfolio rebalancing results in the central bank exchanging bonds for foreign currency, with which the nbps purchase foreign currency bonds. Thus the original exchange of nbps cash for domestic bonds is reversed and the *LM* and *BM* lines shift back to their initial position at A. Thus the open market operation is frustrated by the capital outflow, which returns the money supply to its initial level. Thus the money supply is endogenous in the open economy on a fixed exchange rate, even if there is imperfect asset substitution.

The prospect of sterilising the capital outflow in the very short term requires the authorities to hold the LM_1 curve at B in panel (a). The authorities can do this by buying domestic bonds and selling foreign bonds to the nbps. The problem with this is that they will eventually run out of foreign bonds to sell, at which point the authorities will not be able to continue sterilising and the money supply will contract as the nbps satisfy their demand for foreign bonds by buying from non-residents. The lower panel (b) of **Figure 9.3** shows the identical result

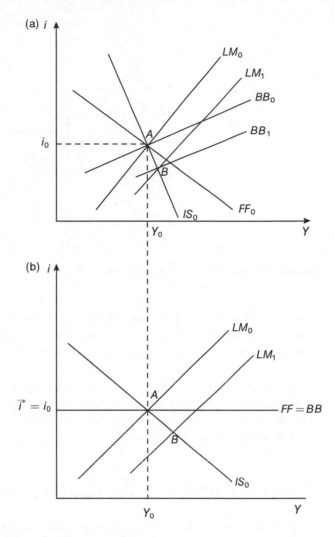

Figure 9.3 *Monetary expansion*

with perfect capital mobility. The initial monetary expansion takes the model from point A to B, where upon a capital outflow takes place and returns the *LM* curve to its initial position. Income and the rate of interest are unaffected. Monetary policy is wholly impotent in an open economy with a fixed exchange rate even if there is less than perfect capital mobility.

The third kind of policy shock is that of an expansionary foreign monetary policy, which is represented by a fall in the foreign rate of interest. It is easiest to see the consequences of this policy when perfect asset substitutability is assumed. In this case, as shown in **Figure 9.4**, the FF_0 line shifts down and the rate of interest falls from $\bar{i}_0^*$ to $\bar{i}_1^*$. The domestic rate of interest initially remains at i_0 which is clearly above i_1^* and so there is a capital inflow at point A. The capital inflow then gives rise to an accommodating expansion in the money supply, which shifts the

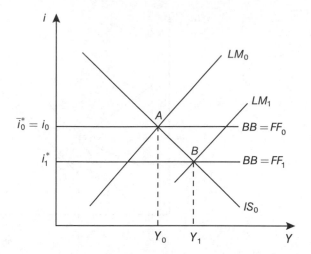

Figure 9.4 *Expansionary foreign monetary policy*

LM_0 curve to LM_1, giving an equilibrium at B. The expansion of the foreign economy has beneficial effects for the domestic economy, in this case, but it follows that a foreign monetary policy contraction will have a contractionary effect on domestic output.

In an open economy under fixed exchange rates, domestic fiscal policy is more powerful than monetary policy in raising domestic output. Foreign interest rate changes also have a more potent effect on the level of domestic output, if there is a high degree of capital mobility.

Economic policy under floating exchange rates

Under floating exchange rates it is possible to extend the *IS–LM* diagram to include an extra quadrant to explicitly demonstrate what happens to the exchange rate. Therefore, in addition to the *IS*, *LM*, *FF* and *BB* lines, **Figure 9.5** also includes the *GM* and *BP* curves in (E, Y) space in the lower section, following Mundell (1963).

The *GM* line in the lower part of the figure represents goods market equilibrium. That is, it is the *IS* curve drawn in (E, Y) space. It has a positive slope because as income rises the trade balance deteriorates unless the exchange rate simultaneously depreciates to maintain the level of demand. Formally, this result can be proved by differentiating the goods market equilibrium equation in Chapter 4 with respect to E and Y. This gives: $(\partial Y / \partial E) = (\delta_2 + \mu_2)/(1 - \alpha_1(1 - \tau_1) + \mu_1) > 0$. This line is therefore drawn for a given rate of interest and level of government spending. The *BP* locus in **Figure 9.5** is the balance of payments equilibrium line, drawn for a zero capital inflow. This line also has a positive slope in (E, Y) space because as income rises net imports increase, which requires a

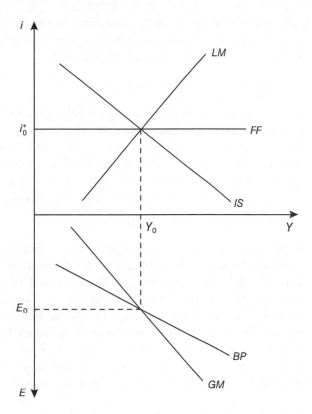

Figure 9.5   The IS–LM *model with floating rates*

depreciation of the exchange rate to restore current account balance. It is assumed that the *BP* line is more responsive to exchange rate changes than the *GM* line, since the latter includes non-traded goods that are not responsive to exchange rate changes. Technically the slope of the *BP* line is given as $\partial Y/\partial E = (\delta_2 + \mu_2)/\mu_1 > 0$, which confirms the relative slopes since the denominator of the *BP* line is clearly smaller than that for the *GM* line. The *BP* line therefore has a larger positive slope. Since the *BP* curve reflects the current account of the balance of payments it is shifted by capital flows. A capital inflow will require an exchange rate appreciation for every level of income and so the *BP* line will move to the right. On the other hand, a capital outflow shifts the BP locus to the left in **Figure 9.5**, as an exchange rate depreciation is needed at each level of income.

With floating exchange rates, capital flows may also be influenced by what agents expect will happen to the exchange rate over the period when they are investing in foreign assets. In other words the expected depreciation, *x*, may be non-zero with floating rates. The reason is that arbitrageurs in the global capital market are expected to switch financial capital from one centre to another on the basis of a comparison of relative rates of return. As noted in Chapter 8, the rate of return on a foreign bond has two components: the interest rate, *i**, and the expected depreciation of the domestic currency, x, during the period for which the investment is made. The expected gain to a domestic resident of investing £P in US dollars for one year will be positive if:

$$P(1+i) < \frac{P}{E}(1+\bar{i}^*)(1-x)E \tag{9.2}$$

where E is measured as the domestic price of a dollar (£/$) and x is the expected proportionate depreciation over the year. This expression compares the expected sterling value of the US investment at the end of the period, allowing for the current purchase price of dollars at the rate E and its subsequent conversion back into sterling at the rate $(1-x)E$, with the option of remaining in sterling and investing in the UK at the rate i. Cancelling and simplifying equation (9.2) reduces to:

$$x(1+i^*) < (i^*-i) \quad \text{or} \quad (i^*-i) > x \tag{9.3}$$

since the product, xi^*, is negligibly small. Equation (9.3) says that the US investment will be more profitable than the UK investment if the interest differential in favour of the US is greater than the expected depreciation of sterling over the year. On these grounds, as demonstrated in Chapter 8, under floating exchange rates the capital flows will depend on the changes in the foreign interest rate adjusted for the expected depreciation of the exchange rate. For the time being, however, the assumption that exchange rate expectations are static is retained. Formally this is written as: $E_t^e - E_{t-1}^e = 0$. Hence the expected value of the exchange rate is the same at time t as at $t-1$ and the proportionate depreciation is:

$$x = (E_t^e - E_{t-1}^e)/E_{t-1}^e = 0$$

As in the previous section, three policy shocks can be considered, this time with a floating exchange rate. In **Figure 9.6** a balanced-budget fiscal expansion with perfect capital mobility causes the IS_0 curve to shift to the right to IS_1 in the upper section, and the GM_0 line to GM_1 in the lower section of the figure. At point B on the initial LM curve the domestic rate of interest exceeds the world rate, leading to a net capital inflow as domestic residents sell their foreign currency assets in exchange for domestic bonds. This excess demand for domestic currency appreciates the exchange rate on the foreign exchange market which causes the IS_1 curve to move back towards IS_0, and the initial equilibrium at A. The IS curve shifts back because with a lower value of E, domestic exports are less competitive on world markets. Therefore demand for domestic exports falls reducing expenditure on domestic output. In the lower part of the figure the capital inflow at point B shifts the BP line to the right to BP_1, to intersect the GM_1 line at C, at the initial level of income Y_0. Fiscal policy is therefore impotent in affecting output. This initial fiscal expansion is completely crowded out by the appreciation of the exchange rate, from E_0 to E_1, which reduces net exports by an amount exactly equal to the amount of the fiscal injection.

With imperfect capital mobility, however, fiscal policy can have some impact on the level of domestic output. In **Figure 9.7** the fiscal expansion shifts IS_0 to IS_1. At point B there is a capital inflow as domestic residents sell their excess

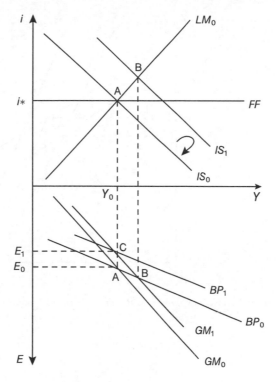

Figure 9.6 *Fiscal expansion with floating exchange rate*

holdings of foreign currency bonds which leads to an appreciation of the exchange rate and starts to shift the IS_1 line back to IS_2. Simultaneously the FF_0 line also moves up to the right to FF_2 to give the final equilibrium at C.[1] Note that in this case the exchange rate appreciation is curtailed, compared to that in **Figure 9.6**, because the domestic rate of interest is able to rise above the world rate of interest and so reduce the need for the exchange rate to appreciate.

A domestic monetary expansion by way of an open market purchase of domestic bonds will lead to a depreciation of the exchange rate and a rise in income as shown in **Figure 9.8**. From the initial equilibrium at A the *LM* line shifts to LM_1. At B there is a capital outflow which leads to a depreciation of the exchange rate, which in turn shifts the *IS* curve to the right to IS_1, as net exports rise. The final equilibrium is at point C, where output is Y_1 and where in the lower part of the figure, the capital outflow has shifted the *BP* line down to BP_1 to cut GM_0 at C. In this case, with perfect capital mobility, the exchange rate depreciation reinforces the monetary expansion so making monetary policy very potent under floating exchange rates.

---

[1] Figure 9.7 assumes that the effect of the exchange rate change on the demand for money is zero, although the domestic bond market schedule (not drawn) will shift up to pass through point C.

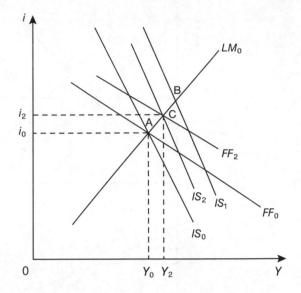

Figure 9.7 *Fiscal expansion with imperfect capital mobility*

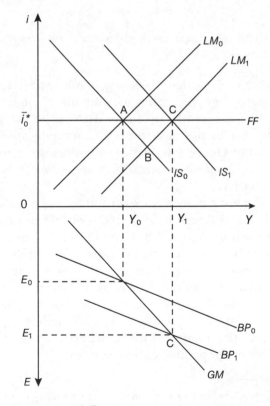

Figure 9.8 *Monetary expansion with floating rates*

With less than perfect capital mobility, the effectiveness of monetary policy is reduced. This is shown in **Figure 9.9**. The open market purchase shifts the LM_0 locus to LM_1. At point B there an excess demand for foreign bonds on the part of domestic residents, which gives rise to capital outflow and a depreciation of the exchange rate. This depreciation shifts the *IS* curve to the right, but also shifts the FF_0 line down to the left as the exchange rate depreciation raises the value of foreign currency assets. The final equilibrium is at point D where IS_2 cuts the FF_1 line and where output is higher at Y_2 , but which is less than Y_1, in the perfect capital mobility case. The lower degree of capital mobility reduces the potency of monetary policy under floating exchange rates.

Finally, consider the case of a reduction in the foreign or world rate of interest. **Figure 9.10** shows that with perfect capital mobility the effect of a cut in $\bar{i}^*$ from $\bar{i}_0^*$ is to $\bar{i}_1^*$ move the economy from point A to point B, and to reduce domestic income from Y_0 to Y_1. Following the cut in the foreign interest rate the domestic rate initially remains at i_0, which generates a capital inflow and an exchange rate appreciation. The exchange rate appreciation reduces the competitiveness of domestic goods on world markets, which sees a fall in net exports and a shift of the *IS* curve to the left, to IS_1. Under floating exchange rates a foreign monetary expansion has a contractionary effect on domestic output. This happens because the exchange rate appreciates thereby reducing the overseas demand for domestic goods. With imperfect capital mobility the qualitative effects are very similar, although of course the multiplier effect on domestic output is smaller.

This section has demonstrated that under floating exchange rates, monetary policy is more potent than fiscal policy in raising the level of domestic output. This is a reversal of the policy effectiveness result from that obtained earlier (pp. 174ff) on fixed exchange rates. The direction of the effects of a cut in foreign interest rates on output is also reversed under floating exchange rates,

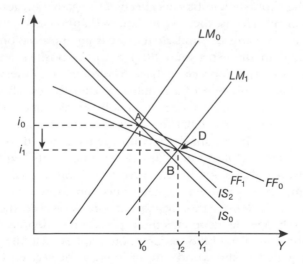

Figure 9.9 *Monetary expansion with imperfect capital mobility*

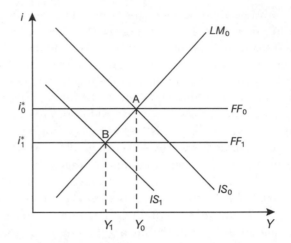

Figure 9.10 *A cut in the foreign rate of interest*

compared to fixed rates.

It is, however, possible to restore some potency to fiscal policy under floating exchange rates if the assumption concerning static exchange is dropped and replaced with the alternative assumption of regressive expectations. Regressive expectations state that following a disturbance the exchange rate is expected to move back towards its previous value. Formally this is:

$$x = \pi[(\tilde{E}/E) - 1] \tag{9.4}$$

where $\tilde{E}$ is defined as the equilibrium exchange rate. If $\tilde{E}$ is initially equal to E then $x = 0$. Thus a depreciation of the exchange rate, causes E to rise above $\tilde{E}$, so the expression in brackets becomes negative suggesting that x will fall in the next period. That is, there is an expected appreciation in the next period as E adjusts back towards $\tilde{E}$. Similarly if there is an appreciation so that E initially falls below $\tilde{E}$, than the expression (9.4) becomes positive and hence x rises in the next period as E depreciates back towards $\tilde{E}$. This method of endogenising expectations is only one of a number of alternatives, although it is not without some empirical support (see for example, Frankel and Froot 1987).

The case of a balanced budget fiscal expansion with perfect capital mobility can now be reconsidered with agents assumed to have regressive expectations. **Figure 9.11** illustrates this case. From the initial equilibrium at A an expansionary fiscal policy shifts the *IS* curve to the right, to IS_1. As before the position at B implies a capital inflow that induces an appreciation of the exchange rate, so that $\tilde{E}/E > 1$. With regressive expectations, however, the current appreciation of the exchange rate generates the expectation of depreciation in the next period. Since the capital mobility assumption implies that the domestic rate of interest is equated to the world rate of interest for a given expected depreciation, that is $i = i^* + x$ and a i^* is unchanged, the domestic rate of interest can increase because

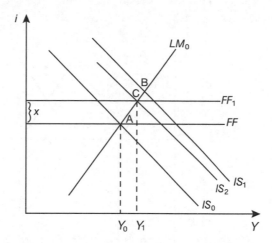

Figure 9.11 *Fiscal expansion with regressive exchange rate expectations*

$x > 0$ and the *FF* line shifts upwards in **Figure 9.11**. The appreciation also shifts the *IS* curve back to the left as competitiveness declines and a new equilibrium is reached at C. Here fiscal policy has some power over output, which rises to Y_1. Paradoxically, the rise in the rate of interest, equivalent of the expected depreciation, is here a condition for a reduction in crowding-out. This result is obtained by assuming that the effect of the expected depreciation of the exchange rate on the domestic demand for money is zero. If this effect were non-zero, then the demand for money would decline as the opportunity of holding money increases and the *LM* curve would also be forced to the right giving a larger rise in output.

The optimality of exchange rate regimes

The *IS–LM* model has been a useful construct in examining the effectiveness of fiscal and monetary policy in an open economy with high capital mobility. Before leaving this model an answer to another question is needed: should the authorities prefer fixed or floating exchange rates? The answer is that it all depends upon the source of the shocks expected to hit the economy. There are two basic shocks that can be considered – goods market shocks and money market shocks.

The shocks to the goods market are represented in **Figure 9.12** by movements of the *IS* curve within the range given by the lines IS_L and IS_U. Thus a negative demand shock, such as an autonomous fall in investment, causes the *IS* curve to shift to the left, to a lower value, IS_L. Similarly, a positive demand shock leads to the *IS* curve shifting up to the right to give an upper value of IS_U. Fixing the exchange rate implies that these shocks to the *IS* curve lead to movements in output in the range between Y_L and Y_U. In a fixed rate system the money supply is endogenously determined and so adjusts automatically to movements in the *IS* curve, because of the intervention commitments of the monetary authorities. In

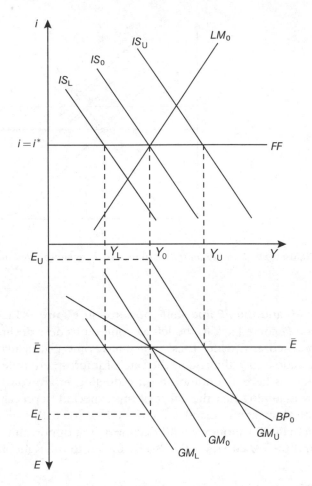

Figure 9.12 *Goods market shocks and the exchange rate regime*

contrast with the alternative of floating exchange rates output stabilisation is perfect, with the exchange rate fluctuating between E_L and E_U. If the objective of the authorities is to stabilise output then floating exchange rates are clearly preferable if shocks originate from the goods market.

On the other hand this conclusion is completely reversed if the random shocks originate from the money market. These money market disturbances are represented in **Figure 9.13** by movements in the *LM* curve within the range given by the loci LM_L and LM_U. Now a floating exchange rate regime produces movements of output between Y_L and Y_U, together with movements in the exchange rate. In a fixed rate regime, however, output can be stabilised perfectly. To see this suppose the *LM* curve has shifted to the right, to LM_U. Fixing the exchange rate forces the authorities to intervene in the foreign exchange market and to sell foreign currency. This reduces the domestic money stock so that the *LM* curve is forced back

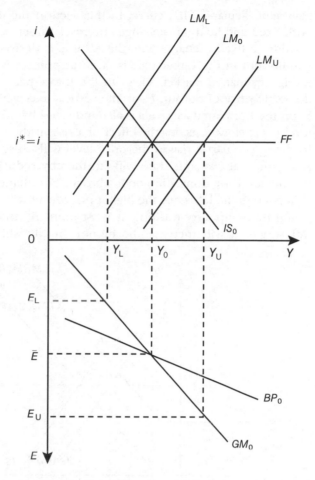

Figure 9.13 *Money market shocks and the exchange rate regime*

to its initial position. Output is unaffected by the disturbance to the demand for money. Thus, faced with monetary shocks a fixed exchange rate regime is to be preferred if the authorities prefer output stabilisation.

This analysis leads to the conclusion that policy rules are inferior to discretion. In the real world shocks occur in both the goods markets and the money markets and as a result neither pure fixed nor pure floating rates are likely to be optimal. The optimal exchange rate regime must lie between these two extremes: that is, there is a *prima facie* case for a *managed* floating system. This is the case for policy activism in the context of this model.

The derivation of the aggregate demand curve

The *IS–LM* model is a short-run model of aggregate demand for domestic output. The model can be further reduced to a single equation, referred to as the aggregate demand (*AD*) curve. In this section the *AD* curve will be derived for both fixed and floating exchange rate cases under perfect capital mobility.

Under a fixed exchange rate the *AD* line is derived in **Figure 9.14.** The initial equilibrium in the upper part is given at point A where the goods, money and foreign exchange markets clear. In the lower part, which depicts the aggregate domestic price of output, *P*, on the vertical axis against the level of real income, *Y*, on the horizontal axis, this is also indicated by point A. At A the assumed price level is P_0. Now consider the effect of a rise in the price level in both quadrants. In the upper part a rise in the price level will cause IS_0 to shift to the left to IS_1, since the real exchange rate will fall thereby reducing the competitiveness and the demand for domestic goods abroad. Simultaneously, the *LM* schedule will shift back to the left since the higher price level will reduce the real money stock, giving the temporary position at B. At point B, however, there will be a capital inflow which will increase the money supply, shifting LM_1 back to the right

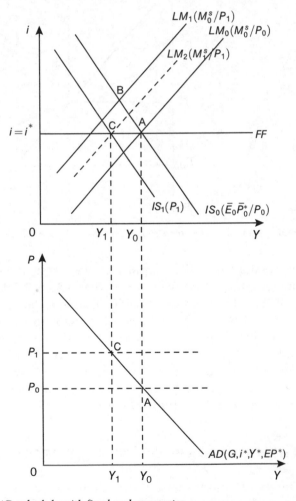

Figure 9.14 *The* AD *schedule with fixed exchange rates*

to LM_2. The new equilibrium is reached at C. In the lower part at C the level of output is lower and the price level is higher (by construction). Hence, joining points A and C in the lower part of the figure gives a downward-sloping *AD* line. This result is demonstrated formally in the Appendix to this chapter.

It is important to note that this line is drawn for given values of *EP**, *G*, *Y** and *i**. Changes in any of these variables therefore cause the aggregate demand line to shift. In particular, a rise in *G*, *Y** or *EP** will cause the *AD* curve to shift out to the right, while a rise in the foreign rate of interest will lead the *AD* curve to shift down to the left. Note also that the *AD* line is independent of the *LM* schedule, being determined exclusively by the *IS* and *FF* lines. This is related to the point made earlier (pp. 172ff) that under fixed rates and perfect capital mobility monetary policy does not affect output. Thus the *LM* curve and the money supply have no bearing on the position of the *AD* curve under fixed exchange rates.

Under floating exchange rates the *AD* curve becomes independent of the *IS* curve since the real exchange rate becomes an endogenous variable, whereas the money supply becomes wholly exogenous under perfect capital mobility. In **Figure 9.15** the initial equilibrium is given by the points A in both parts of the figure. A rise in the price level will shift the *LM* line back to LM_1 and the IS_0 line back to IS_1. At point B there is a capital outflow and a depreciation of the exchange rate, which shifts IS_1 to IS_2 as competitiveness improves. The new equilibrium level of income is at Y_1 that is consistent with the higher price level P_1. Again the slope of the *AD* curve is proved more rigorously in the appendix to this chapter.

Note that in this case the *AD* line is only shifted by M^s and *i**, since, for example, any rise in *G* will be completely offset by exchange rate appreciation leaving the level of demand exactly where it was prior to the increase in government spending. Because fiscal policy expenditures are fully crowded-out in this case it follows that the level of government spending is unable to affect the position of the *AD* curve. A rise in M^s or a fall in *i** will cause the *AD* curve to move up to the right. Thus the variables that shift the *AD* function are different under fixed and floating exchange rate regimes.

Finally, it is important to appreciate that the *AD* curve in macroeconomics is not simply the sum of all microeconomic demand curves. Indeed it is not really a demand curve at all! It is the locus of points at which the planned expenditure on goods and services exactly equals the actual output produced, together with money and bond market equilibrium.

Conclusions and limitations of the *IS–LM* model

In this chapter the effectiveness of monetary and fiscal policy in raising the level of output in an open economy under fixed and floating exchange rates has been examined. Under fixed exchange rates fiscal policy is the more powerful policy instrument, while under floating rates monetary policy is the more powerful tool. In the case of floating exchange rates this is because a fiscal expansion is accompanied by exchange rate appreciation that crowds out the initial demand

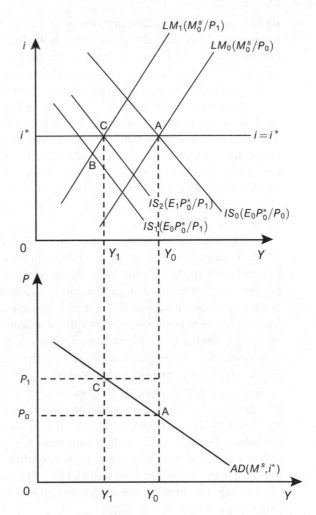

Figure 9.15 *The* AD *schedule with floating rates*

expansion, whereas a monetary expansion leads to exchange rate depreciation which reinforces the monetary expansion. In the case of fixed exchange rates on the other hand, monetary policy is ineffective because changes in the central banks' foreign exchange reserves occur which operate to offset the initial effect of the domestic money expansion on the money supply. Thus under fixed exchange rates the money supply is endogenous (with E exogenous), whereas under floating rates it is the exchange rate that is endogenous (with M^s exogenous).

Although the model developed in this chapter is the benchmark model of open economy macroeconomics, it suffers from a number of defects. For example, it predicts that a monetary expansion leads to a permanent increase in output. This prediction is obtained when the monetary expansion is engineered, in the context of a flexible rate system, or when it comes about from devaluation.

The empirical evidence, however, is very much against this prediction. In particular, there seems to be little or no correlation between the rate at which a currency depreciates and the growth of output over long time periods. There is also doubt about whether countries that maintain a fixed exchange rate can permanently increase output by expansionary fiscal policies. Thirdly, the prediction that an expansionary fiscal policy financed by issuing debt leads to an appreciation of the currency is also subject to doubt. If anything the empirical evidence seems to indicate that a reverse correlation exists: such that countries experiencing increasing budget deficits have experienced currency depreciation.

Not all of the predictions of the model have been refuted, however. For example, the prediction that monetary policy is impotent under fixed rates seems to be fairly robust. The general point is that the model is limited. The principal limitations of the short-run *IS–LM* model of the macroeconomy are that it assumes that non-bank private sector wealth is constant and that prices are fixed. In the next chapter the effect of allowing wealth accumulation into the model is discussed, and the implications of this for the potency of fiscal policy under fixed and floating exchange rates. The potentially most important limitation, however, is the fixed price assumption. This assumption will be relaxed in Part IV of the text when the labour market and supply-side are added to the model.

Summary

- Fiscal policy is more effective when exchange rates are fixed, and monetary policy more effective at raising output when the exchange rate is floating. Fiscal policy is also enhanced by a higher degree of asset substitution (capital mobility).
- The domestic economy is insulated from foreign goods market shocks by a floating exchange rate, but not from foreign monetary shocks. Hence a rise in foreign interest rates raises the demand for domestic output, and a fall in foreign interest rates leads to a fall in the demand for domestic output. Under fixed rates the economy is not insulated from foreign real shocks.
- The analysis suggests that a policy of managed floating is the optimal exchange rate policy for a small open economy with a high degree of capital market integration.
- The *AD* schedule has a negative slope in price–output space, since as the price level falls the real exchange rate rises and hence the demand for domestic goods increases in foreign markets. Under floating rates, assuming perfect capital mobility, the *AD* shifts only in response to monetary policy changes, whereas under fixed exchange rates, it is shifted by autonomous expenditure shocks, including both government spending and real exchange rate shocks.

Suggested further reading

The closed economy *IS–LM* model stems from the seminal paper of Hicks (1937) which was extended by Modigliani (1944). King (1993) links the *IS–LM* model with the New Keynesianism. The open economy version of the model was first elaborated by Fleming (1962) and Mundell (1963), with an extension to include regressive exchange rate expectations by Dornbusch (1976). Pentecost (1993) provides an extensive review of the floating exchange rate form of this model including the implications of alternative assumptions regarding exchange rate expectations. A recent survey of the model and its various extensions is provided by Frenkel and Razin (1987). The effect of goods and money market stochastic shocks was first analysed by Poole (1970) in the context of a closed economy and the choice of an interest rate or a money supply target.

Essay titles

1. How and under what assumptions, does the authorities' decision to pursue either a fixed or a floating exchange rate policy constrain domestic stabilisation policies?
2. 'Monetary policy is highly effective as an instrument to raise output in small, open economies.' Discuss.
3. Critically appraise the usefulness of the *IS–LM* model in examining the macroeconomic behaviour of output, the rate of interest and the price level.

Questions

1. Derive the *LM* curve from the supply and demand for money. Suppose the money supply, instead of being constant, increased with the rate of interest. How would this change the construction of the *LM* curve and what are the implications for the effectiveness of monetary policy?

2. (a) What does the *FF* curve represent?
   (b) How do the income and interest sensitivities of the demand for foreign bonds affect its slope?
   (c) What do points above and below the *FF* schedule imply?

3. Show the effect on domestic output of the following shocks, assuming the authorities follow a fixed exchange rate policy:

   (a) an exogenous fall in private sector investment;
   (b) a devaluation of the domestic currency;
   (c) a rise in world income.

4. Show the effect on domestic output of the following shocks, assuming the authorities follow a floating exchange rate policy:

   (a) an exogenous fall in private sector investment;
   (b) a fall in the domestic money supply;
   (c) a rise in world income.

5. Show that a fiscal policy expansion under floating exchange rates, although ineffective at raising output when exchange state expectations are static, can be effective when exchange rate expectations are regressive.

6. Is external balance a problem that the authorities should be concerned about? Explain your reasons.

Appendix   The derivation of the policy multipliers with perfect capital mobility

$$Y = \frac{\delta - \beta_1 \bar{i} + \bar{G} + \delta_1 \bar{Y}^* + (\delta_2 + \mu_2)(EP^*/P)}{1 - \alpha_1(1 - \tau_1) + \mu_1} \tag{9.1A}$$

$$\frac{M^s}{P} = \lambda_0 + \lambda_1 Y - \lambda_2 i - \lambda_3 i^* \tag{9.2A}$$

$$i = i^* \tag{9.3A}$$

The *IS* curve and the *LM* curve are given by equations (9.1A) and (9.2A) respectively. The third equation represents the bond markets when there is perfect capital mobility and static expectations. Substituting this equation into the *IS* and *LM* relations the policy multipliers can be derived under fixed and floating exchange rates.

Fixed exchange rates

With fixed rates the money supply is endogenous, so we solve the model for income and the money supply. Differentiating the *IS* and *LM* functions and arranging in matrix form we have:

$$\begin{bmatrix} k & 0 \\ -\lambda_1 & 1 \end{bmatrix} \begin{bmatrix} \partial Y \\ \partial M \end{bmatrix} = \begin{bmatrix} -\beta_1 \partial i^* + \partial G + \delta_1 \partial Y^* + (\delta_2 + \mu_2)\partial(EP^*/P) \\ + (M/P^2)\partial P - (\lambda_2 + \lambda_3)\partial i^* \end{bmatrix} \tag{9.4A}$$

where $k = 1 - \alpha_1(1 - \tau_1) + \mu_1$. Inverting the left and 2×2 matrix, assuming that $P = 1$, gives:

$$\begin{bmatrix} \partial Y \\ \partial M \end{bmatrix} = \frac{1}{k} \begin{bmatrix} 1 & 0 \\ \lambda_1 & k \end{bmatrix} \times \begin{bmatrix} -\beta_1 \partial i^* + \partial G + \delta_1 \partial Y^* + (\delta_2 + \mu_2)\partial(EP^*/P) \\ (M/P^2)\partial P - (\lambda_2 + \lambda_3)\partial i^* \end{bmatrix} \tag{9.5A}$$

The policy multipliers are now given as:

$$\frac{\partial Y}{\partial G} = \frac{1}{k} > 0; \quad \frac{\partial Y}{\partial i^*} = \frac{-\beta_1}{k} < 0; \quad \frac{\partial Y}{\partial Y^*} = \frac{\delta_1}{k} > 0; \quad \frac{\partial Y}{\partial E} = \frac{(\delta_2 + \mu_2)}{k} > 0.$$

Because the interest rate is held constant at the world level these are the same multipliers that emerge from the income expenditure model of Chapter 4.

To derive the *AD* curve the top equation from (9.5A) is solved for $\partial P/\partial Y$ which is:

$$\frac{\partial P}{\partial Y} = -\frac{1 - \alpha_1(1 - \tau_1) + \mu_1}{\delta_2 + \mu_2} < 0$$

Thus the slope of the *AD* curve is related to the government expenditure multiplier.

Flexible exchange rates

Under flexible exchange rates the money supply becomes exogenous and the exchange rate endogenous, so the system is now:

$$\begin{bmatrix} k & -(\delta_2+\mu_2) \\ -\lambda_1 & 0 \end{bmatrix}\begin{bmatrix} \partial Y \\ \partial E \end{bmatrix} = \begin{bmatrix} -\beta_1\partial i^* + \partial G + \delta_1\partial Y^* + (\delta_2+\mu_2)\partial(EP^*/P) \\ -\partial M + (M/P^2)\partial P - (\lambda_2+\lambda_3)\partial i^* \end{bmatrix} \qquad (9.6A)$$

With the inversion of the left hand 2×2 matrix we get:

$$\begin{bmatrix} \partial Y \\ \partial E \end{bmatrix} = \frac{1}{-(\delta_2+\mu_2)\lambda_1}\begin{bmatrix} 0 & (\delta_2+\mu_2) \\ \lambda_1 & k \end{bmatrix} \times \begin{bmatrix} -\beta\partial_1 i^* + \partial G + \delta_1\partial Y^* + (\delta_2+\mu_2)\partial(EP^*/P) \\ -\partial M + (M/P^2)\partial P - (\lambda_2+\lambda_3)\partial i^* \end{bmatrix}$$

$$(9.7A)$$

The policy multipliers are now simply:

$$\frac{\partial Y}{\partial M} = \frac{1}{\lambda_1} > 0; \quad \frac{\partial Y}{\partial i^*} = \frac{\lambda_2+\lambda_3}{\lambda_1} > 0.$$

The *AD* curve with flexible exchange rates is given by the top row from equation (9.7A), that is:

$$\frac{\partial P}{\partial Y} = -\lambda_1 < 0.$$

CHAPTER 10

The Government Budget Constraint and the Financing of Fiscal Policy

Aims and objectives

- To examine the implications of introducing government budget financing constraints on the effectiveness of fiscal policy.
- To reexamine the effectiveness of fiscal policy under fixed and floating exchange rates with financial wealth accumulation.
- To consider the rationale for the Maastricht Treaty rules limiting the size of budget deficits and debt to GDP ratios in the EU.

Introduction

In Chapter 9 the *IS–LM* model linked flow equilibrium from the goods market to stock equilibrium in asset markets. This analysis, however, ignored the potential feedback from changes in the demand for assets on the demand for goods and did not allow the stock of financial wealth to change. In other words, only half of the story has been told. A rise in government expenditure will increase the demand for goods and services, but the resulting budget deficit requires financing. The subsequent rise in the money supply and the bond supply to finance the fiscal deficit will feedback onto the demand for goods and services, due to the wealth effects on the demand for goods and services and the demand for assets. These second-round wealth effects and their potential implications for the effectiveness and stability of fiscal policy, are the principal concern of this chapter.

The definition and role of wealth in macroeconomics, with particular reference to fiscal policy, is considered in the next section. The question as to whether or not bond-financed fiscal deficits are expansionary has reemerged as part of the New Classical revival of the late 1970s and 1980s. While the traditional view has been that such deficits are expansionary, the New Classical protagonists have argued that since rational agents can anticipate the future they will appreciate that higher government borrowing today will result in higher levels of taxation in the future. Hence the increased private sector wealth from holding government bonds is offset by higher tax liabilities in the future so that, over time, private sector net wealth is unchanged. We then set out the fixed-price *IS–LM* model of an open economy together with the income–expenditure framework of Part II, to illustrate the notion of full, stock-flow equilibrium and the potential longer-run effects of fiscal policy under fixed exchange rates with perfect capital mobility. This is followed by an examination of the floating exchange rate case, and a brief consideration of the implications of wealth effects in the consumption and demand for money functions for the slope and position of the *AD* curve derived in Chapter 9. Finally we consider the practical issue of how large budget deficits can be consistent with macroeconomic stability and review the fiscal policy constraints imposed by the Maastricht Treaty on members of the European Union (EU).

The importance of wealth effects

In the analysis of the consumption function in Chapter 6 and the demand for financial assets in Chapter 8, it was hypothesised that real consumption and the real demand for assets are positive functions of the non-bank private sector's real wealth. So far non-bank private sector (nbps) financial wealth has been defined to consist of money and bonds. From the point of view of the economy as a whole, financial wealth is only a proportion of the whole, and in particular both real assets and equities have been excluded from consideration. To include both real assets and equities would, however, involve an element of double counting, since equities represent a claim on ownership of physical assets. The exclusion of both real assets and titles of ownership to them, implies that real capital accumulation is to be ignored on the grounds that incremental increases to the capital stock are sufficiently small in the short to medium run and so can be safely overlooked. A second reason for omitting the growth in real capital is that this would require an examination of changes in productivity and economic growth, which requires a different method of analysis, which is left until Chapter 16.

Even confining the analysis to aggregate, non-bank, private sector financial wealth requires a careful distinction to be made between 'inside' and 'outside' wealth. This distinction arises in the aggregate because intra-sector claims and liabilities cancel out. For example, suppose private sector firms borrow funds from the banking sector to finance their business. Suppose these same funds are deposited in the bank by personal-sector savers. Then the private sector as a whole has zero net financial wealth, since the positive wealth of one part of the sector (households) is exactly offset by the borrowing of another part of the same sector (firms). In this case the wealth is 'inside' wealth: that is, it washes out in aggregate. On the other hand, consider the overseas sector issuing bonds that are purchased by the domestic private sector households. The bond is a liability of the overseas government while it is an asset to the household sector. Since there is no offsetting liability within the private sector, foreign bonds count as part of the net wealth of the domestic private sector: that is, they are 'outside' wealth. A similar argument can also be made about debt issued by the public sector. If the government issues a bond which is purchased by the non-bank private sector then the liability is with the public sector whereas the asset is with the private sector, so again the bond held by the private sector is part of the net outside wealth of the sector. In essence, therefore, the definition of 'outside' wealth is those nbps assets which are the liabilities of either the government or the overseas sectors. Thus nbps wealth has consistently been defined as:

$$\frac{A}{P} = \frac{M^s}{P} + \frac{B^s}{P} + \frac{EB_d^*}{P} \tag{10.1}$$

where the money supply (M^s) is the liability of the domestic central bank, the bond stock (B^s) is the liability of the government, and the stock of foreign bonds held by the nbps (B_d^*) are a liability of the overseas government. These financial instruments are therefore all assets to the domestic non-bank private sector.

This is the standard definition of outside wealth, although the extent to which domestic government bonds are outside wealth has become highly controversial, since the seminal paper of Barro (1974) which asked the seemingly simple question: Are government bonds net wealth? The essence of Barro's argument is that government bonds should not be considered as part of the non-bank private sector's net wealth because to pay the interest due on the bond and to subsequently redeem the bond will require the government to levy future taxes on the private sector. Since, at least in Barro's world, agents are attributed with infinite lives and perfect foresight, these nbps agents know that the more bonds the government issues the higher future taxes will have to be to redeem the bonds. Thus the private sector earns a return on government bonds today, only to face higher income taxes in the future when the bond is due for redemption. So the higher asset income stream today is matched by a corresponding higher income tax liability in the future and so government bonds should not count as outside wealth. This is known as the *Ricardian Equivalence Proposition*.

Although this is something of an ingenious argument it is based on a number of highly dubious assumptions. For example, some residents who benefit from higher income streams this period, die before the next period when higher taxation is imposed. For these individuals the public sector bonds are clearly net additions to their wealth, since they earn the extra income without paying the higher taxes. Barro's reply is that this argument takes no account of bequests from one generation to the next. That is, the agents who die before the next period will simply adjust their bequests or gifts to their children to accommodate the increased burden of taxes that they will now have to bear. Although, therefore, individuals have finite lives, they act *as if* they were infinitely lived. The real objection to Barro's contention is that it presumes a degree of fine calculation and rationality that is wholly unrealistic.

A second difficulty faced by advocates of the Ricardian equivalence proposition is that the public and the private sectors face different interest rates. When the government's rate of interest on borrowing is less than the private sector's, as is usually the case, then the nbps gains an increase in its net wealth from any increase in public sector borrowing. To see this consider **Figure 10.1**, where the budget constraint *BC* is the private sector constraint and the line *PS* represents

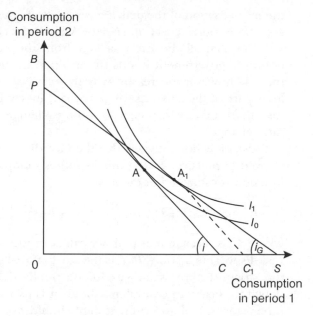

Figure 10.1   *Ricardian equivalence*

the public sector's constraint, reflecting the different interest rates at which each sector can borrow. The private sector's after tax endowment position is assumed to be at point A and total private sector wealth measured in the current period is $0C$, with future income streams discounted at i. When the government reduces taxes today it increases the private sector endowment by the same amount, thereby moving point C to the right to C_1. Taxes will, however, have to be raised in the next period by an amount determined by the government budget constraint, corresponding to the interest rate i_G. Private wealth discounted at the private discount rate, i, is measured by the distance $0C_1$, which is clearly larger than $0C$. The difference, CC_1, represents the present value of the wealth gain that accrues to the public when the government borrows on their behalf. The indifference map shows that the preferred consumption point is now at A_1, which exhibits a higher level of utility than the initial point at A.

A third reason why the Ricardian equivalence proposition may not hold is that taxes, excluding lump sum taxes, are themselves distortionary. For example, taxation on labour incomes may lead some individuals to supply less effort that will reduce output, which in turn reduces wealth. On the other hand, if budget deficits increase the level of economic activity and thereby generate additional income then the associated increase in the public sector debt leads to real wealth creation.

A fourth argument against the Ricardian equivalence proposition is that in the future a government may decide not to raise taxes to fund the deficit, but rather to monetise the deficit. This will, at least partially reduce the Ricardian effect as future tax liabilities are correspondingly reduced. To the extent, however, that the monetisation of the deficit gives rise to higher inflation, the inflation itself is a tax that imposes costs on society. A final objection to the proposition is that it assumes that all the extra savings from the tax cut will be used to purchase domestic government bonds. In an open economy without exchange controls, there is however, no reason why these private individuals should not invest, at least part of their extra savings abroad, in say foreign government debt. In this case there may be real effects as the exchange rate may depreciate and interest rates change.

These objections suggest that the Ricardian equivalence proposition is unlikely to hold in practice. To test this hypothesis empirically an extended consumption function is estimated of the form:

$$C' = \alpha_0 + \alpha_1(Y-T) + \alpha_2\left(\frac{A}{P} - \frac{B^s}{P}\right) + \alpha_3\left(\frac{B^s}{P}\right) + \alpha_4(G-T) \tag{10.2}$$

where C' is measured as real per capita private consumption, $Y-T$ is the level of real disposable income, B^s/P is the stock of real government debt, $(A/P) - (B^s/P)$ is the stock of nbps wealth excluding public debt, and $G-T$ is the real budget deficit. If Ricardian equivalence holds it is expected that $\alpha_3 = 0$, and $\alpha_1 = -\alpha_4$. In other words, real government debt should not influence real consumption and, at the same time, the increase in consumption from the rise in disposable income from a direct tax cut should be exactly offset by the negative effect of a rise in the real budget deficit. Nicoletti (1988) finds that of 16 studies reviewed, the Ricardian equivalence proposition is rejected by nine of the studies. Furthermore, from Nicoletti's own multi-country study he concludes that with the exceptions of Italy and Belgium the full tax-discounting hypothesis does not receive much support from the data, and that in the majority of countries the Barro Model is strongly rejected. It is also interesting to note that in countries with large and probably unsustainable budget deficits the Ricardian equivalence proposition is more likely to hold. This is the case in both Belgium and Italy where it is impossible to reject the Barro Model.

These arguments suggest that the Ricardian equivalence proposition is unlikely to hold empirically, especially in the short-run, and therefore at least some of the public sector's financial liabilities can be counted as part of the private sector's net wealth. On this basis the effects of fiscal policy in a wealth-augmented, medium-run *IS–LM* model are explored in the following sections.

The wealth augmented *IS–LM* model with fixed exchange rates

The open-economy *IS–LM* model can now be set out fully, integrating the interactions between real side flows of expenditure and changes in the holdings of financial assets. The first key relationship is the national income accounting identity, which is:

$$S - I = G - T + X - M = \Delta A \tag{10.3}$$

Equation (10.3) says that net private sector savings must be equal to the sum of the public sector deficit and the overseas sector's current balance deficit, and that additions to private sector savings will enhance private sector wealth. In steady-state equilibrium, that is when all stocks are constant, $\Delta A = 0$. In this case, from a rearrangement of equation (10.3) it is clear that:

$$T - G = X - M \tag{10.4}$$

This says that the public sector surplus must equal the current balance surplus of the home economy in equilibrium. This is equivalent to assuming that the desired level of demand is exactly equal to supply or, in the context of the income–expenditure model, the model is on the 45-degree line.

In terms of the financial sector, both the public sector deficit and the current balance deficit have to be financed. The public sector deficit is assumed to be covered by either a sale of bonds to the central bank or to the nbps which increases the volume of domestic credit (ΔD) outstanding, or the bond supply ΔB^s respectively. So the government budget constraint is simply:

$$G - T = \Delta D + \Delta B^s \tag{10.5}$$

In addition, the current account balance must be equal to the capital account balance and the change in official reserves under a fixed exchange rate system. This can be represented as:

$$X - M = \Delta B_d^* + \Delta R \tag{10.6}$$

where ΔB_d^* is the private sector's accumulation of foreign assets and R is the change in official reserves. Combining these two identities gives:

$$G - T + X - M = (\Delta D + \Delta B) + \Delta B_d^* + \Delta R = \Delta A \tag{10.7}$$

where ($\Delta D + \Delta R = \Delta M^s$) is the change in the domestic money supply and equation (10.7) denotes the components of wealth which are likely to be changing. It is through these identities that the real sector is linked to the financial sector.

The final link in the model is the direct link between changes in financial wealth and the demand for financial assets and goods and services, as noted in Chapters 6 and 8. The consumption function, as in Chapter 6, depends upon disposable income and the stock of real wealth, so that:

$$C = \alpha_0 + \alpha_1(Y - T) + \alpha_2 A \tag{10.8}$$

The demand for money also depends positively upon wealth, as indicated in Chapter 8, such that:

$$\frac{M^s}{P} = \lambda_0 + \lambda_1 Y - \lambda_2 i - \lambda_3 i^* + \lambda_4 A \tag{10.9}$$

where the price level, P, is fixed and normalised to unity. Since perfect capital mobility is part of the maintained hypothesis in this chapter it is not necessary to specify the bond market equilibrium equations. From equations (10.8) and (10.9) it follows that the *IS* curve and the *LM* curve will depend directly upon the level of real private sector wealth, according to the size of the coefficients α_2 and λ_4 respectively.

The full model of stock–flow interaction is set out in **Figure 10.2**. This figure presents the wealth-augmented *IS–LM* model in the upper part where domestic and foreign bonds are perfect substitutes, with the income–expenditure flow equilibrium shown in the lower part. As nbps wealth rises consumption rises, which leads toa higher demand for output and the *IS* curve will shift to the right. The *LM* curve will shift to the left as private sector wealth increases, since the demand for money will be higher for a given supply, so necessitating a rise in the rate of interest to maintain money market equilibrium. If, however, the increase in nbps wealth comes about through a rise in outside money, so that the money supply increases, then the *LM* curve will move to the right since the effect of a higher money supply dominates the effect of higher wealth on the demand for money. Formally, that is: $\lambda_4 < 1$.

In the lower part the $T-G$ line slopes down, indicating that as income increases the tax receipts increase, so for a given level of spending by the government the budget surplus rises. The $X-M$ line slopes up since for a given value of exports and real exchange rate, imports rise with income, so reducing the current balance surplus as income rises. From (10.4), only at the intersection of the $T-G$ and $X-M$ lines is nbps wealth unchanging. Therefore, for the model to be

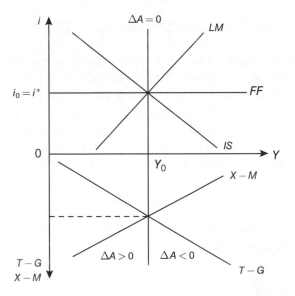

Figure 10.2 *The complete stock–flow model*

in equilibrium requires a level of income to be reached which is consistent with $(T-G)-(X-M)=0$. In all the figures below this is denoted by the vertical line labelled $\Delta A=0$. To the left of the vertical $\Delta A=0$ line the budget surplus is less than the current balance surplus and so nbps wealth is increasing. On the other hand, to the right of $\Delta A=0$ the current balance surplus is less than the budget surplus and so nbps wealth is decreasing.

There are several general points to note at the outset of the analysis. Firstly, there are no wealth effects linked with monetary policy changes, since monetary policy involves the private sector holding more money and less government bonds. Since with an open market operation $\Delta M^s = -\Delta B^s$ there is no change in the non-bank private sector outside wealth. Therefore in this chapter only the effectiveness of fiscal policy is considered.

Secondly, with regard to fiscal policy there are now three alternative ways of financing a rise in government spending:

1. The government could raise taxes so as to raise revenue by the exact amount of the higher spending. As shown in Chapter 5, the balanced budget multi- plier is strictly greater than unity so a balanced budget increase in spending has a positive effect upon the level of income.
2. In the case of a budget deficit, where G rises for a given value of T, the deficit can be financed by either an increase in the money supply or an increase in the sale of government debt to the nbps. When the budget deficit is financed by an expansion of the money supply the level of non-bank private sector wealth increases. This causes the LM curve to shift to the right, since the sup- ply effect is greater than the demand effect through the rise in wealth.
3. If the budget deficit is financed by the sale of bonds to the non-bank private sector again nbps wealth rises. In this case, however, the LM curve shifts to the left, as the demand for money rises for a given supply. In this case especially in a closed economy context, there is the possibility of instability if the wealth effect on the demand for money exceeds that on the consumption function.

These three alternative forms of financing fiscal deficits are considered below.

Figure 10.3 examines the case of a balanced budget fiscal expansion. In the lower part the $T-G$ schedule is unchanged since both T and G have risen by the same amount. Therefore the initial and final levels of wealth are the same. Therefore the line $\Delta A=0$ is the same in the initial and final equilibrium. In the upper quadrant the IS curve shifts to the right, to IS_1 to give a temporary equilib- rium at B, which is equivalent to the closed economy balanced budget expan- sion. At B, however, the domestic rate of interest has risen above the world rate leading to a capital inflow and an expansion of the domestic money supply, which shift the LM curve to the right to LM_1. At point C, although from the top part of **Figure 10.3** the model looks to be in full equilibrium, but wealth is falling because the current balance surplus is less than the budget surplus, as indicted by the distance HF in the lower part. Since non-bank private sector wealth is falling, the IS_1 curve will shift back to the left towards IS_0 as consumption spend- ing falls. For the LM curve at point C, the falling level of wealth will lower the

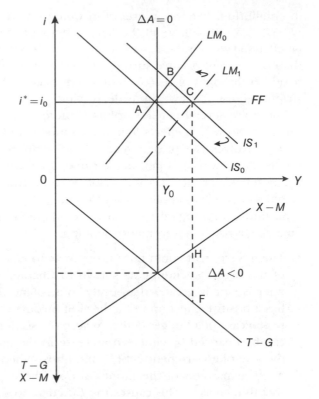

Figure 10.3 *Balanced budget fiscal expansion*

demand for money, which will tend to push the LM_1 line further to the right beyond LM_1. This effect, however, will be swamped by the capital outflow that will take place as soon as the rate of interest falls below i^*. This will reduce the money supply, which shifts LM_1 back to LM_0. The final equilibrium is back at A. Therefore a balanced budget fiscal expansion has no effect on the level of income in an open economy with a fixed exchange rate, perfect capital mobility and wealth effects. This result is in contrast to the usual positive balanced budget multipliers when there are no wealth effects, as in Chapter 5 and Chapter 9.

Figure 10.4 shows the case of a pure money-financed fiscal expansion, whereby the increase in government spending is financed by the authorities selling domestic bonds to the central bank, which results in an increase in the supply of outside money. Thus in the upper part of the figure the increase in spending shifts the *IS* curve to the right, to IS_1 and the *LM* curve to LM_1. The shift of the *LM* curve to the right is due to a rise in both domestic credit creation from the central bank purchase of government debt, and from an inflow of foreign currency reserves due to the domestic interest rate temporarily rising above the world rate. Point C is the usual open economy equilibrium position where the IS_1 and LM_1 lines intersect on the $i = i^*$ line. In the lower part of the figure, however, the rise in government spending has shifted the $T - G_0$ schedule to the right to $T - G_1$, thus at Y_1, below point C, nbps wealth is still increasing as the current

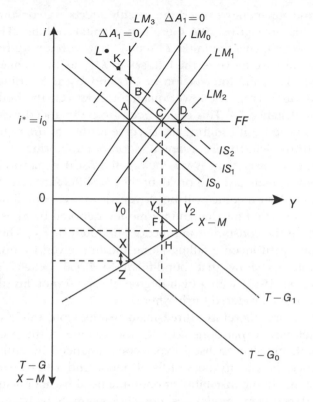

Figure 10.4 *Money and bond-financed fiscal expansions*

balance surplus is greater than the budget surplus, given by the distance FH. The increase in wealth will enhance consumption, shifting the IS_1 line to IS_2. The rise in wealth will also tend to push the LM_1 back towards LM_0, but the rise in the rate of interest that this provokes, gives rise to a large capital inflow that increases the money supply, shifting the LM_1 curve to LM_2. The final equilibrium is at D in the upper part, which is consistent with the new constant wealth line, $\Delta A_1 = 0$. Thus a money-financed fiscal expansion has a greater effect on output with wealth effects than without such effects. The potency of fiscal policy is enhanced.

The third method of financing a budget deficit is by selling bonds on the open market to the non-bank private sector. In this case of a pure bond-financed fiscal expansion, the fiscal policy multiplier will also be enhanced in an open economy with high or perfect capital mobility, because the higher rate of interest causes a capital inflow and a simultaneous increase in the money supply. The increase in the money supply dominates the wealth effect on the demand for money, as a result of the higher bond stock, which tries to push the *LM* curve to the left. As long as the *LM* curve shifts to the right the new stable equilibrium can be reached. In this case the outcome is again as shown in **Figure 10.4**.

With pure bond-financed fiscal deficits, however, instability can arise when the degree of capital mobility is relatively low and if the wealth effects on the demand for money exceed the wealth effects on consumption. To see this suppose that in **Figure 10.4** there is no capital mobility. The point B is where the new *IS* curve cuts the initial *LM* curve, but with a pure bond-financed deficit the *LM* would also move to the left, say to LM_3, as the demand for money rises with wealth. Thus the intersection of LM_3 and IS_2 at K would be the new short-run equilibrium. From the lower quadrant, however, the budget deficit at K is given by the distance ZX. This deficit needs to be financed by a further issue of bonds which raise wealth shifting the *IS* curve further to the right and the LM_3 curve further to the left, to give a new temporary equilibrium at, say, L. At L the level of income is lower than it was before the fiscal expansion. Moreover, every time the government issues more debt the *LM* shifts further left than the *IS* does to the right, and so income will be driven down without limit. (This is because the wealth effect on the demand for money, denoted by λ_4, is greater than the wealth effect on the consumption function, denoted by α_2.) The budget deficit is destabilising, with income falling along the line given by points AKL. Although it is possible to show that bond-financed fiscal deficits may be unstable (see Pentecost, 1983) with a high degree of capital mobility, this is not very plausible and is not considered further here.

There are, therefore, three main results from this analysis. Firstly, balanced-budget fiscal expansions do not raise income in the presence of wealth effects. Second, unbalanced fiscal expansions, financed by either money or bonds, do enhance the effectiveness of fiscal policy under fixed exchange rates. Third, the possibility of the instability of bond-financed fiscal deficits that is characteristic of closed economy models, is not a problem here if there exist internationally mobile capital flows.

The wealth augmented *IS–LM* model with floating exchange rates

The analysis under floating exchange rates is much more complicated than under fixed rates, although the principal result is that there is no enhanced potency for unbalanced fiscal expansions with wealth effects, although the balanced budget multiplier is non-zero in this case.

Figure 10.5 shows the effect of a balanced budget fiscal expansion under flexible exchange rates. The mechanisms in operation here are rather complex, but crucial to the story is that there are no equilibrating capital flows, but rather exchange rate changes. The balanced budget expansion leads the *IS* curve to shift to the right, to IS_1. At point B there is a fall in wealth as the budget surplus exceeds the current balance surplus, given by the distance FH in the lower quadrant. The fall in wealth shifts the *LM* curve to the right, since the wealth effect reduces the demand for money for a given supply a fall in the rate of interest is needed to clear the money market. The fall in wealth also tends to push the *IS* curve back to left, as consumption spending is reduced. This leftward movement in the *IS* curve is reinforced by the fact that at B the domestic interest rate is

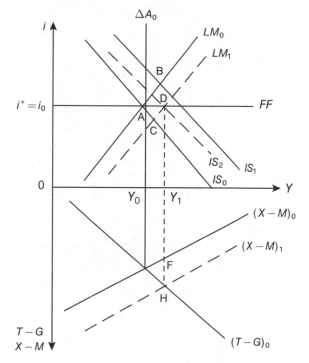

Figure 10.5 *Balanced budget fiscal expansion with floating exchange rates*

above the foreign rate, there by giving rise to exchange rate appreciation. The *IS* curve shifts towards IS_0, to cut the LM_1 line at C. At C, however, there is a potential capital outflow with the domestic rate of interest below the foreign rate provoking a depreciation in the home currency. This shifts the *IS* curve out to IS_2 and the current balance line to the right to $(X-M)_1$ to give the final equilibrium at point D. At this point income is higher than at A, implying a higher level of imports offset by a lower exchange rate.

Figure 10.6 shows the effect of an unbalanced fiscal expansion using the same set-up as before, with the model initially in equilibrium at point A. A rise in government spending shifts the $T-G$ line up to the right and the *IS* curve up to the right to IS_1. The potential capital inflow, caused by the rise of i above i^*, leads to an appreciation of the domestic currency. This exchange rate appreciation leads to a deterioration in competitiveness and the net trade balance deteriorates, which shifts the *IS* curve back to IS_0 and in the lower part of the figure the appreciation also shifts the $X-M$ line back to the left, to $(X-M)_1$. The model returns to equilibrium at Y_0. Fiscal policy has been totally ineffective. This is exactly the same result as without wealth effects: fiscal policy is ineffective under floating exchange rates with perfect capital mobility. In the absence of perfect capital mobility the two results need not be the same. Conventional analysis implies the possibility of some income expansion in these conditions, with a current account deficit matched by a capital inflow attracted by higher interest rates, but with no

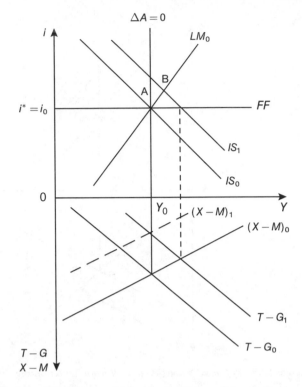

Figure 10.6 *Unbalanced fiscal expansion under floating exchange rates*

guarantee that the current account and budget deficits are exactly matching, althoughthis is a condition in wealth-augmented analysis. The existence and stability of such equilibria are problematic and not considered further in this text.

Derivation of the AD curve with wealth effects

In Chapter 9 the *AD* curve was derived from the *IS–LM* model ignoring wealth effects on the consumption and demand for money functions. In this chapter it has been demonstrated that under floating exchange rates wealth effects do not enhance the effectiveness of real budget shocks on the level of income. Thus, under floating exchange rates the *AD* curve is the same as that derived in Chapter 9.

On the other hand, with fixed exchange rates wealth effects have the effect of augmenting the effect of fiscal policy. In this case, therefore, the *AD* line will have a flatter slope than that in Chapter 9. To see this consider **Figure 10.7**. Starting from the initial equilibrium at point A, assume that the price level falls to P_1. Under fixed exchange rates this makes domestic output more competitive shifting the *IS* curve to the right to IS_1. The resulting capital inflow leads to an increase in the money supply, which reinforces the fall in the price level, to shift the *LM* curve to the right, to LM_1. At B there is a new equilibrium, which gives point C on the *AD* line AD_1 in the lower quadrant. However, in addition to these effects, the lower price level

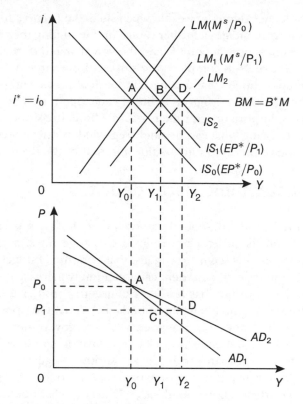

Figure 10.7 *The* AD *schedule with wealth effects*

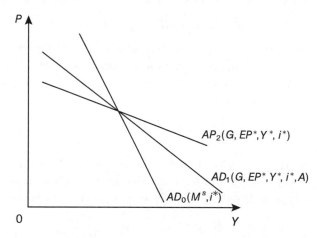

Figure 10.8 *Alternative* AD *Schedule*

stimulates domestic wealth which shifts the *IS* curve further to the right to IS_2, which in turn stimulates a further capital inflow shifting the *LM* curve to LM_2. The final equilibrium is now at point D and the new demand curve is given by the flatter AD_2 line.

Figure 10.8 compares the slopes of the three *AD* schedules derived so far. The steepest line is that attained under floating exchange rates (shown by AD_0), while the flattest line is given by fixed exchange rates and wealth effects (AD_2). Perhaps more importantly, for the text as a whole, the slope of the *AD* line is negative, with there being what can be safely regarded as only a technical difference between the slope of the fixed rate *AD* line and that of the fixed-rate line with wealth effects.

Sustainable fiscal deficits

In the model described earlier (pp. 201–2) it was shown that bond financed fiscal deficits, at least under fixed exchange rates, augmented the level of national income. This seems to suggest that continual budget deficits financed by the issue of more government debt can indefinitely increase the level of output. This unintuitive proposition has lead economists to consider if there are any natural limits on the size or the financing of budget deficits. One possible limit, of course, is inflation. It is not clear, however, why any government should wish to expand fiscal policy when there is no lack of effective demand, so this is not really a good candidate to constrain fiscal deficits. Another suggestion, due to Sargent and Wallace (1981), is that there is some natural limit to the debt to GDP ratio, B^s/Y. The empirical evidence, however, does not bear this claim out. For example, in 1996 the debt to income ratio was about 60 per cent in the UK, France, Germany and the USA, but 81 per cent in Japan, 101 per cent in Canada and 125 per cent in Italy.

A more fruitful exercise is to pose the question the other way around and ask what size of structural budget deficit the government is able run, while holding the debt to GDP ratio constant? To answer this question a slightly different form of the budget constraint is needed which distinguishes the structural budget deficit from interest repayments on the outstanding stock of debt, that is:

$$G - T + rB^s = \Delta M^s + \Delta B^s \tag{10.10}$$

where the product rB^s is the value of interest payments made by the government each period on the outstanding stock of debt. Since equation (10.10) is in real terms, r is defined as the real rate of interest. Dividing (10.10) through by the level of income gives:

$$g - t + rb + \frac{\Delta M^s + \Delta B^s}{Y} \tag{10.11}$$

where g, t, and b denote their respective variables as a ratio to income, so that $g = G/Y$, $t = T/Y$ and $b = B^s/Y$. The next step is to write down an expression for the change in the debt to income ratio, b. This is:

$$\Delta \left(\frac{B^s}{Y} \right) = \frac{\Delta B^s}{Y} - \frac{B^s}{Y} \frac{\Delta Y}{Y} = \frac{\Delta B^s}{Y} - bz \tag{10.12}$$

where $z = \Delta Y/Y$. The final step is to use (10.12) to substitute for $\Delta B^s/Y$ in (10.11). Substituting and rearranging yields:

$$\Delta b = (g-t) + (r-z)b - \Delta M^s/Y. \tag{10.13}$$

Although equation (10.13) does not suggest any formal limits to pure bond-financed fiscal deficits (that is, when $\Delta M^s = 0$) it does show that persistent budget deficits lead to a rising debt to GDP ratio.

Equation (10.13) has two other implications. First, since it is a first-order difference equation in b, it gives a formal condition for the stability of the debt to income ratio. This is simply $r - z < 0$, which means that the real rate of interest must be less than the growth rate of income for the debt to income ratio to be convergent over time. Alternatively, expressed in nominal terms, if the nominal interest rate exceeds the growth in nominal income, such that $i > \pi + z$, where π is the expected rate of inflation then the debt to income ratio will rise over time.

Second, the European Union (EU) adopted fiscal targets in the Maastricht Treaty of 1991 by which the maximum size of the budget deficit is 3 per cent of GDP and the maximum debt to GDP ratio is set at 60 per cent. These figures imply that in order to keep the debt to GDP ratio from rising, the nominal growth of income must exceed the nominal interest rate by 5 per cent. Even with low nominal interest rates of, say, 2 per cent per annum, this requires money income to grow by at least 7 per cent annum.

Conclusions

This chapter has showed how stocks and flows are an integral part of a simple macroeconomic model because of the accumulation identities that relate particular stock and flow variables. In this context it was demonstrated that the effectiveness of fiscal policy is enhanced under fixed exchange rates and a high degree of capital mobility, although without a high degree of capital mobility and with a relatively large wealth effect on money demand, pure bond-financed deficits could be unstable. This analysis also seemed to imply that there is no limit to the expansion of income by way of bond-financed fiscal deficits. This led on to a discussion of the potential limits to bond-financing from which it was concluded that although there are no natural limits, the fact that bond-financed deficits require servicing, large fiscal deficits in one period may result in fiscal policy not being an available policy option in the future.

The ultimate issue of macroeconomic policy is which instruments of policy are to be set, and which are to be left to be residually determined. Since the late 1970s, macroeconomic policy in many countries has been focused on monetary growth targets as a constraint on fiscal decisions, an approach which has led to extreme reliance on bond-financed deficits and a dramatic increase in debt to GDP ratios. The analysis of this chapter suggests that it might be more appropriate for monetary policy to be determined residually, as Friedman (1948) originally proposed. As long as the fiscal parameters are set so that the budget deficit averages zero, this arrangement would control the longer-run growth in the money supply and therefore the underlying inflation rate. It would also have the advantage of avoiding the potential instabilities associated with bond financing.

Summary

- The Ricardian equivalence proposition argues that debt-financing and tax-financing of fiscal deficits are equivalent, since the private sector with rational expectations, realise that current income received from holding government stock will be needed in the future to pay off their higher tax liabilities when the debt is redeemed. Empirically, however, this proposition receives little support.
- Fiscal policy is more potent under fixed exchange rates when wealth accumulation is permitted, although under floating exchange rates the effectiveness of fiscal policy is not enhanced and instability may result.
- In the open economy context the potential instability of debt-financed fiscal deficits, under fixed exchange rates, is ruled out if there is a sufficiently high degree of capital mobility.
- The requirement that the debt to GDP ratiobe stabilised requires that the real rate of interest must be less than the growth of income. In the context of the EU and the fiscal targets adopted in the Maastricht Treaty, the growth in nominal income must exceed the nominal interest rate by 5 per cent. Even with low nominal interest rates of, say, 2 per cent per annum, this requires money income to grow by at least 7 per cent per annum.

Suggested further reading

The literature on the government constraint was instigated by Ott and Ott (1965) and Christ (1968) and developed by Blinder and Solow (1973, 1976) and Tobin and Buiter (1976). The most accessible papers for students are Silber (1970), Currie (1976, 1979) and Artis (1979), of which the latter two authors wrote with students in mind. Scarth (1975) extends the analysis to the open economy as does Pentecost (1983) which also provides a largely diagrammatic treatment. The debate about Ricardian equivalence stems from the seminal, but difficult paper of Barro (1974), although students will find Barro (1989) easier. Seater (1993) provides a thorough survey of the empirical evidence. The development of fiscal rules stems from Sargent and Wallace (1981) and De Grauwe (1997) provides an easier exposition in the EU context.

Essay titles

1. Explain the so-called Ricardian equivalence proposition and comment on its empiricalrelevance.
2. Show how private sector asset accumulation is related to the public sector and overseas deficits. What influence might wealth effects have on economic activity?
3. Why does the explicit consideration of the government's budget constraint figure so crucially in discussions of the crowding-out effects?
4. 'Bond-financed government deficits crowd out private expenditure but money-financed deficits never do.' Discuss.

Questions

1. (a) Distinguish between 'inside wealth' and 'outside wealth'. Why is this distinction important?
   (b) Does it make any difference whether the government pays for its expenditures by raising taxes or by issuing debt?
   (c) What are the principal objections to the Ricardian equivalence view?
2. To what extent does the flow equilibrium in the goods market determine the stock equilibrium in the asset markets? What are implications of this for the stock of nbps wealth?
3. Use a wealth-augmented *IS–LM* model to demonstrate the effect of a balanced budget contraction, that is a simultaneous and equal cut in tax revenue and government spending.
4. Show how bond-financed fiscal deficits are always likely to be stable, even in the presence of a relatively large wealth effect on the demand for money, when the authorities follow a fixed exchange rate policy and there is a high degree of capital mobility.
5. (a) Distinguish between the structural and the cyclical budget deficits. To what extent do we need to worry about the debt-servicing component in the budget?
   (b) Why is it more useful to look at the ratio of debt to GDP than to discuss the absolute value of the debt?
6. On the Maastricht definition the debt to income ratios of France, the Netherlands and Belgium in 1996 were approximately 57%, 79% and 130% respectively. If the growth rates for each country are assumed to be 2% and the rate of interest is assumed to be 3%, how large should the primary budget surplus be in each country in order to stabilise the debt to income ratio, without resorting to monetary financing of the deficit?

CHAPTER 11
The Demand for Money

Aims and objectives

- To investigate the determinants of the aggregate demand for real money balances from the microeconomic foundations.
- To compare the monetarist approach to the demand for money to the post-Keynesian analysis of the demand for money.
- To examine the empirical evidence for a stable aggregate demand for money function and the size of the interest rate elasticity of demand.

Introduction

Having completed an examination of the financial markets and their interaction with the goods market in the theory of aggregate demand, and especially the crucial role they play in financing the budget deficit, it is time to take a more detailed look at the demands for these financial assets. The focus of this chapter is on the demand for money, since this is assumed to be of the greatest importance for the macroeconomy. In particular, the determinants and stability of the aggregate demand for money are crucial for the operation of monetary policy. For example, if the demand for money is independent of the rate of interest then the *LM* curve will be vertical and fiscal policy will have no purchase on domestic output. This issue was one of the initial points of dispute between the monetarists and Keynesians in the late 1960s and early 1970s. The monetarist's favoured a vertical *LM* curve, making monetary policy all-powerful, whereas the Keynesians believed, liked Keynes, that the demand for money function was sensitive to the rate of interest and therefore the *LM* curve was positively sloped, giving fiscal policy leverage on output. Although the Keynesian position is largely accepted today there still remains the question of stability. If the demand for money is unstable then a policy that is aimed at influencing the economy by controlling the money supply is not feasible. For monetary policy to be feasible the demand for money function needs to be stable so that it is possible to predict how changes in the money supply will affect interest rates and output. Thus the determinants and the stability of the demand for money are crucial for the operation of monetary policy as it has been described in Chapters 8–10.

In Chapter 8 the demand for money was identified as depending on the demand for cash for both transactions purposes and for speculative purposes. In the next section the transactions demand for money is examined with specific reference to developments since the *General Theory*, and this is followed by a consideration of Keynes' speculative motive for the demand for money. This analysis was modified in the 1950s by Tobin (1958), although there is a debate as to whether Tobin's extension of Keynes' speculative motive is really not a precautionary motive for holding cash balances (see, for example, Harris, 1981). For this reason Tobin's asset demand for money is considered in a separate section which examines the asset or precautionary demand for holding money balances. Friedman's restatement of the Classical Quantity Theory of Money as a demand for money (Friedman, 1956) is then examined to give an alternative view of the micro-foundations for holding money in which the demand for money is viewed simply like the demand for any other commodity. The final section completes the chapter with a brief review of the problems in estimating and appraising the empirical evidence on the aggregate demand for money.

The transactions demand for money

The Classical economists regarded money primarily as a medium of exchange and unit of account. Money was therefore held primarily for the commodities and services that it could buy. Since the purchases of goods and services are closely related to income, the demand for money should also be directly related to nominal income. Thus Keynes, following the approach of Marshall and other Cambridge economists, specified the transactions demand for money as proportional to nominal income, that is:

$$M^d = kPY \tag{11.1}$$

where P is the aggregate price level, Y is the level of real output and k is the factor of proportionality. Expressed in real terms the demand for (real) cash balances is proportional to real income. This simple expression reflects the fact that spending reflects income and to spend agents need to hold cash, therefore cash holdings are directly related to income. An alternative interpretation for equation (11.1) is that money is held to smooth out the difference between frequent income receipts and continual expenditure payments.

This view of the transactions demand for money assumes that individuals hold all of the proportion of their income that they intend to spend in any one period in cash. Cash balances are, however, typically non-interest bearing and so it is costly for individuals to hold large amounts of cash. Individuals therefore generally choose to hold only the cash they need for current transactions, while leaving the rest in a bank or building society deposit where it earns interest. Baumol

(1952) showed that this type of behaviour gives rise to the transactions demand for money also depending inversely on the rate of interest.

Formally consider an individual household with a nominal income of £y_b per month, all of which is spent during the month at a uniform rate. **Figure 11.1** panel (a) shows the individuals' demand for money when all the income is held as cash. The average cash balance held over the month is simply $(y_b/2)$. Suppose now that the household only withdraws half of the money from the bank, at the start of the period and withdraws the other half at the start of the third week. Panel (b) of **Figure 11.1** shows that the average cash balance is now is $(1/2)(y_b/2)$. Furthermore panel (c) shows that if the household makes four (weekly) cash withdrawals the average cash balance held is only $(1/2)(1/2)(y_b/2) = (y_b/8)$. This example shows that the average cash balance held by the individual household falls as the number of cash withdrawals increase. This simple story can be generalised alittle by defining the number of withdrawals over any period as n. Then the household's average cash balance can be written as:

$$m_b = \frac{1}{2}\,(y_b/n) \tag{11.2}$$

since when $n=1$, $m_b=(y_b/2)$ and when $n=2$, $m_b=(y_b/4)$ just as in the example above. This prompts the question as to what determines, n, the number of withdrawals? There are two main factors. First, since a bank or building society deposit account offers interest on the funds remaining in the account, as interest rates rise the household will economise on its holdings of idle cash balances, thereby increasing, n, the number of withdrawals per period. At the mid-point of the period the building society deposit is $(y_b/2)$, as shown in **Figure 11.1**, less the amount withdrawn in cash at the mid-point, which according to (11.2) is $(1/2)(y_b/n)$ So the net interest earned will be simply $i[(y_b/2) - (1/2)(y_b/n)]$, which is the rate of interest multiplied by the unspent income less the amount withdrawn in cash at the half-way point. This expression increases as n rises. The second factor that determines the size of n, is the cost in terms of time and trouble of making frequent visits to the bank or building society in order to affect cash withdrawals. If the average cost of each withdrawal is b, the total cost of cash withdrawals are bn. A rational, profit-maximising household will wish to choose the value of n to maximise net interest earnings, z, which are the sum of the two elements which determine the size of n, that is:

$$z = i\left(\frac{y}{2} - \frac{1}{2}\frac{y}{n}\right) - bn \tag{11.3}$$

where i is the rate of interest paid on the average balance held. From the expression for the average cash balance n can be written as: $n = (1/2)(y_b/m_b)$ and the whole expression re-expressed as:

$$z = i\left(\frac{y_b}{2} - m_b\right) - b\frac{1}{2m_b}y_b \tag{11.4}$$

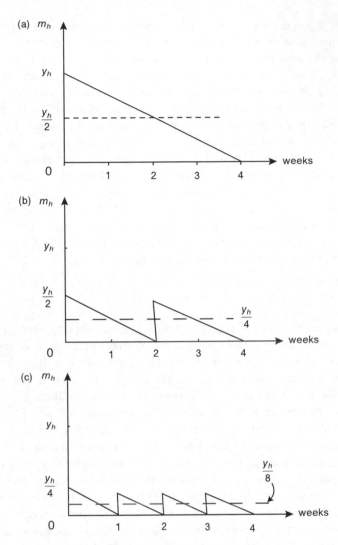

Figure 11.1 *Individual's transaction demand for money*

Maximising the net earnings with respect to m_b thus yields:

$$\frac{\partial z}{\partial m_b} = -i + \frac{1}{2}by_b\frac{1}{m_b^2} = 0 \tag{11.5}$$

from which the optimal money holding, m_b, can be found as:

$$m_b = \sqrt{\left(\frac{1}{2}b\frac{y_b}{i}\right)} \tag{11.6}$$

This is known as Baumols' square-root rule which identifies a specific relationship between an individual's demand for real cash balances, m, income, y, and the rate of interest, i. Disregarding the specific form, equation (11.6) shows that the transactions money demand depends directly on income and inversely on the rate of interest.

To move to the aggregate money demand for each representative consumer whose money demand is given by equation (11.6), there is assumed to be someone on the other side of the market. Suppose, for example, that the consumer buys goods from a representative firm and that the firm periodically converts its money-holdings into bonds. The firm's pattern of bond and money holdings would follow the same saw-tooth pattern exactly complementary to the consumer's pattern in **Figure 11.1**. Thus the firm's demand for money would also be given by the square-root rule. The aggregate money demand in the transactions model is therefore the sum of the households demands and that of the firms on the other side of the market. This means we must double, m_b in equation (11.5) to get the aggregate demand for real money transactions balances, M_T^d/P:

$$\frac{M_T^d}{P} = 2m_b = \sqrt{\left(\frac{2bY}{i}\right)} \tag{11.7}$$

where Y is now national income. Thus the aggregate demand for real money balances for transactions purposes also follows the square root rule. This implies that the elasticity of demand for real balances with respect to both income and the rate of interest is $+0.5$ and -0.5 respectively.

There are a number of implications of this model for the aggregate demand for money. First, the demand for money is directly related to the level of transactions costs, b. The higher money-conversion costs the greater will be the demand for money. Moreover, if transactions costs were zero, there would be no transactions demand for money. Second, the transactions demand for money depends inversely upon the rate of interest. This will increase the sensitivity of the demand for money to the rate of interest, making the LM curve more interest elastic. Third, whereas Keynes' demand for transactions balances was strictly proportional to income, Baumol's model implies possible economies of scale in money-holding by giving a non-proportional relationship between cash balances and income.

The speculative demand for money

The principal difference between Keynes' theory of the demand for money and the Classics' was Keynes' speculative demand for money. Keynes argued that individuals would hold money not only for transactions purposes, but also as a way of avoiding expected capital losses. Thus individuals would be inclined to speculate about bond price movements. If individuals perceived that bond prices would rise in the future they would hold bonds in order to make a capital gain. On the other hand, if the individuals believed that bond prices would fall they would hold cash, so as to avoid the prospect of capital losses. If it is assumed that there is no set date for the redemption of the bond and the interest quoted in the market on such a bond is simply the ratio of the annual coupon to the price of the bond (p_b), then setting the coupon to unity for simplicity gives the rate of interest, i, as $i = 1/p_b$. The total expected gain from holding such a bond for a period (such as a year) is:

$$R = i + g = \frac{1}{p_b} + \frac{p_b^e - p_b}{p_b} = \frac{1 + p_b^e - p_b}{p_b} \tag{11.8}$$

where p_b^e is the bond price expected at the end of the period and $(p_b^e - p_b)$ is the anticipated gain. Thus the total return, R, comprises of the yield $i = 1/p_b$ and the capital gain, g, which is the expected change in the price of the bond as a proportion of the initial price. The investor will compare this gain from holding a bond to the gain from holding money over the same period. The gain from money is zero, since there is neither a capital gain nor interest yield. So the speculator, who is assumed to expect the rate of interest with certainty, will simply buy bonds (and run down money balances) if $R > 0$, or sell bonds (and increase his money holdings) if $R < 0$.

Recalling the relationship between the price of the bond and the rate of interest, the speculator will be indifferent between bonds and money when $R = 0$, that is when:

$$R = \frac{1 + (1/i^e) - (1/i)}{1/i} = 0 \tag{11.9}$$

Multiplying both sides by $1/i$, replacing 1 by i^e/i^e, and simplifying yields:

$$i = \frac{i^e}{1 + i^e} = i^c \tag{11.10}$$

This equation says that the value of the rate of interest at which the prospective gains from holding bonds are zero is something less than the value of the expected rate of interest itself. This particular rate of interest is called the critical rate of interest, i^c, and denotes the point at which the individual's portfolio is switched from bonds to money. If the current rate of interest is below the critical rate the speculator will wish to hold all of the portfolio in money whereas if the rate of interest is above the critical rate the speculator will hold all his wealth in bonds.

Figure 11.2 shows the individual's speculative demand for money as a right-angled schedule, kinked at the level of i^c, given by the line Bi^cB'. The argument is that for any rate of interest that is below the current expected rate, capital losses are in prospect, since interest rates are expected to rise back to i^e and bond prices move inversely with the interest rate. At a current rate that is at the critical level, however, the prospect of the bond coupon is just enough to offset this capital loss. At a current rate above the critical level, but below the expected rate, capital losses are in prospect but are less than the coupon, while for values of the rate of interest that are currently higher than the expected rate, capital gains are in prospect. On this basis a rate of interest below the critical

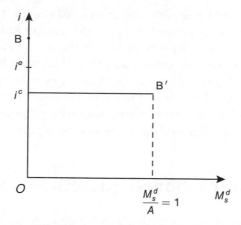

Figure 11.2 *Individual's speculative demand for money*

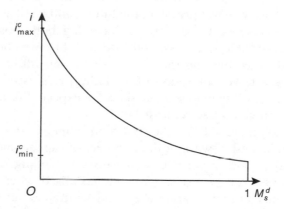

Figure 11.3 *Aggregate speculative demand for money*

rate implies capital losses that outweigh the coupon and indicate a negative gain from bonds; above the critical rate the prospect of a net gain is positive.

If all the individuals in the economy were to have close agreement as to the expected rate of interest, then small movements in the rate of interest around the critical value would precipitate a movement of funds into or out of bonds (and money). This would imply a step-like aggregate demand for money function very much like that in **Figure 11.2**. Correspondingly, the movement would be more gradual if speculators differ greatly in their views of the expected rate of interest. In this case as the current rate fell (rose) only a proportion of all investors would find that it had fallen (risen) below (above) their individual critical rates and the consequent shift from bonds to money (money to bonds) would be limited to the portfolio shifts of the investors affected. Therefore the aggregate demand for money would resemble the downward-sloping function in **Figure 11.3**. At this stage the source of market expectations about the rate of interest are unimportant. One reasonable hypothesis is that these expectations are greatly influenced by recent and current values, and thus it is unlikely that investors will continue to entertain for very long the expectation that the interest rate should be much different from what it is and has recently been. In this case the speculative demand for money is likely to be only a short-run phenomenon, as a change in the rate of interest may indicate large-scale switching between money and bonds.

The precautionary (asset) demand for money

In Keynes' model of the speculative demand for money, individuals are certain in their own minds as to the rate of interest they expect to prevail in the future and consequently hold their entire wealth in either money or bonds. By holding either bonds or money these individuals are speculating on interest rate movements. In the real world, however, most individuals are not certain as to what interest rate will prevail in the future, and if risk-averse they will tend to maintain a diversified asset portfolio including both bonds and money. Tobin (1958) showed that risk-averse individuals hold diversified portfolios and therefore the individual demand for money as an asset will be inversely related to the rate of interest. The allocation of an individual's asset portfolio between money and bonds will therefore depend on the expected returns on bonds and the riskiness attached to these returns.

Tobin argued that the return on money is zero, so $R_m = 0$, but that it is also a riskless asset, without the prospect of capital gain or loss. The return on bonds can be either positive or negative depending on expected bond price movements. Returns are potentially maximised when all of the portfolio is held in bonds, but this is also the most risky strategy since bond prices may not move as expected. The probability of capital gains is assumed to follow a normal distribution which is uniquely characterised by its mean and standard deviation. Thus the mean is the average return and the standard deviation is a measure of the riskiness of the mean return. The total return on an investor's portfolio is given as $R = i + g$, where i is the interest yield and g is the capital gain. If the individual invests B pounds in bonds then the expected (mean) return on the whole portfolio is R given as:

$$\overline{R} = B(i+g) \tag{11.11}$$

Similarly if the standard deviation of return on a bond is σ_b and all bonds are alike then the standard deviation or risk of the total portfolio is given by:

$$\sigma_T = B\sigma_b \tag{11.12}$$

This positive relationship between the riskiness of the total portfolio and the proportion of the portfolio held in bonds is shown in the lower panel of **Figure 11.4**.

Risk is maximised when the whole portfolio is held in bonds, as at one, and zero when the whole portfolio is held in money.

The individual now has to choose how much of the portfolio to invest in bonds, given that he wishes to maximise the return on the portfolio but also to minimise the risk. Substituting for B in (11.11) using (11.12) and rearranging gives:

$$\bar{R} = \frac{\sigma_T}{\sigma_b}(i + \bar{g})$$

(11.13)

In this formula the rate of interest is known, determined in the bond market. The investor also implicitly knows, $\bar{g}$ the mean capital gain, and the standard deviation of g, σ_b, from the probability distribution of returns. Thus the expression in equation (11.13) can be regarded as known. Differentiating (11.13) gives:

$$\frac{\partial \bar{R}}{\partial \sigma_T} = \frac{i + \bar{g}}{\sigma_b} > 0$$

(11.14)

which shows the trade-off between risk and return, faced by the individual investor. This is illustrated in the upper panel of **Figure 11.4**, by the line $0L$. $0L$ is the

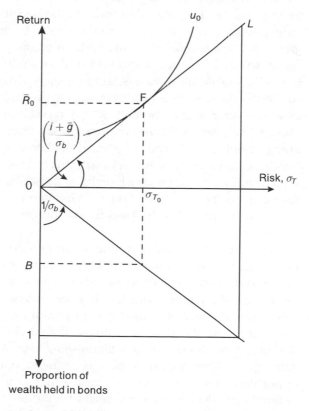

Figure 11.4 *The asset demand for money*

opportunity locus between risk and return, which has a slope given by equation (11.14) above. Hence a rise in the rate of interest (or in the mean capital gain) makes the slope steeper, causing the $0L$ line to swivel upwards, while an increase in the riskiness of bonds causes the line to swivel downwards. When all the portfolio is held in money there is no risk, but also no return: thus the model is at the origin. As the share of the portfolio held in bonds increases so the risk rises, as does the return. At 1, in the lower part of the figure, for example, the whole portfolio is held in bonds. How far the vertical axis extends beyond the horizontal axis depends on the total level of wealth. In order to locate the individual's optimal combination between risk and return the individual's indifference map needs to be added to the diagram.

Since risk-averse individuals dislike risk and like returns, individual utility, U, depends positively upon returns and negatively on risk; that is: $U=U(\bar{R},\sigma_T)$ $U_{\bar{R}}>0$, $U\sigma_T<0$ where the subscripts denote the partial derivatives of the utility-function. In the case of a risk-averse individual the in difference curves will have positive slopes, indicating that the individual demands higher expected returns in order to be willing to take on more risk. The point of tangency between the highest indifference line and the opportunity locus gives the individual's optimal combination of bonds and money for given levels of interest rates, risk and wealth. In **Figure 11.4** the individual is a diversifier. As risk increases by equal increments the diversifier demands increasing increments of return, so that the indifference curves are convex to the origin. In this case the expected return is given as R_0, with risk of σ_{T_0} and with $0B$ of the portfolio in bonds and $1-B$ of the portfolio in money. **Figure 11.5** shows different kind of preferences that individuals might hold. Panels (a) to (c) show risk-averse individuals, while panel (d) shows the case of a risk-lover, who is prepared to take on more risk even if expected returns are lower. Panel (a) reproduces the diversified individual of **Figure 11.4**. Panels (b) and (c) illustrate another class of risk-averter: a plunger. Plungers hold non-diversified portfolios, choosing to hold either all money or all bonds, as in panels (b) and (c) respectively. Since the world is characterised by diversification, it can be concluded that most asset holders are diversifiers. Thus the situation shown in panel (a), with indifference curves representing increasing risk aversion, provides the basis for the portfolio balance model of the demand for money.

The aggregate demand for money can be derived by examining the effects of increasing the rate of interest. In **Figure 11.6**, as the rate of interest rises from i_1 to i_2 and then to i_3, the $0L$ locus swivels upwards from $0L_1$ to $0L_2$ and to $0L_3$, giving points of tangency with indifference curves at points F, G and H. The line connecting points F, G and H is the optimum portfolio curve. With each rise in the interest rate the amount of the portfolio held in bonds increases, as does the risk of the portfolio, but at a diminishing rate. An increase in expected capital gains, g, will have the same effect as an increase in the interest rate, rotating the opportunity locus up and increasing the amount of financial wealth held in bonds and decreasing the demand for money. On the other hand, an increase in uncertainty would increase the riskiness of bond holdings. This increase in

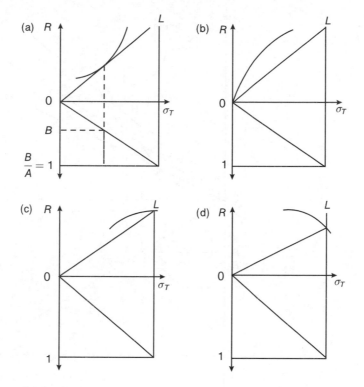

Figure 11.5 *Individual preferences*

uncertainty would rotate the opportunity locus in the upper part of the figure downwards, while rotating the line in the lower part upwards. Thus bond holdings fall on two counts: first, the riskiness of each bond is higher, as σ_b rises, but secondly the total desired risk, σ_T also rises.

In aggregate, however, Keynes' and Tobin's demand for money functions look similar, as in **Figure 11.7**. Keynes assumed that investors would all have different assessments of the expected rate of interest and so, although individuals hold non-diversified portfolios, in aggregate for any given level of the rate of interest some individuals will be holding bonds and some money to give an aggregate diversified portfolio. In Tobin's approach to the demand for money all risk-averse individuals hold diversified port-folios and so in aggregate there is an inverse relationship between the rate of interest and the asset demand for money. In these models a rise in the rate of interest means that individuals become less liquid and lower the aggregate demand for money, while simultaneously raising the demand for bonds.

Friedman's restatement of quantity theory

Friedman (1956) does not distinguish between the transactions, speculative and precautionary motives for holding cash. Instead, the demand for money is treated

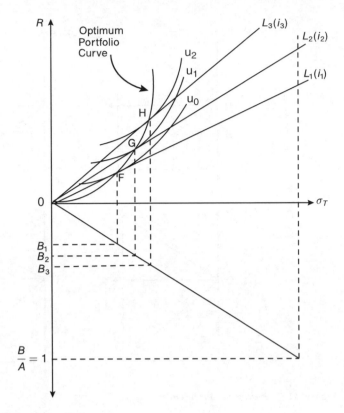

Figure 11.6   *Optimum portfolio curve*

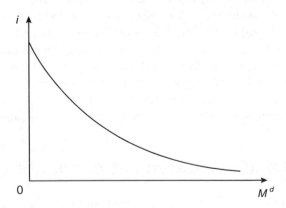

Figure 11.7   *The aggregate precautionary demands for money*

in exactly the same way as the demand for any other good or service. Money is assumed to yield utility to the holder, on account of its convenience as a medium of exchange in which function it incurs no transactions costs. Like other real demands for goods and services it varies inversely with its own price and the price of substitutes, and directly on income, tastes and the prices of complemen-tary assets.

To be more explicit, Friedman writes the demand for real money balances as:

$$\frac{M^d}{P} = k(Y, i_b, i_E, i_m, \hat{P}^e, t, h) \tag{11.15}$$

where i_E is the expected return on equity, i_b is the expected return on bonds, i_m is the expected return on money, $\hat{P}^e$ is the expected rate of inflation, which denotes the expected return on commodities, t is tastes and h is wealth, measured as the ratio of human to non-human wealth. The demand for money balances is assumed to depend directly upon income, the rate of return on money and tastes and negatively upon the returns on other assets and commodities. To simplify this model some of these rates of return can be omitted from the analysis. For example, the return on money, i_m, can be assumed to be zero. The return on bonds, i_b, can be assumed to serve as a proxy for the yield on bonds, equities and bank deposits that yield interest. Capital gains on bonds and equities are assumed to be proportional to the rate of inflation, which also provides the implicit yield on consumer durables. As prices rise the purchasing power of money falls, but the value of durable goods remain roughly constant, as durable goods prices rise in line with inflation. Hence an increase in expected inflation should lead to a shift out of money into consumer goods. Since the expected inflation rate raises the gain on equities there is also likely to be a movement into equities, although the relationship is complicated. Furthermore, the terms in tastes and the ratio of human to non-human wealth, can also be excluded on practical grounds as they are impossible to measure, and if it is assumed that expected and actual inflation are equal then the money demand function can be written as:

$$\frac{M^d}{P} = k(Y, i_b, \hat{P}), \quad k_Y > 0, \ k_{i_b} < 0 \ \ k_{\hat{p}} < 0 \tag{11.16}$$

Friedman further assumes that the demand for real money balances are homogenous of degree one in Y, which means (11.16) can be written as:

$$\frac{M^d}{P} = k(i_b, \hat{P})Y \tag{11.17}$$

In this form it is clear that Friedman's demand for money is a restatement of the quantity theory, in that $k(\cdot)$ is the reciprocal of the Classical concept of velocity of circulation, V. To see this note:

$$MV = PY \text{ therefore } \frac{M}{P} = \frac{1}{V}Y \text{ and hence } k(i_b, \hat{P}) = \frac{1}{V} \tag{11.18}$$

Velocity therefore increases with the rate of interest on bonds and the rate of inflation, as individuals attempt to economise on their holdings of depreciating cash balances.

The principal difference, therefore, between Friedman's demand for money and the Keynesian theories is the inclusion of the rate of inflation as a determinant of money demand. In terms of the primarily static model developed here, adding inflation to the demand for money function will not greatly affect the qualitative nature of the static model unless large variations in inflation are expected. There are, however, empirical implications that have received extensive treatment by economists.

Empirical evidence on the demand for money

There is a huge empirical literature on the demand for money. The interested reader would be well advised to refer to Laidler (1994) or Artis and Lewis (1991) for a more complete discussion of the empirical issues than can be given here. In this section little attempt is made to provide a comprehensive review of the empirical results, but rather to review some of the contentious issues and problems that arise when estimating an aggregate demand for money function together with a small sample of empirical results. There are perhaps three methodological issues that require discussing before considering any econometric results: the definition of money, the variables to be included in the demand for money function and the method used to model the dynamic adjustment process.

The definition of money is by no means clear-cut in modern economies, with a variety of assets having medium-of-exchange and store-of-value capacities. The narrowest definition of money is M0, which includes cash held by the non-bank private sector (nbps) plus banker's balances at the Bank of England. The M1 definition of money also includes nbps current account balances. The broader definitions of money also include deposit accounts and building society accounts. Studies of the demand for money are therefore divided between the 'narrow' and the 'broad' money studies. Moreover, the theoretical formulations of the demand for money give very little guidance on this question with the transactions models having in mind a narrow definition whereas the portfolio balance approach implies that a broader definition is appropriate. In the absence of any clear guidance as to what measure is appropriate, Friedman's advice to use whatever definition of money performs best is frequently employed.

The second conceptual problem is that of what variables to include in the aggregate demand for money function. The existence of both transactions and asset theories of the demand for money means that it is not obvious whether income or wealth should be the scale variable in the function. Until recently the absence of data on wealth meant that income predominated as the scale variable, although in some cases a measure of permanent income has been used, the lack of a reliable means of estimating this concept makes the concept redundant. The portfolio approaches to the money demand emphasise that wealth-holders have a choice between holding money and a variety of financial and real assets such as bills, bonds, equities and commodities. In an open economy foreigners may also hold domestic currency in the form of bank deposits and other short-term paper, while domestic residents hold foreign securities and other foreign currency claims, so that interest rates on foreign securities also influence the demand for money. In most instances, however, the selection of one representative rate of interest, such as the yield on long or short-term securities, has proved to be adequate. So far as long rates are concerned government bond yields are most commonly used, while money market rates such as local authority rates (UK) and the commercial paper rate (US) are popular because they vary more during periods of monetarydisturbances.

The impact of inflationary expectations upon the demand for money has not been resolved theoretically. Friedman (1956) has money substituting for both securities and real assets, so that both nominal interest rates and the anticipated inflation rate enter the demand for money equation. On the other hand the theoretical Keynesian position views the margin of substitution, given financial wealth, between money and bonds. In practice it seems that inflation expectations are incorporated into nominal interest rates, so that the cost of holding money relative to securities is the real rate of interest plus the expected fall in the purchasing power of money. Therefore the impact of expected inflation is taken up by the nominal rate of interest, and hence the rate of inflation is omitted in most empirical work. Though most of the early empirical studies of the demand for money omitted the rate of return on money, i_m, more recent studies have tended to include this variable as deregulation, financial innovation and the advent of high inflation and high interest rates have made it more explicit. Since the cost of holding money depends on the difference between i and i_m, the use of i alone is based on the assumption that the own rate on money adjusts only sluggishly, if at all, to market forces. Although such an assumption was plausible in the context of the UK banks' interest rate cartel prior to 1971, it is less easily justified today.

The third conceptual problem with estimating the demand for money is that of specifying the short-run dynamics so that the problem of short-run instability can be investigated. The most common solution to the dynamic problem has been to augment the long-run demand for money function with a partial adjustment hypothesis. With all variables transformed into logarithms (denoted by lower case letters for M, P and Y) the long-run function can be written as:

$$(m_t - p_t)^* = a + by_t - ci_t + u_t \tag{11.19}$$

where u_t is a random error term. Some studies employ a real balance adjustment hypothesis (Chow, 1966; Laidler and Parkin, 1970; Goldfeld, 1973), which is written as:

$$(m_t - p_t) - (m_{t-1} - p_{t-1}) = \theta[(m_t - p_t)^* - (m_{t-1} - p_{t-1})] \tag{11.20}$$

which says that the actual demand for real money balances adjusts at a rate of θ, to the new desired level, where $0 < \theta < 1$. Substituting the equilibrium equation (11.19) into the lower adjustment equation (11.20) gives:

$$(m_t - p_t) = a\theta + b\theta y_t - c\theta i_t + (1 - \theta)(m_{t-1} - p_{t-1}) + \theta u_t \qquad (11.21)$$

which shows that if actual real money balances are not at their desired level their movement is always towards it. This specification suffers from two problems. First, this representation shows that the speed of adjustment affects all variables in an identical fashion, with each long-run coefficient multiplied by the speed of adjustment, θ. Second, there is an asymmetry in the adjustment of nominal money balances since individual prices, interest rates and income should be taken as given in the short run, with nominal balances providing the buffer. The specification (11.21) above, however, carries the implication that nominal money balances adjust fully and instantaneously to prices, while responding only partially to movements in all other variables. For this reason other studies (Goodhart and Crockett, 1970; Goldfeld, 1976) accordingly preferred the nominal adjustment hypothesis, which can be written as:

$$m_t - m_{t-1} = \theta(m_t^* - m_{t-1}) \qquad (11.22)$$

which when combined with the long-run equation gives:

$$m_t - p_t = a\theta + b\theta y_t - c\theta i_t + (1 - \theta)(m_{t-1} - p_t) + \theta u_t \qquad (11.23)$$

Equation (11.23) differs from (11.20) only by the penultimate term. In practice they are likely to perform similarly.

An alternative approach to modelling dynamics was suggested by Hendry and Mizon (1978), who suggested that an error correction model (ECM) was the most suitable way to capture dynamic behaviour. This approach can be illustrated by assuming that the long-run demand for money is homogenous in income and prices and independent of the rate of interest such that, $m_t = p_t + y_t$, but that the dynamics are given by changes in the other variables. The estimating equation is therefore:

$$\Delta m_t = a_0 + a_1 \Delta p_t + a_2 \Delta y_t - a_3 \Delta i_t + b(m - p - y)_{t-1} \qquad (11.24)$$

The a_i's are the short-run coefficients with b the coefficient on the error correction term, which shows the speed of adjustment back to equilibrium. In addition extra lags might be added to (11.24), but at each stage the coefficients are tested for significance, with insignificant coefficients dropped from the final model. The dynamics are therefore determined empirically by a process of trial and error. More recently, the co-integration approach to time series modelling has embodied the notion that short-run dynamics can be modelled separately from the long-run equilibrium. The difference with the co-integration approach is that the long run can be estimated independently of the short-run dynamics, whereas in the Hendry and Mizon method both short-run and long-run equations are estimated together. For examples of the co-integration approach to the demand for money see Hendry and Ericsson (1987) and Hall *et al.* (1989).

It is now time to move on to briefly consider some of the empirical findings. In terms of the long-run demand for money there seems to be a consensus that interest rates are significant, the income elasticity is about unity and nominal money demand is homogenous in prices. These results apply to both the UK and the USA, although there are not insubstantial departures from the line of best fit in the war years and in the early 1970s in the UK, when Competition and Credit Control was in operation. In the USA, Friedman and Schwartz (1982) claimed to find similar results. While these long-run studies show some support for the theory of the aggregate demand for money, the short-run studies have been rather less successful.

Up until the mid-1970s studies of the short-run demand for money in the UK consistently yielded three results: (1) a general form of the demand for money function seemed capable of explaining the course of monetary behaviour in the UK (as in the USA); (2) the income elasticities of time deposits and savings bank deposits were found to be greater than unity, that of current deposits or M1 around or slightly less than unity, and that of broad money sometimes well over unity; (3) at least one interest rate had a significant effect on the demand for money, and in most cases the response was found to be inelastic and sometimes less than −0.5.

From the mid-1970s, however, it became clear that the formerly stable short-run demand for money function had broken down. There are several aspects to this breakdown. First, when existing studies from the 1950 and 1960s were used to forecast the demand for money into the 1970s large forecast errors appeared. For example, Hacche (1974) showed that the Bank of England's demand for money function seriously underpredicted actual monetary growth. Second, when existing models were re-estimated using data from the 1970s, the coefficient on the lagged dependent variable increased markedly showing that the nature of the adjustment process had changed. Third, in order to accommodate the additional data from the 1970s many studies found it necessary to add additional variables not previously thought to be important in explaining the demand for money. These extra variables included dummy variables to allow for policy and regulatory changes (Hacche, 1974) and gross wealth, which includes money (Grice and Bennett, 1984).

Attempts to explain the short-run instability of the demand for money function abound in the modern literature. Judd and Scadding (1982) note the fundamental importance of financial innovation in explaining the collapse of the US narrow money demand equation in the early 1970s. Such innovation is associated with automated cash machines, financial deregulation and the switch towards quantity controls. The abandonment of fixed exchange rates and the arrival of a period of volatile exchange rates, commodity price rises and activist economic policies seem likely to have led to expectations of higher inflation, so leading people to switch out of money balances thereby raising the velocity of circulation. If this is true the demand for money should increase in the late 1980s and early 1990s as inflation has subsided.

On the other hand, Brittain (1981) has argued that the instability of national demand for money functions is due to currency substitution, whereby changes in the non-resident demand for the home currency destabilises the domestic monetary aggregates. More recent tests (see Mizen and Pentecost, 1994; Milner, Mizen and Pentecost, 1996) suggest that this reason is not likely to be important in the advanced industrialised countries like the USA or northern Europe, but is potentially very significant in developing countries where hyper-inflation is a serious problem. This has, however, not prevented a number of studies (see for example Kremers and Lane, 1991) investigating the stability of the international demand for money, especially in the European context. These studies, however, still seem to suffer from the same instability as their national counterparts (see Barr, 1992 and Artis *et al.*, 1993). The continued instability of the short-run demand for money function can be interpreted as suggesting that to target any single monetary aggregate, like M4, is not a sound policy in the open economies of western Europe.

Conclusions

The alternative theories of the demand for money discussed in this chapter suggest that in the aggregate the demand for money should depend directly on the level of real income and inversely on the rate of interest. This relationship is confirmed by the empirical evidence, although other possible variables, such as inflation and the level of wealth, have not really been widely tested. The instability of the short-run demand for money is a particularly important result, since it warns against the use of monetary policy in influencing the macroeconomy through the demand for money. Thus the control of an intermediate target variable such as the growth of M4 is not a reliable indicator of the stance of monetary policy nor suitable as a policy tool.

This completes Part III of this book, where a fixed-price assumption has been in force throughout. In Part IV this stringent assumption is relaxed and a model of the supply side of the macroeconomy developed. This extension will lead to some of the results of this section being modified, although many will be found to be robust even in a more complex setting.

Summary

- The demand for money is a demand for real money balances which are held for transactions, precautionary and speculative purposes.
- There are a range of alternative measures of the money supply from M1, which is cash plus current accounts, to broad money (M4) which also includes deposit accounts and accounts with building societies as well as banks.

- The inventory theoretic approach shows that an individual's real money balances vary inversely with the rate of interest and directly with the level of income and the cost of transactions. According to this approach the income elasticity is expected to be about 0.5 which shows there are economics of scale in money-holding. The interest elasticity is also about 0.5.
- The asset demand for money indicates that the demand for money also varies inversely with the rate of interest and directly with the level of financial wealth. Money is held in the portfolio of assets, despite its low or zero yield, because it is less risky than other assets.
- The empirical evidence supports a positive income elasticity that is usually close to unity, and a negative interest elasticity of money demand, with the short-run elasticities in general smaller than the longer-run elasticities.
- Since the mid-1970s there have been questions about the stability of the aggregate demand for money function. This instability has been variously explained by: financial innovation, currency substitution or a change in the behaviour of the monetary authorities. Without a stable demand for money, however, monetary policy changes have an unpredictable effect on the real economy.

Suggested further reading

The origin of the transactions, precautionary and speculative motives for holding money is in Keynes (1936), Chapters 11–13. The most accessible account for students is Laidler (1993), which is a classic in this area, although students will also find Harris (1981) and Cuthbertson (1985) useful. The original work on the transactions motive is to be found in Baumol (1952) and Tobin (1956), and on the asset demand in Tobin (1958). Friedman (1956) is the source of the Restatement of the Quantity Theory and Friedman (1959) reports the first empirical tests of this hypothesis. A recent review of the empirical evidence is to be found in Artis and Lewis (1991), Laidler (1993) and Judd and Scadding (1982). The currency substitution hypothesis is reviewed in Pentecost (1997) in a European context, while the contributions of Kremers and Lane (1991) and Barr (1992) offer a European angle on the stability of the demand for money question.

Essay titles

1. 'In Keynes' analysis the individual is certain about what the future interest rate is going to be. In Tobin's analysis the individual is uncertain about future interest rates.' Explain and discuss.
2. Compare and contrast Tobin's risk-aversion theory of the demand for money with Friedman's restatement of the quantity theory of money as a demand for money.
3. Why did the stability of the demand for money function break down in the 1980s and to what extent is this an important problem for the operation of monetary policy?

Questions

1. Explain the concept of the opportunity cost of holding money.
2. The demand for nominal balances rises with the price level. At the same time, inflation causes the real demand to fall. Explain how both of these assertions can be correct.
3. Consider an individual who earns £2000 per month, who can earn 0.5% interest per month on a savings account and who faces a transactions cost of £1:
   (a) using Baumol's square root rule, compute the individuals' average monthly cash balance.
   (b) suppose the rate of interest falls to 0.02% per month. By how much does the individual's average cash balance fall?
4. Using Tobin's model of the asset demand for money, show the effect on the individual's demand for money of a fall in the rate of interest. Is your result theoretically unambiguous? If not, what assumptions do you need to make for this to be the case?
5. Consider the estimated demand for money function, based on the model of equation (11.21) of the text, where lower case letters denote the logarithms of the natural numbers with the exception of the interest rate:

$$m_t - p_t = -0.610 + 0.125y_t - 0.032i_t + 0.778(m_{t-1} - p_{t-1})$$

   (a) compute the value of the partial adjustment coefficient, θ;
   (b) noting that $b\theta = 0.125$ and $c\theta = -0.032$ using the result from (a), compute the structural parameters of the long-run demand for money function;
   (c) interpret the results from (b) in view of the expected theoretical sizes of the parameters.

PART IV
The *AD–AS* Framework

CHAPTER 12
The Classical Theory of the Labour Market and Aggregate Supply

Aims and objectives

- To present the neo-classical analysis of the aggregate labour market from its microeconomic foundations and to distinguish between the real consumption wage and the real product wage rate.
- To derive the neo-classical aggregate supply schedules for an open economy under alternative assumptions regarding the extent of global product market integration.
- To consider the characteristics and types of voluntary unemployment and the concept of the natural rate of unemployment.

Introduction

In Parts II and III the demand side of the economy was studied in some detail, based on the assumption that the aggregate price level, P, could be treated as exogenously determined. Thus the aggregate demand curve derived in Chapter 9 is drawn for various values of P. The task in this part of the text is to develop a model of the supply side of the macroeconomy and to integrate this with the demand side. This is more difficult than it may at first seem because this is an area of very great controversy, and hence there is far less agreement about the supply side than there is about the demand side. This partly stems from the fact that in Keynes' *General Theory of Employment, Interest and Money* the supply side of the book is not fully consistent with the demand side of the model. Secondly, it stems from the fact that unemployment and the flexibility of wage rates are highly contentious political, as well as economic, issues. The question as to the nature of unemployment is an important theme of this part of the book, although the empirical analysis of unemployment in the UK and continental Europe is left until Chapter 15.

In this chapter the microeconomic foundations of a competitive aggregate labour market are explored and an aggregate supply function for an open economy derived. In Chapter 13 Keynes' and the Keynesian aggregate supply functions are derived and contrasted with the classical models of this chapter. Chapter 13 concludes with a discussion of supply shocks and their impact on the aggregate supply function. In Chapter 14 the *AD–AS* model of the macroeconomy will be developed to show the short-run effects of policy changes on prices, output, employment, wages and exchange rates. Finally in Chapter 15 a more detailed look at the microeconomic foundations of labour markets under imperfect competition is considered together with the limitations of the simple model developed in this chapter, in an attempt to explain the persistently high level of European unemployment since the mid-1970s.

The labour market, like all other markets, has both a demand side and a supply side. In this chapter we first develop the theory of the aggregate demand for labour and then briefly develop the aggregate supply of labour. This is followed by an examination of the aggregate labour market under perfectly competitive conditions, and finally, the aggregate labour market demand and supply curves are combined with an aggregate production function to derive a classical (or equilibrium) aggregate supply function.

The demand for labour

The demand for labour is a derived demand. That is to say, firms do not demand labour for its own sake, but for what it is able to produce for sale in conjunction with other factors of production, such as capital. It follows, therefore, that firms will only demand labour if it is profitable for them to do so. It will be profitable to employ more labour only if the marginal revenue earned from the sale of the extra output exceeds the marginal cost of producing that output. Hence the demand for labour, for the individual firm operating in competitive markets, is based on the notion of profit maximisation. Profit maximisation implies that additional labour will be demanded until the marginal cost of labour (the wage rate) just equals the marginal revenue of labour obtained from the sale of the extra output produced by the marginal worker.

To understand the decisions being taken by the firm it is necessary to understand the underlying determinants of the firm's marginal revenue and marginal cost functions. This will depend in part on the state of technology and the nature of the production function. **Figure 12.1** shows the production function, which describes real output, Y, as a function of labour input, N, and the capital stock, K. The capital stock is fixed at $\bar{K}$, which implies that this model of the labour market is strictly a model of the short run. Other inputs are held constant or vary in direct proportion to labour in the short run. The shape of the production function, $Y = Y(N, \bar{K})$, shows Y increasing with labour input, so that $\partial Y/\partial N = Y_N(N, \bar{K}) > 0$. Initially output increases at an increasing rate with the first additions of labour to the capital stock, shown over the range $0N_1$ in **Figure 12.1**. Beyond the level of employment given by N_1, however, Y begins to increase at a decreasing rate, exhibiting diminishing marginal returns as the fixed capital stock is shared among more and more workers.

The lower panel of **Figure 12.1** shows the relationship between the production function shown in the top panel and the average and marginal products of labour. The average product of labour (*APN*), defined as output per head, *Y/N*, is represented by the slope of a line from the origin to any point on the production function. It can be seen that as employment rises the average product of labour first increases, up to N_2 and then decreases, beyond N_2. Thus the *APN* line in the lower panel has an inverted U-shape. The second line in the lower panel of **Figure 12.1** is the marginal product of labour (*MPN*) schedule, which represents the additional output produced by the last worker employed, and is derived from the slope of the production function. The slope of the production function can be represented by the slope of a straight line drawn tangent to the production function. Thus from **Figure 12.1** the slope is initially rising, peaking at N_1 the point of inflexion where the production function changes from convex to concave, and then falling beyond N_1. It is notable that the *MPN* line cuts the *APN* line at the point of maximum *APN*, and that the *MPN* is zero at N_3, when the production function becomes flat (and so has a zero slope). Beyond N_1 the marginal

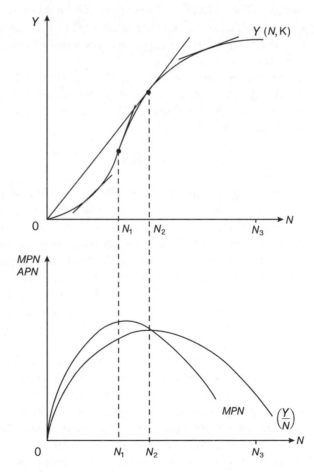

Figure 12.1 *The production function*

product of labour therefore falls with N, that is $\partial^2 Y/\partial N^2 = Y_{NN}(N, \overline{K}) < 0$, and the *MPN* schedule exhibits a diminishing marginal product of labour.

With this information a firm's labour demand decision can be examined. The employment of one more worker will lead output to rise by the *MPN*. If this addition to total output is sold in a competitive market, such that the price it sells for is the same as that for all previous units, then the marginal revenue received by the firm is the price of the firm's output, P, multiplied by the marginal product of labour (*MPN*). The product of the price and *MPN*, $P \times MPN$, is called the marginal revenue product of labour (*MRP*). Thus the profit-maximising condition whereby the marginal cost of the extra worker is the money wage, W, equals the marginal revenue product of labour is given as:

$$W = P \times MPN \quad \text{or} \quad \frac{W}{P} = MPN \tag{12.1}$$

This says that the competitive firm will employ labour up to the point where the real wage is equal to the *MPN*. Since, as **Figure 12.1** shows, the *MPN* falls as N increases, beyond N_1, the firm's demand for labour is inversely related to the real wage rate. Since the price deflator used in this calculation of the real wage rate is the price of the firm's output, this measure of the real wage rate is often referred to as the real *product* wage.

In the aggregate it is assumed that the demand for labour is the horizontal sum of all individual firms' labour demand curves, which gives the downward-sloped function depicted in **Figure 12.2.** The aggregate demand for labour function is therefore denoted as:

$$\frac{W}{P} = \phi(N) \quad \text{or} \quad W = P.\phi(N) \tag{12.1'}$$

where $\phi(N)$ denotes the economy-wide *MPN* schedule. Because the marginal product schedule falls as N increases, $\phi_N(N) < 0$, and the real product wage is inversely related to the aggregate demand for labour. **Figure 12.2** plots the relationship between the real product wage rate and the marginal product of labour in the upper panel and the similarly inverse relationship, between the money wage and the aggregate marginal revenue product, in the lower panel. Both parts of this diagram convey identical information, although occasionally both frames will be used. To understand the way the labour market works it is vital to appreciate the difference between the money wage rate, W, and the real (product) wage rate, $W/P = w$.

There are two other important things to note about the aggregate demand for labour. First, its negative slope is due to diminishing marginal productivity of labour as more labour is applied to a given capital stock. Thus in a perfectly competitive world with a fixed output mix, the demand for labour curve $\phi(N)$ is the aggregate *MPN*. Second, since profit-maximising firms are interested in the real wage they pay, that is the price of labour input relative to the price of output, the price level enters the money wage version of the demand for labour function multiplicatively. The importance of this point will become clearer later on.

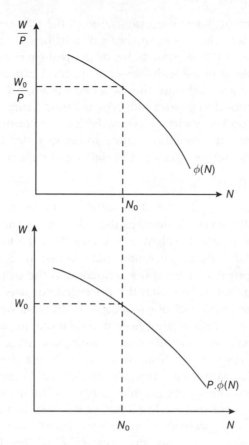

Figure 12.2 *The aggregate demand for labour*

The supply of labour

The individual supplier of labour is assumed to supply labour in direct proportion to the real (consumption) wage. The problem with even this simplistic definition is that the definition of the real (consumption) wage is by no means unambiguous to the worker.

First, although the worker will have full information about the nominal or money wage, he or she will only be able to guess as to the real wage. This is because they may not know in advance exactly what products they will need to purchase with their money wages, and second, even if they did, they would not know the exact prices of these goods in advance. Suppose that the individual is an average consumer and buys the same basket of goods as included in the consumer price index (CPI). The worker can then use the CPI, which includes the prices of imported products in addition to domestically produced goods and services, to deflate his or her money wage. It is, however, not possible for the worker to know the exact value of the CPI over the length of the nominal wage contract. Hence the worker will only be able to guess the expected future value of the CPI, and estimate his or her real wage rate. In order to keep the analysis as simple as possible, however, price-level expectations are disregarded in this part of the text, although they will become important in Part V when dynamic models are considered more fully. For the time being, it is assumed that workers act as if they do know with certainty the level of consumer prices over the next year.

Since the consumer price index includes both home and foreign produced goods and services, the CPI deflator is defined as:

$$P_c = (1 - \rho)P + \rho EP^* \tag{12.2}$$

where $(1 - \rho)$ is the share of domestic output in the consumers' consumption bundle, so that ρ denotes the share of expenditure on imported goods, where E is the nominal exchange rate and P^* is the foreign price level. Thus a depreciation of domestic currency, that is a rise in E, will lead to an increase in the consumer price index and a reduction in the worker's real consumption wage. It is important to note that the price deflator used by the worker, when deciding on the amount of labour to supply, is different from the price level used by the producer in determining how much labour to employ. These two real wages rates are referred to as the real consumption wage, W/P_c, and the real product wage, W/P, respectively. Note, however, that in a closed economy the real product and the real consumption wage are identical because $\rho = 0$ and so from (12.2) $P = P_c$.

Individual workers, like other economic agents, have preferences and face budget constraints. In particular it is assumed that workers prefer more leisure, L and more income, y, where the lower case y denotes individual real income. Therefore each worker faces a utility function, given as $U = U(L, y)$, where $U_L(L, y) > 0$ and $U_y(L, y) > 0$, so that utility is increasing in both leisure and income. The individual suppliers of labour then attempt to maximise their utility subject to a constraint. The constraint each worker faces is that the total hours available for work are limited, given the need for rest. So the constraint is written as:

$$y = (H - L)\frac{W}{P_c} \tag{12.3}$$

where H is the total hours available to the worker and L is the number of leisure hours taken (including sleep). The solution to the utility maximisation problem is given in **Figure 12.3.** When individuals spend all their hours on leisure $H = L$ and income earned is zero. This is given by point H in the figure, which since this corresponds to zero income assumes that the individual has no unearned income and that there are no unemployment benefits. On the other hand, if workers spend all their time working, earned income becomes the real wage multiplied by H, since $L = 0$, which is denoted by point A in **Figure 12.3.** The locus AH denotes the constraint that has a slope of $\partial y / \partial L = -(W/P_c)$.

From the properties of the utility function the indifference curves will be convex to the origin, since individual workers will only forgo income if they can have more leisure. Thus U_0 and U_1 denote indifference curves, along which workers

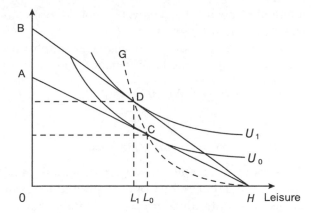

Figure 12.3 *Individuals' labour supply*

enjoy a constant level of utility. At point C the indifference curve U_0 is tangential to the budget constraint, indicating that when the real wage rate is W_0/P_c the workers take $0L_0$ hours leisure and supply $(H-L_0)$ hours of work. A rise in the real wage to W_1/P_c, causes the budget line to swivel, so that the maximum level of income the individual can now earn is given by point B. Point D is the new point of tangency between the new income constraint and the indifference map. As drawn in **Figure 12.3**, the increase in the real wage initially reduces the amount of leisure taken by the individual, or conversely, increases the hours worked to $H-L_1$. By joining all points of tangency between the budget lines and indifference curves for various real wage rates with H held constant, the dotted labour supply curve for the individual is given by *HG*. The individuals' labour supply curve may seem to be negatively, rather than positively sloped, in **Figure 12.3**, but because leisure is plotted on the horizontal axis, rather than hours worked, this curve will have a positive slope when plotted in wage–work space.

The individual labour supply curve slopes up because it has been assumed that the substitution effect of a wage rise outweighs the income effect. The substitution effect in this case is the extra hours of work supplied by the individual in response to the wage rise. In other words, because the wage rise increases the opportunity cost of leisure, the individual substitutes work for leisure. The income effect, on the other hand, tends to reduce the labour supplied, since with a higher wage rate an individual can maintain the same level of income while working fewer hours. The assumption that the substitution effect dominates the income effect may not be valid for all occupations. This is most likely to be in occupations where wage rates are relatively high, which implies that in some industries or parts of the labour market the labour supply curve may be backward-bending.[1] If, however, it is assumed that the labour force is homogenous and faces a single wage rate, then all the individual labour supply curves can be

---

[1] In fact the empirical evidence suggests that the labour supply for males is backward-bending at high wage rates, but that for female workers is not.

summed to obtain the aggregate labour supply function for the entire economy. This is shown in **Figure 12.4**.

For a given value of P_c the aggregate supply curve of labour shown in **Figure 12.4** can be represented mathematically as:

$$\frac{W}{P_c} = \omega(N), \quad \omega_N(N) > 0 \tag{12.4}$$

or

$$W = P_c \omega(N) = [(1-\rho)P + \rho EP^*]\omega(N) \tag{12.4'}$$

The symbol, ω denotes the aggregate supply of labour function and represents workers' preferences for work as opposed to leisure. **Figure 12.4** again has two panels. The only difference is, as before, that the top panel is drawn in real wage–employment space whereas the lower panel is in money wage–employment space. Note that in the upper panel to make the vertical axis consistent with that of the demand for labour schedules in **Figure 12.2**, both sides of the money wage equation have been multiplied by the ratio of the consumption price index to the price of domestic output. Thus equation (12.4) becomes:

$$\frac{W}{P_c}\frac{P_c}{P} = \frac{W}{P} = \frac{P_c}{P}\omega(N) \tag{12.5}$$

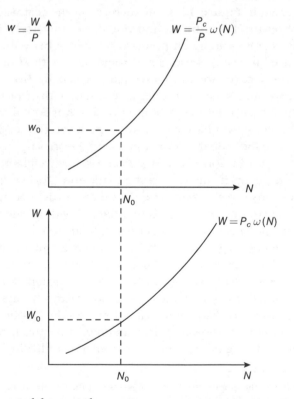

Figure 12.4 *Aggregate labour supply*

This operation allows the real product wage to be measured on the vertical axis of **Figure 12.4**, for both labour demand and supply curves. Because the aggregate labour supply function depends on the relative price of consumer goods to domestic output, unless these price indices move in the same proportion, labour supply conditions will change. For example, a devaluation of the exchange rate, which leads to a rise in P_c, will result in an upward shift of the labour supply function since a higher real product wage rate will be required to maintain the purchasing power of the money (consumption) wage.

Labour market equilibrium

Now that both the demand and supply functions of labour have been derived, labour market equilibrium can be examined. Equilibrium occurs where the planned demand for labour is exactly equal to the planned supply. This is at point A in **Figure 12.5**. Note that again both real wage and money wage panels have been drawn. At point A the labour market clears, but this does not imply that there is zero unemployment. To see this, note that if all workers are in employment then the supply of labour curve would become vertical, since no matter how high real wages were pushed up, there could be no increase in employment because all workers are already employed. In **Figure 12.5** this level of full employment is given at N_F. The distance $N_F - N_0$ therefore denotes the level of *voluntary* unemployment.

The level of voluntary unemployment expressed as a percentage of the total workforce, is usually referred to as the *natural rate of unemployment*, which in this context is the rate of unemployment that is consistent with aggregate labour market clearing. This natural rate of unemployment is regarded as voluntary because there are sufficient vacancies at the going real wage for the unemployed to secure jobs. These jobs remain unfilled either because these individuals have excessively high reservation wages below which they are not prepared to work, or because of labour market frictions whereby it takes time for workers to search for new jobs and for employers to hire new workers. Thus even when the aggregate labour market is in equilibrium there is always some (voluntary) unemployment and some vacancies.

The voluntary unemployment due to labour market frictions is frequently believed to consist of two specific kinds of unemployment, namely *frictional* unemployment and *structural* unemployment. Frictional unemployment is explained by the special characteristics of the labour market which distinguish it from most product or services markets. Most importantly it takes time to match workers to jobs. The equilibrium model of the aggregate labour market discussed above assumes that workers and all jobs are the same and therefore that each worker is equally well-suited to each job. If this were really true then frictional unemployment would be zero. In fact workers have different preferences and abilities and jobs have different characteristics. Moreover, the flow of information about employment opportunities is imperfect and the geographical mobility of

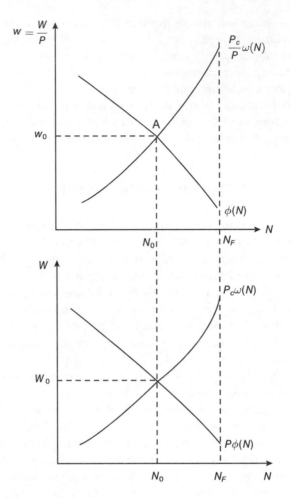

Figure 12.5 *The labour market*

workers is often low. Searching for a job takes both time and effort and because different jobs require different skills and pay different wage rates, unemployed workers may not accept the first job offer they receive. The unemployment caused by the time it takes workers to search for a job is called frictional unemployment.

Although job-search theory can explain frictional unemployment in individual labour markets which are in equilibrium, as structural changes occur in the economy some industries and some regions of the country may decline and some labour skill categories become redundant as others expand. This can lead to structural unemployment. This results from sectoral labour market disequilibria where there is excess labour supply in contracting sectors and excess labour demand in expanding sectors. Labour will move from declining sectors into expanding sectors, partly in response to wage differentials, but such adjustment takes time and may remain incomplete. Moreover, the displaced workers are likely to have different skills to those required by the new employment opportunities; they may also live in different locations to where the new job opportunities are to be found. Retraining takes time and some displaced workers may find it very difficult to be retrained. The mobility of workers will also be restricted by difficulties with re-housing or strong personal preferences for their current location. Technical change may also contribute to structural unemployment by altering the balance of demand and supply in specific product markets and by improving labour productivity.

Thus the natural rate of unemployment, or the level of unemployment consistent with aggregate labour market clearing, is voluntary in the sense that the number of job vacancies is equal to the number of workers seeking jobs. There is unemployment because of mismatch in the labour market and the slowness of adjustment of the labour market.

The classical (or equilibrium) view of aggregate supply

The classical aggregate supply curve is derived from the aggregate labour market and production function to give a direct relationship between output and the price-level, for a given state of technology, the work–leisure preferences of workers and import prices measured in domestic currency.

The aggregate supply curve is derived for the classical (or equilibrium) case in **Figure 12.6.** The upper panel shows the aggregate labour market, below which is the production function. In the lower panel is the aggregate supply schedule, denoted as AS. To derive the AS line begin from labour market equilibrium at point A, where the money wage is W_0, the level of employment is N_0 and the domestic price level is fixed at P_0. This point A translates via the production function to output level Y_0 and to point A' in the bottom right-hand panel. Next, assume that the price level rises from P_0 to P_1. In the upper panel the higher price level shifts the demand curve to the right, to $P_1\phi(N)$. The rise in the price level can be shown as the vertical distance AB, because the price level is combined multiplicatively with the marginal product of labour. On the supply side of the labour market, the higher price of domestic output translates into a higher consumer price index, so workers will perceive a fall in their real wages and so contract their labour supply to the market. Crucially, however, in an open economy context, the supply curve does not shift up as far as the demand curve because the domestic price level enters the consumer price level with a weight of $(1-\rho)$, which is strictly less than unity. Therefore, the supply of labour curve only shifts up to the left to $P_{c1}\omega(N)$. If, for example, the value of ρ was 0.3, then the supply curve shifts up by two-thirds of the distance between A and B, cutting the demand schedule at point C. At point C the real (product) wage is lower and the equilibrium level of employment is higher, as is the money wage rate, which results in a higher level of output being produced. Tracing the line round the

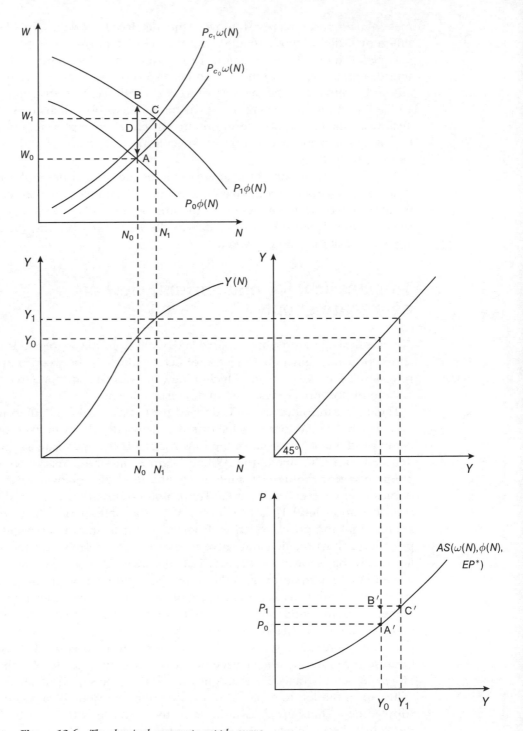

Figure 12.6 *The classical aggregate supply curve*

figure gives point C' in the lower quadrant, which must be a point on the *AS* curve. Hence the *AS* curve has a positive slope.

The reason behind this upward-sloping *AS* curve is that the real product wage has fallen, which encourages employers to demand more labour and to increase production, as marginal revenue has increased by more than marginal cost. The fact that the real product wage rate has fallen can be seen from the labour market diagram. The price level has risen by the distance AB, while the money wage has only risen by the distance AD. The money wage rate has only risen by AD, because the consumer price index has not risen by as much as the domestic output price index since import prices have been assumed constant. Thus in an open economy the classical supply curve is upward sloping if import prices and the exchange rate are constant. The real consumption wage is constant along this *AS* curve, although the real product wage falls, which is why the line has an upward slope. Along the classical (equilibrium) *AS* curve the labour market always clears, so that any changes in employment are entirely voluntary.

In fact the *AS* curve may be vertical in the open economy case if import prices measured in domestic currency change in exactly the same proportion as domestic prices. This is clear since if both elements of P_c rise by the same amount then P_c must also rise by the same amount. For example, if P rises by 5 per cent and EP^* rises by 5 per cent, then regardless of the degree of openness, denoted by the value of ρ, P_c will also rise by 5 per cent. In this case where P and EP^* change by the same amount, the real exchange rate, defined as EP^*/P, is constant. This is referred to as purchasing power parity (PPP). This will be the case, *inter alia*, if international goods markets are competitive, fully integrated and not subject to tariff barriers. The very strict conditions that are required for PPP to hold suggest that in practice it is likely to be invalid. It is therefore no surprise that the empirical evidence does not support this hypothesis in the short to medium run with the implication that the *AS* curve is likely to have an upward slope. In the long run, however, empirical support for PPP is stronger, albeit if not entirely convincing.[2] If this is assumed to be the case then the real exchange rate will be constant and the classical aggregate supply curve will be vertical at the level of output corresponding to the natural rate of unemployment. For short-run policy purposes, however, it is more appropriate to consider the *AS* curve as positively sloped.

In a closed economy, however, the *AS* curve will always be vertical. To understand this point set $\rho = 0$, so that there are no imported goods. In this case the consumer price index, P_c, will be identical to the domestic output price index, P, since there are, by assumption, no imports. In this case it is easy to see that the supply curve for labour will shift up to the same extent as the demand curve for labour. Hence the closed economy labour supply curve will shift up to pass through point B. At B the level of employment and output will be unchanged from N_0 and Y_0, although prices are higher at P_1. The point B therefore translates

---

[2] See Pilbeam (1998) for a non-technical review of the empirical evidence for PPP. Rogoff (1996) and Lothian (1997) offer more technical reviews.

Box 12.1   Technical derivation of the classical *AS* curves

Technically, labour market equilibrium generates the equilibrium wage rate and level of employment. Given a specific technology, incorporated in the production function, the market clearing level of employment can produce a specific amount of output. To see this consider the labour market equilibrium condition derived earlier (pp. 244ff and **Figure 12.5**):

$$W = P\phi(N) = P_c\omega(N) \tag{B12.1}$$

where $\phi(N)$, denotes the marginal product of labour and $\omega(N)$ is the function which captures the workers' choice between work and leisure. Therefore in the aggregate the marginal cost (W) equals the marginal revenue, $P\phi(N)$, which equals the value of the marginal utility derived from supplying effort. Totally differentiating this equilibrium condition, with $P = P_c = 1$ we get:

$$\partial P\phi(N) + \phi_N(N)\partial N = \partial P_c\omega(N) + \omega_N(N)\partial N \tag{B12.2}$$

where it will be recalled that $\partial P_c = \rho\partial P_m + (1 - \rho)\partial P$, which says that the change in consumer prices is a weighted average of the change in import prices and domestic output prices and where ρ denotes the degree of openness of the economy. Gathering terms this expression becomes:

$$\partial P[\phi(N) - (1 - \rho)\omega(N)] = \rho\partial P_m + [(\omega_N(N) - \phi_N(N)]\partial N \tag{B12.3}$$

Finally, from the production function, $Y = Y(N)$, we know that $\partial Y = Y_N\partial N$, so that $\partial N = \partial Y/\phi(N)$. Substituting for the change in employment from the production function into the labour market equilibrium condition gives the final expression for the classical *AS* curve, which is:

$$\frac{\partial P}{\partial Y} = \frac{1}{\phi(N)}\frac{[\omega_N(N) - \phi_N(N)]}{[\phi(N) - (1 - \rho)\omega(N)]} = \frac{\gamma_1}{\gamma_2} > 0 \tag{B12.4}$$

since $\phi(N) > 0$, $\phi_N(N) < 0$ and $\omega_N(N) > 0$. In a closed economy, $\rho = 0$, and so the denominator becomes simply $\phi(N) - \omega(N)$. Moreover, in a closed economy $\phi(N) = \omega(N)$ and so the denominator becomes zero. Therefore the *AS* curve has a slope of infinity: that is, it is vertical. In the open economy $0 < \rho < 1$, so $(1 - \rho)\omega(N) < \phi(N)$, in which case the denominator is positive and hence the *AS* curve has a positive slope.

into point B′ in the lower panel and hence the closed economy classical *AS* curve is vertical and the real wage is constant along this line. This case has received an inordinate amount of attention in the macroeconomics literature since it implies that demand management policy is impotent and that money is neutral. In reality, even in a closed economy this is only likely to be the case if labour markets exhibit perfect wage flexibility. Since a high degree of wage flexibility is uncharacteristic of Western labour markets, it seems unlikely that the *AS* curve will be vertical. On the other hand, the open economy version is not only more general, but also permits some potential policy effectiveness in the short run, due to international goods markets being less than perfectly integrated and hence imperfectly competitive. It therefore seems safe to postulate an upward-sloping classical aggregate supply in the short run over the time horizon when PPP does not hold.

Conclusions

In this chapter an analysis of the competitive labour market has been used to derive the aggregate supply of output schedule. The classical approach yields an aggregate supply function whose position depends upon the productivity of labour, the preferences of workers for work and leisure, and the domestic currency price of imported goods. This aggregate supply function assumes that the workers' real consumption wage is constant along its length, so there is no tendency for this curve to shift in response to demand shocks. (This is why it is also referred to as the equilibrium supply function.) In the extreme case of PPP, the *AS* line will be vertical as it is in the closed economy version of the model.

Summary

- Firms will employ labour up to the point where the marginal product of the extra worker is equal to the real wage rate. In aggregate the demand for labour varies inversely with the real product wage rate and directly with the level of productivity.
- The individual supply of labour depends on individual preferences for income and leisure and the real consumption wage. In aggregate the labour supply function is an increasing function of the real consumption wage and the preference of individuals for work.
- The aggregate neo-classical labour market is assumed to be perfectly competitive and continuously clears at a non-zero level of unemployment. This level of unemployment is entirely voluntary and referred to as the natural level of unemployment.

- The natural rate of unemployment is made up of frictional and structural unemployment – that is those between jobs and those who have become unemployed because of a structural decline in their industry.
- The neo-classical aggregate supply (*AS*) curve has a positive slope, indicating that more output will be supplied as output prices rise, if purchasing power parity (PPP) does not hold, even if workers have perfect foresight. The *AS* curve will become vertical if international goods markets are fully integrated and PPP holds. In this case the *AS* schedule is shifted only by changes in productivity or work–leisure preferences. In the upward-sloping case it may also be shifted by changes in relative prices.

Suggested further reading

Keynes (1936) offers a review of the classical system and defines voluntary (frictional) unemployment in Chapter 2. The microeconomic foundations of the demand and supply of labour are outlined in most labour economics texts of which Sapsford and Tzannatos (1993) is one example. The best account of the full classical system, however, remains Hagen (1966). The open economy aspects of the supply side have received attention in the literature, although De Grauwe (1983) is an exception. In contrast, there is a vast literature on PPP, the best survey is that of Officer (1976), with Rogoff (1996) and Pilbeam (1998) offering a more up to date review of the empirical findings. MacDonald and Taylor (1992) also review the literature on PPP as part of a general survey on exchange rate economics.

Essay titles

1. To what extent is the natural rate of unemployment 'natural?'
2. 'Since the neo-classical labour market is assumed to always clear there can be no unemployment.' Discuss.
3. 'As the neo-classical model of the labour market postulates an inverse relationship between the real product wage and the level of employment, while the empirical evidence shows that wages and employment are probably pro-cyclical, the model is unable to account for the current level of unemployment.' Discuss.

Questions

1. Using the microeconomic foundations of the individual's work–leisure choice demonstrate the effects of a rise in unemployment benefit on the individual's supply of effort. On what assumptions does your result depend?
2. Distinguish between the real consumption wage rate and the real product wage rate. Under what circumstances are these real wage rates identical?
3. What do you understand by the following terms and how are they related:

    (a) the natural rate of unemployment;
    (b) structural unemployment;
    (c) voluntary unemployment.

4. Examine the effects on the neo-classical labour market, where the demand for labour depends upon the real product wage and the supply schedule depends on the real consumption wage, of:

    (a) a rise in the productivity of labour;
    (b) a rise in the nominal wage rate;
    (c) a rise in the price of imported consumption goods.

5. Derive the short-run neo-classical aggregate supply (*AS*) curve from the labour market where workers and firms use different price deflators for the money wage rate:

    (a) what happens to the real consumption wage as you move up this *AS* curve?
    (b) what are the main variables that shift this curve and how?
    (c) what would be the shape of this *AS* curve if purchasing power parity (PPP) is assumed to hold?

6. Are there any theoretical reasons as to why PPP is likely to be invalid? Is there any empirical evidence to support this?

CHAPTER 13

The Keynesian Theory of Aggregate Supply and Supply-side Shocks

Aims and objectives

- To develop Keynes' view of the labour market and to define the concept of involuntary unemployment.
- To examine and evaluate Keynes' special reasons for the invalidity of the self-adjusting mechanisms of the Classical system and the potential for unemployment equilibrium.
- To explore an alternative view of the Keynesian labour market associated with Kalecki and the post-Keynesians, which emphasises the importance of imperfect competition.

Introduction

In Chapter 12 the neo-classical (or equilibrium) aggregate supply function was derived from a labour market that was assumed to be perfectly competitive such that each firm was on its demand for labour curve and each worker was on his or her supply of labour curve. Keynes argued on the basis of casual empirical evidence that workers were frequently away from their presumed neo-classical labour supply curves and hence that the labour market did not clear as the classics argued. Instead, the suppliers of labour were constrained by firms' demand for labour, which was in turn constrained by the same firms' inability to sell any additional output produced. This led Keynes to develop the concept of involuntary unemployment and an alternative model of the labour market and aggregate supply function, which are the principal subjects of this chapter. This analysis of the labour market is highly important having implications not only for the adjustment of the labour market but for the economy as a whole, in that according to Keynes the economy could become stuck in unemployment equilibrium.

In the next section we therefore start with a constant money wage model of the labour market and develop the specifically Keynesian concept of involuntary unemployment. We then combine this analysis of the aggregate labour market to derive Keynes' fixed money wage model of aggregate supply. The implications of this theory of supply for the automatic adjustment of the economy as a whole are then explored, and an alternative Keynesian model of aggregate supply the horizontal – or constant marginal product *AS* curve is developed. This will also serve to introduce some of the basic ideas underlying the so-called New Keynesian theories of the labour market that are the subject of Chapter 15. In the final section we consider the impact of shocks to the various aggregate supply functions.

Keynes' view of the labour market and involuntary unemployment

In the *General Theory* Keynes made it clear that he accepted the neo-classical analysis of the demand for labour schedule and that where he differed from the Classics was on the shape of the aggregate supply of labour function. Keynes argued that the aggregate labour supply curve was horizontal at a given level of *money* wages. This assumption reflected the mass excess supply of labour in the Great Depression of the 1930s and the apparent failure of money wages to fall to clear the market.

There are perhaps three principal reasons as to why Keynesians believe that money wages are rigid in a downward direction:

1. The first explanation is due to Keynes. He argued that workers are interested in their relative as well as their absolute wage. There exists in any labour market a set of wage differentials between workers with different trades and skills. Much of the wage bargaining process is to arrive at a wage structure that is acceptable to both labour and management. Wage differentials can be measured by relative money wages, since price-level changes affect all wage rates symmetrically. Therefore Keynes believed that one reason why workers would resist money wage cuts, even if the demand for labour fell, was that they would see wage cuts as unfair changes in the structure of relative wages. Workers in one firm or industry would see changes in money wage rates as changes in relative wages because they would have no assurance that if they accepted a cut in wages, workers in other industries would do the same. A decline in the real wage as a result of a rise in prices would not be seen by labour as affecting the structure of relative wages. Because of this, Keynes believed that a decline in real wages caused by a price-level increase would meet with much less resistance from labour than an equivalent fall in the real wage from a money wage cut.

2. The institutional structure of the labour market is another potential cause of money wage rigidity. In the unionised sector of the labour market wages are set by labour contracts in which the money wage is fixed for the duration of the contract. The money wage will not respond to events, such as a decline in labour demand over the life of the contract. Even in situations where the contracts are renegotiated annually, it is usual for money wage settlements to reflect previous rather than future rates of inflation, and for any wage rises to be less than previous price rises hence ensuring a fall in the real wage rate.

3. Even in sectors of the labour market where there are no unions or explicit contracts fixing the money wage rate, there is frequently an implicit agreement between employers and employees that money wage rates will remain fixed over some period of time. In particular, implicit contracts prevent employers

cutting money wage rates in the face of a fall in the demand for their products and labour demand. Keynesians believe, therefore, that contractual arrangements are central to an understanding of how labour markets work. This is in sharp contrast to the auction market view of the neo-classical economists. In the Keynesian view, according to Okun (1981):

> Wages are not set to clear markets in the short run, but rather are strongly conditioned by longer-term considerations involving... employer–worker relations. These factors insulate wages... to a significant degree from the impact of shifts in demand so that the adjustment must be made in employment and output. (p. 223)

Thus in a Keynesian model the supply of labour is assumed to be perfectly elastic with respect to the current money wage rate. **Figure 13.1** therefore shows the Keynesian labour supply schedule as $W_0 S$, its position depending fundamentally upon the money wage rate, W_0. The demand for labour is identical to the classical demand for labour derived in Chapter 12 and is represented in **Figure 13.1** as $P_0\phi(N)$. As the money wage rate rises the real wage also rises along the demand curve, since the price level is given at P_0. Given a money wage rate of W_0 and a price level of P_0 only N_0 units of labour are demanded, while the of supply labour given by the neo-classical supply curve $P_{c_0}\omega(N)$ is at N_2 when the money wage rate is W_0. The labour market does not clear and there is unemployment, given by the distance $N_2 - N_0$. In the neo-classical model the excess supply of labour at W_0 would result in a fall in the money wage rate to W_1, which would lead to the labour market clearing with employment N_1. With rigid money wages, however, there is no mechanism for the wage rate to fall and persistent unemployment of $N_2 - N_0$ prevails at W_0. The excess supply of labour, or unemployment, is given by the distance $N_2 - N_0$ and is partly voluntary and partly involuntary unemployment. Because $N_2 - N_1$ are only prepared to work at real wage rates which exceed the

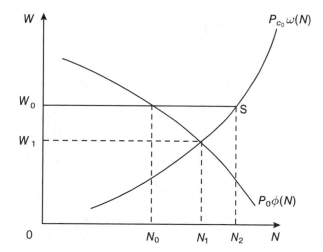

Figure 13.1 *Keynes' labour market*

market clearing real wage rate of W_1 (denoted by W_1/P_0), this leaves $N_1 - N_0$ as the amount of involuntary unemployment at W_0 and P_0.

Involuntary or *Keynesian* unemployment occurs when unemployed workers are willing to work at or below the current real wage but are unable to find jobs. In fact Keynes gave a more precise definition of involuntary unemployment in the *General Theory*. Involuntary unemployment exists if, following an increase in the price level with an unchanged money wage:

(a) the supply of labour still exceeds the existing level of employment; and
(b) the demand for labour is greater than the current level of employment.

The need for this elaborate definition of involuntary unemployment can be seen from **Figure 13.2**, which assumes for simplicity that domestic and foreign prices are identical through purchasing power parity (PPP), so that $P = P_c$. Given a money wage of W_0 and a price level of P_0, $0N_2$ units of labour are supplied, but at this real wage only $0N_0$ units are demanded. If the price level increases from P_0 to P_1 and the real wage rate falls to W_0/P_1 from W_0/P_0, the demand for labour increases from $0N_0$ to $0N_3$, thus passing the second of Keynes' conditions that the demand for labour must be greater than the current level of employment. At the lower real wage the amount of labour willing to work $0N_4$, still exceeds the original level of employment, $0N_0$, and so the first necessary condition for involuntary unemployment is also satisfied. The real wage rates W_0/P_0 and W_0/P_1 are wage rates above the equilibrium real wage. Once the price level has risen to reduce the real wage to the market-clearing level, W_0/P_2, and employment is at N_1, conditions for involuntary unemployment no longer exist. To show this, if the price level is raised again, above P_2 say to P_3, the real wage will fall below W_0/P_2 and the supply of labour will fall below $0N_1$, the current employment level, to $0N_3$. Therefore the first condition for involuntary unemployment no longer holds.

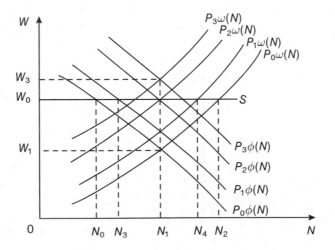

Figure 13.2 *Keynes' concept of involuntary unemployment*

Thus when the Keynesian labour supply function is operative, labour is said to be off the neo-classical labour-supply function. In Keynes' analysis this will occur at levels of employment below the market-clearing amount of employment: that is, when the real wage is stuck at a level which exceeds the equilibrium real wage rate.

The fixed money wage aggregate supply curve

The derivation of the fixed money wage, aggregate supply curve is shown in **Figure 13.3**. In the top panel is the labour market in money wage–employment space. In the middle panel is the production function and in the lower panel is the fixed money wage aggregate supply curve. Starting at point A, the demand for labour is N_0, which for the price level P_0 translates via the production function into output Y_0. A rise in the price level from P_0 to P_1, will shift the demand for labour curve upwards, raising the level of employment to N_1. In the middle panel the higher level of employment generates a higher level of output Y_1, which in the lower panel is associated with a higher price level P_1. Thus for a given money wage rate and marginal product of labour the aggregate supply curve has a positive slope and is represented by $AS(\overline{W}, \phi(N))$.

This aggregate supply curve does not depend upon the foreign price level or the exchange rate, since in Keynes' model workers disregard changes in consumer prices. Moreover, it also ignores the workers' decision between working and not working, reflecting the fact that the workers' labour-supply decision is irrelevant, since the wage is fixed and firms can purchase all the labour they need at that wage rate. These assumptions reflect the economic circumstances of the Great Depression. Workers clearly wanted to work, but could not find jobs. Moreover, prices actually fell during the depression and so the possible effect of rising prices was not a major issue for Keynes in the early 1930s. This constant money wage supply curve will therefore have a flatter slope than the neo-classical constant real consumption wage supply curve, since as domestic prices rise and firms' demand for labour increases, the supply of labour will rise to meet the higher demand even though real wages are falling. Workers suffer from 'money illusion', in that they base their labour supply decisions on the money wage rate offered rather than the real wage in prospect.

The conditions for unemployment equilibrium

There remain, however, some serious questions to be asked of the above analysis of the labour market. First, because the fixed money wage AS curve has a positive slope, showing that output rises with the price level, it is inconsistent with the income–expenditure and the IS–LM models which assume a fixed price level and which are also derived from the *General Theory* (see Parts II and III of this text). Second, since the Classics were aware of the rigidity of money wages, and if all Keynes really did was to graft the assumption of rigid money wages on to the neo-classical model, why is the *General Theory* regarded as having brought about

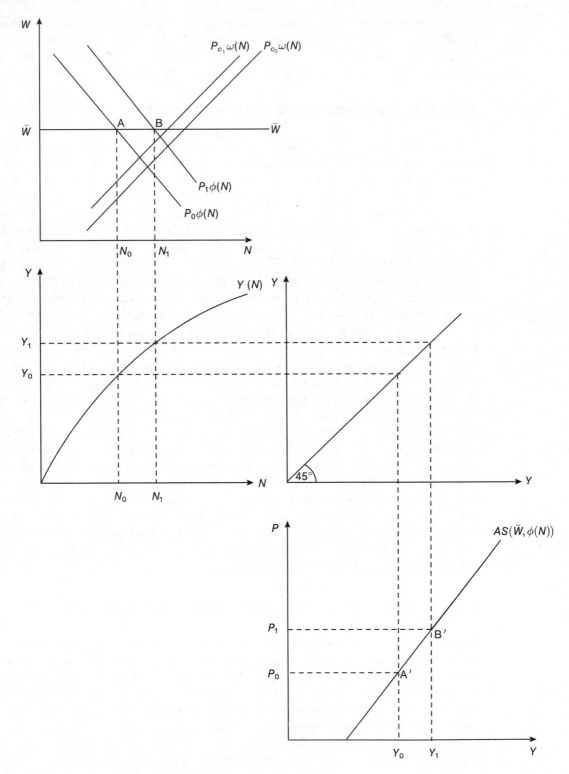

Figure 13.3 *The fixed money wage supply curve*

a revolution in macroeconomics? The first question is held over until the next section, while in this section the second question regarding the contribution of Keynes is considered, although these two questions are in fact closely related.

As to the second question, the crucial argument of Keynes was that even if real wages were to fall the economy would not return automatically to full employment as in neo-classical analysis. For the neo-classical analysis to be correct prices must fall less rapidly than money wages, so that the real wage rate falls to induce a higher demand for labour and hence a higher supply of output. Keynes argued that even if real wages did fall this would only serve to reduce the workers' ability to buy the extra output produced – hence, without more demand for output, firms would not expand production. If the firms did expand output then the extra output would simply make the excess supply of goods greater and so drive down prices and wages further. Indeed, Keynes argued that there was a serious danger of a downward price–wage spiral, with no limit on how far prices and wages could fall. He therefore argued that rigid money wage rates were a useful stabilising influence on the economy and not the reason why full employment could not be reached.

Keynes believed that the failure of the economy to automatically return to full employment was because the fall in prices did not affect the level of aggregate demand. For Keynes the mechanism by which falls in the price level fed through into aggregate demand involved the money market. A fall in the price level, for a given money supply, leads to a higher real money supply, which causes the rate of interest to fall, which in turn stimulates investment and causes a multiple increase in aggregate demand. Keynes argued that this transmission mechanism could be broken at one of two places: either the rise in the money supply would not result in a fall in the rate of interest or, even if interest rates fell, these would not affect the level of investment. In the context of the 1930s, interest rates were very low and were not expected to fall further. Hence, even if the money supply was increased there would be no downward effect on the rate of interest and hence no effect on aggregate demand. This special case is called the *liquidity trap* scenario and is illustrated in **Figure 13.4.**

The top panel of **Figure 13.4** shows a flat *LM* curve and a standard *IS* curve, while the middle panel shows the Keynesian labour market where there is involuntary unemployment. A fall in the price level will raise the real money supply, but has no effect on the rate of interest and so the level of demand is given by Y_0 and hence the demand for labour is given by N_0. Regardless of how much the real money supply increases it is impossible to increase the demand for labour. The economy is in 'equilibrium', but stuck at a position where there is involuntary unemployment given by the distance $N_F - N_0$.

The second possible break in the causal chain is the link between interest rates and investment. Even if interest rates were to fall, Keynes argued that with business confidence so very low and the rates of return on investment correspondingly small, then investment would simply not be forthcoming even if interest rates fell. In other words, investment was interest-inelastic. This second special case is also shown in **Figure 13.4,** by using the middle and lower panels. In the bottom panel the *IS* curve is vertical since the level of investment is unresponsive to changes in the rate of interest. As the price level falls, even though the real money supply increases shifting the *LM* curve from LM_0 to LM_1, there is no change in the level of demand which remains stuck at Y_0. Hence, as before, the demand for labour is also stuck at N_0, in the middle panel, with involuntary unemployment in equilibrium.

Neither of these arguments, however, is sufficient to establish Keynes' case. In the first place, in an open economy context the goods market equilibrium depends on the level of the real exchange rate, EP^*/P, of which the domestic price level is an element. Hence, when the price level falls, other things remaining constant, domestic goods become more competitive on world markets and demand for them rises.

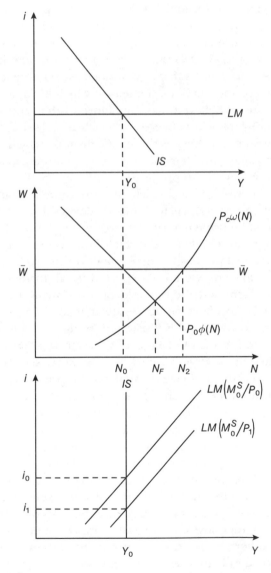

Figure 13.4 *Keynes' special cases*

As the demand for exports rises so too does aggregate demand. Thus as prices fall the IS_0 curve in the upper and lower panels of **Figure 13.4** shifts to the right increasing aggregate demand until full employment equilibrium is restored. This direct link between the demand for goods and the price level in an open economy nullifies both of Keynes' special cases of the liquidity trap and interest inelastic investment.

Furthermore, these special cases can also be nullified in a closed economy if the demand for goods also depends upon real wealth. As Pigou (1943) argued, consumption demand might depend on both the flow of income and on the stock of real wealth (see Chapter 6). Hence, as the price level falls the level of real wealth rises, raising the aggregate demand for domestic output and shifting the IS_0 curve to the right in **Figure 13.4**. This so-called *Pigou effect* yields exactly the same outcome as when aggregate demand depends on the real exchange rate: that is, Keynes special cases for unemployment equilibrium are theoretically invalid, leaving the Keynesian system based solely on the assumption of rigid money wage rates. It should not be surprising therefore that the reasons for wage rigidity are central to the Keynesian research agenda.

An alternative interpretation of Keynes' model of the labour market

The first question raised at the beginning of the previous section concerned the apparent inconsistency between the fixed-price income–expenditure and *IS–LM* models, both of which imply a horizontal *AS* curve, and the upward-sloping money-wage aggregate supply curve suggested by Keynes. In fact it is possible to derive a horizontal *AS* curve and to simultaneously provide a rationalisation for wage and price rigidity which, as noted above, forms the bedrock of Keynesian economics. To do this, however, the neo-classical demand for labour function, based on the diminishing marginal productivity of labour, has to be dropped although Keynes himself believed it to be appropriate.

In order to obtain a horizontal aggregate supply curve from the labour market model that has been developed so far requires the very special assumption of constant marginal productivity of labour. This is consistent with a linear production function of the form:

$$Y = \bar{\phi} N \tag{13.1}$$

such that the average and marginal product of labour is $\bar{\phi}$, which is constant and invariant with labour input. Since the marginal product of labour is constant and since the real wage must equal the marginal product of labour, then the real wage must also be constant. Thus the demand for labour schedule is horizontal: the firm can obtain all the labour it needs at this constant real wage rate. At any higher real wage rate it will demand zero labour, since marginal costs will have risen relative to the marginal revenue, while at any lower real wage its demand for labour will become infinite – constrained only by the available supply of labour.

In terms of aggregate supply, for a given money wage rate W_0, a rise in the price level will reduce the real wage and the firm will expand both output and the demand for labour until the labour supply constraint at full employment is reached. Thus in **Figure 13.5**, the *AS* curve is horizontal at P_0, until full employment output Y_F is reached. On the other hand, a fall in the price level below P_0 leads to a rise in the real wage and a fall in the marginal revenue relative to the fixed marginal cost, such that the firm's demand for labour falls to zero. Thus aggregate supply becomes zero at all price levels below P_0. This analysis produces the step-shaped *AS* curve in the lower panel of **Figure 13.5**, although the analysis should be confined strictly to the flat section of this curve, since it is this section that is relevant when prices are fixed at P_0. To keep to this part of the step-shaped *AS* function, the price level also needs to be held constant at P_0.

As noted by Kalecki (1939), however, in markets where there is some monopoly power firms may set prices as a mark-up on average costs. Therefore, if wage costs are the biggest element in average costs, then the price level is simply given as:

$$P = (1+m)\overline{W} \tag{13.2}$$

where m in this context is the mark-up over average (wage) costs. Thus a flat *AS* curve can be justified by assuming that firms operate in goods markets which are characterised by a degree of imperfect competition. In this case the price level is independent of aggregate demand. Whereas in the complete neo-classical model with PPP, output is determined solely by supply and prices solely by demand, in this extreme Keynesian framework the dichotomy is reversed: that is, the price

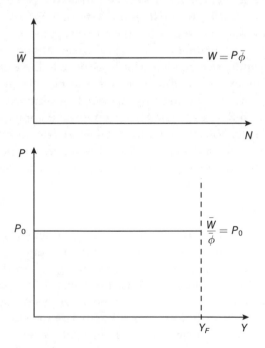

Figure 13.5 *The perfectly elastic* AS *schedule*

level is determined entirely by costs of production and output and employment by the level of aggregate demand.

From the point of view of the labour market in **Figure 13.5**, the demand for labour schedule is flat, but the demand for labour is indeterminant as far as the labour market is concerned. The factor that determines the level of employment is the level of aggregate demand, denoted in **Figure 13.6** by the vertical D lines. So with demand at D_1 the level of employment will be N_1, while at a higher level of demand such as D_2 the level of employment will be given by N_2. Thus firms are demand-constrained. They will only take on more workers if aggregate demand is higher. This justifies Keynes' view that raising the level of demand is essential to raising employment, but note that it is also inconsistent with the downward-sloping demand curve for labour to which Keynes subscribed. Note also, however, that reducing the real wage rate is wholly irrelevant in this framework. At point A in **Figure 13.6**, for example, a money wage cut will have no effect on employment: the firm will just move down the vertical D_1 line. Hence, a cut in money wages to W_1 will reduce the real wage to B, since B is on the notional neo-classical supply of labour curve, but will not raise employment. Until full employment is reached at point C, real wage cuts have no employment-enhancing effects, since employment is determined exclusively by the level of aggregate demand.

Thus a horizontal AS curve can be derived from a model of the labour market, but it is important to note that this requires some very special assumptions; in particular, that the marginal product of labour is constant. It is therefore perhaps best regarded as an AS function characteristic of a deep recession since for the most part Keynes assumed rising marginal costs, which imply an upward-sloping aggregate supply function. It follows, therefore, that the $IS–LM$ and income–expenditure models of Parts II and III should be regarded as 'short-run' models, where the 'short-run' in this context is defined as a period over which prices and costs are constant. To the extent that the New Keynesians emphasise the role of imperfect competition (see Chapter 15), then Kalecki can be regarded as a forerunner of this school of modern economic thought.

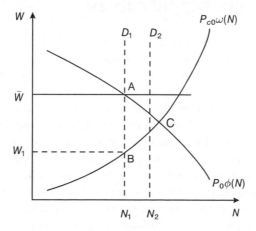

Figure 13.6   *Demand constrained labour demand*

Box 13.1 Technical derivation of the Keynesian *AS* curves

Technically, labour market equilibrium generates the equilibrium wage rate and level of employment. Given a specific technology, incorporated in the production function, the market-clearing level of employment can produce a specific amount of output. In this case the equilibrium is given where the fixed money wagerate, W, is equal to the marginal revenue product of labour, that is:

$$W = P\phi(N) \tag{B13.1}$$

where $\phi(N)$ denotes the marginal product of labour. Totally differentiating this equilibrium condition, with $P = 1$ we get:

$$\partial P\phi(N) + \phi_N(N)\partial N = \partial W \tag{B13.2}$$

Finally, from the production function we know that $\partial Y = Y_N(N)\partial N$, so that $\partial N = \partial Y/Y_N(N)$. Substituting for the change in employment from the production function into the labour market equilibrium condition, with $\partial W = 0$ gives the final expression for the keynesian *AS* curve, which is:

$$\frac{\partial P}{\partial Y} = \frac{-\phi_N(N)}{\phi(N)Y_N(N)} > 0 \tag{B13.3}$$

Hence the Keynesian fixed money wage *AS* curve slopes up.

In the special case, where the MPN is constant, then $\phi_N(N) = 0$, such that the numerator is zero and the *AS* curve is perfectly elastic at the given level of prices.

A comparison of neo-classical and Keynesian supply curves

This chapter has derived two alternative Keynesian aggregate supply curves for labour and in Chapter 12 two alternative neo-classical supply curves were also derived. The question that this short section poses is simply: which aggregate supply curve?

Figure 13.7 shows the four alternative aggregate supply curves. Since the Keynesian supply curves are only relevant at less than full employment of output, only the part of these schedules to the left of Y_F are drawn. This is the first major difference between the theories of supply. At points on AB or CB there is involuntary unemployment and the labour market does not clear in the sense that the workers are off their labour supply schedules. Along the aggregate supply curves given by DBF or EBG there is no involuntary unemployment. It is also the case that as the aggregate supply schedules become steeper so the degree of labour market and goods market flexibility increases. Along AB money wages, output prices and the marginal product of labour are fixed. Along BC, although the money wage is fixed the demand for labour is characterised by a diminishing marginal product of labour. Along DBF the marginal product of labour is diminishing and money wages are perfectly flexible, but goods market imperfections mean that domestic prices do not move directly in proportion to world prices. Finally, the vertical AS curve denoted by EBG is the neo-classical AS curve where domestic and foreign prices also move together in accordance with purchasing power parity theory (PPP).

The degree of steepness of the various AS curves may also be taken as a guide to the period of time assumed to be relevant for policy analysis. Thus the Keynesian supply curves are relevant for the short period, perhaps a year or so, over which money wages are fixed and workers do not have the opportunity to renegotiate work contracts and hence raise their money wages as their expectations about the future level of prices change. On the other hand, the vertical AS curve suggests that not only are real wages constant, since workers continually adjust their money wages, but the level of domestic output prices exactly reflects world prices. It is clear that such market conditions may never actually materialise even over a relatively long period of calendar time, since they depend on a complete absence of trade barriers and market imperfections. It would seem plausible, therefore, to argue that the AS curve is positively-sloped in all but the very short run, and therefore macroeconomic policy can influence both the level of output and prices in the economy in the short to medium term.

In **Figure 13.7**, starting from the general equilibrium at B, consider the effect of a fall in aggregate demand from AD_0 to AD_1. The output and employment consequences of this shift in demand are smaller the greater the degree of price flexibility, or, alternatively, the longer the period of time allowed for the shock to work its way through the system. Thus with rigid wages and prices, output falls from Y_F to Y_3; if prices are permitted to fall then output only falls to Y_2. If both money wages and prices can fall, output falls by less to only Y_1. Moreover, if in

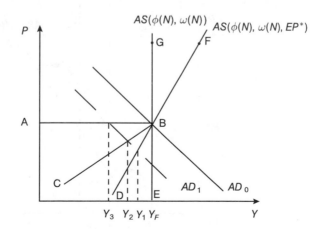

Figure 13.7   *Alternative* AS *schedules*

addition the domestic currency price of foreign output falls by the same extent as the domestic output price, say due to an appreciation of the home currency, then the level of output can be maintained at its initial level of Y_F.

Supply-side shocks

The neo-classical equilibrium and Keynesian aggregate supply curves derived in Chapter 12 and in this chapter are all drawn for a given production function and a given marginal product of labour function $\phi(N)$. Therefore changes in production technology or in the demand for labour will affect all *AS* curves. Supply-side shocks may also emanate from the supply of labour function, including changes in import prices, in the neo-classical case, or from changes in money wage rates in the Keynesian cases. Changes in any of these exogenous variables will have the effect of shifting the whole aggregate supply curve in (P, Y) space. In this section each of these exogenous variables is changed in turn.

Consider the effect of an upward shift in the labour-supply function as illustrated in **Figure 13.8.** In the upper panel the labour-supply function shifts up

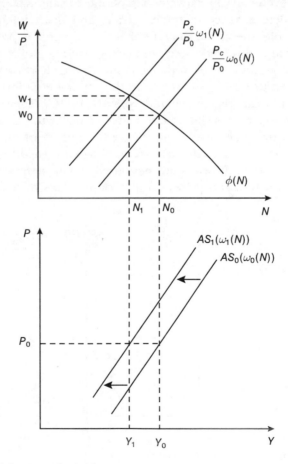

Figure 13.8 *A labour supply shock*

from $\omega_0(N)$ to $\omega_1(N)$. This could be the result of a change in tastes of the workforce between income and leisure in favour of more leisure or, what is analytically equivalent, an increase in unemployment benefits. The upward shift in the labour supply function reduces equilibrium employment from N_0 to N_1, at the preexisting price level. The reduction in employment is reflected in a lower level of output which translates into a shift in the *AS* curve in the bottom panel as output is lower at all prices.

Another potential supply-side shock that operates through the supply of labour function is an increase in the domestic price of imports. This could come about through a devaluation of the exchange rate (a rise in E) or through a rise in foreign (world) output prices. In this case the qualitative effect is the same as for the shift up in the labour-supply function, with the *AS* curve shifting to the left for all price levels. This case is complicated, however, by the fact that for the *AS* curve to shift as described above, requires the change in the consumer price index to exceed the change in the domestic output price index. In other words purchasing power parity (PPP) is assumed not to hold. As noted in Chapter 12 and above this is likely to be the case in the short to medium time horizon over which policy is generally believed to be effective.

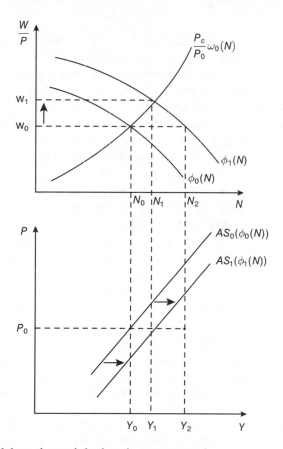

Figure 13.9 *A labour demand shock and aggregate supply*

Figure 13.9 shows the effect of a change in technology on the demand for labour. In general a technical improvement will lead to a shift in the production function and an increase in the productivity of labour, which causes the demand for labour schedule to shift up to the right. In **Figure 13.9** the demand for labour shifts from $\phi_0(N)$ to $\phi_1(N)$, which raises the level of employment from N_0 to N_1 if labour supply is neo-classical, and to N_2 if labour is supplied at a constant money wage. This shifts the aggregate supply function out to the right in the lower panel of the figure, increasing the supply of output to Y_1 in the neo-classical case, and to Y_2 in the Keynesian fixed money wage case (not drawn).

The horizontal aggregate supply curve is shifted by changes in either average costs, that is money wages rates W, or productivity $\bar{\phi}$. A rise in money wage rates will lead to a shift up in the aggregate supply function, since with higher input costs, firms earning only normal profits will be forced to raise prices to cover higher costs of production. A rise in the marginal product of labour will lead to a shift down in the *AS* curve, as new entrants enter the industry taking advantage of the more efficient production technology and bid down prices.

Conclusions

This chapter has illustrated that, unlike the aggregate demand curve, there are many alternative forms for the aggregate supply of output schedule, which make the supply side rather more complex than the demand side. There are, however, two basic approaches: the classical (equilibrium) approach and Keynes' (fixed money wage) approach.

The classical approach yields an aggregate supply function whose position depends upon the productivity of labour, the preferences of workers for work and leisure and, at least in the short run, the domestic currency price of imported goods. Keynes' fixed money wage approach, on the other hand, views the *AS* function as being independent of the supply of effort and the price of imported goods, but dependent instead on the level of money wages in addition to productivity. Because money wages are given along the Keynesian supply function, workers' real wages fall as output is increased. Such falls in the real wage are likely to lead to claims for money wage increases, which if achieved would serve to shift the $AS(\overline{W})$ curve up to the left, thus justifying the point that this *AS* curve is a short-run schedule. The neo-classical supply function, on the other hand, assumes that workers' real consumption wages are constant along its length, so there is no tendency for this curve to shift as prices or wages change – indeed this is why it is referred to as the equilibrium supply function. For this reason it is useful to think of the Keynesian fixed money wage supply curve as a short-run aggregate supply curve, and the classical curve as a medium-term supply curve where, although the capital stock remains fixed, workers do not suffer from money illusion. That is to say, workers do not confuse money and real wage rates. It should also be noted that the horizontal Keynesian *AS* curve is also a short-run curve and is shifted by productivity and money wage rate changes, in addition to import price changes if these are part of average costs. Thus this horizontal *AS* curve may therefore be interpreted as a further simplification of the fixed money wage rate supply function where in addition to fixed money wages labour productivity is also assumed to be invariant with labour demanded.

This analysis of the supply side means that the demand-side equilibrium developed in Chapters 9 and 10 can now be combined with the supply side of the macroeconomy developed in this chapter. This leads to a consideration of the most complete macroeconomic model, the *AD–AS* model, in Chapter 14.

Summary

- For Keynes the labour supply schedule was horizontal at a given money wage rate and thus the level of employment was exclusively determined by the demand for labour. If the demand for labour is insufficient to generate full employment at the going money wage then involuntary unemployment will exist.
- Keynes' *AS* curve slopes upwards because as prices rise the real product wage falls inducing firms to demand more labour and expand production.
- The neo-classical automatic adjustment mechanism whereby the price level falls, to stimulate demand is inoperative according to Keynes for two reasons. First, due to a liquidity trap, a rise in the real money supply following a fall in the price level does not reduce the rate of interest; or, second, because although the interest rate falls investment is interest-inelastic and so demand is unaffected.
- The Pigou effect nullifies Keynes' reasons for the neo-classical system not self-equilibrating in the context of a closed economy. In an open economy context the real exchange rate effect also serves to dispose of Keynes' special cases, independently of the Pigou effect.
- Keynes' theory of involuntary unemployment is based on the rigidity of money wages downwards, but although money wages are too high to cut wages only makes the unemployment problem worse as workers will have less income to spend and so reduce their demand for goods further.
- Keynes' aggregate supply schedule is inconsistent with the demand side of the model based on fixed prices. This inconsistency may be overcome by assuming that marginal product is constant at all levels of output or that goods markets are imperfectly competitive, such that prices are based on a mark-up on unit costs. In this case the *AS* curve becomes horizontal and independent of aggregate demand.
- The flat *AS* curve is shifted up by rises in money wages or other elements in unit costs and shifted down by rises in productivity. The upward-sloping *AS* curve due to Keynes is also shifted upwards by money wage rises and downwards by productivity rises. These Keynesian *AS* schedules do not shift as a result of changes in workers' preferences for work and leisure, since unemployment is assumed to be involuntary.

Suggested further reading

Keynes (1936) defines involuntary unemployment in his Chapter 2, but the theory of aggregate supply given in Chapter 21 is rather difficult. Smith (1956) gives a good diagrammatic treatment of the Keynesian and classical models. Pigou (1943) is the original source of the Pigou effect. The fixed money wage in Keynes is assumed to be part of the institutional structure of the labour market, the modern role of which is explored in Okun (1981). The post-Keynesian view of the aggregate supply function presented in this chapter stems from Kalecki (1939), that found contemporary empirical support from Hall and Hitch (1939).

Essay titles

1. Explain the concept of involuntary unemployment. How does it differ from classical unemployment?
2. 'The Pigou effect disposes of Keynes' concept of unemployment equilibrium.' Discuss.
3. Compare and contrast the neo-classical and Keynesian models of the labour market. To what extent are these differences important for the policy recommendations put forward to reduce unemployment?

Questions

1. Draw a supply and demand diagram of the aggregate labour market and show the effects of a rise in the money wage rate on employment in a Keynesian and neo-classical model.
2. Explain the difference between structural and cyclical unemployment. What policies might you recommend to address these kinds of unemployment?
3. Explain the Pigou or real balance effect. Explain how it restores automatic full employment in the Keynesian special cases of liquidity trap and interest-inelastic investment.
4. Provide a justification for a flat, short-run *AS* curve. What assumptions are required to attain such a result from a standard neo-classical model of the labour market?
5. Show the effect on the Keynesian aggregate supply curve of:

   (a) a rise in the money wage rate;
   (b) a rise in the marginal product of labour;
   (c) the introduction of a successful prices and incomes policy.

6. To what extent do the shapes of the various *AS* schedules reflect different views as to the time horizon over which the labour market clears?

CHAPTER 14
The *AD–AS* Model of Economic Policy

Aims and objectives

- To combine the aggregate demand relation and the aggregate supply relations to give a general comparative static equilibrium model of the macroeconomy.
- To understand the interactions between the product, financial and labour markets that determine the level of output, employment, prices, wages, the interest rate and the exchange rate.
- To be able to understand and predict the effects of demand-side policy shocks and supply-side shocks on the equilibrium levels of employment, output, the price level and wage rates.

Introduction

In Chapter 9 the aggregate demand (*AD*) curve was developed taking the aggregate price level as exogenous. In Chapters 12 and 13 the labour market and the production technology were combined to derive an aggregate supply (*AS*) curve, still maintaining the price level exogenous. In this chapter aggregate demand and aggregate supply relations are combined to give a general equilibrium model for the price level P, output Y, employment N, the wage rate W, and the rate of interest i.

To keep the model as simple as possible, it is assumed that domestic and foreign bonds are perfect substitutes in the portfolios of domestic residents. Thus the domestic rate of interest, i, is identical to the foreign interest rate, $\bar{i}^*$, and hence exogenously given. This assumption helps avoid potential difficulties concerning the reconciliation of stock and flow equilibria (see Chapter 10), since under perfect capital mobility stock and flow equilibria are equivalent. It also implies that under floating exchange rates agents' expectations about future exchange rate changes are static. This implies not only that $i = \bar{i}^*$, but that any current account balance deficit can be financed indefinitely by the inflow of private capital without the domestic authorities facing a binding financing constraint or foreign investors loosing confidence in the ability of the domestic economy to pay interest on their capital.

In addition to the potential problems caused by integrating stocks and flows there is a further concern: the flexibility of wages and the integration of goods

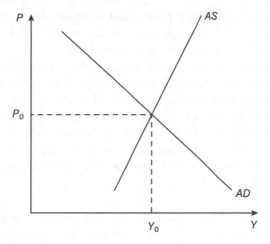

Figure 14.1 *The general* AD–AS *model*

markets. From Chapters 12 and 13 it is clear that there are alternative aggregate supply schedules, depending on the assumed flexibility of money wage rates and the degree of goods market integration. In the general case when goods markets are not fully integrated internationally, the open economy supply curve will be upward-sloping, the steepness of which depends on the flexibility of money wages. On the other hand, with purchasing power parity (PPP), the aggregate supply schedule will be vertical and demand management policies wholly ineffective. Since the empirical evidence in support of PPP is weak, the upward-sloping aggregate supply curve is taken to be the general case. This is the version of the *AD–AS* model illustrated in **Figure 14.1**, where money wages are perfectly flexible and the real consumption wage is constant along the *AS* curve.

The structure of this chapter is as follows. We first consider the neo-classical model with PPP and show that demand disturbances are unable to affect the level of output, while supply-side shocks are unable to affect domestic prices. This is the famous dichotomy of the classical model. We then examine supply-side shocks to the general model without PPP, and use the same model to examine demand-side shocks. Foreign interest rate and price shocks are then considered. Finally, the results are reviewed and we attempt to draw some general conclusions about the relative effectiveness of macroeconomic policies.

The neo-classical (or equilibrium) model with PPP

On the demand side of the *AD–AS* model if domestic and foreign goods are perfect substitutes, then they must sell for the same price when measured in a common currency: that is, $P = P^*E$ where P^* is the foreign price level and E is the exchange rate. Therefore, as with a firm in perfect competition, the domestic economy will be a price-taker from the world market. The home country will be able to sell all it is able at the world price and nothing at a higher price. In other words, the aggregate demand curve is horizontal. More formally, this implies that the parameters δ_2 and μ_2, which denote the price responsiveness of export and import volumes to changes in the real exchange rate, both tend to infinity; that is δ_2 and $\mu_2 \to \infty$. Therefore with both export and import volumes infinitely price-elastic with respect to the real exchange rate, the *AD* schedule will be horizontal. This is shown in **Figure 14.2**, where the aggregate demand curve is given by $AD_0(P_0{}^*E_0)$. In this context the only variables that can shift the *AD* line are the exchange rate and the foreign price level.

With PPP the aggregate supply curve is independent of the price level and hence given by $AS_0(\phi(N), \omega(N))$. The *AS* curve will be shifted by the marginal product of labour ϕ, and any factors that change the tastes of workers between work and leisure, ω. This indicates that neither fiscal nor monetary policy can be effective in this model, although this is considered more formally by reference to **Figure 14.3** which shows the complete macroeconomic model that has been constructed in segments throughout this text. In the centre panel (b) is the neo-classical *AD–AS* model with PPP, which is taken from **Figure 14.2**. The bottom panel (c) shows the labour market, which is taken from **Figure 12.3**, where the real wage is inversely related to the marginal product of labour and the labour supply curve depends only upon the parameter representing the work–leisure choice of workers since $P_c/P = 1$. In the top panel (a) of **Figure 14.3** is the financial sector, adapted from Chapter 9, which shows the money market equilibrium schedule denoted as *LM*, and the horizontal *FF* line denoting that domestic and foreign bonds are perfect substitutes. The exchange rate is not explicitly represented, but it can be assumed to be either fixed or floating. To understand how this model of the macroeconomy 'hangs together' the implications of any shock have to be considered for all markets, as these markets are, by definition,

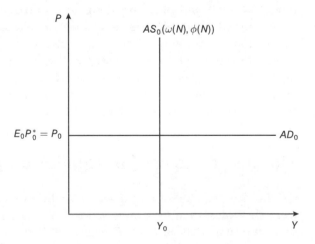

Figure 14.2   AD–AS *model with PPP*

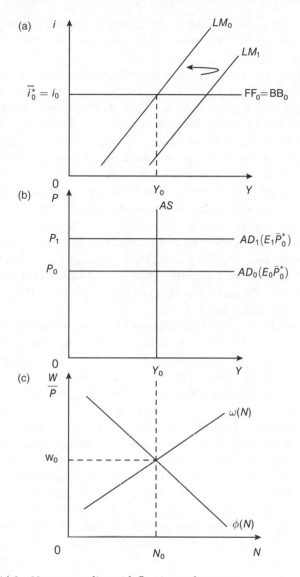

Figure 14.3 *Monetary policy with floating exchange rate*

interdependent. Setting out the model in three panels as in **Figure 14.3**, is convenient since with demand shocks you begin in panel (a) and 'work down' the figure, whereas with supply-side shocks you start is panel (c) and 'work up' the figure. This principle will become clear as this chapter progresses.

Starting from the initial, full equilibrium denoted by $(i_0^*, Y_0, P_0, N_0, w_0)$ several shocks to the model can be considered. Let us begin with demand shocks. From Chapter 9 we know that fiscal policy is ineffective under floating exchange rates and that monetary policy is ineffective under fixed exchange rates, so these cases can be excluded, *a priori*. We know also, however, that fiscal policy is highly effective under fixed exchange rates, and that monetary policy is highly effective under floating rates, so these cases would most likely yield interesting policy implications.

Consider, therefore, a monetary expansion with a floating exchange rate regime. The effect of a rise in the money supply would be to shift the LM_0 curve to the right to LM_1. Since an increase in the money supply lowers the rate of interest below the world rate, there will be a potential capital outflow from the domestic economy that will cause a depreciation of the exchange rate. The depreciation of the exchange rate leads to an increase in the price level in panel (b), which is represented as a shift of the AD_0 line up to AD_1. At the same time, the higher price level reduces the real money supply, shifting the LM_1 line back to LM_0. Hence, in the final equilibrium the levels of wages, output, employment and the rate of interest are all unchanged, while the domestic price level and exchange rate are higher. Thus the monetary expansion does not raise output or employment, only the price level. Because the initial increase in the money supply does not affect real income, employment or the real wage rate money is neutral in the neo-classical model. That is, a change in the money supply will not affect any real variable.

A rise in government spending will have no effect in this model even under fixed exchange rates. All that happens is that the increase in public demand is exactly offset by a fall in private demand. There is complete crowding-out. Therefore, the initial equilibrium level of output, prices, employment and the interest rate is also the final equilibrium. Fiscal policy has no effect on output, prices, interest rates, wage rates or employment.

Demand shocks have no effect on the level of output in the classical model with PPP. It can also be demonstrated that foreign price and interest rate shocks also have no effect on output in this framework with either fixed or floating exchange rates. Consider a rise in the foreign rate of interest. This will cause the $FF_0 = BB_0$ line to shift up in the top panel of **Figure 14.3**. Under fixed exchange rates, this will give rise to a capital outflow from the home country, which will reduce the money supply, shifting the LM curve back to the left, until it intersects $FF_1 = BB_1$ at the initial level of output. There are no implications for the goods or labour markets and output remains at its initial level. Under a floating exchange rate the capital outflow will lead to a depreciation of the exchange rate, which will lead to a rise in the price level, shifting up AD_0 to AD_1. As the price level rises the real money supply will fall, shifting the LM curve back to intersect $FF_1 = BB_1$ at the initial level of income. Therefore the level of output is unaffected by changes in the level of world interest rates.

A rise in the foreign price level will cause the domestic price level to rise with a fixed exchange rate system, shifting AD_0 up to AD_1. A higher price level will reduce the real money supply leading to a temporary rise in the rate of interest, sufficient to induce a capital inflow into the home economy and hence shift the LM line back to its initial position. On the other hand, under a floating exchange rate system the rise in the foreign price level will be completely offset by an appreciation of the exchange rate so that $P_0 = P_0^* E_0 = P_1^* E_1$, and domestic output and prices are unchanged. This result is the same as that noted in Chapter 9: floating rates insulate the domestic economy from foreign goods market shocks, but not from foreign money market shocks, as witnessed by the fact that the rise in the foreign interest rate caused the domestic price level to rise. Note, however, that output has not changed in response to any demand-side disturbances.

Figure 14.4 examines the effect of a supply-side shock in the neo-classical model with internationally integrated goods markets. From the initial equilibrium given by

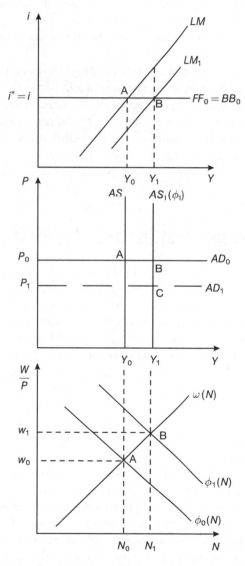

Figure 14.4 *Supply-side shock in the classical model with PPP and a fixed exchange rate*

the points marked A, assume that there is an increase in the level of productivity. This is indicated by a rise in the marginal product of labour, $\phi(N)$. A rise in ϕ from ϕ_0 to ϕ_1 shifts the demand for labour curve up to the right. This leads to an increase in the real wage rate and the level of employment, from w_0 to w_1 and N_0 to N_1 respectively. At the same time the aggregate supply curve shifts to the right to AS_1. The higher level of output causes the rate of interest to rise above the world rate, leading to a capital inflow which swells the money supply shifting the LM_0 curve to the right to intersect $FF_0=BB_0$ at B where the new permanently higher level of income is Y_1. Under a floating exchange rate system the higher domestic rate of interest would give rise to an exchange rate appreciation. This would lower domestic prices, causing AD_0 to fall to AD_1. The lower price level would simultaneously raise the real money supply, causing the LM line to shift to the right to intersect the capital market line at B, but prices would be permanently lower at P_1.

Thus in response to a supply-side shock the level of real output rises as does the real wage rate. The implications for the price level vary with the exchange rate system in operation. Prices remain constant under a fixed exchange rate system, but fall under floating exchange rates. The essential classical dichotomy remains: that is, prices are determined exclusively by demand, and output determined exclusively by supply. In other words macroeconomic policy can have no effect upon output when prices and wages are perfectly flexible.

The general model: demand-side shocks

The neo-classical model, because it is a fully dichotomised model, gives clear-cut policy results. This model is useful as a first approximation, but it is not very plausible in the real world where goods markets are not perfectly integrated and money wages and prices are not fully flexible. In this section a more general model is developed with an upward-sloping aggregate supply curve to consider the effects of demand-side shocks on the five main macroeconomic variables. In the following two sections supply-side shocks and foreign shocks will also be examined in the context of the same model.

Without the assumption of purchasing power parity the aggregate demand and supply curves take the usual shapes given in **Figure 14.1**. Throughout it will be assumed that the upward- sloping *AS* curve is the fixed money wage *AS* curve, although occasionally the neo-classical, open economy supply curve will be drawn on the same picture for purposes of comparison.

Figure 14.5 shows the effect of a monetary expansion under a floating exchange rate system. The three panels represent the financial sector, the goods market and the labour market respectively downwards. Starting from the initial equilibria marked by an A, an increase in the money supply will shift the LM_0 line to the right to LM_1 in the upper panel. This results in a fall in the interest rate, which gives rise to a potential capital outflow and a depreciation of the exchange rate. This

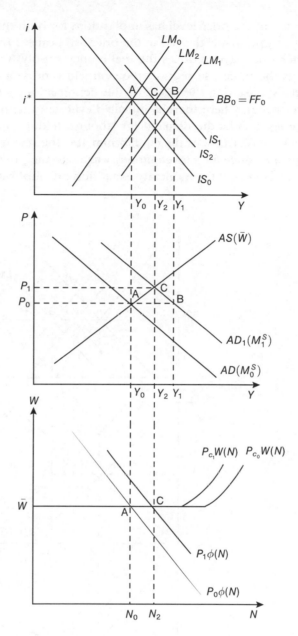

Figure 14.5 *Monetary policy with a floating exchange rate and fixed money wages*

depreciation shifts the *IS* curve to the right to give a temporary equilibrium at point B, with output at Y_1. Taking the line from Y_1 down to the middle panel, at the initial price level P_0, demand is at point B on AD_1, which lies to the right of AD_0 due to the increase in the money supply. At point B in the middle panel there is an excess demand, given by the horizontal distance AB and hence prices rise to P_1 to give a new equilibrium at point C, where output is given by Y_2.

The rise in the price level has implications for both the other panels in **Figure 14.5**. In the upper panel the rise in the price level causes LM_1 to move back to LM_2, as the higher price level reduces the real money supply. The IS_1 line also moves back to IS_2, as the price rise reduces the competitiveness of domestic production, thereby partially offsetting the effect of the depreciation, giving equilibrium at C. In the lower panel, where there is initially Keynesian unemployment at A, the rise in the price level shifts the demand for labour schedule up to $P_1\phi(N)$ and employment rises from N_0 to N_2. At the equilibrium at C the real wage rate is lower than the real wage at A, since for a given money wage rate the price level at C is higher than at A. The real effect of the monetary expansion on employment comes about because the

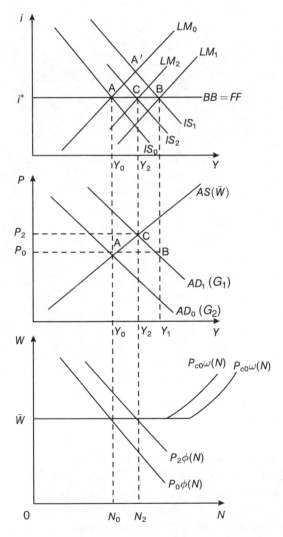

Figure 14.6   *Fiscal expansion with fixed exchange rates and rigid money wages*

real wage rate has fallen and the domestic price level has increased by more than the exchange rate has depreciated. That is, there has been a fall in the real exchange rate EP^*/P.

Figure 14.6 shows a rise in government spending on output and employment when there is a fixed exchange rate system in operation. In the top panel the increase in government spending shifts the *IS* curve to the right to IS_1, which leads to a net capital inflow as the domestic interest rate rises temporarily above the world rate (at point A′) inducing a rightwards shift in the *LM* curve to LM_1. The new level of output is now at Y_1, which is consistent with an upward shift in the AD_0 schedule in the middle panel to AD_1. At the initial price level P_0 there is now an excess demand for domestic output given by the distance AB in the middle panel, and hence the price of domestic output will rise along the supply curve to point C. Point C is the new short-run equilibrium, with the price level at P_2 and output at Y_2. As in the case of the monetary expansion, this higher price level has implications for both the upper and lower panels of the diagram. The rise in the price level will reduce the real money supply and the level of competitiveness of domestic production, which will cause the LM_1 and IS_1 schedules to shift back to the left to LM_2 and IS_2 in the upper panel. In the lower panel the rise in the price of domestic output will shift the demand for labour schedule to the right, reducing the real wage rate and raising the level of employment to N_2. The final equilibrium is therefore given by the points labelled C, where output, prices and employment are higher than in the initial equilibrium, and where the real wage rate is lower.

The crucial point to note is that in both of these cases a demand expansion is effective at raising output and employment in the short run because workers are assumed to accept a real wage cut in the short run. This has the effect of raising the firms' marginal revenue relative to marginal cost, encouraging firms to increase profits by raising labour demand and output. On the other hand, the extent of the rise in output relative to the rise in the price level depends on the slope of the *AS* curve. If a classical open economy supply curve had been assumed, rather then the Keynesian fixed money wage supply curve, then the rise in output and employment would have been smaller and the rise in the price level correspondingly greater. This is because workers would have responded to a rise in the price of domestic output by negotiating a higher money wage rate, to fully offset the rise in the consumer price level and so maintain their real consumption wage.

Supply-side shocks

There are a number of potential supply-side disturbances that can affect the level of output and employment in the model. A rise in productivity by shifting the labour demand function is one possibility; a shift in workers' tastes between work and leisure is another possibility which shifts the supply of labour. The shock which shifts both the Keynesian fixed money wage supply curve and the

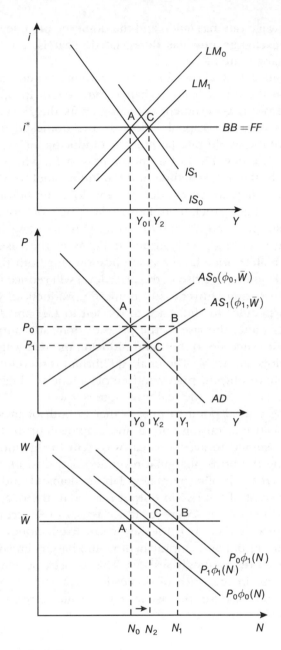

Figure 14.7 *A rise in productivity*

neo-classical open economy supply curve is a productivity shock, so this is adopted as the principal supply-side shock. **Figure 14.7** considers the effect of a rise in the productivity of labour under fixed and floating exchange rates, and **Figure 14.8** uses the neo-classical *AS* curve to consider the effect of a change in the tastes of the workers between work and leisure.

In **Figure 14.7** the impact of a rise in the productivity of labour is to shift the demand for labour schedule to the right from ϕ_0 to ϕ_1 in the lower panel, and the *AS* curve from AS_0 to AS_1 in the middle panel. With a fixed money wage rate the level of employment initially rises to N_1, but at P_0 in the middle panel there is now an excess supply of output at point B, which causes the price level to fall to P_1. The fall in the price level reduces output from Y_1 to Y_2 in the middle frame and causes the demand for labour curve to move back to the left, to $P_1\phi_1(N)$ in the lower panel, which reduces employment to N_2 as the marginal revenue product of labour falls. In the upper panel the financial sector responds to the lower

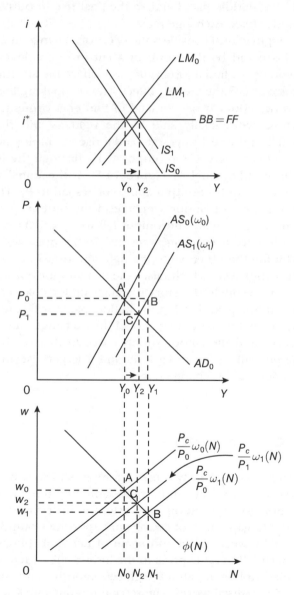

Figure 14.8   *A labour supply shock*

price level, which simultaneously increases the real money supply shifting the *LM* locus to the right to LM_1 and improves the competitiveness of domestic output shifting the *IS* curve to the right to IS_1.

Under a floating exchange rate system the principal difference in the transmission mechanism is that the adjustment in the upper panel, following the fall in the price level, is by way of a combination of exchange rate appreciation and price level falls. To ensure that the *IS* curve does shift to the right, however, it is necessary that the price level falls by more than the exchange rate appreciates, so that the real exchange rate rises. Strictly this will also cause AD_0 to shift to the left in the middle panel and so the final rise in output is likely to be less than ½ as under fixed exchange rates.

Figure 14.8 considers the effect of a change in tastes between work and leisure. This could be the result of a cut in unemployment benefit, which encourages workers to find a job in the case where the substitution effect of the cut in benefits exceeds the income effect. Thus by making leisure more expensive relative to work, labour is encouraged to find employment. In this case the labour supply curve will initially shift to the right as will the *AS* curve. This will lead to a fall in the real wage rate and a rise in employment. The rise in employment to N_1 generates a rise in output to Y_1, through the implicit production function, in the middle panel of **Figure 14.8**. At the initial price level P_0 there is now an excess supply of output and so prices fall to P_1. The fall in the price level reduces the supply of labour schedule in the bottom panel since P_1 rises relative to P_c and employment and output fall to N_2 and Y_2 respectively. In the upper panel, with a fixed exchange rate, the lower price level enhances the money supply shifting the *LM* curve to the right and the *IS* curve to the right as competitiveness has improved, which raises the demand for output to Y_2.

Interestingly, the story is similar under floating exchange rates except that the fall in the price level in the middle panel will result in an exchange rate appreciation. In this particular model an exchange rate appreciation will shift the AS_1 curve and the labour supply curve further to the right. This will give rise to a larger fall in the price level and a larger rise in output and employment than under fixed exchange rates.

Foreign shocks

There have been two major foreign shocks which have hit the UK economy in recent years that can be represented by this model. The first was the oil export embargo imposed on the western industrialised world by the members of OPEC (the Organisation of Petroleum Exporting Countries) in 1973–4, as a result of the war between Israel and some of her Arab neighbours in the Middle East. The sharp fall in oil exports to the industrialised nations led to the world price of oil quadrupling in about eighteen months and stagflation in the oil-importing, industrialised world. The second foreign shock was the effect of a rise in German interest rates in the early 1990s which ultimately led to the UK suspending its membership of the exchange rate mechanism (ERM) of the European monetary system in September 1992.

Figure 14.9 shows the effect of the OPEC oil embargo on the *AD–AS* model. The initial effect is to reduce the productivity of labour and to shift the demand for labour curve to the left to $P_0\phi_1(N)$. The productivity of labour fell because oil was an essential complementary factor of production with labour and capital in the production process, so that the oil shortage led to the production function

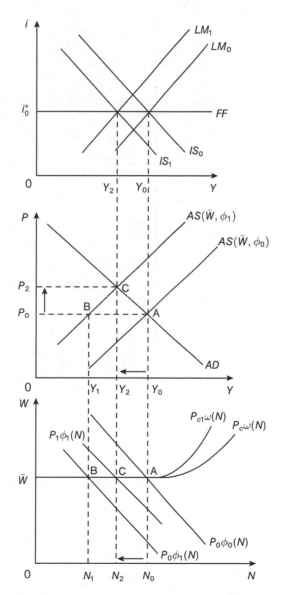

Figure 14.9 *An oil embargo*

shifting inwards, hence reducing the demand for labour. Along with the fall in the demand for labour the *AS* curve shifts to the left from AS_0 to AS_1 in the middle panel of **Figure 14.9**. At the initial price level P_0 there is now an excess demand given by the horizontal distance AB in the middle panel, and so the general level of prices rises to P_2. The higher price of output raises the marginal revenue product of labour in the lower panel and the demand for labour shifts to the right to $P_1\phi_1(N)$, cutting the money wage line at C. In the upper panel the *IS* and *LM* curves are shifted to the left by the rise in the general level of prices.

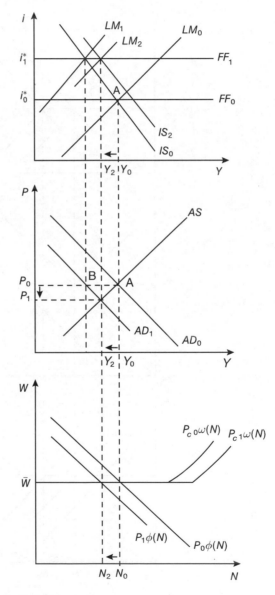

Figure 14.10 *A foreign interest rate rise*

The effect of the oil embargo is therefore a rise in the price level and a fall in employment, output and the real wage rate.

In the UK in 1973–74 the price level implications were made considerably worse by two additional factors. First the Labour government in an effort to protect employment increased demand. Thus the *AD* curve at C in **Figure 14.9** was shifted to the right which had the effect of raising prices further, although it did mitigate the fall in employment. Second, with rising prices money wage rates were bid up, so shifting the *AS* curve to the left from C, thereby reducing employment and raising prices still further. The consequence of the oil embargo was that the UK experienced a wage–price spiral simultaneously with a contraction in output. This phenomenon became known as *stagflation*.

The rise in German interest rates in the early 1990s was a policy change under a fixed exchange rate system. Hence **Figure 14.10** is drawn for a fixed exchange rate with a Keynesian, fixed-money wage *AS* curve. The effect of the German interest rise is to raise the i_0^* line in the upper panel of the figure i_1^*. With a fixed exchange rate system the initial equilibrium at point A becomes associated with a capital outflow, which results in the LM_0 curve shifting to the left to LM_1. With a lower demand for output at P_0 in the middle panel there is an excess supply of output at point B and the price level falls to P_1. The fall in the domestic price level shifts both the IS_1 and LM_1 lines back to the right in the top panel to IS_2 and LM_2. In the lower panel the lower price level will shift the neo-classical demand for labour locus to the left, so the real wage rate rises, but the level of employment is reduced from N_0 to N_2. Thus the tightening of German monetary policy in the early 1990s lead directly to a fall in output and employment in the UK and ultimately undermined confidence that the UK could maintain the fixed exchange rate and remain in the ERM.

Conclusions

In this chapter the effects of policy shocks, supply-side shocks and foreign shocks in the most general model of the macro economy have been analysed. Although it is difficult to try and summarise these various effects, because there is a trade-off between the output and the price response depending largely on the slope of the *AS* curve, **Table 14.1** attempts this task. This table, in addition to covering the shocks

Table 14.1 *Summary effects of policy changes*

Shocks (rises in)	Exchange rate regime Fixed		Exchange rate regime Floating	
	Price level	output	Price level	output
Foreign interest rate	−	−	+	±
Foreign price level	+	+	0	0
Money supply	0	0	+	±
Government spending	+	+	−	+
World demand	+	+	−	+

examined in this chapter, also summarises the main results not explicitly treated in this chapter, the validity of which is left as an exercise for the reader to check (note that the formal results are also presented in the Appendix to this chapter).

As with all models the discussion in this chapter has had to be limited in a number of ways. Perfect capital mobility has always been assumed, which means that the consequences of any current account deficits can be ignored. Similarly there has been no treatment of expectations, as agents adjust their behaviour in response to changes in price level expectations. This issue of expectations will be considered in some detail in Part V of the text. A third, and in some ways the most important, limitation is that the treatment of the labour market is rather simplistic and not in accord with empirical evidence. This issue is taken up in Chapter 15.

Summary

- In the neo-classical version of the model with purchasing power parity (PPP), demand policies are wholly impotent in affecting the level of output or employment. Money is neutral – that is, it is unable to influence any real macroeconomic variable. Supply shocks are, however, able to move the level of output, employment and the real wage rate.
- In the Keynesian model, demand policies are effective in raising output and employment, at least in the short run when there is some involuntary unemployment. Supply-side policies, as in the neo-classical case, can also raise employment, output and prices.
- Income tax cuts, if they are assumed to raise the take-home wage, have both a supply-side and a demand-side effect. The empirical evidence suggests that the demand-side effects are stronger than the supply-side effects.
- Foreign interest rate and demand shocks can also affect the level of domestic output, employment, interest rates and prices, but the quantitative effects depend partly on the exchange rate regime.
- The limitation of the *AD–AS* model is that it is based on the anti-cyclical nature of the real wage implied by both the neo-classical and Keynesian models of the labour market, while the empirical evidence suggest that real wages are either non-cyclical or pro-cyclical.

Suggested further reading

There are few specific references on the *AD–AS* model as it has been developed in this chapter. The best textbook treatment is that of Branson (1989), although this is for a closed economy. The open economy treatment in De Grauwe (1983) is technically difficult and, like Branson, does not always allow for international capital mobility.

Essay titles

1. 'Since both neo-classical and Keynesian models are dichotomous, neither model should be trusted to provide neutral policy advice.' Discuss.
2. Use the *AD–AS* framework to show the potential effect on output and employment of a policy change that results in an overvalued fixed nominal exchange rate.
3. 'In the complete absence of money illusion macroeconomic policy will be ineffective.' Discuss.
4. Critically appraise the *AD–AS* model as a model for forecasting the behaviour of output, prices and interest rates following a rise in the budget deficit.

Questions

1. Explain why purchasing power parity is required to give a horizontal *AD* curve in the context of a model of the open economy. Why is the *AS* curve vertical in this case?
2. Demonstrate the effect of a rise in the money wage on output, employment and prices using the fixed money wage *AS* curve in an *AD–AS* model of the economy.
3. Consider the effect of a fall in foreign income on the level of output, employment and real wage of the home economy. In particular, examine the difference between the fixed money wage and the neo-classical cases under both fixed and flexible exchange rates.
4. What might be the effect of a cut in income taxes in the neo-classical *AD–AS* model? Why might the results for output and employment not be straightforward?

Appendix 14.1 The *AD–AS* model policy multipliers

The *AD–AS* model is made up of four principal relations: the *IS* curve, the *LM* curve, the perfect capital mobility line and labour market equilibrium, which are given as equations (14.1A) to (14.4A) respectively:

$$Y(1 - \alpha_1(1 - \tau_1) + \mu_1) = \delta + \overline{G} - \beta_1 i + \delta_1 Y^* + (\delta_2 + \mu_2)(EP^*/P) \qquad (14.1A)$$

$$M^s/P = \lambda_0 + \lambda_1 Y + \lambda_2 i - \lambda_3 i^* \qquad (14.2A)$$

$$i = i^* \qquad (14.3A)$$

$$\gamma_2 \partial P = \partial P_m \omega(N) + \gamma_1 \partial Y \qquad (14.4A)$$

The labour market is written as a derivative, since the labour market and production functions are inherently non-linear. This format is consistent with both the fixed money wage and neo-classical formulations, although the term $\partial P_m \omega(N)$ will be zero in the fixed money wage case. γ_1 and γ_2 are defined in **Box 12.1** in Chapter 12, noting the slope of the *AS* curve is $\gamma_1/\gamma_2 > 0$, where

$$\gamma_1 = [\omega_N(N) - \phi_N(N)]/\phi(N) \text{ and } \gamma_2 = [\phi(N) - (1-\rho)\omega(N)]$$

Fixed exchange rates

With fixed rates equation (14.3A) is substituted into both equations (14.1A) and (14.2A) which are then solved for income Y and the money supply M^s (see the appendix to Chapter 9 for details). The result for income, expressed as a derivative, is:

$$\partial Y = k^{-1}[\partial\overline{G} - \beta_1\partial i^* + \delta_1\partial Y^* + (\delta_2 + \mu_2)\partial(EP^*) - (\delta_2 + \mu_2)\partial P] \tag{14.5A}$$

where $k = (1 - \alpha_1(1-\tau_1) + \mu_1)$. Substituting for ∂P from the labour market equation (14.4A), gives the following expression for ∂Y:

$$\partial Y = [k\gamma_2 + (\delta_2 + \mu_2)\gamma_1]^{-1}\{\partial\overline{G} - \beta_1\partial i^* + \delta_1\partial Y^*$$
$$+ (\delta_2 + \mu_2)(1 - \rho\omega(N))\partial P_m\} \tag{14.6A}$$

Thus the policy multipliers are:

$$\frac{\partial Y}{\partial\overline{G}} = \frac{1}{D} > 0; \quad \frac{\partial Y}{\partial i^*} = \frac{-\beta_1}{D} < 0; \quad \frac{\partial Y}{\partial Y^*} = \frac{\delta_1}{D} > 0;$$

$$\frac{\partial Y}{\partial P_m} = \frac{(\delta_2 + \mu_2)(1 - \rho\omega(N))}{D} > 0$$

where $D = k + (\delta_2 + \mu_2)\gamma_1/\gamma_2 > 0$.

Flexible exchange rates

With flexible rates the model is slightly more complicated, because in addition to Y and P we have to simultaneously solve for E. Arranging equations (14.1A) to (14.4A) in matrix form, having replaced i with i^* yields:

$$\begin{bmatrix} k & (\delta_2 + \mu_2) & -(\delta_2 + \mu_2) \\ -\lambda_1 & -M^s/P^2 & 0 \\ -\gamma_1 & \gamma_2 & -\rho\omega(N) \end{bmatrix} \begin{bmatrix} \partial Y \\ \partial P \\ \partial E \end{bmatrix} = \begin{bmatrix} -\beta_1\partial i^* + \partial G + \delta_1\partial Y^* + (\delta_2 + \mu_2)\partial P^* \\ -\partial M^s - (\lambda_2 + \lambda_3)\partial i^* \\ \rho\omega(N)\partial P^* \end{bmatrix}$$

Let $M^s/P^2 = 1$ then the determinant is: $\Delta = k\rho\omega(N) + (\delta_2 + \mu_2)[\gamma_1 + \lambda_1 (\gamma_2 - \rho\omega(N))] > 0$.

The policy multipliers can then be shown to be as follows:

$$\frac{\partial Y}{\partial G} = \frac{\rho\omega(N)}{\Delta} > 0; \quad \frac{\partial Y}{\partial Y^*} = \frac{\rho\omega(N)\delta_1}{\Delta} > 0;$$

$$\frac{\partial Y}{\partial M^s} = \frac{-[(\delta_2 + \mu_2)\rho\omega(N) - \gamma_2]}{\Delta} \gtrless 0;$$

$$\frac{\partial Y}{\partial i^*} = \frac{-[\rho\omega(N)\beta_1 + (\lambda_3 + \lambda_2)(\delta_2 + \mu_2)\rho\omega(N) - \gamma_2]}{\Delta} \gtrless 0;$$

$$\frac{\partial Y}{\partial P_m} = 0$$

The interesting point to note about these multipliers is that in a closed economy when $\rho = 0$, or in a fixed money wage economy when $\omega(N) = 0$, the fiscal and foreign income multipliers will be zero and the money supply and foreign interest rate multipliers will both be unambiguously positive.

CHAPTER 15

The New Keynesian Theories of Sticky Wages and Unemployment

Aims and objectives

- To reexamine the microeconomic foundations of the labour market under imperfectly competitive conditions and to attempt to explain wage and price stickiness and the non or pro-cyclical nature of real wages.
- To account for the level of unemployment and explain the persistence of unemployment in Europe during the 1980s and 1990s.

Introduction

The neo-classical and Keynesian approaches to the labour market, analysed in Chapters 12 and 13 and which underlie the *AS* curves of Chapter 14, both imply that the real product wage falls as the economy expands. Indeed, the reason why firms wish to employ more workers and expand output is precisely because the marginal revenue product of labour has increased relative to the money wage rate therefore making output expansion profitable. This analysis implies that the real product wage behaves counter–cyclically, rising in a slump and falling in a boom. The empirical evidence, however, suggests that the real wage is either pro-cyclical or non-cyclical. **Figure 15.1**, for example, shows that for the UK over the postwar period the annual growth in real wage rates and the annual growth in output are positively correlated. It follows, therefore, that neither the neo-classical nor the Keynesian theories of the labour market are able to explain this pattern of wage behaviour. Moreover, the neo-classical model of the labour market also concludes that all unemployment is voluntary, which fits uneasily with the large rises in unemployment experienced by many European economies in the 1980s and 1990s, as shown in **Figure 15.2**. Thus both the neo-classical and the traditional Keynesian approaches to the labour market are unable to account for the observed facts. As a result of these deficiencies the so-called New Keynesian economists have focused on the micro-foundations of the labour market and, in particular, on non-competitive behaviour in the labour and goods markets, in an attempt to explain the facts.

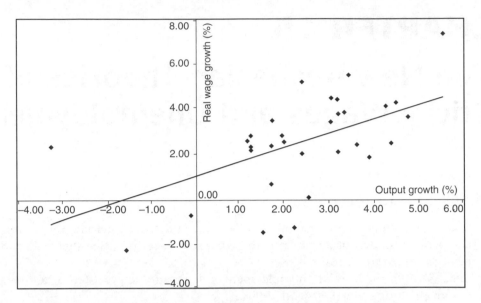

Figure 15.1   *The relationship between UK real wage growth and output*

Table 15.1   *Alternative combinations of price and wage flexibility*

Goods market	Labour market	
	Fixed money wages	Flexible money wages
Fixed output prices		New Keynesian alternative – workers off labour demand curve Involuntary unemployment a possibility
Flexible output prices	Keynes case – workers off neo-classical labour supply curve Involuntary unemployment	Classical case – no involuntary unemployment, flexible real wage rates

Table 15.1 shows three alternative combinations of price and wage rigidities. Whereas Keynes focused on the labour market for the source of rigidities, the New Keynesians have focused more on price rigidities in the goods markets. In this chapter models that focus on institutional rigidities in the labour market and price stickiness in the product markets, arising from imperfect competition are considered, developing some of the arguments briefly outlined in Chapter 13. First we examine wage contract models which in some ways marked the beginning of the New Keynesianism, with their focus on the micro-foundation of the

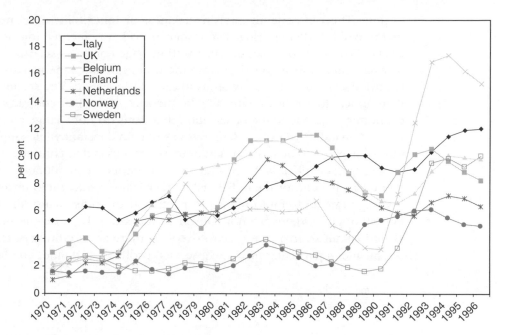

Figure 15.2 *Unemployment, 1970–96*

labour market in circumstances where there was not perfect competition. We then consider the idea that even though wages are flexible there are factors that keep the real wage rate above the market clearing level. These are the efficiency wage theories. Insider–outsider theories of the labour market are then examined as a means of explaining the rise in unemployment since the early 1980s and the concept of hysteresis is introduced. The final sections consider the effect of imperfect competition in the goods market, reflected by sticky prices, on the labour market where money wages are flexible, and a review of the empirical evidence of the causes of the rise in unemployment since the mid-1970s.

Implicit wage contracts

Fluctuations in economic activity result in periods of high and low demand for labour. If households are risk-averse they will try to protect their real income from these disturbances. In most developed market economies wages are not fully flexible because of the existence of contracts between employers and employees, which fix the wage rate for a specific period of time. In the UK this is usually a year, but in the USA it can be for as long as three years. Once a contract is agreed it is unusual to have it renegotiated before its expiry date, and so individual workes are committed to a given money wage rate for a specified period of time. This can certainly explain stickiness or inflexibility of money wage rates that impede market clearing. Two justifications have emerged for these wage contracts. First, it has been argued that setting wage contracts is costly. It is not clear to what extent this is true, but since the notion of adjustment costs is frequently regarded as *ad hoc*, this view tends to carry little weight. The second justification is to appeal to implicit contracts. The theories of implicit contracts are a microeconomic response to the observation that firms do not change their wage scales when demand turns down. Rather wages remain constant while employment and output may vary. The basic insight of these models is that contracts consist of two elements: an explicit wage contract and an implicit commitment about employment. The benefit for the individual worker is the reduction in uncertainty about his wage rate and employment prospects. On the other hand, the firm benefits even though workers are not laid off in recession, because the firm retains its skilled labour so that when recovery comes there are no hiring or training costs.

Consider a particular firm j, whose total profit π_j, is defined in real terms as:

$$\frac{\pi_j}{P} = \frac{P_j Y_j}{P} - \frac{W_j}{P} N_j \tag{15.1}$$

where total revenue is $P_j Y_j$, divided by the general level of prices P, which gives total real revenue $(P_j/P) \, Y_j$. The total real cost is assumed to be the real cost of labour; that is, the money wage rate, W_j, paid by the firm multiplied by the number of employees, N_j, and divided by the general level of prices. The firm chooses the level of labour input in order to maximise its real profits. Differentiating the real profit function with respect to employment gives:

$$\frac{\partial(\pi_j/P)}{\partial N_j} = \frac{P_j}{P} Y_N(N, \bar{K}) - \frac{W_j}{P} = 0 \tag{15.2}$$

From this first-order condition employment is increased until the marginal worker is paid his or her marginal product, that is:

$$w_j = \frac{W_j}{P} = \left(\frac{P_j}{P}\right) Y_N(N, \bar{K}) = (P_j/P) \phi_j(N_j) \tag{15.3}$$

Equation (15.3) gives the downward-sloping demand for labour schedules in **Figure 15.3**, where the general price level index, P, has been normalised to unity for clarity. The higher demand curve $P_1\phi(N)$ is the labour demand in a boom period, and the lower curve denoted by $P_2\phi(N)$ is the relevant demand curve in periods of low demand. The boom and recession states of the world are both assumed to be equally probable.

Suppose there are two types of labour contract. One contract offers a flexible wage rate and no guarantee of a job while the other contract specifies both the level of employment and the money wage rate. If the labour market operates like a neo-classical auction market the real wage rate jumps from w_1 in the high

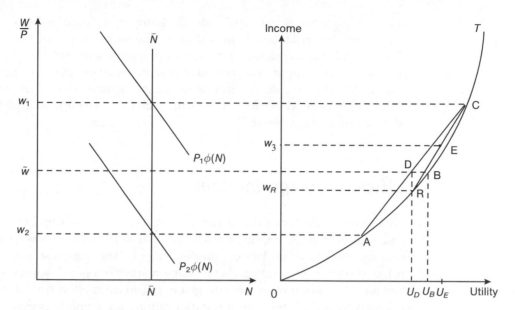

Figure 15.3 *Implicit wage contract model*

demand period to w_2 in the low demand period, in the left-hand panel of **Figure 15.3**, given there is a fixed supply of labour, $\bar{N}$. The reason for the jump in the real wage rate is the fall in the demand for labour from $P_1\phi(N)$ to $P_2\phi(N)$. The jump in the real wage rate would give rise to the individual bouncing between points A and C on the total utility of income curve, given in the right-hand panel as the line $0T$, giving an expected (mean) level of utility at D equal to U_D. The individual, however, could obtain a higher level of utility, equal to U_B, if offered a wage of $\tilde{w}$ without the risk of redundancy. Thus if individuals are risk-averse they will prefer a certain real wage, $\tilde{w}$, and level of employment $\bar{N}$, than the risky prospect of a higher wage but without an employment guarantee.

Suppose now that unemployment benefit is added to the model at a rate greater than w_2. This level of unemployment benefit becomes the reservation wage rate of the individual, denoted w_R, below which it is not worthwhile him or her seeking employment. In this case, because of the existence of state-provided unemployment insurance the individual can choose to risk being laid off in the low demand period, but can try to secure a wage greater than $\tilde{w}$ when working. The right-hand panel of **Figure 15.3** shows this, by joining points R and C, the expected (average) wage will be at the mid-point of RC at E which is w_3, which exceeds $\tilde{w}$. Since point E can be to the right of point B, the agent can choose to risk being laid off and obtain a higher level utility given by U_E.

In this model there are two scenarios. Either the individual is risk-averse in which case he accepts the fixed real wage contract and a permanent job, or this contract is rejected and the individual hopes to earn a high real wage in the boom, but risks lay-off in a slump. The unemployment that arises in the down-turn looks like demand-deficient unemployment, but it is classified as voluntary unemployment. The reason is that the workers *chose* to take the risk of unemployment in order to gain a higher wage rate while they were working. Thus this model while able to explain real wage rigidity, is unable to explain involuntary unemployment.

Efficiency wage models

An alternative theory of the labour market to the risk-sharing between employee and employer in the implicit contracts model, is the efficiency wage model which stresses variations in labour productivity. In the simplest terms the model is based on the proposition that a happy worker is a good worker. It is therefore assumed that workers are encouraged to put in extra effort only if their real wage is relatively high. There are three motivations for a link between effort and the real wage. Leibenstein (1957) argued that high wages allow for better worker nutrition and increased physical strength. Salop (1979), on the other hand, argued that recruitment is expensive for firms and so firms seek to lower labour turnover by offering good working conditions, which simultaneously enhance labour productivity. Finally, Shapiro and Stiglitz (1980) argue that monitoring workers is costly to the firm, and so offering higher wages reduces shirking among the workforce more efficiently than continual monitoring.

In the model developed in this section workers face a trade-off between shirking and working. The more they shirk the lower the marginal product of labour so the lower is the firm's overall demand for workers and the greater the chance of an individual becoming unemployed. Thus the threat of unemployment serves as a mechanism that restricts the extent of shirking at the individual level. It is not rational for firms to try to insure themselves fully against shirking by raising the real wage. If they do so, the resulting increase in labour productivity so increases demand that unemployment falls, which by reducing the chance of being laid off gives workers an increased incentive to shirk. This is the moral hazard aspect of the model: as the firm pays more 'insurance', the likelihood of 'crime' goes up. Therefore agents cannot be expected to choose the optimal level of insurance and thus the unemployment that emerges is not optimal, but rather involuntary. Hence, government stabilisation policies to reduce unemployment can be supported.

Formally, therefore, firms need to choose not only the level of employment but also the real wage rate, since if the market clearing wage rate turns out to be too low, shirking may be encouraged. The output of the firm is assumed to be a direct function of effort, e, so that the production function is $Y = Y(e)$ where $Y_e(e) > 0$. The amount of effort supplied by the employees depends directly on the real wage rate and the number of workers employed. This can be expressed as $e=b(w)N$, where $b_w(w)>0$. The firm's real profit function (with $P=1$) is given as:

$$\pi=Y(b(w)N)-wN \tag{15.4}$$

The firm chooses to maximise profit by choosing both the level of employment and the real wage rate. So differentiating the profit function with respect to both w and N gives the following first-order conditions:

$$\partial\pi/\partial N=Y_e(e)b(w)-w=0 \tag{15.5}$$

$$\partial\pi/\partial w=Y_e(e)b_w(w)N-N=0 \tag{15.6}$$

Rearranging (15.5) shows that $Y_e(e)=w/b(w)$, which by substituting into (15.6) gives:

$$\frac{w}{b(w)}b_w(w)=1=\frac{\partial e}{\partial w}\cdot\frac{w}{e} \tag{15.7}$$

This expression shows that the change in effort with respect to the real wage is a rectangular hyperbola. This is the positively-sloped, non-shirking constraint (NSC) illustrated in **Figure 15.4.**

The figure shows two other schedules. The supply of labour is drawn as perfectly inelastic for simplicity and is at $\overline{N}$. The demand for labour is represented by the marginal product of labour denoted as $\phi(N)$, and is identical to that derived in the previous section, with $P/P_j=1$, when there is no shirking by the workforce.

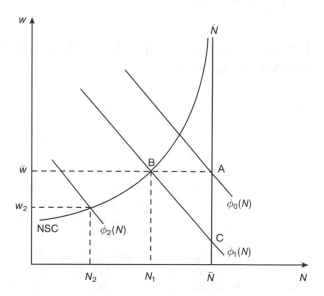

Figure 15.4 *The efficiency wage model*

If there is shirking then the productivity of labour falls and the demand for labour schedule shifts down to the left.

If there is no shirking then the equilibrium is at A in **Figure 15.4**, and there is no unemployment. If, however, there is shirking, then the labour demand curve shifts down to the left to $\phi_1(N)$. In this case the non-shirking constraint also comes into play. Since some workers are shirking the supply of effort is less than the supply of labour and the new equilibrium is at B. At B there is involuntary unemployment given by the distance $\overline{N} - N_1$. The unemployed want jobs at the going real wage rate, but the firm cannot afford to hire these individuals because it knows that the lower real wage that must accompany an increase in employment will induce more shirking and so reduce the firm's profits. Thus the unemployment given by $\overline{N} - N_1$ is involuntary and the real wage rate is constant at $\overline{w}$. Moreover, any further fall in demand beyond $\phi_1(N)$ will result in a much larger rise in unemployment than a fall in wages, due to the shape of the non-shirking locus. Thus a fall in the demand for labour to $\phi_2(N)$, in **Figure 15.4** would reduce the real wage to w_2, but employment would fall to N_2.

The formal model has involved the assumption of homogenous workers. If, however, workers are assumed to be heterogeneous when the demand for labour falls, it does not pay the firm to cut wages because it simply loses its best workers who would voluntarily seek work elsewhere. By maintaining the pre-existing real wage, and by cutting employment through a random assignment of layoffs, the firm can insure that only some of the lost workers are 'good' workers; that is to say, those who shirk less.

The attraction of the efficiency wage model is that is does offer an explanation for involuntary unemployment. A less attractive feature is that although it can rationalise real wage rigidity, it is unable to explain money wage rigidity which Keynes believed was so important.

Insider–outsider models of trades union behaviour

The insider–outsider model of McDonald and Solow (1981) provides a further explanation for real wage stickiness. According to this hypothesis the 'insiders' – those already in employment with a firm – disregard 'outsiders' – those who are unemployed or in low-paid jobs – when setting wage rates. It is useful to think of the insiders as members of trades unions, but any worker with job-specific skills which are of value to the employer has some bargaining power. In the wage bargaining process between the union and the employer neither side achieves exactly what it wants and so the levels of wages and employment may not be optimal.

The firm's objective is to maximise real profits. As in equation (15.1), to achieve this the firm sets the real wage rate equal to the marginal product of labour. Since profits are maximised when this first-order condition holds it follows that if employment is less then profits are lower, and if employment is higher profits are also lower. Conversely, to maintain a given level of profit as employment rises or falls from the optimal level the wage must fall. Therefore an iso-profit line can be sketched in (w, N) space such that it is an inverted U-shape, given by the lines π_i in **Figure 15.5**. Formally the slope of the profit function is obtained by differentiating the real profit function (15.1) with respect to labour (after normalising prices to unity) which gives:

$$\frac{\partial w}{\partial N} = \frac{Y_N(N) - w}{N} \tag{15.8}$$

Thus when the real wage equals the marginal product of labour (that is, $w = Y_N(N)$) the slope of the profit function is zero as the numerator in (15.8) is zero. That is, the profit hill is flat at this point. Thus the profit function is rising when the marginal product exceeds the real wage and falling when the marginal product is less than the real wage. Moreover, for any level of employment a lower wage rate must mean a higher level of profit. So the firm will want to choose the lowest iso-profit line at which the real wage is equal to the marginal product of labour. This is point A in **Figure 15.5**. On the other hand, the higher the real wage the lower the level of profits. The wage that yields zero profits in **Figure 15.5** is w_0, and therefore the line AH is the firm's downward-sloping demand curve for labour.

The trade union may care about a number of issues, such as job security, working conditions, political power as well as wage levels, although to keep the analysis as simple as possible the focus will be on just two objectives – wage rates and employment. More formally the unions utility, V, is assumed to be directly proportional to the wage bill, WN, that is: $V = WN$. Differentiating totally and setting $\partial V = 0$ gives:

$$\partial V = W \partial N + N \partial W = 0 \tag{15.9}$$

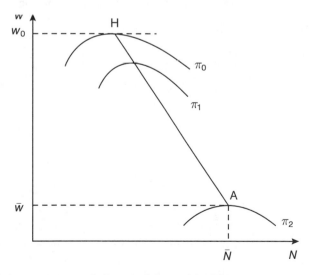

Figure 15.5 *Firm's iso-profit lines and demand for labour*

Rearranging gives the slope of the union indifference curves as:

$$\frac{\partial W}{\partial N} = -\frac{W}{N} < 0 \tag{15.10}$$

which shows that the union's indifference curves are rectangular hyperbolas convex to the origin, as in **Figure 15.6**, showing that higher wage rates can be seen as a compensation for lower employment. Conversely, higher levels of employment are matched with lower wage rates. The union's utility therefore increases in a north-easterly direction away from the origin.

Combining the union's and the firm's positions as in **Figure 15.7**, it is clear that the preferred position for the union is at B, since this is the highest union indifference curve that is tangent to the firm's demand for labour. Point B is consistent with a monopoly union where the union has all the power. The firm's preferred position is at A, which is where the lowest iso- profit line is tangent to the market clearing real wage rate. In this bargaining situation it is assumed that managers have the right to manage, so some intermediate position between A and B will be reached, say at point C. The precise position of C depends on the relative power of the union relative to that of the firm's management. At C unemployment is $\overline{N} - N_1$. To the extent that individuals voluntarily joined the trade union, then this unemployment is classed as voluntary. If the wage negotiated by the union also applies to non-union members, and there individuals subsequently become redundant then they are involuntarily unemployed. It is likely therefore that $\overline{N} - N_1$ is partly voluntary and partly involuntary unemployment.

The problem with this outcome is that it is economically inefficient, since one party can be made better off without making the other party worse off, by moving to a point inside the shaded lens-shaped area to the right of C. For example, at D the firm is no worse off than it is at C, and the union is better off because it is on a higher indifference curve at D than at C. The locus of efficient outcomes is

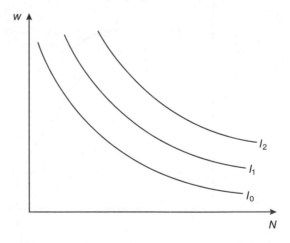

Figure 15.6 *Unions indifference map*

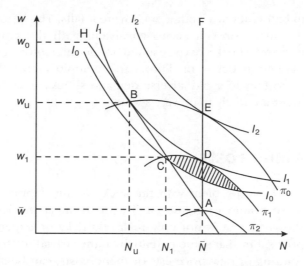

Figure 15.7 *Union bargaining diagram*

in fact given along the contract curve, given by AF, that connects the points of tangency between the union indifference curves and firms iso-profit lines. The slope of the contract curve is given by equating the slopes of the indifference map and the iso-profit map, that is: $-(w/N) = (Y_N(N) - w)/N$, which implies that $Y_N(N) = 0$ and hence as w does not enter this expression the contract curve is independent of w and therefore vertical.

The problem with this microeconomic wage bargaining model is that so far there are not really any macroeconomic consequences. Employment may be the same or less than under competition and in special cases a change in demand may leave the real wage unaltered, but this does not result in aggregate demand affecting output. The crucial point to note is that this is a static one-shot model, whereas the real world is dynamic and hence the bargaining game between employers and unions is replayed each year. To elucidate the nature of this game it is typically assumed that trade union membership is given by last year's level of employment and that insiders only care about their expected welfare. These assumptions then lead to two contradictory results.

First, the insiders will want to consider their future probability of being employed. Lower employment now will tend to imply lower employment in future and thus a higher probability of being out of the inside group. This gives the insiders an incentive to lower the wage rate in bad years and to accept greater real wage flexibility than in the static case. Second, and in opposition to the first effect, if employment does fall the reduction in employment is likely to persist for a long time, because the outsiders are excluded by the insiders when setting the wage bargain. That is to say, there is *unemployment hysteresis*. Hysteresis is when a temporary shock to employment persists for a long time and hence unemployment is permanently higher. It is not clear from the model which of these opposing effects will dominate – whether real wages are reduced in bad years or whether employment falls. The latter effect is often assumed to be dominant since it seems consistent with the empirical evidence that adverse demand shocks have resulted in permanently higher unemployment (see the discussion below on European unemployment). If this is true, then it is very important to avoid adverse demand shocks since the consequences for employment are likely to be very severe.

Menu costs

The basic problem with the sticky nominal price (or wage) hypothesis is how these nominal rigidities spill over to affect the level of output. It needs to be shown that it is not only relatively risky or expensive for firms to adjust their prices, but that some potentially rather trivial microeconomic factors, such as the printing of new price lists or menu costs, can be shown to lead to large welfare losses. Caplin and Spulber (1987) argue that in the presence of imperfect competition, these small menu costs may have a disproportionate effect on aggregate demand. Although the physical cost of altering prices is trivial there are other important considerations, for example, customer goodwill and loyalty. The argument is simply if firms raise prices of existing product lines this may encourage existing customers to look to other suppliers for better deals.

To see how menu costs can be important for aggregate output consider a monopolist who has to set a nominal price before the start of the relevant period, but who can change that price later during the period at a small cost. A situation where the initial price has been set too high is illustrated in **Figure 15.8**. When the firm set its price it did not correctly estimate the future position of its demand curve. As it enters the period, it has posted the price as equal to p_a, but the appropriate price is equal to p_b which corresponds to the lower demand and marginal revenue curves D_1 and MR_1. The firm must decide whether lowering the price to p_b is worthwhile. As far as private profits are concerned, the firm loses an amount equal to area FGH by not lowering the price to p_b, since at q_1 the firm's marginal revenue exceeds its marginal cost – suggesting that a rise in output would add to profits. This area must be small for the firm to decide to keep prices at p_a. The welfare cost to society of the firm not adjusting its price is equal to the area DGHE – potentially a much bigger amount. It is therefore quite possible for even quite small adjustment costs (such as the cost of printing a menu) to be larger than area FGH, but much smaller than the area DGHE. Thus the social gains from price adjustment may far exceed the private gains if all firms act in the same way. This is an example of a demand externality, since the firm is bound by the failure of other firms to cut their prices in the face of a fall in demand.

There are, however, a few limitations of this analysis that also need to be considered. First, **Figure 15.8** shows only the case involving prices that remain too high. If the existing price is set too low, it is still true that firms incur a small

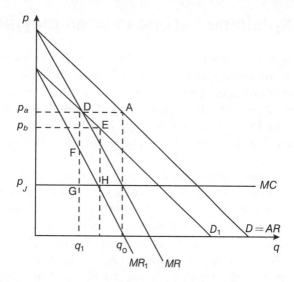

Figure 15.8 *Menu costs*

private cost (in terms of foregone profits) that may easily be dominated by the menu costs if they do not raise prices. It is also true that the implications of not adjusting prices are much larger for society. This time, however, the large area is a welfare gain rather than a welfare loss. Since prices are initially likely to be set too low as often as they are too high, it may be that menu costs on average lead to no significant net effect from society's point of view. A second problem with the menu cost story is that the mechanism does not really work for large changes in demand. If prices fell to say p_j, then the lost profit may well exceed the menu cost. In this case the firms would simply change their prices. A third limitation of the model considered here is that it is entirely static. A more realistic model would permit a succession of shocks over time and permit different firms to be in different positions relative to their optimal price. Caplin and Spulber (1987) point out that if the direction of shocks is always upward, as it may well be in the presence of some inflation, then the effect on aggregate demand washes out on average.

The concept of imperfect competition has been central to the models considered in this chapter. Menu-costs models need marginal revenue to exceed marginal costs, which is incompatible with perfect competition, as are trade union wage bargaining procedures. The traditional notion of imperfect competition suggests that firms match price falls, but not price rises: that is, prices are sticky upwards. Stiglitz (1979) argues that this is because price cuts will attract few new buyers, but higher prices will put off potentially large numbers of existing customers. This rigidity of industry prices upwards implies that moderate increases in aggregate demand are likely to have real effects on aggregate output and employment.

Explaining European unemployment

Unemployment continues to be the most serious macroeconomic problem for the UK and many OECD countries. **Figure 15.9** shows that the average rate of unemployment in the OECD has been on a rising trend since 1970, when it stood at just over 2 per cent. The average rate of unemployment in the OECD peaked in 1994 at about 11 per cent, and by 1997 it had fallen back a little to stand at around 10 per cent. This large rise in unemployment exhibited some specific characteristics:

- Unemployment has risen in a cyclical pattern (see **Figure 15.9**) but the levels of unemployment associated with booms and slumps in the cycle have been rising since the early 1970s. With each successive recovery unemployment has bottomed out at a higher rate than in the previous cycle; whilst in each successive downswing unemployment has peaked at a higher level than before.
- There has been a significant rise in long-term unemployment, which has risen in the OECD area from about 1 per cent in 1979 to over 6.5 per cent in 1994.
- The rise in unemployment in the UK has been most heavily concentrated in unskilled occupational groupings with about half of total unemployment being accounted for by general labourers and other manual workers and being also regionally unevenly distributed. Regions such as the South-east, East Anglia and East Midlands consistently have unemployment rates below the national average, whereas the North, Wales and Scotland have rates which are consistently above the national average.

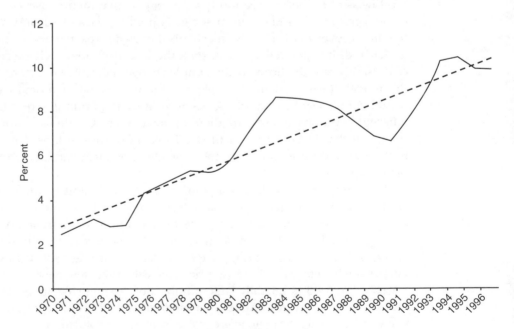

Figure 15.9   *OECD average unemployment rates, 1970–96*

This rise in unemployment has no single cause. It is often attributed to a lack of labour market flexibility especially in France, Germany and Italy (see Siebert, 1997), although in the UK and the Netherlands labour markets are generally accepted to be more flexible, but this has not protected these economies from rising unemployment in the 1980s and 1990s. Bean (1994), while accepting that there is no single cause for the rise in unemployment, notes, in particular, adverse movements in the terms of trade and the effects of counter-inflationary demand policies which have worked to raise unemployment. In this section the extent to which the New Keynesian models of the labour market can help to explain these trends in unemployment is examined.

The implicit contract wage model offers a good explanation of voluntary unemployment when generous unemployment benefits are paid, and when the labour market is characterised by both an implicit contract sector and a competitive sector. Suppose, for example, workers in the contract sector do better than in the competitive sector. In this case potential employees will have an incentive to remain unemployed for longer in the hope of securing a high-quality job in the contract sector, rather than simply taking a job in the competitive sector. Summers (1986) has argued that this 'wait' unemployment is important in the USA, where measures of wage dispersion and measures of wage differences between high-quality and low-quality jobs are strongly associated with different unemployment rates. This kind of explanation is also likely to be important in Europe where reservation wage rates have increased sharply since 1970. The duration of unemployment benefits, the ease of obtaining such benefits, the raising of the minimum wage and the small gap between the lowest wage in the labour market and non-working income in welfare programmes have all made unemployment a lower risk prospect. Thus individuals may well be encouraged not to accept the wage-employment contract on offer, but to try and earn a higher wage while working in the knowledge that should they be fired in the downturn the state will offer comfortable support. To the extent that OECD unemployment is voluntary, then the implicit contract model offers a plausible explanation.

To the extent that OECD unemployment is involuntary the efficiency wage and insider–outsider models should be consistent with the facts. Adverse demand shocks do seem to have had a strong effect on unemployment in the European Union because wage settlements seem less responsive to the level of unemployment than in Japan and in non-EC Europe. That is to say that real wage rigidity is relatively high. This is consistent with all New Keynesian models, but only the insider–outsider model is able to offer an explanation as to why the rise in unemployment should exhibit persistence long after the demand shock has passed.

If insiders' bargaining power is sufficiently great they will set the wage high enough to risk some unemployment, but if the insiders are fully employed with certainty then there is a benefit and no cost. On the other hand, negative demand shocks are likely to lead some of the insiders to lose their jobs, in which case they find it very hard to influence the wage bargain and remain unemployed for a relatively long time. Blanchard and Summers (1986) argue that the structure of

European labour market institutions in the 1980s were exactly ripe for this kind of behaviour. The workers had a good deal of bargaining power in wage setting; there were large negative shocks to demand; and the 'insiders' once on the outside had little or no influence on the wage bargain of the remaining insiders.

Although it is not possible to explicitly test these New Keynesian models of the labour market, they seem to be able to provide a credible explanation for the high and persistent level of unemployment in the EU. The policy advice is to make labour markets more flexible by reducing the costs of hiring and firing, limiting trade union power, reducing reservation wages and improving training. The UK has gone furthest in implementing such policies. A series of laws in the 1980s weakened trade union power by limiting picketing, forcing secret ballots for union elections and strengthening employer power to get injunctions against strikes. In addition, wages councils were abolished and employment protection legislation was weakened and there was a continual decline in how much of wages could be replaced by benefits from 1980 into the early 1990s. In 1996 the duration of unemployment benefits was reduced from one year to six months.

The overall impact of these changes was that labour markets were made somewhat more flexible, and Britain's unemployment rate has fallen since the mid-1908s; although according to Nickell (1997) it is probably still higher than might have been expected after all the institutional changes. To reduce UK unemployment further specific measures have been taken to target specific groups, such as the long-term unemployed or youth unemployment and provide them with local training through the 82 Training and Enterprise Councils in England and Wales and the 21 local Enterprise Councils in Scotland. The common thread that links these diverse but specific reforms and measures is that they are all supply-side orientated.

Conclusions

Unemployment has always been central to macroeconomics, but Keynesian macroeconomics has lacked a proper treatment of supply. The New Keynesian research paradigm attempts to fill this gap by devising models with explicitly microeconomic foundations, inhabited by agents who have rational expectations, which are able to show how nominal rigidities in both goods and labour markets, together with labour institutional structures, are important in understanding observed unemployment. There is, however, no single model to capture this complex phenomenon and it is empirically very difficult to distinguish between the alternative models. Although for the moment it seems that the Keynesian problem of aggregate supply remains unresolved, giant steps have been taken towards a satisfactory resolution.

Summary

- The implicit contract models show that unemployment is voluntary although real wages are sticky if individuals opt for insurance rather than risk layoff. Unemployment benefits set above the individuals' reservation wage will encourage risk-taking behaviour by individuals.

- The efficiency wage model can explain involuntary unemployment because firms are relucant to reduce wage rates since this encourages shirking and reduces profits. Thus real wage rigidity results together with involuntary unemployment.

- The insider–outsider models of the bargaining process lead to an emphasis on the importance of hysteresis effects in explaining the persistence of unemployment, although not all of this unemployment is necessarily involuntary.

- The menu-costs models emphasise that if menu costs are small then firms will not adjust prices, preferring to suffer the reduced profits than to lose market share. Imperfectly competitve goods markets also give rise to sticky prices for reasons that are clear from oligopoly behaviour – the demand curve is price-elastic for price rises, but price-inelastic for price falls.

- Unemployment in the UK is a mixture of demand-deficient unemployment and voluntary unemployment and has no single cause. The demand-deficient unemployment comes as the employment costs of reducing inflation. There is also a substantial amount of structural unemployment that has resulted from the deindustrialisation of the UK from the recessions of the early 1980s and 1990s. It has been argued with regard to the 1980s recession that about half of the rise in unemployment was due to demand deficiency and about half due to structural factors.

- Policies to reduce unemployment in the 1980s and 1990s have been largely supply-side based involving training and retraining programmes, direct tax cuts, reductions in unemployment benefits and the reduction of trade union power in the labour market. These policies are in direct contrast to the demand-side policies pursued from 1950 until the late 1970s.

Suggested further reading

The literature on New Keynesian economics of the labour market is new and diverse. Stiglitz (1992) provides on overview of the New Keynesian methodology. The implict contract literature stems from the works of Azariades (1975), although students might find Timbrell (1989) an easier dicussion of the issues. The insider–outsider model was developed by McDonald and Solow (1981) and reviewed in Solow (1985).The paper on efficiency wages is that of Shapiro and Stiglitz (1984),with Yellen (1984) and Akerlof and Yellen (1986) providing short and long surveys, respectively. In terms of explaining rising European unemployment the survey by Bean (1994) is easily accessible, as are the papers by Siebert (1997) and Nickell (1997). Layard and Nickell(1986) give a break down of UK employment of 1980s and Blanchard and Summers (1986) examine hysteresis effects in European labour markets.

Essay titles

1. Why is the unemployment rate so high at full employment?
2. What do the New Keynesian theories of the labour market add to traditional theories of the labour market?
3. 'The real issue is not the existence of a long-run static equilibrium with unemployment, but the possibility of protracted unemployment which the natural adjustments of a market economy remedy very slowly if at all' (Tobin, 1975, pp. 195–6). Discuss.

Questions

1. Define the following terms: (a) efficiency wages; (b) hysteresis; (c) implicit contracts.
2. Draw the menu costs diagram, **Figure 15.8**, for when the firm initially underestimates the demand for its product. Indicate the areas that represent the menu cost and the welfare gain to society.
3. What basic types of unemployment do the following models predict: (a) the implicit contract model; (b) the efficiency wages model; and (c) the insider–outsider model.
4. Why are the causes of unemployment difficult to identify?
5. What have been the most important causes of European unemployment since 1970? Justify your answer.
6. Show the effect on the wage and the level of employment of a fall in the labour supply in the efficiency wage model.

PART V
Macroeconomic Dynamics

CHAPTER 16
Economic Growth and Technical Progress

Aims and objectives

- To evaluate the contributions to the growth of output from labour and capital inputs and total factor productivity.
- To examine the causes of economic growth with reference to the neo-classical and endogenous growth models, and in particular the role played by technical progress and the enhancement of human capital.
- To consider the policy towards economic growth in the UK and explore some of the reasons for the UK's relatively poor growth performance.

Introduction

In the final part of this book the dynamic behaviour of the macroeconomy is explicitly examined, especially the dynamic behaviour of output (Chapters 16 and 17), the price level (Chapter 18) and the implications of an explicit treatment of time for macroeconomic policy (Chapter 19). The essentially comparative static framework of the earlier parts of the book is put to one side and dynamics explicitly addressed.

These dynamic models require a new notation and a new concept of equilibrium. Since dynamics are concerned with rates of change of key variables over time, $\dot{X}$ is defined as the time derivative of X, that is $\partial X/\partial t$, and the rate of change of any variable X is defined as $\dot{X}/X = \hat{X}$. Furthermore, in models with several variables all growing at the same time, it is important to note that if they grow at different rates then there can be no concept of equilibrium. Therefore in the context of dynamic models the notion of a steady-state equilibrium is defined as a state where all variables grow at the same constant proportionate rate.

This chapter is concerned with economic growth – a central issue to the classical economists of the early nineteenth century, but a topic which witnessed a revival of interest in the immediate postwar years and again in the 1990s. Economic growth can be defined as the expansion of an economy's productive potential over a long period of time. Economic growth is therefore concerned with the long-run trend rise in output rather than its fluctuations, thus this chapter is in contrast to the rest of this book, that focuses on short-run fluctuations in output and prices. In the long run all factors of production are variable, so that both capital and labour inputs must be considered in the production function. In addition, it is also necessary to allow for technical progress, as over the long period both the quantity and quality of factor inputs are likely to be enhanced.

The long-run trend rise in output or productive potential raises two measurement issues. The first is that it can only be measured satisfactorily over long intervals of time or between periods when the utilisation of resources was similar. For example, **Figure 16.1** plots the level of output on the vertical axis against time. The rate of growth is measured as the average slope of the time path of output. If the growth rate is measured between t_2 and t_3, the rate of growth is higher than if it is measured from t_1 to t_3, since the line BC has a steeper slope than AC. It is therefore very important to measure growth rates from the same point of the business cycle.

The second measurement issue is with the concept of productive potential itself. The productive potential of an economy depends upon the resources available. Therefore larger countries with greater resources may have a tendency to grow faster than smaller countries. To overcome this problem it is common to measure the growth of GDP relative to the size of the population, called GDP per capita, to negate the country-size effect. Another problem, which is much more difficult to overcome, is how to compare GDP growth between countries which have different economic structures and currencies. For example, some countries will have a much larger informal economy than other countries that may lead to GDP under-recording of economic activity. If the proportion of the whole economy made up by the informal economy changes over the long period of time relevant for the measurement of economic growth, then the growth of GDP per capita will be distorted. Furthermore because GDP is typically measured in home currency units any comparison between countries must first involve the conversion to a common currency. Usually purchasing power parity (PPP) exchange rates are

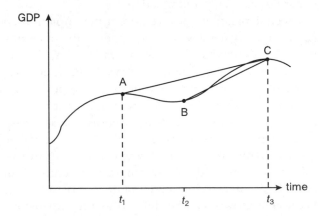

Figure 16.1 *Measuring the growth rate*

used to undertake the conversion to a common currency, although to the extent that there are deviations from PPP over the relevant time period, then the relative measurement of growth rates will be distorted.

To illustrate how growth rates have varied during the twentieth century, **Table 16.1**, gives estimates of the growth in GDP per capita for six major industrial countries. There are four points of note:

1. The large range of growth rates, from 1.15 per cent in France in the 1913–50 period, compared to 9.27 per cent in Japan between 1950–73. This range may not seem so large, but even a 1 per cent difference in the growth rate can make a very big difference over a generation because of the compounding effects of growth. For example, consider two countries 'born' on the same day with equal endowments, but that country A's inhabitants expect to enjoy per capita income growth of 2 per cent per annum whereas country B's residents expect to experience income growth of 3 per cent per annum. In one generation, say 75 years, country A's individuals will have incomes nearly 4.5 times greater than initially, whereas country B's inhabitants will have incomes over 9 times greater than at the outset and twice as large as the incomes of inhabitants in country A.
2. The substantially higher growth rate of Japan in the postwar period compared to the rates of growth in all other countries.
3. For all countries the rate of economic growth was faster in the period 1950–73 than in the period since 1973.
4. The UK's growth rate was relatively low in the period up to 1950, then respectably high in the second period up to 1973, with only Japan surpassing the UK performance, and relatively low again in the period 1973–87. Although including the 1990s would raise the estimate of the UK's post-1970 growth rate, it is interesting that in the early postwar period when UK governments were concerned about the poor growth performance of the UK, **Table 16.1** indicates that in fact the UK was doing rather well.

This chapter is primarily concerned to investigate the determinants of economic growth and to consider policies that may be used to influence the rate of growth.

Table 16.1   *Average annual growth rates (per cent)*

	1913–50	1950–73	1973–87
France	1.15	5.04	2.16
Germany	1.28	5.92	1.80
Japan	2.24	9.27	3.73
Netherlands	2.43	4.74	1.78
UK	1.28	5.92	1.80
USA	2.79	3.65	2.51

Source: A. Maddison (1991) *Dynamic Forces in Capitalist Development: A Long-Run Comparative View* (Oxford University Press).

The next section examines the potential sources of economic growth, followed by a development of the neo-classical growth model due to Solow (1956). This model postulates that the growth rate is driven by the rate of growth of the labour force and technical progress. We then examine alternative classifications of technical progress and consider the principal alternative to the neo-classical growth model – the endogenous growth models. Endogenous growth models suggest that savings are an important factor in determining the level of economic growth and that convergence of incomes is unlikely. The final section concludes by examining recent UK policy towards economic growth.

The sources of economic growth

The study of the potential sources of economic growth stems from the aggregate production function which links factor inputs to output for a given level of technology. That is: $Y=AF(K, N)$, where Y is the level of real output, A represents the state of technology and K and N are the factor inputs – that is, the quantities of capital and labour inputs respectively. To keep the analysis as simple as possible assume that the production function has a specific functional form, given by a Cobb–Douglas constant returns-to-scale production function, which is written as:

$$Y=AK^{\theta}N^{1-\theta} \tag{16.1}$$

where θ is the share of capital in output and $1-\theta$ the share of labour input in output. With this functional form, differentiation of (16.1) with respect to time gives the rate of change of output over time which can be written as:

$$\frac{\partial Y}{\partial t}\frac{1}{Y}=\frac{\partial A}{\partial t}+\theta\frac{\partial K}{\partial t}\frac{1}{K}+(1-\theta)\frac{\partial N}{\partial t}\frac{1}{N} \tag{16.2}$$

or, using the hat notation as:

$$\hat{Y}=\hat{A}+\theta\hat{K}(1-\theta)\hat{N} \tag{16.3}$$

Thus the rate of growth of output is identically equal to the rate of change of technology (technical progress $\hat{A}$), called total factor productivity (TFP), plus the rate of growth of each of the factor inputs multiplied by their respective shares in total output (that is, θ for capital and $1-\theta$ for labour). TFP is the amount by which output would increase as a result of improvements in methods of production with all inputs unchanged and is distinct from labour productivity.[1]

This technical identity enables the potential importance of total factor productivity and labour and capital inputs in the growth process to be computed. The problem with equation (16.3) is that the growth in total factor productivity cannot be measured directly. Solow (1957) derived an estimate of $\hat{A}$ by inverting the equation and deriving $\hat{A}$ as a residual. This measure of total factor productivity is therefore

---

[1] Labour productivity is the ratio of output to labour input, Y/N. Labour productivity may grow because of the improvement in capital inputs per workers.

sometimes referred to as the Solow residual and defined as: $\hat{A}=\hat{Y}-[\theta\hat{K}+(1-\theta)\hat{N}]$. Suppose capital's share of income is about 0.3 and that of labour 0.7. Then if the labour force grows at 1 per cent, the capital stock at 3 per cent with total factor productivity of 1 per cent, then the growth rate must, by accounting identity, be 2.6 per cent. An important point about this calculation is that the growth rates of capital and labour are weighted by their respective income shares, θ and $1-\theta$. Because labour's share is higher, a 1 per cent rise in labour input has a greater effect on output growth than a 1 per cent rise in capital input. Using the numbers above, a 1 per cent rise in the labour force adds 0.7 per cent to the growth rate, whereas a 2.3 per cent rise in the capital stock is needed to make the same contribution to growth. Given that these factor shares are an approximate representation of the actual observed factor shares in the UK, this suggests that labour supply enhancement will raise the growth rate by more than capital enhancement, although economic policy is most frequently directly towards the latter.

Solow (1957) examined the factors contributing to US economic growth over the period 1909–49. He concluded that of the average annual growth rate of 2.9 per cent, 0.32 per cent was attributable to capital accumulation, 1.09 per cent was due to increases in labour inputs and the remaining 1.49 per cent was due to technical progress. Thus, according to this analysis the most important source of economic growth for the USA over the first half of the twentieth century was technical progress. Denison (1985) extended the initial work of Solow using data for the USA spanning the period 1929–82, and found that output growth was 2.92 per cent per annum of which 1.02 per cent was due to technical progress. Moreover, of this 1.02 per cent some two-thirds was due to the 'advance of knowledge'. This is consistent with the view recently made popular by Mankiw, Romer and Weil (1992) that investment in human capital, which is accrued through education and training, is an important source of economic growth.

Recent work on economies other than the USA also highlights the relative importance of the growth in factor inputs and total factor productivity. **Table 16.2** decomposes the growth rates of some of the major OECD economies drawing on Maddison (1991). The first point to note is that for all countries over all time periods the capital input always contributes more to the growth of output than does labour input. Second, total factor productivity contributes more to the growth rate than the factor inputs for both Germany and the UK, although the factor inputs are more important than TFP in France, the Netherlands and Japan. Indeed in a study of the Asian 'tiger' economies Young (1995) finds that the remarkable rates of growth achieved between 1966 and the early 1990s were largely due to a rapid growth of the factor inputs of labour and capital, rather than in total factor productivity. Third, in **Table 16.2** the labour input is sometimes negative, as in the UK since 1973, indicating the move towards a shorter working week and longer vacations. In many countries the impact of these reductions in the average hours worked per worker on GDP offset the positive effects of higher labour force participation rates and improvements in workers' skills. Fourthly, **Table 16.2** shows that there has been a major change in the importance of total factor productivity in the postwar period. From 1950 until 1973, total factor productivity grew rapidly

Table 16.2 *The sources of economic growth*

	1913–50	1950–73	1973–87
France			
Labour input	−0.17	0.18	−0.25
Capital input	0.65	1.84	1.49
Total input growth	0.48	2.02	1.24
Productivity growth	0.67	3.02	0.92
Output growth	1.15	5.04	2.16
Germany			
Labour input	0.38	0.15	−0.49
Capital input	0.62	2.27	1.28
Total input growth	1.00	2.42	0.79
Productivity growth	0.28	3.50	1.01
Output growth	1.28	5.95	1.80
Japan			
Labour input	0.36	2.51	0.67
Capital input	1.21	2.93	2.28
Total input growth	1.57	5.44	2.95
Productivity growth	0.67	3.83	0.78
Output growth	2.24	9.27	3.73
Netherlands			
Labour input	1.04	0.36	0.09
Capital input	1.05	1.96	1.21
Total input growth	2.09	2.32	1.30
Productivity growth	0.34	2.42	0.60
output growth	2.43	4.74	1.78
UK			
Labour input	0.12	0.01	−0.19
Capital input	0.82	1.75	1.12
Total input growth	0.94	1.76	0.93
Productivity growth	0.35	3.50	1.01
Output growth	1.28	5.92	1.80

Source: A. Maddison (1991) *Dynamic Forces in Capitalist Development: A Long-Run Comparative View* (OUP) Tables 5.10 and 5.19.

in all the economies in the table, but since 1973 there has been a marked decline in productivity growth. The reason for this decline in TFP is something of a mystery: indeed it may even be due to measurement problems in that official statistics may not adequately capture changes in the quality of production.

This review of the growth accounting literature does not explain the growth process: it merely identifies, in a rather simplistic way, the likely contributing factors to economic growth.

The neo-classical model of economic growth

Theories of economic growth are concerned with the rate of long-run equilibrium growth, that is with the rate of growth of output that yields full employment of labour and capital. Rising unemployment of labour would, by definition, violate the full-employment growth assumption, and it would probably be accompanied by deficient demand and falling prices. On the other hand, under-utilisation of the capital stock would drive profits and investment incentives down, reducing investment and the demand for output. The principal theory of equilibrium economic growth is the neo-classical theory, which in contrast to the open economy approach of the rest of this book is based upon economies in which there is no foreign trade or public sector. Unless labour and physical capital are highly mobile internationally, however, the closed economy assumption is arguably potentially less important for growth theory than for many other areas of macroeconomics.

The neo-classical model is based on six assumptions. First, because the economy is assumed to be closed and there is no government sector, in equilibrium investment will equal savings; that is:

$$S=I \tag{16.4}$$

This is simply the national income identity that was discussed at length in Chapter 4. The second assumption is that savings, S, are assumed to be proportional to income, such that:

$$S=sY \tag{16.5}$$

where s is the average and the marginal propensity to save. It is assumed that $1>s>0$. Third, there is assumed to be no technical progress, such that $\hat{A}=0$, in equation (16.3). Fourth, the change in the capital stock K is equal to gross investment I less depreciation δK. Therefore the change over time of the capital stock is equal to investment less depreciation which is:

$$\dot{K}=I-\delta K \tag{16.6}$$

Fifthly, the labour force, N, is assumed to grow at a constant, exogenous rate of n, that is:

$$\frac{\partial N/N}{\partial t}=\hat{N}=n \tag{16.7}$$

The sixth and final assumption is concerned with the production technology. The neo-classical model assumes a constant return-to-scale production function such that $Y=F(K,N)$. Constant returns to scale means that multiplying all factor inputs by say, z, will give rise to an increase in output of z. Formally, that is:

$$zY=F(zK, zN) \tag{16.8}$$

Thus if labour and capital inputs are doubled, such that $z=2$, then output is also doubled. This is what is meant by the assumption of constant returns to scale.

With this assumption, the production function can be written in per capita form. To do this let $z = 1/N$, then the production function becomes:

$$\frac{Y}{N} = F\left(\frac{K}{N}, 1\right) = y = f(k) \tag{16.9}$$

In (16.9) lower-case letters denote variables measured relative to the population. Hence y is output per head, Y/N, and capital per head is $k = K/N$. Equation (16.9) is the per capita production function, in general form, which depends only on capital per head. Increasing the scale of operations by increasing K and N proportionately will not change Y/N. Thus there is no gain in output per head from increasing both labour and capital as long as the K/N ratio, k, is the same because the production function exhibits constant returns to scale.

The per capita production function (16.9) is illustrated in **Figure 16.2**. The marginal productivity of increasing the capital–labour ratio is positive, but diminishing. That is $f_k(k) > 0$, and $f_{kk}(k) < 0$. If the production function is assumed to take the Cobb–Douglas form, as in equation (16.1), then there are constant returns to scale since the factor shares sum to unity. In per capita terms, the Cobb–Douglas form is written as:

$$y = \frac{Y}{N} = \frac{AK^\theta N^{1-\theta}}{N} = \frac{AK^\theta}{N^\theta} = Ak^\theta \tag{16.10}$$

The marginal productivity of k is then given as:

$$MPk = \frac{\partial y}{\partial k} = \theta Ak^{\theta-1} > 0$$

and the second derivative,

$$\frac{\partial MPk}{\partial k} = \frac{\partial^2 y}{\partial k^2} = (\theta - 1)\theta Ak^{\theta-2} < 0$$

which is negative because $\theta < 1$. This shows that the MPk is decreasing with additions to k; that is the production function of **Figure 16.2** is concave downwards as shown.

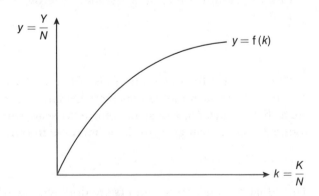

Figure 16.2   *The per capita production function*

From the per capita production function, equation (16.9), it should be apparent that the growth rate of GDP per capita is going to be determined by, *inter alia*, the rate of growth of capital per head, which can be written as (using assumption five):

$$\dot{k} = \frac{\dot{K}}{N} - \frac{\dot{K}}{N}\frac{\dot{N}}{N} = \frac{\dot{K}}{N} - kn \tag{16.11}$$

Using the assumptions that the growth over time of the capital stock is equal to investment less depreciation, equation (16.6), that savings equal investment in equilibrium, equation (16.4), and that savings are directly related to income from equation (16.5), and substituting into equation (16.11), gives:

$$\dot{k} = \frac{sY - \delta K}{N} - kn = sy - (\delta + n)k \tag{16.12}$$

This is the fundamental dynamic equation of the neo-classical growth model. In equilibrium, when $\dot{k} = 0$, equation (16.12) becomes

$$sy = sf(k) = (\delta + n)k \tag{16.13}$$

which says that the proportion of income per head that is saved must equal the rate of growth of capital per head. In other words, to maintain continuous full employment, savings per head must be sufficient to replace worn-out machines, δk, and to purchase new machines in sufficient quantity to keep the growing population employed, nk.

The stability or convergence of the neo-classical growth model can be illustrated graphically as in **Figure 16.3**. The production function is shown as $y = f(k)$. This exhibits diminishing returns and hence is concave to the origin. The per capita savings function is given by $sf(k)$ and exhibits an identical shape to the production function, but lies below at all levels of output because the marginal propensity to save, s is less than unity. There are two rays from the origin, labelled $(n + \delta)/s$ and $(n + \delta)k$. The steeper line is the average product of capital and is obtained by dividing both sides of equation (16.13) by k, that is:

$$\frac{y}{k} = \frac{f(k)}{k} = \frac{n + \delta}{s} \tag{16.13$'$}$$

The flatter of the two rays from the origin is derived by multiplying equation (16.13$'$) by sk. This represents the savings requirement in the model. Note that it intersects the savings function vertically below the intersection of the average product of capital and the production function where the capital–labour ratio is $\bar{k}$. In the lower panel of the figure the dynamics of adjustment are shown such that at any level of k, other than $\bar{k}$, the model automatically converges back to $\bar{k}$. Consider an initial capital–labour ratio of k_1. At this point savings per head of the population, s_1, exceed the savings required simply to replace worn-out machines and fully employ the workforce, i_1. Thus there is a rise in the capital–labour ratio.

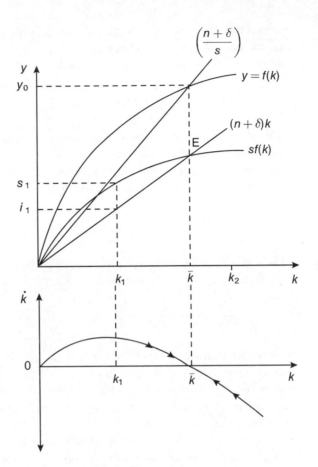

Figure 16.3 *Neo-classical growth model equilibrium*

Indeed k rises until $\bar{k}$ is reached. Similarly at an initial capital–labour ratio of k_2. The new investment forthcoming from savings is insufficient to keep the growing labour force fully employed, so the capital–labour ratio falls until $\bar{k}$ is reached. At point E the capital stock per head is growing at just the right rate to keep the growing population fully employed. Since the population growth is at rate n, the capital stock must be growing at rate n and hence the economy as a whole is growing at rate n.

The model can now be used to understand the determinants of economic growth. There are two experiments that can be undertaken with this model: (1) an increase in the savings rate, and (2) an increase in the rate of population growth.

An increase in the savings rate can come about from a cut in the (implicit) tax rate on savings or through a change in the tastes of individuals between consumption and savings. A rise in the saving rate in **Figure 16.4**, shifts up the savings line from $s_0 f(k)$ to $s_1 f(k)$. The level of income per head rises from y_0 to y_1 and the capital–labour ratio from k_0 to k_1. There is, however, only a transitory rise in the growth rate, while the savings rate exceeds the required investment

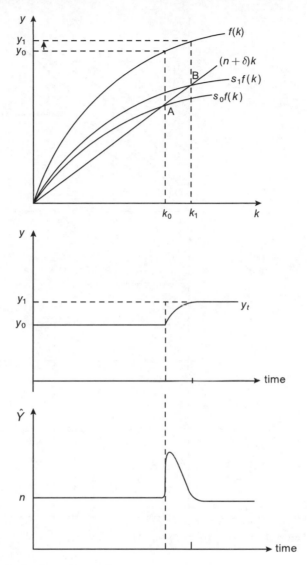

Figure 16.4   *A rise in the savings ratio*

rate between k_0 and k_1. The new steady-state equilibrium position at B is on the same growth path as the initial steady-state position at A. The lower panels of **Figure 16.4** show that income per head is permanently higher, but that the growth rate of the economy returns to its initial steady-state level following a transitory increase that prevails only or so long as savings exceed the required investment rate. Thus the neo-classical growth model has a growth rate that is independent of the savings ratio.

An increase in population growth is illustrated in **Figure 16.5**. This amounts to a rise in n, which causes the $(n_0 + \delta)$ line to swivel upwards, $(n_1 + \delta)$. The new

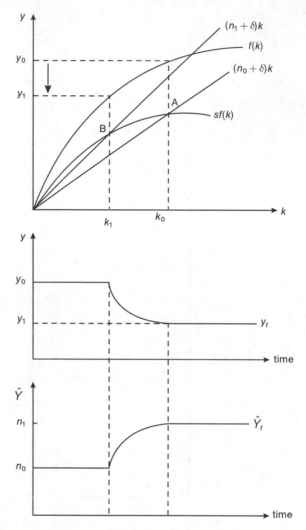

Figure 16.5 *An increase in population growth*

steady-state equilibrium is now at point B. Income per head is lower than at A, as is the capital–labour ratio, but the rate of growth is permanently higher. This result may seem paradoxical but it is typical of many developing countries. The logic is that because of the higher population growth rate, income per head is lower now, but the growth of the labour force means that output can rise faster as labour is substituted for capital in the production process.

These experiments have important implications for economic convergence. Since in the steady state all variables grow at rate n, economies with identical technology, savings rates and population growth all tend to the same level of income per head. This is called *absolute* or *unconditional* convergence. This implies that regardless of current levels of income, if poor countries use the same technology and have the same savings ratios and population growth as a rich country they will eventually catch up, since the model implies absolute convergence in income per head. If countries have different savings rates, then income per head will differ, but there will be a convergence in the growth rates. This is called *conditional* convergence.

Technical progress

The neo-classical growth model of the previous section excluded consideration of technical progress, which is a major potential source of economic growth as shown earlier (p. 320). Technical progress can be 'disembodied' and apply equally to all inputs falling like manna from heaven on to all machines and workers, or it can be 'embodied' technical progress which affects only certain types of equipment and certain sectors of the labour force. There are three ways of specifying disembodied technical progress, which are distinguished in **Figure 16.6**.

If the production function is Cobb–Douglas then:[2]

$$Y = (MPK)K + (MPN)N \tag{16.14}$$

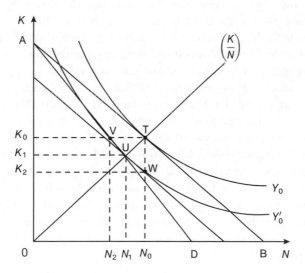

Figure 16.6 *Technical progress*

---

[2] To prove this write the Cobb–Douglas production function as $Y = AK^\theta N^{1-\theta}$ from which the marginal products are $MPK = \theta Y/K$ and $MPN = (1-\theta)Y/N$. Substituting these marginal products into equation (16.12), gives $Y = K\theta Y/K + N(1-\theta)Y/N = Y$.

This can be rearranged and written as:

$$K = \frac{Y}{MPK} - \frac{MPN}{MPK} \cdot N \qquad (16.14')$$

Equation (16.14′) gives the slopes of the lines AB and AD in **Figure 16.6**, where the intercept is Y/MPK and the slopes are $-(MPN/MPK)$. The output isoquants are derived by totally differentiating the production function and setting the change in output to zero which gives, for the Cobb–Douglas case, $(\partial K/\partial N) = -[(1-\theta)/\theta](N/K) < 0$, which indicates a rectangular hyperbola. Less labour and capital are required to produce Y_0 after the technical advance than before, so Y'_0 lies inside Y_0. Thus after technical advance Y_0 can be produced using either K_0 capital and N_2 labour, or K_1 capital and N_1 labour.

Before the technical advance the firm produces at T, employing N_0 units of labour and K_0 units of capital. *Hicks neutral technical progress* occurs when the Y_0 isoquant shifts inwards in such a way that the ratio of the marginal products remains unchanged when the capital–labour ratio remains unchanged. In **Figure 16.6** the line from the origin denotes a constant K/N ratio and the new equilibrium at U has the same ratio of marginal products as the initial equilibrium at T. The shift is therefore Hicks-neutral. In this case the whole production function has shifted upwards so that both marginal products are higher than before the technical change. This can be written as equation (16.1), which is $Y = AF(K, N)$, where A is the index of technical progress. In terms of the Cobb–Douglas function this is $Y = Ae^{\mu t}K^{\theta}N^{1-\theta}$, where μ is the rate of growth of technical skills.

Harrod neutral technical progress occurs when the Y_0 isoquant shifts in such a way that the capital–output ratio remains unchanged when the marginal product of capital is unchanged. From the first condition if output is unchanged at Y_0, capital must remain unchanged at K_0 such that K_0/Y_0 is unchanged. At T the ratio of the marginal product of labour to capital is given by the slope of AB and the intercept of AB equals Y_0/MPK from equation (16.14′). As both Y_0 and MPK are unchanged (from the second condition), this intercept must remain the same for Harrod neutral technical progress. Thus after technical change the economy moves from T to V on line AD, which has a changed slope reflecting more efficient use of labour inputs, but with a fixed intercept. This technical change is labour-augmenting as it allows the same output to be produced with the same capital and less labour (N_2 rather than N_0). It can generally be expressed as:

$$Y = F(K, AN) \qquad (16.15)$$

In (16.15) the technical progress applied only to labour inputs. In the case of the Cobb–Douglas form, labour-augmenting technical progress is denoted as:

$$Y = K^{\theta}(AN)^{1-\theta} \qquad (16.15')$$

Solow neutral technical progress, is the opposite of Harrod neutral technical progress, in the sense that the N/Y ratio remains unchanged when the marginal product of labour is unchanged and the economy moves to a position such as W in **Figure 16.6**. In this case technical progress is capital-augmenting. This capital-augmenting technical progress can be written in general terms as $Y = F(AK, N)$ or in the Cobb–Douglas case as $Y = (AK)^\theta N^{1-\theta}$.

To examine the effect that technical progress has in the neo-classical growth model, consider a Harrod neutral (labour-augmenting) technical change on the production function. Dividing (16.15) by N gives the per capita production function: $y = f(k, A)$, such that A is a shift factor. A continual rise in A at rate g, will result in a continual upward shift in the production function and hence give long-run growth in output per head. The relevant measure of the labour force is now the effective labour force EL, where $EL = AN$, since a continual rise in the productivity of labour is conceptually equivalent to a rise in the labour force. Thus the growth rate of the effective labour force is $\hat{EL} = \hat{A} + \hat{N} = g + n$. The growth rate of the labour force, n, is now augmented by an extra amount, g, due to labour-augmenting technical progress. Hence effective labour input grows at rate $n + g$, rather that at n. It follows that the fundamental equation of the neo-classical model becomes:

$$sf(k, A) = (n + g + \delta)k \tag{16.16}$$

In terms of **Figure 16.7**, from the initial equilibrium at A both the production function and the savings function move up as A rises over time, yielding a continual rise in income and capital per head. The growth rate is now $(n + g)$ rather than in the former model. The analysis of the steady state is the same except that the presence of technical progress gives a higher rate of economic growth. Thus in the neo-classical model the rate of growth depends on technical progress, which allows income per head to grow over time.

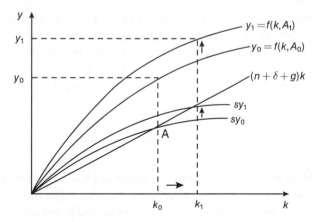

Figure 16.7 *Exogenous technical change*

The theory of endogenous growth

Whereas the neo-classical model predicts the convergence of income per capita between rich and poor economies, this is not fully consistent with the empirical evidence. Thus this alternative model of the growth process seeks to explain why the rich get richer; that is, why the supply of capital does not flow from the rich countries to the poorer countries where the marginal product of capital is higher. The reason must be that the marginal product of capital does not fall in the rich countries despite a rising capital–labour ratio. The new growth theory, therefore, is ultimately concerned with removing the assumption of diminishing returns to reproducible factors of production, such as capital. This is achieved by endogenising technical progress. In neo-classical theory technological progress drives economic growth, although it does not offer any explanation for technological progress. In other words g, the rate of labour-augmenting technical progress, is exogenous. The endogenous growth theories, on the other hand, postulate that the extent of labour-augmenting technical progress is endogenous to the model, depending on the capital–labour ratio. That is to say, that better technology is produced as a by-product of capital investment.

To be specific, assume that technology is proportional to the level of capital per worker, so that

$$A = \eta K/N = \eta k \tag{16.17}$$

where η is the relationship as to how capital and labour are combined to give the production technology (that is, the capital–labour ratio). Second, assume that technology is labour-augmenting, so the Cobb–Douglas production function can be written as (16.15′). Substituting for A gives:

$$Y = K^{\theta}\left(\eta \frac{K}{N}\, N\right)^{1-\theta} = aK \tag{16.18}$$

where $a = \eta^{1-\theta}$. This specification of the production function does not exhibit diminishing returns to capital, since the second derivative of the production function is not negative; that is $\partial Y/\partial K = a$ and $\partial^2 Y/\partial K^2 = 0$. Therefore in per capita terms equation (16.18) becomes $y = ak$ and the growth rate of output per capita is given as $\hat{y} = \hat{k}$. Substituting for $\dot{k}$, the fundamental dynamic equation now becomes:

$$\hat{y} = \dot{k}/k = \hat{k} = sy/k - (n+\delta) = sa - (n+\delta) \tag{16.19}$$

Thus the rate of growth of output per capita depends positively upon the savings rate and negatively on the population growth. Unless $sa = n + \delta$ there is no convergence to any steady-state value of k. Indeed if $sa > (n+\delta)$ capital intensity grows without bound and a higher savings rate permanently raises the growth rate.

The problem with this technical solution as to how the savings rate can affect growth is that it violates the standard principal of diminishing marginal returns – by assumption there are non-decreasing returns to capital as the production function is linear. To explain why capital may not exhibit diminishing returns the concept of capital is usually broadened to include human capital. Romer (1986), for example, has suggested that firms may not reap all of the benefits of capital in that some of the benefits are external to the firm. In this case, when a firm increases its capital stock the firm's production rises, but so does the productivity of other firms. Such external benefits are often thought of as human capital, particularly investment in education and training. Since the contribution of new knowledge is only partially captured by the creator, there can be substantial external benefits. For example, a firm invests in a worker by training him, but then the employee leaves the firm to work for another company. On these grounds investment in human capital in general and in research and development in particular, are the key to understanding economic growth.

An important policy implication of the endogenous growth model is that if economic growth depends positively on investment in human capital, it follows that the more workers that have acccess to education the better the prospects are for growth. To the extent that education is costly, it has been shown by Galor and Zeira (1993) that greater income equality can result in a faster economic growth and, similarly, income inequalities can lead to lower growth because fewer workers have access to education and training.

Policies for economic growth and the UK's performance

Table 16.2 showed the growth record of several of the major industrial countries from 1913 to 1987. **Table 16.3** concentrates on the UK growth record since the mid-1950s, using ten-year averages. Between 1955 and 1997 the average annual rate of growth of the UK economy was 2.4 per cent, with the periods 1955–64 and 1995–97 being periods of relatively faster growth at 2.9 per cent per annum. The decade from 1975–84 exhibits much slower growth, probably due largely to the two oil price shocks in 1973–74 and 1979–81. The relatively smooth path in **Table 16.3** obscures three short periods of negative growth for the UK: in 1974–75, 1980–81 and 1991–92 when the average annual growth rates

Table 16.3   *UK postwar economic growth*

	1955–64	1965–74	1975–84	1985–94	1995–98
UK growth of GDP (average % p.a.)	2.91	2.60	1.48	2.52	2.90

Source: *Economic Trends*, Annual Supplement, 1998.

were − 1.19 per cent, − 1.75 per cent and − 0.73 per cent, respectively. These periods correspond exactly with the two oil price shocks and UK membership of the European exchange rate mechanism (ERM) between October 1990 and September 1992, but are such short time periods that they are perhaps better regarded as cyclical fluctuations around the long-run trend, rather than as a downturn in the trend itself.

The slowdown in economic growth after 1973 is a common experience for most major economies and is associated with a decline in productivity growth. Although the initial cause for the decline in productivity was probably the oil price hoist of 1973–74, it is difficult to explain why such a shock has persisted in restricting productivity growth, especially as oil prices fell in the mid-1980s. Other explanations include a worsened age–skill mix of the labour force, with the baby-boom generation and more part-timers coming into the labour force; or an increase in government regulation, which includes anti-pollution legislation and workforce protection legislation, including trades union restrictive practices. None of these reasons seem to apply universally and the fall in productivity growth remains something of an unsolved mystery.

The UK's growth performance, however, has been worse than other industrial economies over the whole postwar period, despite the claims from the Thatcher government that the UK had the highest growth rate in Europe at the end of the 1980s. This particular piece of propaganda, now shown to be false, does not explain the fact that despite a supply-side growth-orientated strategy, the UK authorities have been unable to permanently raise the rate of economic growth. The policies pursued are well-known – tax cuts to stimulate effort and enterprise, and privatisation and deregulation to stimulate competition. It would seem that to explain the UK's inferior performance we must go back to more deep-seated problems of longer standing. Indeed, the period of highest growth was the period from the mid-1950s to 1970, and even that was insufficient to prevent the UK growth rate from falling behind that of her competitors.

It is difficult even with hindsight to pinpoint the reasons for Britain's relatively poor growth performance, and there have been three principal competing explanations. First is that put forward by Kaldor (1966) who argued that the manufacturing sector was short of labour. Because of the UK's early industrial start, there was no more labour that could be transferred from agriculture to industry as there was in many other countries. Thus the growth rates in manufacturing were constrained by the labour supply. A similar argument was put forward in the 1970s by Bacon and Eltis (1978) who argued that the manufacturing sector was being squeezed by the public sector, which absorbed the best quality labour in relatively unproductive jobs. Neither thesis has been conclusively supported. Indeed the Bacon and Eltis thesis seemed somewhat disingenuous in the 1980s when there were relatively high levels of unemployment and hence an excess supply of labour.

A second explanation is that macroeconomic policy has not been conducive to growth. First there was the stop–go phase of demand-management policy throughout the 1950s and 1960s. The argument at this time was that the exchange rate was a constraint on economic growth, since as soon as a boom developed the UK current account balance ran into deficit that necessitated a tighter demand policy in order to maintain the fixed exchange rate. Then there were the oil crises and high rates of inflation during the 1970s, followed by two periods of substantial overvaluation of sterling in 1980–82 and again in 1990–92. Sharply contractionary demand policies, especially in 1980–82 and 1990–92, reduced inflation but severely damaged economic growth in the process as high real interest rates reduced investment and an overvalued exchange rate discouraged exports. If it is believed that the manufacturing sector is the engine of economic growth, then it is plausible to argue that the reduction in UK manufacturing capacity in 1980–81 permanently reduced the ability of the UK to generate high levels of economic growth. This is perhaps to push the argument too far in that since the mid-1990s the UK has experienced a rise in the growth rate back up to the levels of the 1950s and 1960s. It is more plausible to argue that the severe demand contraction had a prolonged, but not a permanent effect on the growth rate.

The third explanation for the relatively poor UK growth performance is that manufacturing industry has been capital-constrained. There are two aspects to this argument. First, that the overall investment to GDP ratio is too low due to punitive taxation and hence low profit expectations. Although the UK investment to GDP ratio is the second lowest among the industrial countries at 15 per cent (Sweden is the lowest at about 14 per cent for the 1990s), compared to 17 per cent in the USA, 22 per cent in Germany and 29 per cent in Japan, this argument overlooks the fact that the UK has some of the lowest corporate tax rates in Europe. The second argument is that capital is being misallocated into sectors with extravagant capital–output ratios, due to tax-induced distortions of capital towards land and property and away from industrial plant and equipment. Again there is little hard evidence to support this assertion.

Conclusions

In this chapter the sources and causes of economic growth have been explored in an attempt to be able to generate policy advice on how to stimulate economic growth. Theory suggests that capital inputs, including human capital inputs, technical progress and productivity growth are the principal means available to industrial countries to stimulate economic growth. It is, however, clear that no broad consensus as to the ultimate reasons for Britain's comparatively poor postwar growth performance can be formulated. Whilst the current emphasis on supply-side policies, if successful, may produce a once-and-for-all increase in productivity, this may not of itself be able to permanently raise the rate of economic growth. Worryingly, the advent of North Sea oil in the late 1970s does not appear to have raised the trend rate of economic growth, and future membership of the deflation-biased EMU is likely to further constrain the UK's growth ambitions.

Summary

- The neo-classical growth model has it that economic growth can be explained by capital and labour inputs with the relative importance of each factor depending on its factor share. Labour inputs are the most important for economic growth since labour share is some three times larger than that of capital in the UK and most EU countries.

- Long-run growth only results from exogenous technical progress in the neo-classical model. In the endogenous growth models technical progress is assumed to be labour-augmenting, such that human capital increases. Human capital is enhanced by savings.

- In the absence of technical progress the neo-classical model predicts that output per head will eventually converge to a steady state, which depends positively upon the savings rate and the rate of growth of population. This suggests that poor countries will eventually catch up with rich countries.

- UK growth policy has traditionally focused on the need to raise physical investment rather labour inputs or human capital.

Suggested further reading

There are several classic texts on economic growth, including Jones (1975), Hacche (1979) and, more recently, Barro and Sala-i-Martin (1997). Hahn and Matthews (1964) is still an excellent survey, albeit a little dated. On growth accounting the work of Denison (1967, 1985) and Maddison (1987, 1991) is the most important, although Jorgenson (1988) suggests that the growth of the capital stock is underestimated in the growth accounting method. The original sources for the neo-classical growth model are Solow (1956) and Swan (1956). Kaldor (1966) is the principal post-Keynesian alternative. The endogenous growth models based on research and development include those of Romer (1990) and Aghion and Howitt (1992), while those focused on human capital include Lucas (1988) and Mankiw, Romer and Weil (1992). Temple (1999) reviews the now extensive empirical literature, while Peaker (1974) gives a very short readable account of economic growth the UK up to 1970.

Essay titles

1. 'A rise in the savings ratio causes a rise in income per head, but no rise in the growth rate.' Discuss in the context of the neo-classical growth model.
2. What contribution does the endogenous growth model make to the literature on economic growth?
3. 'The road to rapid economic growth depends on the growth of factor inputs.' Discuss.

Questions

1. Examine the relationship between population and economic growth. In what sense is population an economic variable?
2. Use the neo-classical growth model to show:

   (a) the effect of an increase in immigration on the rate of economic growth;
   (b) the effect of the government reducing the rate of tax on savings.

3. Distinguish between alternative types of technical progress. Show how labour-augmenting technical progress can be incorporated into the neo-classical growth model.
4. Distinguish between unconditional (or absolute) and conditional convergence in the context of the neo-classical growth model.

5. (a) What is endogenous economic growth and how does this compare with the neo-classical view of economic growth?
   (b) How do the implications of an increase in saving with regard to both the level and the growth rate of output differ between the neo-classical and endogenous growth models?

6. How can a government promote economic growth? Would such schemes be desirable?

CHAPTER 17
Business Cycles

Aims and objectives

- To investigate the potential sources of business cycles as suggested by alternative models.
- To explain the leading monetary and real models of business cycles.
- To evaluate the evidence in favour of the alternative models.

Introduction

All industrialised societies are subject to recurrent fluctuations in economic activity. These fluctuations are primarily movements in output, and are referred to as business or trade cycles. The classification of cycles is fairly simple, with **Figure 17.1** depicting the symptoms of all cycles – a series of oscillations with constant amplitude and periodicity. If the variable on the vertical axis was output then the economy can be thought of as moving through four distinct phases: phase B (a boom), phase D (a downturn), phase S (a slump) and phase U (an upturn).

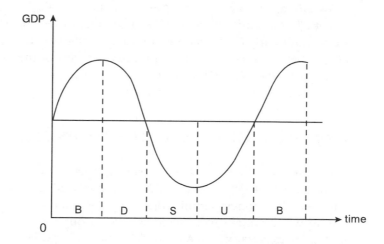

Figure 17.1 *Phases of the cycle*

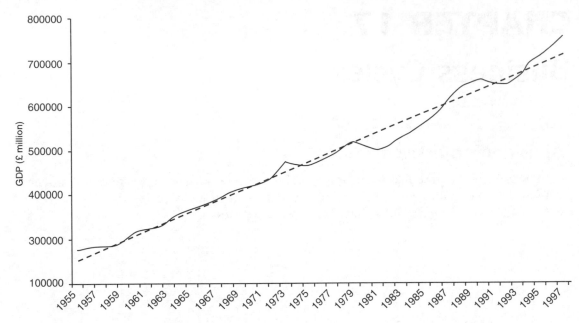

Figure 17.2 *UK GDP 1955–97 at constant prices*

Although this classification is useful to fix ideas, it is misleading in that it abstracts from the long-run trend growth in economic activity. **Figure 17.2** shows a plot of (the logarithm) of real GDP for the UK economy over the period 1956–97. It is clear that over the period as a whole, GDP has increased steadily as indicated by the dotted trend line, with business cycles seen as fluctuations around or deviations from this trend. The focus in this chapter is on how economists attempt to explain the causes of these cyclical fluctuations in economic activity. To this end the approach will be more or less chronological, starting with some of the early Keynesian theories of the cycle due to Samuelson (1939), Hicks (1950) before considering the monetary theories of the cycle. We than move on to examine the New Classical equilibrium theories of the business cycles and finally to consider the equilibrium real business cycles approach.

Keynesian theories of the business cycle

The Keynesian theories of the business cycle grew out of the *General Theory* from the late 1930s onwards. These models all assume that prices are fixed and that the money supply adjusts to the quantity of output. It is therefore output which adjusts to demand shocks, through what Samuelson (1939) called multiplier-accelerator interaction. The process works as follows. An expected increase in output generates a demand for additional capital and leads to an increase in investment. The rise in investment causes output to rise by an amount equal to the increase in investment times the income multiplier. The increase in income causes investment to rise further and so the multiplier-accelerator process continues. These models have progressed through several stages of development which show the effects of including a government sector. In all cases, however, the models are strictly based on the closed economy and are dependent on some basic knowledge of second-order difference equations. It is therefore necessary to start off with an elementary discussion of difference equations.

A difference equation is simply an equation that represents how a variable responds over time. A second-order difference equation for income can be represented by the expression

$$Y_t = \pi_0 + \pi_1 Y_{t-1} - \pi_2 Y_{t-2} \tag{17.1}$$

This says that current income depends upon previous levels of income, according to the parameters π_i. In equilibrium, when the level of income is unchanged, then it follows that $Y_t = Y_{t-1} = Y_{t-2} = \bar{Y}$. Hence from equation (17.1) the equilibrium level of income is given as $\bar{Y} = \pi_0/(1 - \pi_1 + \pi_2)$. More important for the purposes of this chapter, however, is the time path of Y such that equation (17.1) always holds for any values of t, $t-1$ and $t-2$. The time path may take various shapes depending on the parameters π_1 and π_2. Among the possible shapes are some that are characteristic of the fluctuating time path of national income over the business cycle. In other words, only a path $Y(t)$ that oscillates with a regular cycle will ensure that equation (17.1) is satisfied, when the parameters π_1 and π_2 take on certain values. **Figure 17.3** shows several possible time paths for $Y(t)$. Path A shows an explosive cycle. These occur when the solution to equation (17.1) is $\pi_1^2 < 4\pi_2$ and $\pi_2 > 1$. Path B shows a damped cycle. These occur when the parameters of equation (17.1) have the following values: $\pi_1^2 < 4\pi_2$ and $\pi_2 < 1$.

The Keynesian theories of the business cycle rely on the interaction between the accelerator and the multiplier. In particular, it is the investment demand equation that lies at the heart of the business cycle. The following model is based on the work of Samuelson (1939) and Hicks (1950). There are three equations:

$$Y_t = C_t + I_t \tag{17.2}$$

$$C_t = \alpha_0 + \alpha_1 Y_{t-1} \tag{17.3}$$

$$I_t = \nu(Y_{t-1} - Y_{t-2}) + \beta_{0t} \tag{17.4}$$

Equation (17.2) is the goods market equilibrium condition when there is assumed to be a closed economy and no government sector. Equation (17.3) is the consumption function which was investigated in Chapter 4, and which here is simply assumed to depend the upon income last period, with the marginal propensity to consume assumed to lie between unity and zero. The most important equation is the investment equation, which is an accelerator-type equation, such that the investment is determined by the change in income between period $t-1$ and $t-2$, and autonomous investment β_{0t}. Substituting the consumption and investment equation into the income identity gives the following equation for income:

$$Y = \alpha_0 + (\alpha_1 + v)Y_{t-1} - vY_{t-2} + \beta_{0t} \tag{17.5}$$

This has the same form as equation (17.1), where $\pi_1 = \alpha_1 + v$ and $\pi_2 = v$. Since it is expected that the acceleration coefficient, v, exceeds unity and the marginal propensity to consume, α_1, is less than unity, it seems likely that the time path will resemble that of path A in **Figure 17.3.** To see this, substitute in some sample values. Suppose that $\alpha_1 = 0.8$ and $v = 1.2$; then $\pi_1 = 2$ and $\pi_2 = 1.2$. This implies that $\pi_1^2 = 4$ and $4\pi_2 = 4.8$. Therefore $\pi_1^2 < 4\pi_2$ and the cycle is explosive. This implies that any deviation from the initial level of income will result in an ever-increasing or ever-decreasing level of income.

Figure 17.4 shows three dotted trend lines EE', FF' and LL' in addition to the time path for income. These trend lines come from the autonomous investment part of equation (17.5). If autonomous investment grows over time at the same rate as the economy, then $\beta_{0t} = \beta_0(1+g)^t$, where g is the 'natural' rate of growth of the economy. Thus the equilibrium time path of national income, $Y(t)$ is composed of two parts as in:

$$Y_t = Y_0(1+g)^t + F_t \tag{17.6}$$

where the first term reflects the underlying growth rate of the economy, and $F(t)$ is the fluctuating path corresponding to the relationship that must hold between the succeeding values of $Y(t)$, $Y(t-1)$ and $Y(t-2)$. Therefore in **Figure 17.4** start with national income on its steady growth trend, which is represented by the curve EE'. In time period $t=1$ there is a small, unforeseen rise in income above

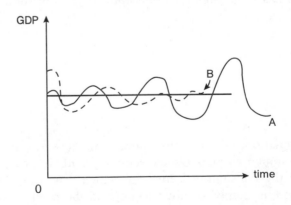

Figure 17.3 *Explosive and damped cycles*

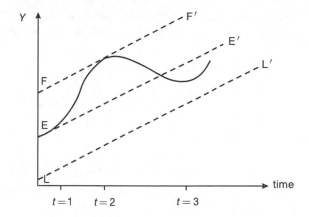

Figure 17.4 *Hicks model of the cycle*

the trend which leads to a rise in investment over and above what is needed to remain in the steady state. The accelerator effect dominates, with a greater than usual rise in income producing a greater than usual rise in investment which, in turn, has a multiplied effect upon income. The effect is to drive income further and further away from the steady-state growth path given by EE'. In principal there is nothing to stop income being driven up forever. Hicks (1950) argues, however, that in practice there are bottlenecks; so as full employment is approached income will not be able to rise at this rate. Instead it will hit the FF' line at $t=2$. At time $t=2$ it follows that income must be rising at a rate which is lower than between $t=1$ and $t=2$. Hence as the rise in income slows then, via the accelerator, investment will fall which will drive down income via the multiplier mechanism. Thus income is now on a downward path from FF' towards LL'.

The problem with this story is that it implies that in the downward phase investment is negative. That is to say, businessmen destroy their capital stock. This is implausible, although the capital stock may be reduced by a policy of non-replacement in which as capital goods wear out they are not replaced. Because it is implausible to argue that businessmen destroy their capital stock in a recession, Hicks believed that the accelerator mechanism did not work in the downswing of the cycle. Therefore the fall in income from the ceiling at FF' is slower and more steady than in the upswing phase of the cycle. As the falling level of income reaches the rising floor LL', which is growing at the rate g, then the accelerator is brought back into play. Hence even before the floor is reached the decline in actual income turns around and another upward phase begins.

Hicks' theory of the income fluctuations offers little help to governments trying to combat the cycle. All Hicks did was to show that the cycle could be unstable, although to some extent self-adjusting. Baumol (1961) extended Hicks' model by introducing a government sector, which would explicitly show the scope for counter-cyclical macroeconomic policy. As it turns out this is a doubled-edged sword, especially in a dynamic situation. To simplify the model the growth factor can be ignored so the model is now written as four equations:

$$Y_t = C_t + I_t + G_t \tag{17.2'}$$

$$C_t = \alpha_0 + \alpha_1 Y_{t-1} \tag{17.3}$$

$$I_t = \nu(Y_{t-1} - Y_{t-2}) \tag{17.4'}$$

$$G_t = \gamma(\overline{Y}_t - Y_t) \tag{17.7}$$

The principal addition is the inclusion of G in the income identity. Rather than assume G to be exogenous Baumol suggested that the authorities could adjust G according to the economic cycle. Equation (17.7) says that government spending will rise as the gap between $\overline{Y}_t$ and Y_t increases. That is, as the gap between the full employment level of income and actual income increases, so the authorities will raise spending. Similarly, if current income rises above full employment income then government spending will be reduced to prevent inflationary pressures from arising. The crucial question is what does this extension of the model do to the time path of income?

Substituting the elements of the modified model into equation (17.2') the dynamic equilibrium condition obtained is:

$$Y_t = (\alpha_1 + \nu)Y_{t-1} - \nu Y_{t-1} + \alpha_0 + \gamma(\overline{Y}_t - Y_t) \tag{17.8}$$

Therefore, rearranging yields:

$$Y_t(1+\gamma) = (\alpha_1 + \nu)Y_{t-1} - \nu Y_{t-1} + \alpha_0 + \gamma \overline{Y}_t$$

$$Y_t = \left(\frac{\alpha_1 + \nu}{1+\gamma}\right)Y_{t-1} - \left(\frac{\nu}{1+\gamma}\right)Y_{t-2} + \left[\frac{\alpha_0 + \gamma \overline{Y}_t}{1+\gamma}\right] \tag{17.9}$$

Ignoring the final term in the square brackets, this model also reduces to two parameters, which again correspond to π_1 and π_2. In this case $\pi_1 = (\alpha_1 + \nu)/(1+\gamma)$ and $\pi_2 = \nu/(1+\gamma)$. This has important implications for the time path of income which is illustrated in **Figure 17.5. Figure 17.5** plots the parameters π_1 and π_2 on the vertical and horizontal axes respectively. The curve divides the diagram into three areas labelled I, II and III. In area II the conditions exist for explosive cyclical behaviour since $\pi_1^2 < 4\pi_2$ and $\pi_2 > 1$ prevail, whereas in area III $\pi_2 < 1$ so cycles are damped. In the model due to Hicks where there is no government sector, cycles are explosive. Therefore the model dynamics are consistent with the dynamics in area II. To be precise, assume that the specific point is H. In Baumol's model both parameters are divided by $(1+\gamma)$, a positive number greater than one, so both parameters will be smaller, moving the model to a position such as B. Since a fall in the value of π_1 increases the frequency of the cycle, while a rise in the value of π_2 raises the instability of the model, a move from H to B in **Figure 17.5** has the effect of making the model more stable, but with more frequent cycles. Thus government fiscal policy has a stabilising effect on the economy.

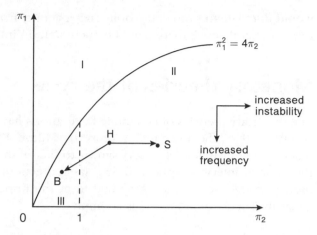

Figure 17.5 *Stability for the Hicks–Baumol model*

Interestingly, counter-cyclical policy may not always be beneficial. Baumol's model is able to show that counter-cyclical policy may result in increased instability in the model. To formally demonstrate this potential instability assume that the government only changes fiscal policy after a two-period lag. Hence equation (17.7) becomes:

$$G_t = \gamma \, (\overline{Y}_{t-2} - Y_{t-2}) \tag{17.7'}$$

With this policy reaction function, the difference equation for national income has the form:

$$Y_t = (\alpha_1 + \nu)Y_{t-1} - (\nu + \gamma)Y_{t-2} + [\alpha_0 + \gamma\overline{Y}_{t-2}] \tag{17.10}$$

Equation (17.10) shows that the parameters π_1 and π_2 now have values $(\alpha_1 + \nu)$ and $(\nu + \gamma)$ respectively. While the value of π_1 is the same as it was at H, the value of π_2 has risen. Thus with a lagged response of the government to income deviations the model moves from point H to point S in **Figure 17.5**, indicating greater instability. Thus the cycles have a greater amplitude, but with the same frequency as at H. This is an extremely important result because it shows, even within the context of a simple model of the goods market, that discretionary fiscal policy may destabilise the economy rather than stabilise it, if the government is unable to respond immediately to economic information.

These models although formally closed economy models can easily be extended to the open economy by adding the current balance to the national income identity (as in Chapter 4). In this case the level of foreign income could be a source of the business cycle. With a fixed exchange rate regime the cycles of one country would be transmitted to other countries, so giving rise to an international business cycle. With floating exchange rates, however, the exchange rate would fluctuate to protect the domestic economy from foreign goods market disturbances and hence there would be no common international business cycle.

Monetary theories of the cycle

The monetary theories of economic fluctuations have been made popular in the second half of the twentieth century by Milton Friedman, although in many respects Friedman's work is very similar to that of the neo-classical economists of the pre-and interwar years. The neo-classical economists emphasised the role of money in the cycle, which stemmed from the importance they attached to the Quantity Theory of Money. This is simply:

$$\overline{M^s} = kPY \tag{17.11}$$

where $\overline{M^s}$ is the money supply, P is the price level, Y is the level of output and k is the factor of proportionality, which is inversely related to the velocity of circulation. The monetary theorists argue that in the long run output is determined by the supply side of the economy to give a level of output consistent with full employment. In this case changes in the rate of growth of the money supply only lead to changes in the price level. In the short run, however, changes in the money supply can cause fluctuations in the level of output. Thus the crucial features of this story are that causality runs from the money supply to output, and that output and the money supply are not related in the long run. Much of Friedman's work has been devoted to demonstrating that this is an appropriate view of the business cycle.

Friedman and Schwartz (1963a, 1963b) consider the contraction of the money supply to be primarily responsible for the severe contractions of the US economy in 1873–9, 1892–4, 1907–8, 1921–2, 1929–33 and 1937–8. Since the money supply has continued to rise during the less severe recessions, Friedman and Schwartz relate fluctuations in the rate of change of the money supply to variations in economic activity. From this exercise they are able to show that, on average, decreases in the rate of change of the money supply precede the reference cycle peak by seven months, while increases in the rate of change of the money supply lead the reference cycle trough by four months. The standard deviation of the lead in the money supply series is eight months at the peak and six months at the trough. From this and other evidence Friedman and Schwartz conclude that changes in the rate of growth of the money supply cause changes in the same direction in real output which occur after a long and variable lag. This conclusion leads them to eschew the use of discretionary monetary policies as a means of damping the cycle.

This approach to explaining business cycles has been highly controversial for two main reasons. The first concerns the issue of timing. To observe that changes in one variable, M^s, precede changes in another variable, Y, does not justify the conclusion that the change in M^s *caused* the change in Y. The change in both variables could, for example, have been caused by a change in another variable, Z.

A second doubt about Friedman's explanation of the cycle is the extent to which money supply changes are endogenously determined by the cycle. It is likely that the public's currency to deposits ratio will vary as income changes, as may the banks' own reserve ratio. As the demand for money grows less rapidly in relation to its supply, the rate of interest is predicted to fall. If a fall in the interest rate increases the currency to deposits or reserve to deposits ratios, the money supply will contract, given a constant money base. In this case the direction of causality is from income to the money supply so that the money supply is an endogenous variable. A similar argument was put forward before the First World War by Hawtrey (1913) who argued that the money supply was partly determined by endogenous forces. In a recession, central bank policy may be expansionary so that trade is stimulated. It is likely, however, that the monetary expansion will be maintained after recovery has begun. This might be reinforced by changes in the distribution of income, since as the level of prices rise, income is transferred to business owners and away from fixed income earners (including the labour force). This transfer can maintain the recovery without further expansion of the money supply. The end comes when the central bank restricts monetary growth and the economy spirals downwards in a reverse of the upswing.

The business cycle in these monetary theories is clearly dependent on banking policy and the interaction between income and the money supply. In this sense Friedman's analysis is somewhat simplistic when compared to those early twentieth century theorists. This overemphasis was perhaps in part due to the need to convince the profession that Keynesian fine-tuning was not a feasible strategy for economic policy. The monetary theories of Friedman and Schwartz and the early real theories of the cycle due, *inter alia*, to Samuelson and Hicks all focused on fluctuations in aggregate demand as causing the business cycle.

Modern theories of the business cycle, however, have emphasised the microeconomic foundations of the supply side of the economy, rather than demand-side aggregates such as investment or the money supply. There are two basic models: the Lucas price level misperceptions theory which is based on agents faced with limited information, and Kydland and Prescott's theory of real business cycles which is based on technology shocks. Both models assume that markets always clear and that agents have rational expectations. These are the models considered in the next two sections.

The new classical misperceptions theory of the cycle

The new classical view of the business cycle is related to the monetarist view in that fluctuations in the money supply process are the underlying cause of the cycle. The crucial element in this view is how these fluctuations in the money supply are transmitted to fluctuations in output. In this transmission mechanism individual producers play a key role, since it is their inability to distinguish between changes in the general level of prices and changes in relative prices that give rise to the business cycle. The problem faced by producers is that they are not able to observe the aggregate price level in the current period, although they are assumed to have expectations as to what it will be. If these expectations are correct then there is no business cycle. More likely, agents' expectations about the price level will not be wholly correct, which means that agents will have confused the extent of relative price changes compared to changes in the general level of prices which lead to fluctuations in output.

To formalise this statement the supply of output in market i can be written as:

$$y_i - \bar{y}_i = \zeta(p_i - p_i^e) \qquad (17.12)$$

which says that the deviation of the log of output, y_i, from its trend level, $\bar{y}_i$, is due to the deviation of the log of the actual price level, p_i, from the log of the expected price level, p_i^e. If the expected and actual price levels are identical then there is no deviation of output from its trend. The problem faced by suppliers is that both the average expected price level and the local price term are subject to random shocks, which cannot be separately identified. This is vital to suppliers because they will only want to increase their supply if there is an increased relative demand for their product. If there is a general rise in the level of prices, then there is no need to supply more goods because it is a nominal increase and not due to a higher real demand. So when p_i rises the problem for the supplier is to determine whether this rise is due to a rise in p_i^e or to an increase in the real demand for the product. This is called the *signal extraction* problem.

To understand how agents attempt to extract the relevant information assume that agent i's price is made up of two elements, the general price level p and a stochastic demand shock z_{it}:

$$p_{it} = p_t + z_{it} \qquad (17.13)$$

The relative demand shock is assumed to be a normally-distributed random variable with a mean of zero and a constant variance equal to σ_z^2, that is $z_{it} \to N(0, \sigma_z^2)$. The general level of prices is also normally distributed with a mean of $\bar{p}$ and a variance of σ_p^2. By assumption, p_t and z_{it} are independent so that $Cov(p, z_i) = 0$. Because p_t and z_{it} are independent then the variance of p_i, $Var(p_{it})$, is simply the sum of the variances of p_t and z_{it}, that is: $Var(p_{it}) = Var(p) + Var(z_{it}) = \sigma_p^2 + \sigma_z^2$. Since the mean of z is zero, it follows from equation (17.13) that the mean of p_{it} is equal to the average price level: that is $\bar{p}_{it} = \bar{p}$. Agents are also assumed to form their expectations about p_i rationally. That is to say, agents will use all available information to them and the forecasts will be unbiased and correct on average. Formally:

$$p_i^e = E(p_i | I_t) = E(p | I_t) = E(p | p_i) \qquad (17.13')$$

where E is the expectations operator and I_t denotes the information set available at time t, when the expectation or forecast is made. Thus the best guess that agents can make about the general level of prices is to use the information observed in their own market to estimate it. Agents can forecast the expected price level by running a simple regression of the general price level on the actual price level in market i, that is to estimate $p = a + bp_i + u$. From an ordinary least-squares regression the parameters a and b are given as:

$$\hat{b} = Cov(p, p_i)/Var(p_i) = \sigma_p^2/(\sigma_p^2 + \sigma_z^2) \quad \text{and} \tag{17.14}$$

$$\hat{a} = \bar{p} - \hat{b}\bar{p}_i = (1 - \hat{b})\bar{p} \tag{17.15}$$

Thus, substituting for $\hat{a}$ and $\hat{b}$ in the regression equation the expected price level can be written as:

$$p^e = (1 - \hat{b})\bar{p} + \hat{b}p_i \tag{17.16}$$

Thus the parameter $\hat{b}$ is the weight attached to the observed local price in the forecast of p. From equation (17.14) it is clear that the size of $\hat{b}$ depends on the relative variances of inflation and the stochastic demand shock in market i. If inflation is constant then $\sigma_p^2 \to 0$ and $\hat{b} \to 0$. This means that the expected average price level is equal to the average price level, $p^e = \bar{p}$, so that any change in p_i would be interpreted as a shift in relative prices. Similarly if inflation was highly variable such that $\sigma_p^2 \to \infty$, then $\hat{b} \to 1$ and any change in p_i would be interpreted as due to inflation.

To understand the effect this signal extraction problem poses for the supplier substitute equation (17.16) into equation (17.12) to give:

$$y_i = \bar{y}_i + \zeta(p_i - (1 - \hat{b})\bar{p} - \hat{b}p_i) = \bar{y}_i + \zeta(1 - \hat{b})(p_i - \bar{p}) \tag{17.17}$$

Thus, output in market i exceeds its trend level only if local prices exceed the general level of prices. Furthermore, as $\hat{b} \to 1$ then $y_i = \bar{y}_i$, since all price shocks are interpreted as being due to inflation and hence suppliers will not wish to change their output levels. On the other hand, if $\hat{b} \to 0$ then $y_i > \bar{y}_i$, if $p_i > \bar{p}$ since the relative rise in p_i will be interpreted as due to a rise in the demand for the product in market i. Aggregating over all markets the aggregate Lucas 'surprise' supply curve is derived, which can be written as:

$$y_t - \bar{y}_t = \zeta(1 - b)(p_t - \bar{p}_t) \tag{17.18}$$

This says that output will grow faster than the trend if actual prices rise faster than expected average prices. This comes about because if suppliers believe they observe their prices rising faster than inflation, they are encouraged to raise output above the normal levels. When they realise that they have made a mistake and that the rise in their prices was just a rise in the average price level, output falls back to its trend rate. Thus business cycles are generated by agents' misperceptions of their prices relative to the average price level.

The Lucas supply curve of equation (17.18) is illustrated in **Figure 17.6**. If agents' expectations are correct then $\hat{b} \to 1$ so that equation (17.18) reduces to $y_t = \bar{y}$ and output is independent of the price level. This is shown as the vertical line, $\bar{y}$, in **Figure 17.6**. Alternatively, suppose $\hat{b} < 1$; in this case the AS curve is upwards-sloping since $\partial p/\partial y = 1/\zeta(1 - b) > 0$. This is the $AS(\bar{p}_0^e)$ schedule. The AD curve is given by the quantity theory of money from equation (17.11), which can be shown to be a rectangular hyperbola and drawn for a given level of the money supply.[1]

If the authorities announce a monetary expansion from m_0 to m_1, the AD line shifts up and the producers will anticipate that the general level of prices will rise. Thus the model moves from point A to point B, prices rise as expected and there is no change in output because relative prices have not changed. On the other hand, if the authorities increase the money supply unexpectedly, agents will be surprised when their local market prices are observed to be rising. They will perceive this as a relative price change and seek to expand output along the supply curve $AS(\bar{p}_0^e)$ towards C. In the next period when they are able to observe the actual general price level, they will immediately reduce output back to $\bar{y}$. The rise in output was only temporary, but sufficient to generate a cyclical movement in output and solely due to agents confusing nominal and real price movements.

There are several criticisms of this theory of the business cycle. The most important limitation in this context is that the model is unable to explain the persistence of cycles. The theory assumes that random shocks are uncorrelated and therefore implies that only serially uncorrelated, and hence unpredictable monetary disturbances will affect the deviation of output from the trend. The movements in output that actually occur over the business cycle, however, are serially correlated. The new classical school attempt to explain this inconsistency by arguing that either there are lags in obtaining information or that the capital stock and employment levels can only change with a lag. This, of course, is

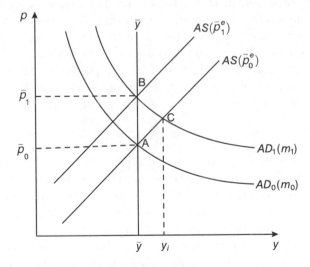

Figure 17.6 *The new classical model of the business cycle*

---

[1] Formally, differentiating the log-linear version of equation (17.11) assuming k is constant gives $\partial \bar{m} = \partial p + \partial y$. Rearranging gives the slope of the AD curve as $\partial p / \partial y = -1$ where the money supply is unchanged.

entirely *ad hoc* and something the new classical school initially sought to avoid in their rigorous microeconomic foundations approach to macroeconomic fluctuations. Such lags and bottlenecks, however, can be captured empirically by adding a lagged output term to equation (17.16), which becomes:

$$y_t - \bar{y}_t = \zeta(1-b)(p_t - \bar{p}_t) + \lambda(y_{t-1} - \bar{y}) \tag{17.19}$$

Now output is serially correlated with its lagged value even though the forecast error is independent of the previous period's forecast error. Thus the divergence of actual prices from expected prices is insufficient of itself to generate the observed serially-correlated time series in output and employment.

A second criticism of the new classical approach is that the model relies on incomplete information to produce cyclical fluctuations. That is to say, output fluctuations occur when traders misperceive general price changes as relative price changes. Output changes may, however, also occur in response to correctly perceived price changes. Suppose there is an increase in military expenditure to finance a war, for example, which causes the real value of output to rise temporarily and traders to increase their current output. Such random real shocks, however, are treated as uncorrelated and are regarded as insufficient to generate cyclical fluctuations. Hence there is a need to specify that important cyclical fluctuations may arise from traders mistaking general price changes for changes in relative prices due to real factors, rather then simply to monetary factors.

A final criticism is that markets are always assumed to clear. This is in contrast to both the Keynesian and monetarist theories of the cycle. The assumption of continuous market clearing, however, is more a methodological device than reflecting believed real world conditions. However, it is so unrealistic as to detract from the model.

Real business cycle theory

As noted above, the Lucas approach to cycles is about agents' misperceptions in prices, which since the general level of prices is determined by the money supply leads to a monetary propagation theory of the cycle. Real business cycles have many features in common with the Lucas model, but they emphasise real shocks as the propagation mechanism for business cycles. The classic treatment is that due to Kydland and Prescott (1982), for whom cycles in economic activity are generated by shifts in labour productivity reflecting technological changes. These shocks are both the source and the propagation mechanism of business cycles. They are therefore a natural phenomenon and not a sign of the malfunctioning of the economy.

The starting point of this class of models is with the production function. Assume that there is a favourable shock to technology. This shifts up the production function, which increases production, the demand for labour and the current real wage rate. Individual agents must decide how to respond to this shock, and in part their response will depend whether they perceive the shock to be transitory or permanent: that is, they too face a signal extraction problem. To the extent that workers perceive the shock to be transitory, the real wage is perceived to be high relative to future real wages, and workers will try to work more hours today and take more leisure later, when the real wage falls again. This is referred to as the *intertemporal substitution of labour* and is a key feature of the real business cycle transmission mechanism and ensures that current period output rises.

Figure 17.7 shows the production function $Y=A_0F(N, K)$ where labour input is initially at N_0. The tangent to the production function at E, vertically above N_0, gives the marginal product of labour which under competitive conditions is equal to the real wage rate, w_0. A technology shock that shifts the production function to $A_1F(N, K)$, leads to a rise in the real wage rate to w_1 at N_0 and a rise in output to Y_1. In this case the rise in output has been achieved by the employees working overtime in response to the higher real wage rates. The firm could have decided to also employ more workers, up to N_1, since between F and G the marginal product of labour is higher on the new production function than at E and the real wage rate is correspondingly higher. In the next period the shock is reversed, the real wage rate falls and the employees work less hours.

To the extent that producers estimate the shock to be permanent, they will begin the construction of new capital in order to provide for increased production in the future. The construction of new machines, however, takes time so that output increases some time after the initial shock and increases for some time. If there are no further shocks to technology, producers might eventually find themselves with too much capital compared with what is needed to maintain steady-state growth. In this case the optimal strategy would be to slow investment down until capital depreciation brings the capital stock back to its steady-state path. Output and employment would also fluctuate with the capital stock.

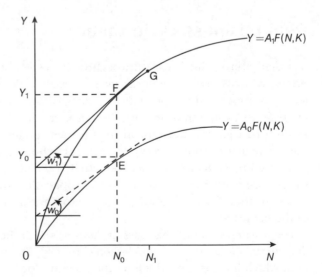

Figure 17.7   *Real business cycle model*

The case for real business cycle models is that they can closely mimic real world business cycles. In particular, employment and the real wage rate vary procyclically, which is consistent with the data as noted in Chapter 15.

A second type of evidence offered is purely statistical. Suppose output grows along a trend, with business cycle fluctuations superimposed. Such a model might be:

$$y_t = at + by_{t-1} + \varepsilon_t \tag{17.20}$$

where t is a deterministic time trend and ε_t is a random error. If there is a shock to ε_t, output rises above the trend. Since y_t depends on y_{t-1} the shock is also transmitted to future periods, generating the serial correlation typical of business cycles, but with $|b| < 1$ the effect of a shock to ε_t on future output gradually diminishes and output reverts to the trend. A similar, but different model of output is that which follows a random walk with drift, in which case the time series process is:

$$y_t = at + y_{t-1} + \varepsilon_t \quad \text{or} \quad \Delta y_t = at + \varepsilon_t \tag{17.21}$$

Equation (17.21) is like equation (17.20) with the exception that now $b = 1$. This difference is crucial, since a shock to ε_t causes output not only to rise in the current period, but in every future period. There is no reversion to trend in equation (17.21) and hence no business cycle. Nelson and Plosser (1982) test specifications similar to both equations (17.20) and (17.21) for output employment and industrial production, *inter alia*, and find that most aggregates are better described as random walks than as fluctuations around deterministic trends. This evidence has been interpreted as supporting the real business cycle model rather than the monetary model of the cycle, since cycles do not appear to be fluctuations around a trend, but rather fluctuations in the trend itself. Since money is presumed to be neutral in the long run, such permanent fluctuations in output could not be caused by a monetary model of the cycle. This, however, is not a clinching argument. Suppose that b, although close to unity is actually less than unity, say $b = 0.999$. In this case there will be mean reversion but it will be very slow. The random walk model would fit well, since b is close to unity, but it would give incorrect long-run properties for output.

There are other limitations of the real business cycle approach to economic fluctuations. Suppose, for example, that technology shocks are in general fairly small. If this is the case then the ability of the model to explain the business cycle is severely limited. Second, the intertemporal substitution of labour which is the underlying propagation mechanism for the cycle is empirically very small, partly because few workers have the flexibility of hours that the model requires. Thirdly, the complete neglect of monetary factors from the theory seems inappropriate. If monetary factors are non-neutral then their omission is a serious limitation of this approach.

Conclusions

In this chapter four alternative theories of the business cycle have been examined. In each case it has been shown how cycles are generated and why they persist. It is, however, very difficult to assess the empirical validity of these theories. The real business cycle model does seem to fit the facts, but is theoretically unconvincing since technology shocks may be small or infrequent. On the other hand, in Lucas' monetary model, given the extensive public information available on price levels and the expected rate of inflation, it is likely that price level misperceptions will also be relatively small. The traditional multiplier-accelerator interaction and monetary theories seem to have more intuitive appeal, partly perhaps because they are not based on continuous market clearing or demanding information requirements, although they are theoretically *ad hoc* and there is little hard evidence to support their contentions.

Summary

- The traditional models of the cycle emphasise the interaction between the investment accelerator and multiplier in a simple Keynesian model, or the role of fluctuations in the money supply in a monetary model of the cycle.
- Modern theories are based on microeconomic foundations and attempt to explain the business cycle in terms of a general equilibrium model. The new classical theory emphasises that cycles are caused because rational agents – facing a signal extraction problem – confuse changes in aggregate prices with changes in relative prices. These new classical models lack a robust propagation mechanism.
- The real business cycle models suggest that cycles are caused by technology shocks. These cycles are propagated because of the time it takes to build capital equipment and change the size of the capital stock. These models minimise the role played by the monetary sector.
- The empirical evidence suggests that there is a long memory in output fluctuations. That is, economic fluctuations are highly persistent, and hence, according to some economists, are unlikely to be due to changes in aggregate demand. This interpretation is supportive of the real business cycle approach.

Suggested further reading

The traditional approach to business cycles stems from Keynes (1936) Chapter 22, and Samuelson (1939) which was the source of the simple multiplier-accelerator interaction model. The monetarist approach is due to Friedman and Schwartz (1963b), drawing on the early neo-classical literature sketched in Chapter 1. The modern equilibrium approach to cycles stems from the classic paper of Lucas (1975). Kydland and Prescott (1982) expound the real business cycle model with supporting empirical evidence from Nelson and Plosser (1982). These modern theories are surveyed in Mullineux, Dickinson and Peng (1993) and Stadler (1994), who concentrates on real business cycles. Other recent and accessible surveys include Mankiw (1989), Plosser (1989), Romer (1999) and Basu and Taylor (1999).

Essay titles

1. Compare and contrast any two theories of the business cycle.
2. 'All explanations of the business cycle revolve around the mismatch between savings and investment.' Discuss.
3. Explain the signal extraction problem. What role does this problem play in the new classical theory of the business cycle?

Questions

1. Why are economists interested in business cycles?
2. Compute the equilibrium level of income and comment on the stability of the time path of output, Y in each of the following cases: (a) $Y_t = 5 + 0.5Y_{t-1} - 2Y_{t-2}$; (b) $Y_t = 4 + Y_{t-1} - 0.8Y_{t-2}$.
3. Explain the role that may be played by expectations in the multiplier-acceleration models of the cycle. What are the limitations of the multiplier-accelerator theories of the business cycle?
4. Explain Friedman's view of the business cycle. To what extent is this theory in contrast and consistent with the Keynesian view of the cycle?
5. (a) Can you think how to capture the new classical model of the business cycle in terms of a diagram using the *AD–AS* framework? (Hint: the *AD* curve is downward-sloping as usual and the *AS* curve can be drawn from equation 17.18).
   (b) Use this model to show the effect of a monetary expansion on the level of output and prices in a closed economy when (i) agents have full information and do not mistake price signals and (ii) agents have only imperfect information and face a signal extraction problem.
6. Describe a propagation mechanism used in real business cycle theory and explain briefly how it works.

CHAPTER 18

Inflation

Aims and objectives

- To examine alternative approaches to the causes of inflation.
- To consider the costs and benefits of inflation.
- To examine anti-inflation policy in the UK.

Introduction

Inflation is defined as a persistent tendency of the general level of prices to rise. The word 'persistent' is important because it indicates a dynamic phenomenon that only makes sense over time. In other words inflation is different from a once-and-for-all rise in the price level: it refers only to a continual rise in the price level over time. The general level of prices refers to a measure of the average price level in the economy as a whole. This may be measured by a consumer price index, such as the CPI, or by the GDP deflator. Which measure of aggregate prices is used depends largely on the use to which the calculation is to be put. In practice, as most price indices move together the choice is rarely crucial. A third point to note is that the inflation rate is usually measured as an annual rate. That is, it is the percentage increase in the price level today compared to prices a year ago. This is important because when computing the inflation rate from quarterly data the formula is:

$$\hat{P} = \frac{P_t - P_{t-4}}{P_{t-4}} \times 100 = ((P_t/P_{t-4}) - 1) \times 100 \tag{18.1}$$

For monthly data the price lags need to be 12 and for annual data only 1. This is perhaps obvious, but a point commonly and erroneously overlooked in empirical work.

Figure 18.1 shows the annual rate of inflation for some of the principal Western economies since the late 1960s. At the start and end of the period the inflation rate for each country is less than 5 per cent per annum, but between 1968 and 1997 there are three periods of relatively high inflation, 1975–76, 1980–81 and to a lesser extent 1990–91 when inflation exceeded 10 per cent per annum. The pattern is broadly the same for all countries, perhaps suggesting a

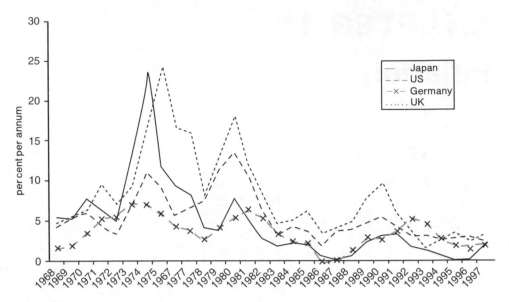

Figure 18.1 *Inflation, 1968–97*

common cause, or at least a contribution from a common factor, although the three peaks are the most pronounced for the UK and the less pronounced for Germany. In particular, the UK inflation rate is the only rate over 10 per cent in 1990–91, suggesting that this peak may be more to do with the UK rather than a general problem.

The approach in this chapter is to consider the causes, consequences and cures of inflation – the three Cs. The causes of inflation are usually classified as demand-pull or cost-push, although the principal dynamic model used in this chapter – the Phillips Curve – is consistent with both demand-pull and cost-push theories of inflation. That said, the analysis of the causes of inflation begins with an examination of the Quantity Theory of Money, which is exclusively a demand-pull theory, but which is the oldest and often regarded as the most important theory of inflation. We then set out the Phillips Curve model and the theoretical foundations of Phillips' trade-off based on labour market adjustment due to Lipsey (1960). The role of trade unions in the inflation process is then examined with particular reference to their potential effect on the shape and position of the Phillips Curve Friedman's expectations-augmented Phillips Curve is introduced and the concept of the NAIRU – the non-accelerating inflation rate of unemployment – to give the most complete explanation of inflation. Finally, the consequences of inflation, both the benefits and costs, are considered together with the empirical evidence on inflation and policy recommendations to reduce or curtail it.

The quantity theory

The oldest and perhaps the most popular cause of inflation is that of an excessive expansion in the money supply (see Chapter 1). This idea stems from the classical *Quantity Theory of Money* made popular in the late 1960s and 1970s by Milton Friedman. The theory states that the nominal value of GDP, that is the volume of output, Y, multiplied by the average price of output, P, is identically equal to the stock of money, M^s, multiplied by the velocity of circulation, V. That is:

$$M^sV = PY \tag{18.2}$$

Thus the flow of monetary expenditures must be equal to the nominal value of GDP.

To convert this identity into a theory of inflation requires three assumptions to be made. First, the money supply is assumed to be exogenously determined by the monetary authorities and hence independent of the level of national income. This assumption is crucial to establishing the direction of causality in the model, although in practice, especially for small open economies it is a highly questionable assumption. The second assumption is that the velocity of circulation is assumed to be constant. The speed at which money circulates around the economy partly reflects the frequency of payment of wages, or the use of credit cards that are largely institutionally determined. It is, however, also affected by the rate of interest and the expected rate of inflation. For example, in periods of very high inflation individuals will not wish to hold money as it depreciates in their hands, so no sooner do they receive income in the form of cash that they spend it on commodities. This is especially the case with hyper-inflation, but even without hyper-inflation high rates of interest will encourage agents to economise on cash holdings, as their bank deposits earn a higher rate of return. In the absence of hyper-inflation and of financial innovation the assumption that velocity is constant is not a strong assumption. The third assumption is that the level of output is exogenously determined and independent of demand. This implies that the level of output is wholly supply-determined and that the labour market is perfectly competitive so that wages are perfectly flexible to ensure the establishment of continuous full employment as in neo-classical theory.

With these assumptions, the equation of exchange becomes the quantity theory of nominal income growth:

$$\bar{M}^s = kPY \tag{18.3}$$

where k is a constant denoting the constant ratio $(1/V)$, or expressing (18.3) in terms of rates of change:

$$\hat{\bar{M}}^s = \hat{P} + \hat{Y} \quad \text{or} \quad \hat{P} = \hat{\bar{M}}^s - \hat{Y} \tag{18.3'}$$

Because of the assumption that the money supply is exogenously determined, denoted by a bar over the M^s, it follows that causality in the model must flow from the rate of growth money supply to the rate of growth of nominal income. With output growth determined wholly by supply-side developments, it follows that if the money supply grows faster than the level of real output then inflation will be positive. Similarly, if the money supply grows less fast than the real economy then there will be a negative rate of inflation: that is, a general fall in the level of prices. Hence the only cause of inflation is an excessive growth of the money supply. This implies that all inflation in this model is, by definition, of the demand-pull type.

Although it is rarely noted, this monetarist view of inflation is only valid in the context of a closed economy or in an open economy with a freely floating exchange rate. The reason is that if the economy is closed the authorities are able, at least in principle, to control the money supply, since as was demonstrated in Chapter 2 in an open economy the balance of payments position may cause the money supply to change endogenously. Similarly, in an open economy with a freely floating exchange rate the authorities do not intervene in the foreign exchange markets, and so the money supply is again independent of the balance of payments position. In an open economy with a fixed exchange rate however, the authorities will continually intervene in the foreign exchange markets to maintain the predetermined exchange rate. Therefore, in the absence of sterilisation policies, any surplus on the balance of payments will result in an increase in the money supply, and any deficit in a decrease in the money supply. Since the authorities are unable to influence the actions of millions of private agents trading goods and assets with each other, they are unable to control the national money supply. The money supply becomes endogenous and the monetarist view is implausible, to the extent that inflation is not determined by the monetary authorities.

The monetarist analysis may be saved, however, by taking a global perspective. The so-called global monetarists argue that since the world is a closed economy, then under fixed exchange rates a global money supply can be defined that is exogenous and the excessive growth of which can cause global inflation. If exchange rates are fixed, then the money supply in each country can be converted into a common currency to give a world money supply measured in a common currency, say US dollars. Furthermore, the existence of international goods market arbitrage, whereby goods prices in different countries are equalised by traders buying in markets where the good is cheap and selling in markets where it is dear, implies that purchasing power parity holds, such that $P = P^*E$. With exchange rates fixed it follows that national inflation must equal world inflation. The determinant of world inflation is, as in the closed economy case, the excess growth in the global money supply over the rate of growth of world output.

Empirical evidence relevant to this global monetarist inflation model is relatively sparse. If the period 1955–71 is regarded as one of effectively fixed exchange rates, then a stable global money demand function needs to be identified for there to be a predictable relationship between global inflation and the exogenous, global excess supply of money. Although a few papers have claimed some support for this model, the evidence is not particularly convincing (see, for example, Gray *et al.*, 1976 and Swoboda, 1977).

Wage inflation and the Phillips curve

An alternative approach to the quantity theory of inflation is to focus on wage inflation, rather than price inflation. The relationship between the rate of increase of money wages and unemployment is known as the Phillips curve in recognition of Phillips' (1958) path-breaking empirical analysis. Phillips's work consisted of a statistical analysis of the relation between the level of unemployment and the rate of change of money wages in the UK over the period 1861–1957. **Figure 18.2** shows the Phillips curve as a non-linear, inverse relationship between the growth in money wages and the rate of unemployment. It may also be seen from the figure that at a rate of unemployment of about 5.5 per cent, money wages would be constant, that is $\hat{W} = 0$. Of potentially greater relevance to policy-makers, the curve also shows that at a rate of unemployment of about 2.5 per cent wages would rise at around 2 per cent per annum. This rate of growth of money wages was believed to be consistent with price stability, since the trend growth of productivity was thought to be about 2 per cent per annum. At its crudest the principal policy implication was that price stability could be achieved if policy was able to stabilise the rate of unemployment at about 2.5 per cent.

The Phillips curve quite clearly had important implications for policy, but it lacked any rigorous theoretical foundations. It was Lipsey (1960) who attempted to provide a theoretical rationale for the curve by looking at wage behaviour in micro-labour markets. A micro-labour market is defined as a market within which labour is more mobile than it is between markets. Lipsey argued that in any particular labour market an excess demand for labour would lead to upward pressure on the wage rate. **Figure 18.3** shows a particular labour market, j, where the demand and supply curves are drawn with respect to the money wage and given as N_j^D and N_j^s respectively. The equilibrium wage is $0W_0$. At a lower wage, such as $0W_1$, there is an excess demand for labour, equal to AB and hence

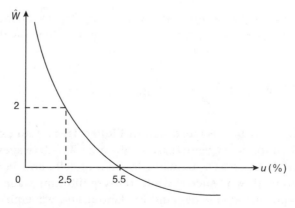

Figure 18.2 *The schematic Phillips relation*

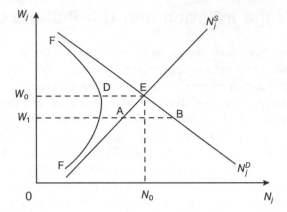

Figure 18.3 *The labour market*

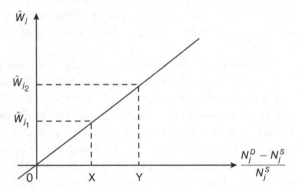

Figure 18.4 *The excess demand for labour*

upward pressure on the wage rate. Lipsey postulated that the speed of wage adjustment, from $0W_1$ to $0W_0$, is dependent on the ratio of excess demand for labour to the total supply, that is:

$$\hat{W} = a\frac{(N_j^D - N_j^S)}{N_j^S} \qquad \text{where } a > 0 \tag{18.4}$$

This function is illustrated in **Figure 18.4.** With excess demand for labour of 0X, the money wage increase is given by $\hat{W}_{j1}$. As wages increase, as shown in **Figure 18.3**, the excess demand for labour falls and hence the rate of wage increase slows down. After a while the equilibrium wage, $0W_0$ will be reached. At this point the excess demand for labour and wage growth are zero – as at the origin in **Figure 18.4.**

The next step is to relate the rate of change of money wages to the level of excess demand for labour. Since there is no direct way of measuring the excess demand for labour both Phillips and Lipsey used the aggregate unemployment rate as a proxy measure of excess demand. The supply of labour consists of those in work (N) and those unemployed (U), while the demand for labour consists of jobs filled (which is the same as employment, N) and job vacancies, V. The excess demand for labour is therefore:

$$N_j^D - N_j^S = (N+V) - (N+U) = V - U \qquad (18.5)$$

In the absence of data on vacancies, if it can be assumed that vacancies have a stable inverse relationship to unemployment, it follows that unemployment will be a good proxy for excess demand. Consider again **Figure 18.3**. At the market clearing wage rate, the demand and supply of labour are equated, and in the absence of any frictions in the market there would be no unemployment at this wage. If, however, some workers are changing jobs and it takes time for them to find a new job, there will be both unemployment and job vacancies in equilibrium. Such unemployment is called frictional unemployment. The curve FF in **Figure 18.3** shows the frontier of effective employment once frictional unemployment is allowed for, hence DE measures the equilibrium level of frictional unemployment and also the number of vacancies.

At wage $0W_1$, where there is an excess demand for labour, the level of frictional unemployment falls, since as the surplus of vacancies over job-seekers increases, the average time it takes to find a suitable job will fall. Whatever the level of excess demand, however, frictional unemployment can never become negative: the FF curve can come very close to the supply curve but can never cross it. It follows that in conditions of excess demand the relationship between excess demand and unemployment is non-linear. This relation is shown in **Figure 18.5**. In equilibrium, when demand equals supply, unemployment is positive and the equilibrium rate of frictional unemployment is u_0. As excess demand increases unemployment falls, but the relationship is non-linear as illustrated by the part of the curve to the left of u_0. If the wage is higher than the market clearing wage there is an excess supply of labour and unemployment is measured as the distance between the FF curve and the N_j^S curve in **Figure 18.3**. In so far as unemployment is now largely a consequence of market disequilibrium, the level of unemployment itself becomes quite a good measure of the excess supply. Therefore in conditions of excess supply the unemployment excess demand relationship is approximately linear as is shown in **Figure 18.5** by the shape of the curve to the right of u_0. This non-linear relationship between unemployment and the excess demand for labour can now be summarised as:

$$u_j = f\left(\frac{N_j^D - N_j^S}{N_j^S} \right) \quad \text{where } f' < 0 \qquad (18.6)$$

Combining equations (18.4) and (18.6) an expression for the micro-market Phillips relation is obtained, which can be written as $\hat{W}_j = g(u_j)$, where $g' < 0$. This

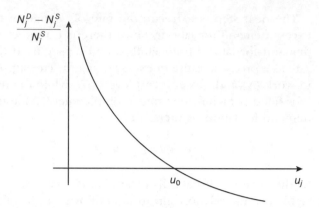

Figure 18.5 *Excess demand for labour and unemployment*

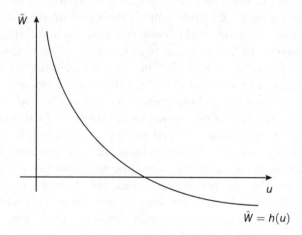

Figure 18.6 *The theoretical Phillips curve*

is the labour market reaction function for market j. By assuming that the micro-reaction functions for all markets are identical, Lipsey aggregates over all markets to obtain the macroeconomic Phillips relation, which is illustrated in **Figure 18.6** and can now be written as:

$$\hat{W} = h(u) \qquad h' < 0 \tag{18.7}$$

The aggregation procedure does raise some inconsistencies. For example, the microeconomic analysis assumes that wages and prices in the rest of the economy can be taken as given, but this assumption is not strictly valid when macroeconomic changes are being considered. If firms find their supply of labour curves shifting because of wage increases in other sectors, they may find it worthwhile to attempt to anticipate such shifts when deciding what wage rate to offer. If they do, the wage increases in each sector depends in part on the expected level of wage increases in other sectors. Despite this limitation, however, the empirical evidence was largely supportive of the Phillips curve in the 1960s, but by the end of the decade the Phillips curve appeared to lose almost all of its explanatory power. The empirical breakdown was observed in most industrial countries, although it was most marked in the UK. The essence of the problem was that inflation showed a tendency to persist and to accelerate, while at the same time unemployment rose to levels far higher than those experienced in the 1950s and early 1960s. This analysis suggested that the Phillips curve had shifted upwards, such that higher inflation was consistent with higher unemployment. To explain this shift two alternative theories were put forward: cost-push pressures from trade union power and militancy, and inflation expectations.

Cost-push theories of inflation and trade union militancy

The most notable feature about the role of trade unions in the labour market is their ability to influence and negotiate wage rates – the process of 'collective bargaining.' Collective bargaining, while unable to affect the rate of wage inflation *per se*, is however a special form of machinery for fixing wages since it is intended to reduce or eliminate the competitive element in the supply of labour and to affect the market adjustment process as a result. Equation (18.4) shows how wages respond to excess demand for labour in competitive market circumstances. If the effect of collective bargaining is to modify the wage adjustment equation, equation (18.4) can be written more generally as:

$$\hat{W} = b\left(\frac{N^D - N^S}{N^S}\right) + z \tag{18.8}$$

where $b < a$ and $z > 0$.

Equation (18.8) differs from equation (18.4) in three ways. First, this is a model of aggregate wage adjustment, whereas equation (18.4) really represented wage adjustment in a micro-market. This distinction is unimportant to the argument here and equation (18.4) can be regarded as equally valid at the aggregate level. Second, equation (18.8) allows for the possibility that collective bargaining may bring about wage increases even in the absence of excess demand for labour. This effect is denoted by $z > 0$. Third, it suggests that collective bargaining may dampen the responsiveness of wage bargains to changes in the pressure of demand in the labour market, since $b < a$. In the extreme case of cost-push inflation, wage increases are independent of excess demand in the labour market and $b = 0$.

Figure 18.7 shows how these alternative wage adjustment hypotheses translate into Phillips curves (which have been drawn as straight lines for convenience).

Case [A] is where the activities of trade unions are neutral and the process of wage bargaining yields the same outcome as the competitive market process ($b=a$ and $z=0$). In case [B] the trade union achieves a higher money wage increase at each level of demand through its exercise of market power, but the outcome of the wage bargain remains as responsive to the pressure of demand as in a competitive market ($b=a, z>0$). In **Figure 18.7** case [B] is therefore drawn parallel to case [A] and vertically above it. Case [C] is the situation when the trade union is able to affect the slope as well as the position of the Phillips curve ($b<a, z>0$), corresponding to the idea that wage settlements are less responsive to market forces under collective bargaining. Finally, in case [D] trade unions merely serve to slow down the responsiveness of wage increases to the pressure of demand ($b<a, z=0$).

The principal advantage of this cost-push model is that it is able to explain an upward shift in the Phillips Curve through the shift parameter z. Tests of this hypothesis for the UK were undertaken by Hines (1964), who used the unionised proportion of the labour force as a proxy to try to capture the effect of trade union power on money wage rates. Although Hines found strong econometric evidence for his model, the hypothesis has not been confirmed by subsequent analysis. Indeed the hypothesis is generally regarded as implausible since variations in trade union membership were very small until the 1980s and the measure takes no account of changes in wage pushfulness in sectors that are already fully unionised. Moreover, in addition to trade unions there were other institutional factors that affected the growth of money ware rates during the 1960s and early 1970s, most specifically incomes policies.

The use of incomes policies will have had just the opposite effect to trade unions in the labour market. A successful incomes policy would work to reduce

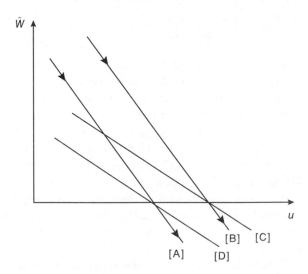

Figure 18.7 *Alternative Phillips curves*

the rate of growth of money wages, which could be interpreted as a factor which reduced the size of z, and hence shifted the Phillips curve inwards towards the origin. Empirical studies of the effects of incomes policies relating to the UK economy up to 1970, show the effects of these policies to be largely small and insignificant (see, for example, Parkin, Sumner and Jones, 1972, or Henry and Ormerod, 1978).

The problem with these cost push theories is that they do not offer a complete theory of the wage bargaining process. For example, trade union behaviour may equally be interpreted as raising unemployment for a given level of wage inflation, or as raising the rate of inflation, at each level of employment.

Inflation expectations and the Phillips curve

At the same time that the Phillips curve was under empirical attack, Milton Friedman launched a theoretical attack on the entire notion of an inflation – unemployment trade-off as suggested by the Phillips curve. Friedman (1968) argued that there were two fundamental problems with the theory underlying the Phillips curve. First, it had prices (wages) depending upon quantities (unemployment), whereas neo-classical economic analysis always postulated quantities varying with price. In this sense the direction of causality is incorrect. Second, and much more important, the Phillips curve is based on money wage rates whereas neo-classical theory suggests that it is the *real* wage rate which underlies the labour supply decisions of workers (see Chapter 12).

The essence of Friedman's argument is that at full employment it is the real wage rate that is constant, not the money wage rate. If money wages are rising at full employment they do so because workers are expecting prices to be rising. Thus, rather than equation (18.7) Friedman argued the appropriate specification should be:

$$\hat{W} = b(u) + \hat{P}_c^{\,e} \tag{18.9}$$

where $\hat{P}_c^{\,e}$ is the expected rate of consumer price inflation defined as $\hat{P}_c^{\,e} = (1-\rho) \hat{P}^{\,e} + \rho(\hat{P}^{\,*e} + \hat{E}^{\,e})$ where, as in Chapter 12, ρ is the degree of openness of the economy, such that when $\rho = 0$, the economy is closed to trade. In the general case when $1 > \rho > 0$, not only will domestic output price inflation influence workers' inflation expectations, but foreign price inflation will influence those expectations too. Equation (18.9) is often referred to as the 'expectations-augmented' Phillips curve. It follows from this that there is a Phillips curve corresponding to each level of inflation expectations. The expected rate of inflation term acts as a shift variable for the original Phillips curve just as the z variable does in the cost-push model of inflation. Thus, each Phillips curve is an identical copy of all other curves, but is displaced in either an upwards or downwards direction. **Figure 18.8** shows a family of expectations-augmented Phillips curves. It is important to note that the curve which cuts the horizontal axis at u_N (where actual inflation is zero) is drawn for an expected rate of inflation of zero. Thus if workers perceive that inflation is growing faster than their money wages their expected real wages will be falling and they will reduce their supply of effort (or increase their demand for leisure). This would cause each Phillips curve to shift up and $h(u) + \hat{P}_c^e$ would rise. Employers would now have to offer larger wage increases to obtain the same amount of labour as before the change in tastes of the workers.

Friedman's extension of the Phillips curve is important for two additional reasons. First, it is now necessary to link wage inflation and expected price inflation, and, second, to specify how inflation expectations are related to observed rates of inflation. This leads to a more complete model of the inflationary process.

From the analysis of labour demand in Chapter 12, the real product wage rate is directly related to the level of labour productivity, that is $W/P = \phi(N)$. It follows that in a dynamic context the rate of change of the real wage must equal the rate of change of productivity, that is: $\hat{W} - \hat{P} = \hat{\phi}$. This relation can now be used in equation (18.9) to give a model of price inflation, by substituting for $\hat{W}$. Using the expression for consumer price inflation gives:

$$\hat{P} = h(u) - \hat{\phi} + (1-\rho)\hat{P}^e + \rho(\hat{P}^{*e} + \hat{E}^e) \tag{18.10}$$

Rearranging gives:

$$\hat{P} - \hat{P}^e = h(u) - \hat{\phi} + \rho(\hat{P}^{*e} + \hat{E}^e - \hat{P}^e) \tag{18.11}$$

This says that *unanticipated* inflation, defined as the difference between actual inflation and expected inflation, depends upon the level of unemployment, the rate of productivity growth and the expected rate of depreciation of the real exchange rate. The presence of the expected real exchange rate term, due to the

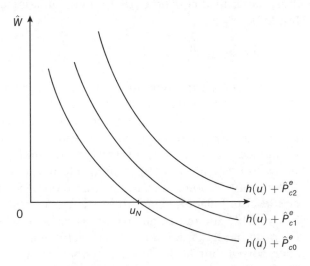

Figure 18.8   *Inflation augmented Phillips curves*

fact that workers' expectations of inflation are based on consumer prices, indicates that this is also a model of inflation for an open economy.

In a closed economy, when $\rho=0$ and all inflation is anticipated such that $\hat{P}=\hat{P}^e$, the rate of unemployment will be independent of inflation, that is $h(u)=\hat{\phi}$. In other words, the Phillips curve is vertical with no trade-off between inflation and unemployment. In the open economy, if PPP holds continuously then the final term in equation (18.11) will always be zero and the closed economy analysis of the equilibrium (or long run) Phillips curve remains valid and there is no-trade-off between inflation and unemployment. **Figure 18.9** combines this vertical Phillips curve with the short-run or disequilibrium curves of **Figure 18.8**.

Figure 18.9 merits careful interpretation. On the vertical axis is plotted both the rate of change of money wages (left-hand scale) and the rate of change of producer prices (right-hand scale) with the rate of unemployment on the horizontal axis. With the assumption of a closed economy or of PPP, consumer price and producer price inflation are identical. At all points to the left of u_N, the level of unemployment is less than u_N and therefore $h(u)-\hat{\phi}>0$, which implies that along the short-run curve to the left of u_N, $\hat{P}>\hat{P}^e$. That is, to the left of u_N actual inflation is greater than agents expect. Similarly, to the right of u_N, the actual inflation rate is less than agents expect. Only when $\hat{P}=\hat{P}^e$ – that is along the vertical Phillips curve – is inflation neither accelerating nor decelerating. This led Tobin (1972a) to label u_N the NAIRU – the non-accelerating inflation rate of unemployment. This concept is similar to Friedman's concept of the natural rate of unemployment, but it makes clear that u_N refers to the rate of unemployment

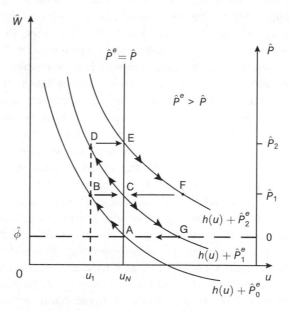

Figure 18.9 *Disequilibrium inflation*

that holds inflation constant, rather than that which equilibrates the labour market.

The second question is what is the relationship between actual inflation and expected inflation? In the Friedman version of the model workers only learn to adjust their expectations of inflation because they observe actual rates of inflation rising. More precisely, it was assumed that agents adjusted their expectations only *after* they observed higher than expected rates of inflation. This is consistant with adaptive expectations behaviour. Formally adaptive expectations can be written as:

$$\hat{P}_t^e - \hat{P}_{t-1}^e = \lambda(\hat{P}_{t-1} - \hat{P}_{t-1}^e) \tag{18.12}$$

where $0 < \lambda < 1$. This adjustment mechanism relates expected inflation to past actual rates of inflation. This can be confirmed by rewriting equation (18.12) as:

$$\hat{P}_t^e = \lambda \sum_{j=1}^{\infty} (1-\lambda)^j \hat{P}_{t-j} \tag{18.13}$$

Thus current expectations of inflation are formed on the basis of a weighted average of past actual rates of inflation, where the weights decline over time. This theory of expectations is vitally important for the dynamics of inflation and macroeconomic policy: namely, that to try to maintain unemployment at a level below the NAIRU will result in accelerating inflation.

To understand this point suppose in **Figure 18.9** that at point A the authorities expand monetary or fiscal policy in an effort to reduce unemployment. The economy moves up the short-run Phillips curve to point B. At B the rate of unemployment is u_1 and the rate of price inflation $\hat{P}_1$. The workers, however, are expecting inflation to be zero, which is consistent with a rise in both money wages and real wages. When the workers realise at point B that inflation is greater than they expected and that there has been no change in their real wage, then they will reduce their supply of effort and employment will fall back to u_N, but inflation will remain at $\hat{P}_1$. That is, the economy is now at point C in **Figure 18.9.** Thus, as workers adjust to the prospect of positive inflation the authorities' efforts to reduce unemployment are frustrated. At C, therefore, the authorities may attempt a further permanent expansion in demand, this time pushing the economy up to point D. The movement up the short-run Phillips curve is again only successful while the workers are fooled into thinking that the rise in money wages is a rise in real wages. Once they realise that inflation is rising faster than they initially believed they will again reduce their supply of labour accordingly. Alternatively, if the authorities wish to maintain unemployment at u_1, then they have to accept accelerating inflation; that is, the economy will move from B to D. Furthermore, it is also the case that if inflation is to be reduced from E then higher unemployment must result in the short run as the economy moves down the Phillips curves in a sawtooth pattern from point E to F then to C, G, and back to A.

This analysis is important for policy-making since it means that the authorities are unable to trade-off unemployment and inflation in anything other than the short run. More technically, points like B and D, are not equilibrium positions. This analysis is equivalent to arguing that demand-management policy can only be used to combat unemployment if workers are slow to adjust their expectations of inflation. To see this, assume instead that workers have perfect foresight expectations. This means that workers on average do not make systematic prediction errors, therefore in this context $\hat{P} = \hat{P}^e$ at all times. From **Figure 18.9**, $\hat{P} = \hat{P}^e$ holds only on the vertical or equilibrium Phillips curve. Thus with perfect foresight expectations there is no trade-off between inflation and unemployment even in the short term, and demand policy is only ever available to combat inflation.

So far the open economy effects of inflation on the Phillips curve have been put to one side to the extent that continuous PPP or a closed economy have been assumed. To show the implications for the Phillips curve when $1 > \rho > 0$ subtract $\rho\hat{P}$ from both sides of equation (18.11) and rearrange. This gives:

$$\hat{P} - \hat{P}^e = \frac{1}{1-\rho}[b(u) - \hat{\phi}] + \frac{\rho}{1-\rho}(\hat{P}^{*e} + \hat{E}^e - \hat{P}) \tag{18.14}$$

Equation (18.14) says that even if actual and expected domestic rates of inflation are equal there will be a trade-off between inflation and unemployment providing actual domestic inflation is not identical to expected future global inflation. Thus setting $\hat{P} - \hat{P}^e = 0$ and rearranging equation (18.14) gives:

$$\hat{P} = \frac{1}{\rho}[b(u) - \hat{\phi}] + (\hat{P}^{*e} + \hat{E}^e) \tag{18.15}$$

If expected world inflation is zero then (18.15) reduces to

$$\hat{P} = \frac{1}{\rho}[b(u) - \hat{\phi}] \tag{18.16}$$

Thus the inverse relationship between domestic inflation and unemployment is restored for given levels of productivity growth, but the trade-off is less favourable in that it is steeper than the initial short-run trade-off, since $\rho < 1$. This steeper 'equilibrium' trade-off is shown in **Figure 18.10**, where $\hat{P}^e_{c1} > 0$ and $\hat{P}^e_{c0} = 0$. Should the government decide to run the economy at some unemployment rate u_1, then eventually the rate of inflation would converge on $\hat{P}_1$ where inflationary expectations are fulfilled. To be able to exploit this trade-off, domestic inflation expectations are adjusted to actual inflation faster than actual domestic inflation adjusts to global inflation expectations. Thus this trade-off can perhaps be regarded as relevant in the medium run, when due to the slowness of goods market arbitrage, domestic prices can differ from foreign prices, even though domestic agents have fully adjusted their inflation expectations to actual inflation. This is the dynamic equivalent of the upward-sloping neo-classical aggregate supply curve derived in Chapter 12, which is conditional on constant import prices. This does, however, assume that workers suffer from persistent

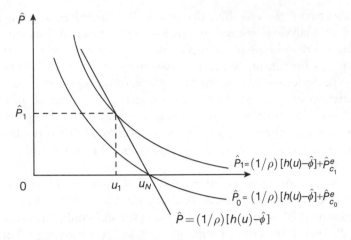

Figure 18.10 *Open economy tradeoff when 0 < p < 1*

'money illusion' in the wage bargain in that world inflation is not immediately and fully incorporated into the money wage rate.

Thus in the open economy, if goods market arbitrage is imperfect in the medium term, the modified Phillips curve trade-off may be exploitable over the time horizon relevant for macroeconomic policy. The empirical evidence for the existence of a Phillips curve trade-off is considered in the next section after a brief review of the consequences of inflation.

The consequences of inflation

The effects of inflation on the economy are almost certainly biased towards the view that inflation is harmful to economic well-being. Although there are costs of inflation these costs are small at relatively low, say single digit, levels of inflation. Moreover, low levels inflation do have some benefits for the economy.

Inflation that is fully anticipated has little effect on the economy. The most important effect is likely to be the welfare cost of non-bank private sector agents holding lower cash balances, but even this is small if the demand for money is interest inelastic as the empirical evidence suggests (see Chapter 11). **Figure 18.11** shows these costs. If real money balances can be produced at zero marginal cost and no interest is offered by the government on these balances, then the demand for money balances is downward-sloping with respect to the nominal rate of interest, as in **Figure 18.11**. When the interest rate on alternative assets is i_0 and the inflation rate is zero, the rectangle $0i_0$DA shows the gains from the non-payment of interest available to the government from the holdings of real money balances equal to 0A. Since these earnings could be remitted to the private sector, the net welfare loss from the practice of not paying interest, given

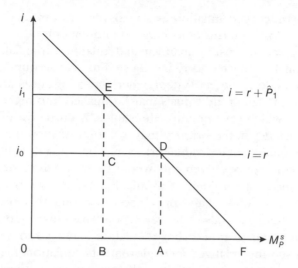

Figure 18.11 *The costs of inflation*

that the social cost of providing the cash balances is zero, is the triangle DAF. A fully-anticipated rise in inflation from zero to $\hat{P}_1$, will lead to a rise in the nominal rate of interest to i_1, thereby leading to a reduction in the demand for cash balances to 0B. The 'inflation tax' raised is measured by the area $i_1 i_0 CE$ and the uncompensated loss to consumer is now given as BADE. The size of this area depends on both the interest rate elasticity of money demand and on the actual rate of inflation. Since the interest elasticity of money demand is low, then the welfare loss is also likely to be low. To the extent that agents economise on their holdings of cash due to the inflation then this will result in more frequent trips to the bank to convert their interest-bearing assets into cash for spending purposes. These extra trips are a cost to the individual – shoe leather costs – but they are unlikely to be particularly important, except perhaps in cases of hyperinflation.

Unanticipated inflation is more important than anticipated inflation in so far as the costs on society are greater. There are a number of effects here. First, the effect of inflation on long-term contracts. If inflation turns out to be higher than expected at the start of the contract there is a windfall gain to net monetary debtors and a corresponding loss to monetary creditors. In this category the losers are perhaps pensioners who saved during their lifetime to provide for old age, but find that on retirement the provision made is unsatisfactory because its real value has been reduced by inflation. In contrast, it is generally believed that the middle-income groups do well out of inflation in the UK because they typically hold real assets (houses) and have monetary debts (mortgages). The government is certainly a big gainer from inflation, since it is the largest monetary debtor. The main creditors are the pension funds and insurance companies, that is to say households at one remove. Thus a typical household may benefit from unanticipated inflation as a taxpayer and through reduced mortgage debts, but may lose in terms of its pension entitlements.

A second cost of unanticipated inflation is the failure of various types of institutional arrangements to be adjusted to take account of inflation. The most obvious example is the tax system, where tax allowances are set in nominal terms. Thus with inflation individuals may be pushed into higher marginal income tax brackets, which have nominal thresholds. A third cost of inflation is its effects on the efficiency of the price system. Without inflation the general level of prices would be stable, but individual prices may be rising or falling. In the absence of inflation relative price movements would be transparent, and the allocation of resources adjusted accordingly. With inflation agents may confuse rises in the general level of prices with relative price rises, so leading to a misallocation of resources.

There are also, however, perhaps two important benefits of inflation. Although, as noted above, inflation may lead to a misallocation of resources by obscuring relative price movements, inflation may actually help in achieving equilibrating relative price adjustments, since it makes it possible to change relative prices without having to cut any price in money terms. This is particularly important in the labour market where it is difficult to cut money wage rates, but where inflation does often work to reduce real wages. A second benefit of inflation is that it ensures that nominal interest rates are positive. Very low, or zero, inflation may seriously curtail the central bank's ability to cut interest rates in response to contractionary shocks to the economy.

Policies to combat inflation and the UK experience

Figure 18.1 shows that the UK has experienced above average rates of inflation since the late 1960s, but that this is related to three specific inflationary episodes in 1973–74, 1980–81 and 1990–91. To the extent that any of these episodes are due to cost-push type inflation then the Phillips curve should show an upward shift to the right according to the models developed above. On the other hand, if the cause of the inflation is primarily demand-pull inflation then we might expect to see movements up a single short-run Phillips curve. **Figure 18.12** shows the plot inflation and unemployment for the UK from 1960, which clearly shows that there was no stable Phillips curve trade-off over this period. This figure, however, is useful in both justifying the principal causes of inflation and the policies adopted to deal with the problem.

One argument for the rise in inflation in 1974–75 is that it was caused by the OPEC oil embargo and the subsequent quadrupling of oil prices. This story is consistent with the cost-push theory of inflation, and if true the Phillips curve should have shifted up to the right. Compared to the points in the bottom left corner of the figure, which were on the 1960s Phillips curve, it is clear that the Phillips curve could have shifted to the right. From 1975 to 1979, inflation fell in the UK with only a moderate rise in the rate of unemployment. This was partly due to the use of incomes policies to reduce wage inflation and shift the Phillips

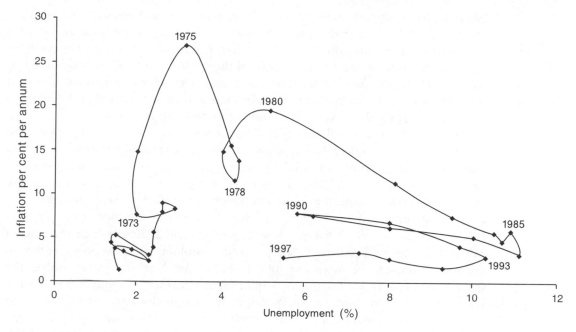

Figure 18.12   *UK inflation and unemployment, 1960–97*

curve inwards. The second oil shock in 1979–80 sees another upward shift of the curve, but this time without the use of incomes policy unemployment rises until 1985 and from about 5 per cent to 11 per cent, as the demand contraction moves the economy along the Phillips curve. Thus, although the second oil shock only resulted in a doubling of oil prices, the employment consequences were much more severe as the Conservative government countered with a sustained contraction in monetary policy. The reason it may have taken such a big rise in unemployment to bring down inflation is because people's expectations of inflation were slow to change and so the Phillips curve did not shift inwards as quickly as expected. By the mid-1980s, however, inflation was into single digits in the UK and a new low-inflation culture established.

The Lawson boom then leads to a rise along a lower Phillips curve between 1986 and 1989, with unemployment falling from 11 to 6 per cent, before the ERM-induced demand contraction shifts the economy back to the right along the same curve. Thus the movements in prices and unemployment between the mid-1980s and 1990s are consistent with movements along a stable, albeit rather flat Phillips curve. Finally, the movement to the left along the lowest curve on **Figure 18.2** show the effect of the falls in unemployment during the 1990s. If the current inflation target is maintained for all time then all subsequent substantial movements will be lateral, at a rate of inflation around 2.5 per cent per annum.

The final point to note from **Figure 18.12** is that it is consistent with the hysteresis theory of unemployment discussed in Chapter 15. The natural rate of unemployment or the NAIRU was stable at around 2 per cent during the 1960s, but rose due to the oil price shocks to 4 per cent then perhaps to 7 or 8 per cent by the mid-1980s. The reduction of inflation, however, did not bring about a fall in unemployment until the late 1980s, when it rose sharply again due partly to demand deflation in the UK as a result of the government's ERM commitments. Since 1993 steady demand reflation combined with special measures aimed at reducing long-term unemployment have managed to reduce unemployment to about 5 per cent – the lowest rate of unemployment since 1980.

How should UK anti-inflation policy be assessed and are there any lessons to be learned for the future? The appropriate policies to curtail inflation depend in part on the other objectives of policy-makers. If the reduction of inflation is the primary objective of policy, then it would seem that some reduction in aggregate demand is needed. A specific recommendation could be that the authorities need to bring about a sustained fall in the rate of growth of the money supply. This will reduce the demand for goods and services and hence reduce the rate of inflation by demand deflation. The potential problem with this policy is that in an open economy the money supply is not an instrument of policy unless the exchange rate is freely floating and international capital mobility is low. In the modern world with high capital mobility any rise in domestic interest rates to reduce money demand, leads to a capital inflow, which will appreciate the exchange rate. Hence, although aggregate demand is reduced, the effects of this policy are very severe on the traded goods sector of the economy. It is the export industries that are the hardest hit, while the non-traded sectors are relatively little affected. Hence a monetary contraction will have serious consequences for industries engaged in foreign trade and employment, and those industries may well be put in jeopardy. This was certainly an important feature of the UK anti-inflationary scenarios during the early 1980s, with nearly 20 per cent of manufacturing capacity lost between 1980 and 1982 by a combination of exchange rate appreciation and low aggregate demand.

An alternative policy that seeks to reduce aggregate expenditure is to raise income taxes. A sharp, short-run increase in the rate of income tax will reduce consumption without reducing investment (through higher interest rates), and simultaneously reduce the demand for imported goods which will be increasing and so jeopardising the current balance if domestic inflation exceeds that overseas. This may be fairer in terms of distributional effects, but there would still be a downward pressure on demand and a likely rise in unemployment. There are also potential political problems with this policy, in that politicians are reluctant to raise taxes for electoral reasons and there is the fear that if taxes are raised then there is inertia in reducing them again in the future.

If the policy objective is to maintain employment while simultaneously reducing inflation, then an incomes policy, at least in the short run, seems to be an important feature of the policy framework. Legislation to curb wage increases will have the effect of reducing real wages and hence encouraging production rather than spending. The problem with such incomes policies is that although they may work for a short time they seem to be ineffective in the longer term, as workers may resort to industrial action to maintain their real wages. This kind of policy may be regarded in some sense as an alternative to income tax rises. Incomes policies were a key feature of the UK's anti-inflation policy during the 1960s and most especially in the 1970s, but not in the 1980s or 1990s which, as noted above, may partly explain why unemployment rose so much over the 1980s. That said, part of the reason why incomes polices were not used was because they were deemed to be ineffective in the long run, difficult to enforce and discriminatory in their effects.

If inflation is not established and the authorities are keen to maintain a low level of price inflation, then economic policy should be focused on a nominal economic variable such as the money supply, the price level or the exchange rate. Which nominal variable is the best to target is a difficult question. In the context of an open economy, the money supply does not seem to be a sensible target variable since it is influenced by the balance of payments position, in which case an exchange rate or price level target is preferable. The UK experience with anti-inflation policy since the mid-1970s has seen all three targets adopted at one time or another. An intermediate money target was introduced in 1976, effectively abandoned in 1982, to be replaced with an informal exchange rate target. This became an official exchange rate target in 1990, when the pound joined the exchange rate mechanism (ERM). This target was abandoned in September 1992 when, after some time, it was replaced with an inflation target. Indeed, UK policy as of 1999 is based on an inflation target of some 2.5 per cent per annum. The principal policy instrument used to achieve this inflation target is the short-term interest rate as set by the Bank of England's monetary policy committee. As **Figure 18.12** shows, to date this policy of inflation targeting has been very successful with inflation on target since the inception of the policy in 1994.

Summary

- Inflation, defined as the persistency of prices to rise, can be due to demand-pull or cost-push factors.
- The traditional quantity theory views inflation as caused by excessive growth of the money supply. This view is only relevant for a closed economy or an open economy with a freely floating exchange rate. Under a fixed exchange system the quantity theory predicts inflation to be caused by excessive growth in the global money supply. The evidence to support the global monetarist view of inflation is weak.
- The Phillips curve denotes a potential trade-off between inflation and unemployment in the short run. In the longer run this trade off may become unstable as inflation expectations change and eventually disappear as expectations fully catch up with actual inflation.
- The main benefits of a stable, low rate of inflation are that relative prices are able to change without some prices falling, which fosters a more efficient allocation of resources and that nominal interest rates are positive.

- The costs of inflation are larger when the inflation is unanticipated. The costs of inflation include the erosion of savings-maintained nominal assets and the redistribution of income towards property, the welfare loss of holding money balances and the possible misallocation of resources caused by agents misperceiving relative price movements.
- Policies to reduce inflation have varied in the UK from the widespread use of incomes policies in the 1960s and 1970s, to sharp contractions in aggregate demand in the 1980 and 1990s. This change in policy reflects a change in the authority's attitudes towards maintaining full employment.
- Current UK anti-inflation policy is based on an explicit inflation target which is achieved by the Bank of England's manipulation of the short-term interest rate.

Suggested further reading

There is a vast literature on inflation most of which stems from the 1970s when inflation was regarded as the major macroeconomic problem. There are a number of good survey papers on the causes of inflation, including Bronfenbrenner and Holzman (1963), Laidler and Parkin (1975) and Gordon (1976) and numerous textbooks of which those by Frisch (1983), Jackman, Mulvey and Trevithick (1982) and Flemming (1976) are especially recommended. The classic statements of the expectations-augmented Phillips curve are Friedman (1968, 1975). Surveys of the inflation–unemployment trade-off are Santermero and Seater (1978) and Sumner (1984). The view that inflation may be generated by cost-push factors has become unfashionable, but a good account of the wage inflation hypothesis is given in Artis (1989).

Essay titles

1. 'Inflation is always and everywhere a monetary phenomenon' (Milton Friedman). Discuss.
2. Critically appraise the monetarist view of the inflation process in the light of the UK experience since the mid-1970s.
3. 'The so-called Phillips curve is based on theory which is incorrect, but on evidence which is indisputable.' Explain and discuss with reference to recent UK experience with inflation and unemployment.

Questions

1. Use a static *AD–AS* diagram to illustrate both cost-push and demand-pull inflation. To what extent do movements in output allow economists to distinguish between these two sources of inflation?

2. (a) Outline the quantity theory explanation of inflation.
   (b) Assume that the money supply and output are fixed and that the velocity of circulation depends directly on the rate of interest. What is the relationship between prices and the rate of interest? Provide an economic rationale.

3. On what grounds does Friedman argue that the Phillips curve does not provide a trade-off between inflation and unemployment in equilibrium? Does this argument need to be modified in the context of an open economy?

4. Using Friedman's expectations-augmented Phillips curve, show that the cost of reducing inflation to zero is higher short-term unemployment. To what extent is this higher unemployment due to workers being slow to change their expectations of inflation.

5. Are there any benefits from low, stable rates of inflation?

6. (a) Explain the concept of an incomes policy.
   (b) How might an incomes policy be a useful instrument of policy in helping to reduce inflation?
   (c) What are the limitations of such incomes policies?

CHAPTER 19
The Dynamic Theory of Macroeconomic Policy

Aims and objectives

- To examine the case for and against discretionary stabilisation policies.
- To evaluate the role of rational expectations in the design and formulation of economic policy.
- To review the policy implications of an independent central bank for both UK and EU monetary policy.

Introduction

Prior to the publication of Keynes' *General Theory of Employment, Interest and Money* there was virtually no theoretical justification for interventionist macroeconomic policy, although there were calls for various kinds of public works to help relieve unemployment, especially in the USA. The Keynesian revolution transformed this state of affairs, and very soon the idea of budget deficits to maintain full employment became the norm. With the passage of time, however, this view came to be challenged, especially due to the rise of inflation in the early 1970s and the rise of monetarism. The view emerged that whereas the business cycle was initially believed to have been caused by demand fluctuations, it was clearly possible, as the oil price hoist of the early 1970s demonstrated, that supply-side shocks could also disturb the economy. Not only was demand management less able to deal with these shocks, but demand management could be a source of instability in this case. Today there is no clear consensus over the desirability of macroeconomic stabilisation policies. It is, however, possible to identify two approaches following Fischer (1988):

> One view and school of thought, associated with Keynes, Keynesians and new Keynesians, is that the private economy is subject to co-ordination failures that can produce excessive levels of unemployment and excessive fluctuations in real activity. The other view, attributed to classical economists, and especially espoused by

monetarists and equilibrium business cycle theorists, is that the private economy reaches as good an equilibrium as is possible given government policy. (p. 294)

Thus the issue is whether the macroeconomy is viewed as being inherently unstable – subject to random shocks generating lost output, unemployment and inflation – or whether one views the economy as being naturally stable and basically efficient. In the first case, monetary and fiscal policy are seen as useful to counteract undesirable fluctuations, whereas in the latter, mistaken and badly conceived policies are seen as a major cause of large and inefficient departures from the natural rate of unemployment and output.

This chapter is divided into five sections, which outline in chronological order the development of the arguments both in favour and against discretionary short-run stabilisation policy. First the traditional static approach to macroeconomic policy is considered: the optimising and fixed targets approaches due to Theil (1964) and Tinbergen (1952), respectively. Friedman's rebuttal of the case for discretionary policy is then examined, followed by an outline of the dynamic approach to macroeconomic policy-making through a consideration of optimal control theory, which can be viewed as a response to Friedman's advocacy of a policy rule based on a constant rate of growth of the money supply. We then examine the role of rational expectations in the case against stabilisation policy, and demonstrate that the New Classical policy ineffectiveness results only hold under very special assumptions and that rational expectations are not central for the case against stabilisation policy as shown by the New Keynesians. The final section briefly reviews the recent main issues in the stabilisation policy debate and comments on the current state of macroeconomic policy.

The traditional static approach to macroeconomic policy

The Keynesian approach to economic policy formulation starts by defining a set of target variables and a set of instruments. The target variables are defined as those for which the government seeks desirable values, and the targets are set with a view to maximising social welfare. The precise values of these target variables are chosen by policy-makers who are assumed to be representative of the public interest. The arguments in the policy-makers' objective function are the deviations of the actual values of the target variables from their desired values. The smaller these deviations are, the greater is the policy-makers' utility. More formally, in the case of two target variables, y_1 and y_2, which are set for one period only, the policy-makers' objective function (SWF) can be written as:

$$SWF = f(y_1 - y_2^T, y_2 - y_2^T) \tag{19.1}$$

where superscripts T denote the target values of the variables.

In order to achieve the desired target values of the y variables the authorities are assumed to use their policy instruments, which are those variables which the government can manipulate to achieve its economic objectives. Instrumental variables are necessarily exogenous, as the authorities need to be able to determine their values independently of the other variables in the economic system. For example, tax rates are instruments, but tax revenues are not since their value is determined not only by the tax rates set, but also by the level of national income. In this model the two instrumental variables are z_1 and z_2, both of which are assumed to be under the control of the government. Both target variables are related to both instruments, since a change in either instrument is likely to affect both target variables. Thus a general form of the structural equations of the model, can be written as:

$$y_1 = a_{11}z_1 + a_{12}z_2 + b_1y_2$$
$$y_2 = a_{21}z_1 + a_{22}z_2 + b_2y_1 \tag{19.2}$$

The reduced form of this set of structural equations is obtained by expressing each target variable, y, as a function of the instruments, z; that is:

$$y_1 = (1 - b_1b_2)^{-1}[(a_{11} + b_1a_{21})z_1 + (a_{12} + b_1a_{22})z_2] = \alpha_{11}z_1 + \alpha_{12}z_2 \tag{19.3}$$

$$y_2 = (1 - b_1b_2)^{-1}[(a_{21} + b_2a_{11})z_1 + (a_{22} + b_2a_{12})z_2] = \alpha_{21}z_1 + \alpha_{22}z_2 \tag{19.4}$$

where the reduced form parameters, α, depend upon the structural coefficients a and b. In matrix form this system is:

$$y = Az \tag{19.5}$$

where y is a 2×1 vector of target variables, A is a 2×2 matrix of coefficients and z is a 2×1 vector of instruments. Setting the y's equal to their target values of y_1^T and y_2^T and inverting the A-matrix, values of the instrumental variables can be found which will achieve the target values of y_1^T and y_2^T. Thus

$$z = A^{-1}y^T \tag{19.6}$$

Stabilisation policy requires that policy-makers:

(1) can determine *unique* and *feasible* target values for y;
(2) have a reasonable knowledge of the values of the elements of the A matrix which relate instruments to targets; and
(3) can control the instrumental variables.

Each of these requirements is difficult to satisfy in practice. For example, it is very difficult to define a unique target for a policy variable. Should inflation be 2 per cent per annum or 4 per cent per annum? Would your decision be affected if the lower rate of inflation is associated with a higher level of unemployment? With regards to (3), although the authorities can control some policy instruments, these instruments may be at least partially endogenous. For example, the budget deficit is partly endogenous as are interest rates, since the former is affected by the economic cycle while the latter may well be at least partly determined by foreign interest rates in an open economy with a high degree of capital market integration.

Another important point to note is that the model of the economy is an interdependent model. That is, target y_1 depends upon the level of target y_2 and vice versa. Thus any change in an instrument to influence the target y_1 will also impact upon target y_2. Because of this interdependence, Tinbergen (1952) argued that the authorities need as many independent instruments as they have targets. Thus in this context if the authorities are to be able to achieve both y_1 and y_2 then they need to use both z_1 and z_2. In a more general context where the government has say n targets, it will need n independent policy instruments if it is to be able to simultaneously achieve all the targets. This means that the authorities will need to increase the number of instruments beyond just fiscal and monetary policy, to include, for example, instruments such as incomes policy or exchange rate changes. If it is not possible to increase the number of instruments, Theil (1964) suggested optimising between targets.

Theil's optimising approach to economic policy is therefore to maximise the policy-makers' social welfare subject to the constraints imposed by the economic system. These constraints are given by the structure of the economy as given by equations (19.2) and (19.3). As an illustration of this approach consider the Phillips curve in **Figure 19.1**. The Phillips curve constrains policy-makers' choices of target inflation and target unemployment rates. The social welfare function is assumed to be defined over various combinations of unemployment and inflation, and in the figure they are represented by the concave indifference curves labelled SWF, where the closer these curves are to the origin the greater the level of social welfare. Hence social welfare is greater along SWF_2 than along either SWF_1 or SWF_0. The trade-off between inflation and unemployment, which maximises social welfare, occurs at point A, where the Phillips curve is tangential to the social welfare function.

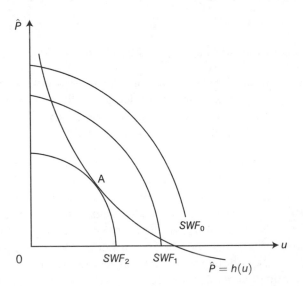

Figure 19.1   *The policy trade off*

The problem with this kind of optimising approach is that it is dependent on the existence of a well-defined social welfare function and a stable Phillips curve. In general it is not possible to determine a unique social welfare function for the economy as a whole and it is difficult, if not impossible, for the policy-maker to maximise social welfare – since social welfare cannot be measured. There will be internal conflict within the government over preferences and the government may also be uncertain as to the preferences it should have. Group decision-making may involve insoluble logical problems and there may be no way to determine group preferences from the preferences of individuals. In particular, the majority voting system as used in the UK will not give rise to an optimum outcome.

The case against stabilisation policy

Friedman (1948) made the case against an activist stabilisation policy largely on the basis of the problem of the timing of such a policy to offset the cycle. He defined two types of output fluctuation. The first is the difference between the market clearing (or equilibrium) level of output, y^E, and the actual value of output, x, that would occur without government intervention. This difference is known as the pure cycle deviation in output and is equal to $x - y^E$. The second type of output fluctuation is the actual output deviation that occurs when demand management policies are in operation. This is measured as $y - y^E$ where y is the level of national output with activist policy which is obtained by adding a policy-induced amount of output u_t to the pure cycle level x_t; that is $y_t = x_t + u_t$. For a perfect stabilisation policy it is necessary for the deviation of actual output with policy from its equilibrium level to be zero, that is:

$$y_t - y_t^E = x_t + u_t - y_t^E = 0 \qquad (19.7)$$

Therefore

$$u_t = -(x_t - y_t^E) \qquad (19.8)$$

Equation (19.8) shows that for perfect stabilisation the policy-induced change in output, u_t, must be of the same magnitude but opposite in sign to the pure cycle deviation. In **Figure 19.2** the pure cycle deviation in output is given by the solid line and the policy-induced change in output by the broken line. When both are added together the deviation of the actual output from the equilibrium output is zero and so the economy travels along the straight line.

The problem for policy-makers is that policy changes have to be synchronised with cyclical changes. Any mistiming of the policy change adds to the pure cycle deviation of output rather than reducing it. Policy is then destabilising as illustrated in **Figure 19.3**, which leads to a greater amplitude in the cycle of national output. The mistiming of policy can come about because of time lags and uncertainties in the policy-making process. In particular, there are a number of potential lags in the system. The *recognition lag* is the time it takes to identify the problem; that is, before a downturn in economic activity shows up in the

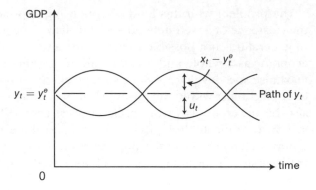

Figure 19.2 *Stabilising policy*

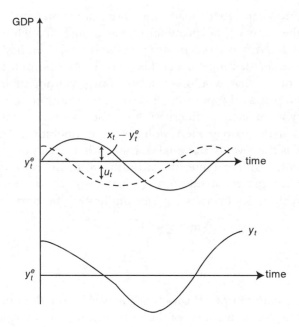

Figure 19.3 *Destabilising policy*

national statistics. This lag can be reduced by improved forecasting procedures and more rapidly produced statistics. A second lag is the *implementation lag*. This is the time taken for policy-makers to agree on the policy change needed and to implement the necessary changes. Finally, there is the *outside lag*, which is the time it takes for the change in the policy variable to affect the target variable. Although these lags delay the policy response, if they are predictable and constant over time they can in principle be appropriately allowed for in the policy-making process.

In addition to the time lags involved, however, there is also the problem of uncertainty which can enter the model in either of two ways. In the case of uncertainty about the exogenous variables, then a feedback rule, called a closed-loop policy in the following section, can still yield a counter-cyclical stabilisation policy. More serious is parameter uncertainty when the parameters of the A-matrix described earlier (p. 381)are not known with certainty or they vary over time. This type of uncertainty is more serious for stabilisation policy as will be demonstrated later when considering the implications of private sector agents using rational expectations to predict an authority's policy actions.

The dynamic stabilisation approach – optimal control theory

An extension of the traditional approaches to stabilisation policy emerged during the 1970s with the introduction of optimal control techniques into economics. The great advantage of this engineering technique was that the authorities' reactions were considered to have a time dimension. Hence, policy outcomes today could be used to feedback onto future values of both the instrument and target variables. Moreover, uncertainty about the values of the exogenous variables is also unproblematic because of the feedback rules employed in this method.

To pursue this approach formally requires the model described above (pp. 381 ff) to be modified. Assume that there is now just one target variable, y, and one instrument, z. The target variable depends upon the value of the instrument as in equation (19.2), but in addition it also depends upon the value of the target variable in the previous period and a stochastic error term, ϵ_t. That is:

$$y_t = a_0 + a_1 z_t + b y_{t-1} + \epsilon_t \tag{19.9}$$

In this one-target model the authorities want to minimise the variance of y around some desired value, y^T. To achieve this the authorities need to set z_t, the instrumental variable, at an appropriate level according to some feedback rule. The general form of the feedback rule is:

$$z_t = \phi_0 + \phi_1 y_{t-1} \tag{19.10}$$

Thus the instrumental variable is adjusted according to the out-turn of the target variable in the previous period. The problem is how to find values of ϕ_1 and ϕ_2 which minimise the variance of y. To do this substitute equation (19.10) into equation (19.9) and solve for y. This gives:

$$y_t = (a_0 + a_1 \phi_0) + (a_1 \phi_1 + b) y_{t-1} + \epsilon_t \tag{19.11}$$

Assuming that in steady-state equilibrium $y_t = y_{t-1} = \bar{y}$, and the stochastic shock ϵ_t is expected to be zero, this can be rewritten as:

$$\bar{y} = \frac{a_0 + a_1 \phi_0}{1 - (a_1 \phi_1 + b)} \tag{19.12}$$

Thus $\bar{y}$ depends on the structural parameters, a_0, a_1 and b and the parameters in the authority's policy rule ϕ_0 and ϕ_1. Furthermore, from equation (19.11) it is clear that the variance of y depends on the variance of y_{t-1} and the variance of the random term ϵ_t, denoted as σ_ϵ^2. The variance of y around its expected or target value is therefore:

$$\text{var } y = (a_1 \phi_1 + b)^2 \text{ var } y + \sigma_\epsilon^2 \tag{19.13}$$

or

$$\text{var } y = \frac{\sigma_\epsilon^2}{1 - (a_1 \phi_1 + b)^2} \tag{19.14}$$

To minimise the variance of y the denominator needs to be set equal to 1 and so the optimal feedback rule is given as $(a_1 \phi_1 + b) = 0$, which gives the optimal value of ϕ_1 as:

$$\phi_1 = -b/a_1 \tag{19.15}$$

By substituting this expression for ϕ_1 into equation (19.12) the optimal setting for ϕ_0 can be calculated. This is $\bar{y} = a_0 + a_1 \phi_0$, so rearranging gives:

$$\phi_0 = (\bar{y} - a_0)/a_1 \tag{19.16}$$

The optimal feedback rule for the instrumental variable z is therefore:

$$z_t = (\bar{y} - a_0)/a_1 - (b/a_1)y_{t-1} \tag{19.17}$$

If this is substituted back into equation (19.9), then we get:

$$y_t = a_0 + (\bar{y} - a_0) - by_{t-1} + by_{t-1} + \epsilon_t = \bar{y} + \epsilon_t \tag{19.18}$$

This is the smallest gap possible between the actual value of the target variable and the desired value. This is equal to the value of the random disturbance. Any other feedback rule will give rise to a greater divergence between y and $\bar{y}$ and so would be sub-optimal. Thus the feedback rule is optimal in this case.

It is possible to show that a feedback rule always dominates a simple rule without feedback, such as a constant growth of the money supply rule as advocated by some monetarist economists, including Milton Friedman. Hence, using optimal control techniques, time lags and variable uncertainty do not pose a serious threat to activist stabilisation policies. Thus the case for discretionary policy is enhanced.

Rational expectations and parameter uncertainty

A more fundamental attack on Keynesian-style stabilisation policy has, however, been mounted by the new classical economists. Lucas (1972, 1976) has provided the most telling criticismof the Keynesian approach arguing that the structural parameters are not invariant over time and vary with policy changes. That is to say, the elements of the A-matrix change with changes in z. To understand this point assume that private sector agents have rational expectations; these expectations then become endogenous within the model. If policy changes, these expectations will also change which, in turn, will affect private sector agents' decisions regarding consumption, investment, labour supply and so on.

The argument that private sector agents' expectations about government policy affect the structural parameters of the model can be illustrated by the following simple New Classical model. The essential feature is the 'surprise' aggregate supply curve due to Lucas (1972) – as discussed in Chapter 17 – which is combined with a simple quantity theory model of the price level. With all equations in log-linear form, the Lucas supply curve and the quantity theory can be written as:

$$y_t - \bar{y} = a(p_t - E_{t-1}p_t) + by_{t-1} + v_t \tag{19.19}$$

$$p_t = m_t - k - y_t \tag{19.20}$$

Equation (19.19) is the New Classical supply curve, with the deviation of output from its equilibrium level, $\bar{y}$, given by the unanticipated price change $p_t - E_{t-1}p_t$, where E_{t-1} is the expectations operator based on information known to agents at time $t-1$, the lagged level of output, y_{t-1}, and a stochastic error term, v_t. If agents correctly forecast the price level then the first term in equation (19.19) will be zero. Equation (19.20) is the naive quantity theory of money, rearranged to give the price level in terms of the money supply and real income.

To solve the model there are three endogenous variables, y_t, p_t and $E_{t-1}p_t$, but only two equations. To be able to solve this system, therefore, another equation has to be generated. This is achieved by taking expectations through equation (19.20) to obtain an equation for the expected price level. Doing so at time $t-1$ gives:

$$E_{t-1}p_t = E_{t-1}m_t - E_{t-1}y_t - k \tag{19.21}$$

where E_{t-1} is the expectations operator based on information known to agents in period $t-1$, and k is a constant and hence unaffected by expectations. Equation (19.21) is the extra equation that is needed to solve the model for all three of the endogenous variables. Substituting both equations (19.21) and (19.20) into equation (19.19) gives:

$$y_t - \bar{y} = a(m_t - E_{t-1}m_t) - a(y_t - E_{t-1}y_t) + by_{t-1} + v_t$$

Assuming that $E_{t-1}y_t = \bar{y}$ then this expression can be rearranged to give:

$$y_t = \bar{y} + \left(\frac{a}{1+a}\right)(m_t - E_{t-1}m_t) + \left(\frac{b}{1+a}\right)y_{t-1} + \left(\frac{1}{1+a}\right)v_t \tag{19.22}$$

The money supply is the instrument of policy and so is now assumed to be adjusted according to a feedback rule, such that as output falls the money supply is expanded and as output rises the money supply is reduced. This is as if the authorities 'lean into the wind'; that is, as if the authorities act counter-cyclically. This is written as:

$$m_t = \bar{m} - cy_{t-1} + w_t \tag{19.23}$$

where $\bar{m}$ is the constant part of the money base, c is the parameter which captures the extent to which the authorities 'lean against the wind', and w_t is a serially independent error term with mean zero ($E_{t-1}w_t = 0$). Taking expectations of equation (19.23) gives:

$$E_{t-1}m_t = \bar{m} - cy_{t-1} \tag{19.24}$$

Substituting equations (19.23) and (19.24) into equation (19.22) gives the final reduced form for output:

$$y_t = \bar{y} + \frac{b}{1+a}y_{t-1} + \frac{1}{1+a}(v_t + aw_t) \tag{19.25}$$

The fundamental characteristic about this final equation is that the level of output is independent of both $\bar{m}$ and c. This is crucial because it is through $\bar{m}$ and c that the authorities can operate to influence the level of output. Thus the authorities are unable to influence the level of output by monetary policy changes in this model. This result, derived by Sargent and Wallace (1976), is referred to as the *super neutrality of money* because the systematic part of the money supply has no effect on real output even in the short run. Thus with rational expectations and a Lucas supply curve, stabilisation policy is not an option.

A Phillips curve-type relation can be obtained from this form of model as output and employment vary with the divergence between p_t and $E_{t-1}p_t$, but the inflation–unemployment trade-off cannot be exploited by the government because systematic variations in the money supply have no effect on output. To illustrate this problem consider the Phillips curve in **Figure 19.4.** At point A the policy-makers attempt to exploit the short-run Phillips curve by expanding monetary policy to move the economy to point B, which the authorities prefer since social welfare is higher at SWF_3 than it is at A (SWF_2). Since private sector agents have rational expectations they will know the model and hence fully understand that the expansion of the money supply will only raise prices. Thus the private sector will expect the rise in the money supply to move the economy to C, rather than to B. Inflation will be permanently higher, but with no change in the level of output or unemployment.

If, on the other hand, private sector agents are initially fooled by the government into thinking that the government will not raise inflation, the economy may actually move to point B in the short term. Once private sector agents realise what has happened, however, they will expect a subsequent movement to point C. Moreover, the private sector will not believe the government in the future since it has lost its 'low-inflation' credibility. Thus it is in the government's own interest not to renege on its promises, since once its reputation is damaged it will find it very difficult to persuade the private sector that its policy pronouncements are genuine.

Using a more formal approach (see **Box 19.1**) it is possible to demonstrate the relative sizes of the welfare losses at the three equilibria, labelled A, B and C in **Figure 19.4**. From the point of view of the authorities, the loss in terms of

---

Box 19.1   The time inconsistency problem

The time inconsistency problem can also be given a technical treatment, based on the model of Kydland and Prescott (1977).

Assume the authorities have a linear Phillips curve, written in terms of output rather than unemployment such that:

$$y = \bar{y} + b(\hat{P} + \hat{P}^e) \quad \text{where } b > 0 \tag{B19.1}$$

The authorities' loss function, L, is assumed to be quadratic such that:

$$L = (y - y^T)^2 + a(\hat{P} - \hat{P}^T)^2 \quad \text{where } y^T > \bar{y}, a > 0 \tag{B 19.2}$$

This says that the authorities dislike deviations in either direction from the target values of both output and inflation, y^T and $\hat{P}^T$ respectively, and that this dislike increases as the deviations become larger. This loss function generates the social welfare preference map in **Figure 19.4**.

Suppose the authorities' target value for inflation is zero, so that $\hat{P}^T = 0$, and they take expectations of inflation as given, then the loss function becomes:

$$L = (y - y^T)^2 + a\hat{P}^2$$

Minimising this with respect to inflation gives:

$$\frac{\partial L}{\partial \hat{P}} = 2a\hat{P} + 2b(\bar{y} + b(\hat{P} - \hat{P}^e) - y^T) = 0$$

and so

$$\hat{P} = \frac{b}{a + b^2}(\bar{y} - y^T - b\hat{P}^e) \tag{B19.3}$$

Agents with rational expectations, however, will work this out for themselves. That is, know $\hat{P}$. Hence $\hat{P}^e = \hat{P}$. Using this gives:

$$\hat{P}_D = \frac{b}{a}(y^T - \bar{y}) \tag{B19.4}$$

Substituting this into the loss function gives:

$$L_D = \left(\frac{a + b^2}{a}\right)(\bar{y} - y^T) \tag{B19.5}$$

Box 19.1 (*Continued*)

Suppose now that the government announces a reduction in inflation to zero, which is believed by all agents. In this case $\hat{P}^e = \hat{P} = 0$. Then minimising the loss function gives:

$$\frac{\partial L}{\partial \hat{P}} = 2a\hat{P} + 2b(\bar{y} + b\hat{P} - y^T) = 0, \text{ and so}$$

$$\hat{P}_R = \frac{b}{a + b^2}(\bar{y} - y^T) \tag{B19.6}$$

Substituting this into the loss function gives:

$$L_R = \left(\frac{a}{a + b^2}\right)(\bar{y} - y^T)^2 \tag{B19.7}$$

Equations (B19.4) and (B19.5) are the solution when the authorities attempt to use discretionary policy to exploit the trade-off. Equations (B19.6) and (B19.7) are when the government announces a zero inflation target and then reneges on the target. When the government pre-commits to zero inflation then the target is achieved and the loss function is simply:

$$L_{PC} = (\bar{y} - y^T)^2 \tag{B19.8}$$

It is now possible to rank these equilibria as follows:

$$L_R < L_{PC} < L_D \tag{B19.9}$$
$$0 = \hat{P}_{PC} < \hat{P}_R < \hat{P}_D \tag{B19.10}$$

The subscripts *PC, R* and *D* denote respectively the pre-commitment solution, the reneging solution and the discretionary solution. From the authorities' point of view the reneging solution is preferable to pre-commitment, since the welfare loss is smaller. The problem is that the reneging solution is not feasible in the long run, so the pre-commitment solution is preferable, both for the government and for the private sector who are assumed to have identical preferences. The problem of time-inconsistency of policy is that in the absence of pre-commitment the economy ends up at the discretionary solution with a rate of inflation higher than either the government or the private sector would wish.

---

deviation from the target levels of output (or unemployment) is minimised when the authorities renege on their commitment not to create inflation; that is, the unannounced policy shift that moved the model from point A to point B. The problem with this policy is that it is *time-inconsistent*. That is, it is not the best solution in the longer term since, as demonstrated in **Figure 19.4**, private sector agents respond to move the model to C where welfare is only SWF_0. Because of this time-inconsistency problem, it is preferable for the authorities to pre-commit themselves to policy rules. In the absence of such rules, the economy ends up at

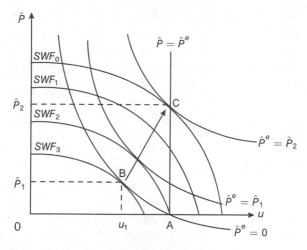

Figure 19.4 *Phillips curve trade-off with rational expectations*

the discretionary equilibrium (at point C) which neither the government nor the private sector want, since welfare at C is less than at A. An example of such a policy pre-commitment is to put inflation control in the hands of an independent central bank. This has become a common policy prescription in Europe, but there are costs in the sense that the independent central bank has no mandate to respond to other economic problems such as rising or persistent unemployment.

The Keynesian response to this policy ineffectiveness result rests on a number of observations. First, the super neutrality result depends on private agents and the government having the same information. If the government has superior information then they are able to offset exogenous disturbances using counter-cyclical policies even when expectations are rational and markets clear. Thus the government is able to change actual prices without affecting price expectations, because the private sector interprets the change in prices as a change in relative prices independent of government, due to its inferior information.

A second way in which Keynesian policy conclusions can be restored while allowing expectations to be rational is to postulate some form of stickiness in wages and prices (see Chapter 15). A specific example of this kind of stickiness is to postulate wage contracts which last for more than on period, or for contracts that overlap. Following Fischer (1977), suppose wage contracts last for two periods and only half the contracts are renegotiated in each period. In the current period, t, money wages are based on price expectations made two periods ago, that is $E_{t-2}p_t$, and cannot be influenced by current policy. Thus the government is able to affect p_t without affecting $E_{t-2}p_t$, and so can influence the level of real output. The existence and widespread evidence of such contracts in practice seems to suggest that short-run macroeconomic policy will have some effect on output. Thus the new Keynesians restore a role for discretionary stabilisation policy by invoking institutional price and wage rigidities, even though private agents are assumed to have rational expectations. The point is that policy ineffectiveness depends on clearing markets rather than on rational expectations. Therefore if markets do not clear quickly then the case for discretionary stabilisation policy is overwhelming.

Conclusions

The theory of economic policy-making outlined in this chapter has suggested either policy discretion or fixed policy rules. The Keynesian case for policy discretion depicts policy-makers as disinterested public servants who can define their objective function and order their priorities. This view of the economic policy-making process totally neglects the political process that decides the objectives of policy. A political perspective on economic decision-making depicts the outcome of bargaining and manoeuvring among many different interest groups, each pursuing its own self-interest. Moreover, civil servants and politicians are not purely disinterested technocrats. Civil servants may be concerned with job satisfaction and enhancement while politicians are likely to be concerned with re-election. This kind of policy-making cannot generate a well-defined objective function since target variables, while easy to identify, are difficult to quantify. The political process therefore introduces a further destabilising element in addition to that of faulty technique discussed earlier (pp. 381 ff). The political dimension helps to explain why so many governments have alternated between inflation and unemployment as their primary concern, rather than pursuing a consistent set of policy objectives.

On the other hand, policy rules allow less scope for political meddling provided that they are adhered to. Even this, however, is not as easy as it may seem. For example, the UK government under John Major's premiership established an exchange rate rule whereby sterling would be fixed at DM 2.95 to the pound. This was the cornerstone of policy from which the government never diverged, but despite this consistency of policy there was a speculative attack on sterling in September 1992 and sterling was forced off its peg and out of the exchange rate mechanism of which it was a part. Thus although the rule was adhered to – at great cost to the real economy – in the end private sector agents did not believe the policy was credible and forced the government to change it. This example suggests that policy rules are not necessarily free from meddling, only that the meddling comes from the private sector rather than the public sector and often with far greater costs than public discretionary policy. The bottom line is that in practice discretionary policy is impossible to avoid. Not only do politicians need to be aware of this fact, but they also need to appreciate that only through a beter understanding of the workings of the macroeconomy can discretionary policy be made more effective in stabilising the economy.

Summary

- The traditional Keynesian view is that the private sector of the economy is potentially unstable and hence there is a need for government intervention to restore and maintain high employment levels.
- There are several difficulties with stabilisation policy: quantifying policy targets; the time lags with which policy operates are long and uncertain; the outcome of the policy change depends upon private sector expectations which are difficult to predict and change with policy; and there is some uncertainty about the structure of the economy.
- Although activist policy is possible, fine-tuning is not. The question is how to change policy and whether policy changes should be announced. Thus there is a trade-off between the certainty about future policy that comes from rules, and the flexibility of policy to respond to economic shocks.
- Central bank independence is one of the routes through which democratic governments pre-commit themselves to low inflation and so mitigate the effects of the time inconsistency problem. The fiscal policy rules enshrined in the Maastricht Treaty can be regarded as a necessary condition for low rates of monetary growth and hence low rates of inflation.

Suggested further reading

This is a technical and extensive literature. The original Tinbergen rules are in Tinbergen (1952). A classic debate on the pros and cons of stabilisation policy is that between Friedman and Heller (1969). B. Friedman (1975, 1990) surveys the targets and instruments approach to economic policy and Curie (1985) gives a non technical discussion of optimal control approach. The new classical policy-ineffectiveness result is in Sargent and Wallace (1975), Lucas (1976) and Minford and Peel (1983). The time-inconsistency problem is discussed in Kydland and Prescott (1977), and in Barro and Gordon (1983) and surveyed by Blackburn and Christensen (1989). The new Keynesian approach to stabilisation policy based on rational expectations and wage contracts is due to Fischer (1977) and Taylor (1979) with Ball, Mankiw and Romer (1988) offering some empirical evidence in a Phillips curve context. The case for central bank independence is considered in Alesina and Summers (1993).

Essay titles

1. Evaluate the case for an activist demand management policy in the UK.
2. 'With rational expectations systematic demand management policies are ineffective.' Discuss.
3. What are the arguments in favour of policy rules rather than discretion?

Questions

1. What economic and political problems may policy-makers consider in setting the targets for macroeconomic policy?

2. (a) Distinguish between inside and outside lags?
   (b) Does fiscal or monetary policy have the smaller inside and outside lag?
   (c) Would you recommend fiscal or monetary policy to be used to offset the effect of a temporary shock to output? Why?

3. Outline Friedman's critique of stabilisation policy. To what extent is this critique redundant if the authorities follow a closed-loop feedback rule?

4. Explain the concept of dynamic inconsistency. How may this arise if the authorities attempt to exploit the short-run trade-off between unemployment and inflation?

5. (a) Using the formal model in **Box 19.1** show the effect on the loss function andthe inflation rates under discretion, pre-commitment and reneging equilibria when the authorities set $\bar{y}=y^{T}$.
   (b) Choose parameter values for a and b where the gap between the natural rate and the target level of income is 1, to confirm the ranking of the solutions given in equation (B 19.9).

References

Aftalion, A. (1927) 'The Theory of Economic Cycles based on the Capitalist Techniques of Production', *Review of Economics and Statistics*, vol. 9, October, pp. 165–70.

Aghion, P. and Howitt, P. (1992) 'A Model of Growth through Creative Destruction', *Econometrica,* vol. 60, March, pp. 323–51.

Akerlof, G. and Yellen, J. (1986) *Efficiency Wage Models of the Labour Market* (New York: Cambridge University Press).

Alesina, A. and Summers, L. (1993) 'Central Bank Independence and Macroeconomic Performance', *Journal of Money, Credit and Banking,* vol. 25, May, pp. 151–62.

Alexander, S.S. (1952) 'The Effects of a Devaluation on the Trade Balance', *IMF Staff Papers,* no. 2, pp. 263–78.

Alexander, S.S. (1959) 'Effects of a Devaluation: A Simplified Synthesis of Elasticities and Absorption Approaches', *American Economic Review,* vol. 49, March, pp. 23–42.

Allen, P.R. (1973) 'A Portfolio Approach to International Capital Flows', *Journal of International Economics,* vol. 3, pp. 135–60.

Allen, P.R. and Kenen, P.B. (1978) *The Balance of Payments, Exchange Rates and Economic Policy. A Survey and Synthesis of Recent Developments* (Athens: Centre of Planning and Economic Research).

Ando, A. and Modigliani, F. (1963) 'The Life Cycle Hypothesis of Saving: Aggregate Implications and Tests', *American Economic Review,* vol. 53, March, pp. 55–84.

Argy, V. (1994) *International Macroeconomics: Theory and Policy* (London: Routledge).

Artis, M.J., Bladen-Hovell, R.C. and Zang, W. (1993) 'A European Money Demand Function', in P.R. Masson and M.P. Taylor (eds), *Policy Issues in the Operation of Currency Unions* (Cambridge: Cambridge University Press), pp. 240–63.

Artis, M.J. (1979) 'Recent Developments in the Theory of Fiscal Policy: A Survey', in S. Cook and P. Jackson (eds), *Current Issues in Fiscal Policy* (Oxford: Martin Robertson), pp. 15–43.

Artis, M.J. (1989) 'Wage Inflation', in D. Greenaway (ed.), *Current Issues in Macroeconomics* (Basingstoke: Macmillan), pp. 91–109.

Artis, M.J. and Lewis, M.K. (1991) *Money in Britain: Monetary Policy, Innovation and Europe* (Hemel Hempstead: Philip Allan).

Attfield, C.L.F., Demery, D. and Duck, N.W. (1991) *Rational Expectations in Macro-economics*, 2nd edn (Oxford: Blackwell).

Azariadis, C. (1975) 'Implicit Contracts and Unemployment Equilibria', *Journal of Political Economy,* vol. 83, pp. 1183–202.

Backhouse, R. (1985) *A History of Modern Economic Analysis* (Oxford: Blackwell).

Bacon, R. and Eltis, W. (1978) *Britain's Economic Problem: Too Few Producers*, 2nd edn (London: Macmillan).

Baily, M.N. (1978) 'Stabilisation Policy and Private Economic Behaviour', *Brookings Papers on Economic Activity,* no. 1, pp. 11–59.

Ball, L., Mankiw, N.G. and Romer, D. (1988) 'The New Keynesian Economics and the Output–Inflation Trade-off', *Brookings Papers on Economic Activity,* no. 1, pp. 1–65.

Barr, D.G. (1992) 'The Demand for Money in Europe: Comment on Kremers and Lane', *IMF Staff Papers,* no. 39, pp. 718–29.

Barro, R.J. (1974) 'Are Government Bonds Net Wealth?', *Journal of Political Economy,* vol. 82, November/December, pp. 1095–117.

Barro, R.J. (1989) 'The Ricardian Approach to Budget Deficits', *Journal of Economic Perspectives,* vol. 3, Spring, pp. 37–54.

Barro, R.J. (1991) 'Economic Growth in a Cross Section of Countries', *Quarterly Journal of Economics,* vol. 106, May, pp. 407–43.

Barro, R.J. and Gordon, D.B. (1983) 'Rules, Discretion and Reputation in a Model of Monetary Policy', *Journal of Monetary Economics,* vol. 12, pp. 101–21.

Barro, R.J. and Sala-i-Martin, X.X. (1994) *Economic Growth* (New York: McGraw-Hill).

Barro, R.J. and Sala-i-Martin, X.X. (1991) 'Convergence Across States and Regions', *Brookings Papers on Economic Activity,* vol. 1, pp. 107–82.

Basu, S. and Taylor, A.M. (1999) 'Business Cycles in International Historical Perspective', *Journal of Economic Perspectives,* vol. 13, Spring, pp. 45–68.

Baumol, W.J. (1952) 'The Transactions Demand for Cash: an Inventory Theoretic Approach', *Quarterly Journal of Economics,* vol. 66, November, pp. 545–56.

Baumol, W.J. (1961) 'Pitfalls in Contra-Cyclical Policies: Some Tools and Results', *Review of Economic and statistics,* vol. 43, February, pp. 21–6.

Bean, C.R. (1978) 'The Determinants of Consumers Expenditure in the UK', *Government Economic Service Working Paper no. 4.*

Bean, C.R. (1981) 'An Econometric Model of Manufacturing Investment in the UK', *Economic Journal,* vol. 91, pp. 106–21.

Bean, C.R. (1994) 'European Unemployment: A Survey', *Journal of Economic Literature,* vol. 32, June, pp. 573–619.

Beckerman, W. (1968) *An Introduction to National Income Analysis* (London: Weidenfeld & Nicolson).

Beveridge, W.H. (1944) *Full Employment in a Free Society* (London: Allen & Unwin).

Bischoff, C. (1971) 'Business Investment in the 1970s: A Comparison of the Models', *Brookings Papers on Economic Activity,* no. 1, pp. 13–63.

Blackburn, K. and Christensen, M. (1989) 'Monetary Policy and Policy Credibility: Theories and Evidence', *Journal of Economic Literature,* vol. 27, March, pp. 1–45.

Blanchard, O.J. and Summers, L.H. (1986) 'Hysteresis and the European Unemployment Problem', *NBER Macroeconomics Annual,* vol. 1, pp. 15–78.

Blanchard, O.J. and Summers, L.H. (1987) 'Hysteresis in Unemployment', *European Economic Review,* vol. 31, pp. 288–95.

Blaug, M. (1968) *Economic Theory in Retrospect,* 2nd edn (London: Heinemann).

Blinder, A.S. and Solow, R.M. (1973) 'Does Fiscal Policy Matter?' *Journal of Public Economics,* vol. 2, November, pp. 318–37.

Blinder, A.S. and Solow, R.M. (1976) 'Does Fiscal Policy Still Matter? A Reply', *Journal of Monetary Economics,* vol. 6, November, pp. 501–10.

Bond, S. and Jenkinson, T. (1996) 'The Assessment: Investment Performance and Policy', *Oxford Review of Economic Policy,* vol. 12, pp. 1–29.

Branson, W.H. (1968) *Financial Capital Flows in the US Balance of Payments* (Amsterdam: North Holland).

Branson, W.H. (1977) 'Asset Markets and Relative Prices in Exchange Rate Determination', *Sozialwissenschaftliche Annalen,* vol. 1, pp. 69–89.

Branson, W.H. (1989) *Macroeconomic Theory and Policy,* 3rd edn (New York: Harper & Row).

Brittain, B. (1981) 'International Currency Substitution and the Apparent Instability of Velocity in Some Western European Economies and in the United States', *Journal of Money Credit and Banking,* vol. 13, pp. 135–55.

Bronfenbrenner, M. and Holzman, F.D. (1963) 'A Survey of Inflation Theory', *American Economic Review,* vol. 53, September, pp. 593–661.

Cantillon, R. (1755) *Essai sur la Nature due Commerce en General,* ed. H. Higgs, 1931 (London: Royal Economic Society).

Caplin, A.S. and Spulber, D.F. (1987) 'Menu Costs and the Neutrality of Money', *Quarterly Journal of Economics,* vol. 106, August, pp. 683–708.

Carline, D. (1985) 'Trades Unions and Wages', in D. Carline, C.A. Pissarides, W.S. Siebert and P.J. Sloane, *Labour Economics* (Harlow: Longman), 186–232.

Chiang, A.C. (1985) *Fundamental Methods of Mathematical Economics*, 3rd edn (London: McGraw-Hill).

Chirinko, R.S. (1993) 'Business Fixed Investment: A Critical Survey of Modelling Strategies, Empirical Results and Policy Implications', *Journal of Economic Literature,* vol. 31, pp. 1875–911.

Chow, G. (1966) 'On the Long-Run and the Short-Run Demand for Money', *Journal of Political Economy,* vol. 74, April, pp. 111–31.

Christ, C.F. (1968) 'A Simple Macroeconomic Model With a Government Budget Constraint', *Journal of Political Economy,* vol. 76, February, pp. 53–67.

Clark, P.K. (1979) 'Investment in the 1970's: Theory, Performance and Prediction', *Brookings Papers on Economic Activity,* vol. 1, pp. 73–113.

Clower, R.W. (1965) 'The Keynesian Counter-Revolution: A Theoretical Reappraisal', in F. Hahn and F. Brechling (eds), *The Theory of Interest Rates* (London: Macmillan), pp. 103–125.

Clower, R.W. (1967) 'A Reconsideration of the Micro-Foundations of Monetary Theory', *Western Economic Journal,* vol. 6, pp. 1–8.

Coddington, A. (1976) 'Keynesian Economics: the Search for First Principles', *Journal of Economic Literature,* vol. 14, pp. 1258–273.

Coddington, A. (1983) *Keynesian Economics: The Search for First Principles* (London: Allen & Unwin).

Corden, W.M. (1960) 'The Geometric Presentation of Policies to Attain Internal and External Balance', *Review of Economic Studies,* vol. 28, October, pp. 1–22.

Currie, D.A. (1976) 'Macroeconomic Policy and the Government Financing Constraint', in M.J. Artis and A.R. Nobay (eds), *Contemporary Economic Analysis* (London: Croome Helm), pp. 65–99.

Currie, D.A. (1979) 'Stabilisation Policy in an Open Economy', in S. Cook and P. Jackson (eds), *Current Issues in Fiscal Policy* (Oxford: Martin Robertson), pp. 108–22.

Currie, D.A. (1985), Macroeconomic Policy Design and Control Theory – A Failed Partnership?', Economic Journal vol. 95, June, pp. 285–306.

Cuthbertson, K. (1985), *The Demand and Supply of Money,* (Oxford: Blackwell).

Daley, V. and Hadjimatheou, G. (1981) 'Stochastic Implications of the Life-cycle-permanent Income Hypothesis: Evidence for the UK Economy: Comment', *Journal of Political Economy,* vol. 89, June, pp. 596–599.

Davidson, J.E.H.. Hendry, D.F., Srba, F. and Yeo, S. (1978) 'Econometric Modelling of the Aggregate Time Series Relationship Between Consumers Expenditure and Income in the UK,' *Economic Journal,* vol. 88, December, pp. 661–92.

De Grauwe, P. (1983) *Macroeconomic Theory for the Open Economy* (Aldershot: Gower).

De Grauwe, P. (1997) *The Economics of Monetary Integration*, 3rd edn (Oxford: Oxford University Press).

Deaton, A. (1978) 'Involuntary Saving Through Unanticipated Inflation,' *American Economic Review,* vol. 67, pp. 899–910.

Deaton, A. (1992) *Understanding Consumption* (Oxford: Oxford University Press).

Denison, E.F. (1967) *Why Growth Rates Differ* (Washington DC: The Brookings Institution).

Denison, E.F. (1985) *Trends in American Economic Growth, 1929–1982* (Washington, DC: The Brookings Institution).

Dornbusch, R. (1975) 'A Portfolio Balance Model of the Open Economy', *Journal of Monetary Economics,* vol. 1, pp. 3–20.

Dornbusch, R. (1976) 'Expectations and Exchange Rate Dynamics', *Journal of Political Economy,* vol. 84, pp. 1161–76.

Duesenberry, J.S. (1949) *Income, Saving and the Theory of Consumer Behaviour* (Cambridge Mass.: Harvard University Press).

Eckaus, R.S. (1953) 'The Acceleration Principle Reconsidered', *Quarterly Journal of Economics,* vol. 67, May,n pp. 209–30.

Farrell, M. (1959) 'The New Theories of the Consumption Function', *Economic Journal,* vol. 69, pp. 678–96.

Fazzari, S.M., Hubbard, R.G. and Peterson, B.C. (1988) 'Financing Constraints and Corporate Investment', *Brookings Papers on Economic Activity,* no. 1, pp. 141–95.

Ferber, R. (1973) 'Consumer Economics: A Survey', *Journal of Economic Literature,* vol. 11, pp. 1303–42.

Fischer, S. (1977) 'Long-Term Contracts, Rational Expectations and the Optimal Money Supply Rule', *Journal of Political Economy,* vol. 85, February, pp. 191–205.

Fischer, S. (1988) 'Recent Developments in Macroeconomics', *Economic Journal,* vol. 98, pp. 294–339.

Fleming, J.M. (1962) 'Domestic Financial Policies Under Fixed and Under Floating Exchange Rates', *IMF Staff Papers,* vol. 9, November, pp. 369–79.

Flemming, J.S. (1976) *Inflation* (Oxford: Oxford University Press).

Frankel, J.A. and Froot, K.A. (1987) 'Using Survey Data to Test Standard Propositions Regarding Exchange Rate Expectations', *American Economic Review,* vol. 77, March, pp. 133–53.

Frenkel, J.A. and Johnson, H.G. (1976) 'The Monetary Approach to the Balance of Payments: Essential Concepts and Historical Origins', in J.A. Frenkel and H.G. Johnson (eds), *The Monetary Approach to the Balance of Payments* (London: Allen & Unwin), pp. 21–45.

Frenkel, J.A. and Razin, A. (1987) 'The Mundell-Fleming Model; A Quarter Century Later: A Unified Exposition', *IMF Staff Papers,* vol. 34, December, pp. 567–620.

Friedman, B. (1975) 'Targets, Instruments and Indicators of Monetary Policy', *Journal of Monetary Economics,* vol. 1, pp. 443–73.

Friedman, B. (1990) 'Targets and Instruments of Monetary Policy', in B. Friedman and F.H. Hahn (eds), *A Handbook of Monetary Economics*, vol. 2, (Amsterdam: North Holland), pp. 1185–230.

Friedman, M. (1948) 'A Monetary and Fiscal Framework for Economic Stability', *American Economic Review,* vol. 38, June, pp. 245–64.

Friedman, M. (1956) 'The Quantity Theory of Money: A Restatement', in M. Friedman (ed.), *Studies in the Quantity Of Money* (Chicago: University of Chicago Press), pp. 3–15.

Friedman, M. (1957) *A Theory of the Consumption Function* (Princeton, N.J.: Princeton University Press).

Friedman, M. (1959) 'The Demand for Money: Some Theoretical and Empirical Results', *Journal of Political Economy,* vol. 67, August, pp. 327–51.

Friedman, M. (1968) 'The Role of Monetary Policy', *American Economic Review,* vol. 58, March, pp. 1–15.

Friedman, M. (1972) 'Comments on the Critics', *Journal of Political Economy,* vol. 80, September/ October, pp. 906–50.

Friedman, M. (1975) 'Unemployment Versus Inflation: An Evaluation of the Phillips Curve', *IEA Occasional Paper* no. 44 (London: Institute of Economic Affairs).

Friedman, M. and Heller, W.W. (1969) *Monetary ver-sus Fiscal Policy: A Dialogue* (New York: Norton & Co).

Friedman, M. and Schwartz, A. (1963b) 'Money and Business Cycles', *Review of Economics and Statistics,* vol. 45, supplement, pp. 32–64.

Friedman, M. and Schwartz, A. (1963a) *A Monetary History of the United States, 1867–1960* (Princeton: Princeton University Press).

Friedman, M. and Schwartz, A. (1982) *Monetary Trends in the United States and the United Kingdom: Their Relation to Income, Prices and Interest Rates, 1867–1975* (Chicago: University of Chicago Press).

Frish, H. (1983) *Theories of Inflation* (Cambridge: Cambridge University Press).

Froot, K.A. and Frankel, J.A. (1989) 'Forward Discount Bias: Is it an Exchange Risk Premium?' *Quarterly Journal of Economics,* vol. 104, February, pp. 139–61.

Galor, O. and Zeira, J. (1993) 'Income Distribution and Macroeconomics', *Review of Economic Studies,* vol. 60, pp. 35–52.

Goldfeld, S.M. (1973) 'The Demand for Money Revisited', *Brookings Papers on Economic Activity,* vol. 3, pp. 1196–229.

Goldfeld, S.M. (1976) 'The Case of the Missing Money', *Brookings Papers on Economic Activity,* vol. 3, pp. 577–638.

Goldstein, M. and Kahm, M.S. (1985) 'Income and Fute Effects in Foreign Trade', in R.W. Jone and P. B.Kenen (eds) *Handbook of international Economics* vol. II (Amsterdam: Elaevier).

Goodhart, C.A.E. and Crockett, A.D. (1970) 'The Importance of Money', *Bank of England Quarterly Bulletin,* no. 10, pp. 159–198.

Goodwin, R.M. (1947) 'The Multiplier', In S.E. Harris (ed.), *The New Economics* (New York: Knopf), pp. 482–99.

Gordon, R.J. (1976) 'Recent Developments in the Theory of Inflation and Unemployment', *Journal of Monetary Economics,* vol. 2, pp. 185–219.

Gordon, R.J. (1990) 'What is New-Keynesian Economics?' *Journal of Economic Literature,* vol. 28, September, pp. 1115–171.

Gray, M.R., Ward, R. and Zis, G. (1976) 'The World Demand for Money Function: some preliminary results', in J.M. Parkin and G. Zis (eds), *Inflation in the World Economy* (Manchester: Manchester University Press), pp. 151–78.

Greenwald, B. and Stiglitz, J. (1993) 'New and Old Keynesians', *Journal of Economic Perspectives,* vol. 7, pp. 23–44.

Grice, J. and Bennett, A. (1984) 'Wealth and the Demand for £M3 in the United Kingdom, 1963–1978', *The Manchester School,* vol. 52, September, pp. 239–71.

Haberler, G. (1949) 'The Market for Foreign Exchange and the Stability of the Balance of Payments: A Theoretical Analysis', *Kyklos,* vol. 3, pp. 193–218.

Hacche, G. (1974) 'The Demand for Money in the UK: Experience Since 1971', *Bank of England Quarterly Bulletin,* vol. 14, September, pp. 284–305.

Hacche, G. (1979) *The Theory of Economic Growth: An Introduction* (London: Macmillan).

Hagen, E.E. (1966) 'The Classical Theory of the Level of Output and Employment', in M.G. Mueller (ed.), *Readings in Macroeconomics* (New York: Holt, Rinehart & Winston), pp. 3–15.

Hahn, F.H. and Matthews, R.C.O. (1964) 'The Theory of Economic Growth: A Survey', *Economic Journal,* vol. 74, December, pp. 779–902.

Hall, R.E. (1978) 'Stochastic Implications of the Life Cycle-Permanent Income Hypothesis: Theory and Evidence', *Journal of Political Economy,* vol. 86, December, pp. 971–87.

Hall, R.L. and Hitch, C.J. (1939), 'Price theory and business behaviour', *Oxford Economic Papers, no.* 2, May, pp. 12–45.

Hall, S.G., Henry, S.G.B. and Wilcox, J.B. (1989) 'The Long-Run Determinants of the UK Monetary Aggregates', *Bank of England Discussion Paper*, August.

Hansen, A.H. (1953) *A Guide to Keynes* (New York: McGraw-Hill).

Harris, L. (1981) *Monetary Theory* (New York: McGraw-Hill).

Hawtrey, R.G. (1913) *Good and Bad Trade* (London: Constable).

Hayek, F. A. (1931) *Prices and Production*, 2nd edn (London: Routledge & Keegan Paul).

Hendry, D.F. and Ericsson, N.R. (1987) 'Modeling the Demand for Narrow Money in the UK and in the US', *European Economic Review,* vol. 35, pp. 833–86.

Hendry, D.F. and Mizon, G.E. (1978) 'Serial Correlation as a Convenient Simplification, Not a Nuisance', *Economic Journal,* vol. 88, pp. 549–63.

Henry, S.G.B. and Ormerod, P.A. (1978) 'Incomes Policy and Wage Inflation: Empirical Evidence for the UK 1961–1977', *National Institute Economic Review,* vol. 98, pp. 31–39.

Hicks, J.R. (1937) 'Mr Keynes and the Classics: A Suggested Interpretation', *Econometrica,* vol. 5, pp. 147–59.

Hicks, J.R. (1950) *A Contribution to the Theory of the Trade Cycle* (Oxford: Oxford University Press).

Hicks, J.R. (1971) *The Social Framework*, 4th edn (Oxford: Oxford University Press).

Hicks, J.R. (1992) 'The Unification of Macroeconomics', in A. Vercelli and N. Dimitri (eds) *Macroeconomics: A Survey of Research Strategies* (Oxford: Oxford University Press), pp. 3–15.

Hines, A.G. (1964) 'Trade Unions and Wage Inflation in the United Kingdom: 1893–1961', *Review of Economic Studies,* vol. 31, October, pp. 221–52.

Hines, A.G. (1971) *On the Reappraisal of Keynesian Economics* (London: Martin Robertson).

Hoover, K.D. (1985) *The New Classical Macroeconomics* (Oxford: Blackwell).

Jackman, R. , Mulvey, C. and Trevithick, J. (1982) *The Economics of Inflation,* 2nd edn (Oxford: Martin Robertson).

Jenkinson, N. (1981) 'Investment, Profitability and the Valuation Ratio', *Bank of England Discussion Paper* no. 17, September.

Johnson, H.G. (1958) 'Towards a General Theory of the Balance of Payments', in H.G. Johnson, *International Trade and Economic Growth* (London: Allen & Unwin), pp. 153–68.

Jones, H. (1975) *An Introduction to Modern Theories of Economic Growth* (London: Nelson).

Jorgenson, D.W. (1963) 'Capital Theory and Investment Behaviour', *American Economic Review,* vol. 53, pp. 247–59.

Jorgenson, D.W. (1971) 'Econometric Studies of Invest-ment Behaviour', *Journal of Economic Literature,* vol. 9, pp. 1111–147.

Jorgenson, D.W. (1988) 'Productivity and Postwar US Economic Growth', *Journal of Economic Perspectives,* vol. 2, Fall, pp. 23–41.

Judd, J. and Scadding, J. (1982) 'The Search for a Stable Demand for Money Function', *Journal of Economic Literature,* vol. 20, September, pp. 993–1023.

Junankar, P.N. (1972) *Investment: Theories and Evidence* (London: Macmillan).

Juster, F.T. and Wachtel, P. (1972) 'Inflation and the Consumer', *Brookings Papers on Economic Activity,* no. 1, pp. 71–114.

Kahn, R.F. (1931) 'On the Relation of Home Investment to Unemployment', *Economic Journal,* vol. 41, June, pp. 173–98.

Kaldor, N. (1966) 'Marginal Productivity and the Macroeconomic Theories of Distribution', *Review of Economic Studies,* vol. 33, pp. 309–19.

Kalecki, M. (1939) *Essays in the Theory of Economic Fluctuations* (London: Allen & Unwin).

Keynes, J.M. (1936) *The General Theory of Employment, Interest and Money* (London: Macmillan).

Keynes, J.M. (1937) 'The General Theory of Employment', *Quarterly Journal of Economics,* vol. 51, February, pp. 209–23.

King, D.N. (1984) *An Introduction to National Income Accounting* (London: Edward Arnold)

King, R.G. (1993) 'Will New Keynesian Macroeconomics Resurrect the IS–LM Model?' *Journal of Economic Perspectives,* vol. 7, Spring, pp. 67–82.

Kitson, M. and Michie, J. (1996) 'Britain's Industrial Performance Since 1960: Under-Investment and Relative Decline', *Economic Journal,* vol. 106, pp. 196–212.

Knox, A.D. (1952) 'The Acceleration Principle and the Theory of Investment: A survey', *Economica,* vol. 19, August, pp. 269–97.

Kouri, P.J.K. and Porter, M.G. (1974) 'International Capital Flows and Portfolio Equilibrium', *Journal of Political Economy,* vol. 82, pp. 443–67.

Kremers, J.J.M. and Lane, T.D. (1991) 'Economic and Monetary Integration and the Aggregate Demand for Money in the EMS,' *IMF Staff Papers,* no. 37, pp. 777–805.

Kuznets, S. (1946) *National Product Since 1869* (New York: National Bureau of Economic Research).

Kydland, F. and Prescott, E. (1977) 'Rules Rather than Discretion: The Inconsistency of Optimal Plans', *Journal of Political Economy,* vol. 85, pp. 473–91.

Kydland, F.E. and Prescott, E.C. (1982) 'Time to Build and Aggregate Fluctuations', *Econometrica,* vol. 50, pp. 1345–69.

Laidler, D.E.W. (1993) *The Demand for Money,* 4th Edn (New York: HarperCollins).

Laidler, D.E.W. and Parkin, J.M. (1970) 'The Demand for Money in the UK 1955–67: Preliminary Estimates', *Manchester School,* vol. 38, September pp. 187–208.

Laidler, D.E.W. and Parkin, J.M. (1975) 'Inflation: A Survey', *Economic Journal,* vol. 85, December, pp. 741–809.

Laursen, S. and Metzler, L.A. (1950) 'Flexible Exchange Rates and the Theory of Employment', *Review of Economics and Statistics,* vol. 32, pp. 281–99.

Layard, R. and Nickell, S. (1986) 'Unemployment in Britain', *Economica,* vol. 53, supplement, pp. S121–69.

Leibenstein, H. (1957) 'The Theory of Under development in Backward Economies', *Journal of Political Economy,* vol. 65, April, pp. 91–103.

Leijonhufvud, A. (1968) *On Keynesian Economics and the Economics of Keynes* (Oxford: Oxford University Press).

Lerner, A. (1994) *The Economics of Control* (London: Macmillan).

Lipsey, R.G. (1960) 'The Relation Between Unemployment and the Rate of Change of Money Wage Rates in the United Kingdom, 1862–1957: a further analysis', *Economica,* vol. 27, February, pp. 1–31.

Lothian, J. (1997) 'Multi-Country Evidence on the Behaviour of Purchasing Power Parity Under the Current Float', *Journal of International Money and Finance,* vol. 16, pp. 19–35.

Lucas, R.E. (1972) 'Expectations and the Neutrality of Money', *Journal of Economic Theory,* vol. 4, pp. 103–124.

Lucas, R.E. (1975) 'An Equilibrium Model of the Business Cycle', *Journal of Political Economy,* vol. 83, December, pp. 1113–44.

Lucas, R.E. (1976) 'Econometric Policy Evaluation: A Critique', *Carnegie-Rochester Conference Series on Public Policy,* vol. 1, pp. 19–46.

Lucas, R.E. (1977), 'Understanding Business Cycles', in K. Brunner and A. Meltzer (eds) *Stabilisation of the Domestic and International Economy* (Amsterdam: North Holland), pp. 7–29.

Lucas, R.E. (1980) 'Methods and Problems in Business Cycle Theory', *Journal of Money Credit and Banking*, vol. 12, November, pp. 696–714.

Lucas, R.E. (1988) 'On the Mechanisms of Economic Development', *Journal of Monetary Economics,* vol. 22, July, pp. 3–42.

Lucas, R.E. and Rapping, L. (1969) 'Real Wages, Employment and Inflation', *Journal of Political Economy,* vol. 77, September/October, pp. 721–54.

MacDonald, R. and Taylor, M.P. (1992) 'Exchange Rate Economics: A Survey', *IMF Staff Papers,* vol. 39, March, pp. 1–57.

Machlup, F. (1939) 'The Theory Foreign Exchanges', *Economics,* vol.6, pp. 379–97.

Machlup, F. (1955) 'Relative Prices and Aggregate spending in the analysis of Devalution, *American Economic Review*, Vol. 45, pp. 225–278.

Maddison, A. (1987) 'Growth and Slowdown in Advanced Capitalist Economies', *Journal of Economic Literature,* vol. 25, June, pp. 649–98.

Maddison, A. (1991) *Dynamic Forces in Capitalist Development: A Long-run Comparative View* (Oxford: Oxford University Press).

Malinvaud, E. (1977) *The Theory of Unemployment Reconsidered* (Oxford: Blackwell).

Mankiw, N.G. (1985) 'Small Menu Costs and Large Business Cycles: A Macroeconomic Model of Monopoly', *Quarterly Journal of Economics,* vol. 100, pp. 529–39.

Mankiw, N.G. (1989) 'Real Business Cycles: A New Keynesian Perspective', *Journal of Economic Perspectives,* vol. 3, Summer, pp. 79–90.

Mankiw, N.G., Romer, D. and Weil, D.N. (1992) 'A Contribution to the Empirics of Economic Growth', *Quarterly Journal of Economics,* vol. 107, pp. 407–37.

Marshall, A. (1962)[1920] *Principles of Economics,* 8th edn (London: Macmillan).

Marshall, A. (1923) *Credit and Commerce,* (London: Macmillan).

Marx, K. (1970–72)[1867] *Capital,* 3 vols (London: Lawrence & Wishart).

McDonald, I.M. and Solow, R.M. (1981) 'Wage Bargaining and Employment', *American Economic Review,* vol. 71, December, pp. 896–908.

McKinnon, R.I. (1969) 'Portfolio Balance and International Payments Adjustment', in Mundell, R.A. and Swoboda, A.K. (eds), *Monetary Problems of the International Economy* (Chicago: Chicago University Press), pp. 199–235.

McKinnon, R.I. and Oates, W.R. (1966) 'The Implications of International Economic Integration for Monetary, Fiscal and Exchange Rate Policy', *Princeton Studies in International Finance,* no. 16, Princeton University, New Jersey.

Mill, J.S. (1965)[1848] *Principles of Political Economy* (New York: Kelley).

Miller, M. (1985) 'Measuring the Stance of Fiscal Policy', *Oxford Review of Economic Policy,* vol. 1, pp. 44–57.

Milner, C., Mizen, P. and Pentecost, E.J. (1996) 'Trade, Currency Services and Currency Substitution in Europe', *Weltwirtschaftliches Archiv,* vol. 132, pp. 160–71.

Minford, P. and Peel, D. (1983) *Rational Expectations and the New Macroeconomics* (Oxford: Martin Robertson).

Mizen, P. and Pentecost, E.J. (1994) 'Evaluating the Empirical Evidence for Currency Substitution: A Case Study of the Demand for Sterling in Europe', *Economic Journal,* vol. 104, pp. 1057–69.

Modigliani, F. (1944) 'Liquidity Preference and the Theory of Interest and Money', *Econometrica,* vol. 12, pp. 45–88.

Modigliani, F. (1977) 'The Monetarist Controversy, or Should We Forsake Stabilisation Policies?' *American Economic Review,* vol. 67, March, pp. 1–19.

Modigliani, F. and Brumberg, R. (1954) 'Utility Analysis and the Consumption Function: An Interpretation of Cross Section Data', in K.K. Kurihara (ed.), *Post-Keynesian Economics.* (New Brunswick, NJ: Rutgers University Press), pp. 388–436.

Mullineux, A., Dickinson, D.G. and Peng, W. (1993) *Business Cycles: Theory and Evidence* (Oxford: Blackwell).

Mun, T. (1664) *England's Treasure by Forraign Trade, or the Ballance of our Forraign Trade is the Rule of Our Treasure,* London.

Mundell, R.A. (1963) 'Capital Mobility and Stabilisation Policy Under Fixed and Flexible Exchange Rates', *Canadian Journal of Economics and Political Science,* vol. 29, November, pp. 475–85.

Nelson, C.R. and Plosser, C.I. (1982) 'Trends and Random Walks in Economic Time Series: Some Evidence and Applications', *Journal of Monetary Economics,* vol. 10, pp. 139–62.

Nickell, S. (1997) 'Unemployment and Labour Marker Rigidities: Europe versus North America,' *Journal of Economic Perspectives,* vol. 11, Summer, pp. 55–74.

Nicoletti, G. (1988) 'Private Consumption, Inflation and the "Debt Neutrality Hypothesis": The Case of Eight OECD Countries', *Department of Economics and Statistics Working Papers,* no. 50 (Paris: OECD), January.

Niehans, J. (1984) *International Monetary Economics* (Deddington: Philip Allan).

Officer, L. (1976) 'The Purchasing Power Theory of Exchange Rates: A Review Article', *IMF Staff Papers,* no. 23, pp. 1–16.

Okun, A.M. (1962) 'Potential GNP: Its Measurement and Significance', in *Proceedings of the Business and Economics Statistics Section, American Statistical Association,* pp. 98–110.

Okun, A.M. (1981) *Prices and Quantities.* (Washington DC: Brookings Institution).

Ott, D. and Ott, A. (1965) 'Budget Balance and Equilibrium Income', *Journal of Finance,* vol. 20, pp. 71–77.

Oulton, N. (1981) 'Aggregate Investment and Tobin's Q: The Evidence from Britain,' *Oxford Economic Papers,* vol. 2, July, pp. 177–202.

Parkin, J.M., Richards, I. and Zis, G. (1975) 'The Determination and Control of the World Money Supply under Fixed Exchange Rates', *The Manchester School,* vol. 43, September, pp. 293–316.

Parkin, J.M., Sumner, M.T. and Jones, R.A. (1972) 'A Survey of the Econometric Evidence of the Effects of Incomes Policy on the Rate of Inflation', in J.M. Parkin and M.T. Sumner (eds), *Incomes Policy and Inflation* (Manchester: Manchester University Press), pp. 1–19.

Peaker, A. (1974) *Economic Growth in Modern Britain* (London: Macmillan).

Pentecost, E.J. (1983) 'Government Financing Constraint, Wealth Effects and External Balance, *Southern Economic Journal,* vol. 50, April, pp. 1174–81.

Pentecost, E.J. (1993) *Exchange Rate Dynamics: A Modern Approach to Theory and Evidence* (Aldershot: Edward Elgar).

Pentecost, E.J. (1997) 'Currency Substitution and Exchange Rate Policy within the European Union, in P. Karadeloglou (ed.), *Exchange Rate Policies for Europe* (Basingstoke: Macmillan), pp. 110–31.

Petty, W. (1662) *A Treatise of Taxes and Contributions*, London.

Phillips, A.W. (1958) 'The Relation Between Unemployment and the Rate of Change of Money Wages Rates in the United Kingdom, 1961–1957', *Economica,* vol. 25, November, pp. 283–99.

Pigou, A.C. (1927) *Industrial Fluctuations* (London: Macmillan).

Pigou, A.C. (1933) *Theory of Unemployment* (London: Macmillian).

Pigou, A.C. (1943) 'The Classical Stationary State,' *Economic Journal*, vol. 53, pp. 343–51.

Pilbeam, K. (1998) *International Finance*, 2nd edn (Basingstoke: Macmillan).

Plosser, C. (1989) 'Real Business Cycles', *Journal of Economic Perspectives,* vol. 3, Summer, pp. 51–78.

Poole, W. (1970) 'Optimal Choice of Monetary Instruments in a Simple Stochastic Macro Model', *Quarterly Journal of Economics,* vol. 84, May, pp. 197–216.

Ricardo, D. (1951)[1817] *Principles of Political Economy and Taxation* (Cambridge: Cambridge University Press).

Robinson, J. (1933) *The Economics of Imperfect Competition (*London: Macmillan).

Robinson, J. (1937) 'The Foreign Exchanges', in her Collected Economic Papers vol. IV (Oxford: Blackwell).

Robinson, R. (1952) 'A Graphical Analysis of the Foreign Trade Multiplier', *Economic Journal,* vol. 62, September, pp. 546–64.

Rogoff, K. (1985) 'The Optimal Degree of Commitment to a Monetary Target', *Quarterly Journal of Economics,* vol. 100, November, pp. 1169–89.

Rogoff, K. (1996) 'The Purchasing Power Parity Puzzle', *Journal of Economic Literature,* vol. 34, June, pp. 647–88.

Romer, C.D. (1999) 'Change in Business Cycles: Evidence and Explanations', *Journal of Economic Perspectives,* vol. 13, Spring, pp. 23–44.

Romer, D.H. (1993) 'The New Keynesian Synthesis', *Journal of Economic Perspectives,* vol. 7, Spring, pp. 5–22.

Romer, P.M. (1986) 'Increasing Returns and Long-Run Growth', *Journal of Political Economy,* vol. 94, October, pp. 1002–37.

Romer, P.M. (1990) 'Endogenous Technical Change', *Journal of Political Economy,* vol. 98, October, pp. S71–S102.

Salop, S. (1979) 'A Model of the Natural Rate of Unemployment', *American Economic Review,* vol. 69, March, pp. 117–25.

Samuelson, P.A. (1939) 'Interactions between the Multiplier Analysis and the Principle of Acceleration', *Review of Economics and Statistics,* vol. 21, May, pp. 75–78.

Samuelson, P.A. (1948) 'The Simple Mathematics of Income Determination', in P.A. Samuelson (ed.), *Income Employment and Public Policy: Essays in Honour of Alvin Hansen* (New York: Norton), pp. 133–55.

Santermero, A.M. and Seater, J.J. (1978) 'The Inflation-Unemployment Trade-Off: A Critique of the Literature', *Journal of Economic Literature,* vol. 16, June, pp. 499–544.

Sapsford, D. and Tzannatos, Z. (1993) *The Economics of the Labour Market* (Basingstoke: Macmillan).

Sargent, T. and Wallace, N. (1975) 'Rational Expectations the Optimal Monetary Instrument and the Optimal Money Supply Rule Policy', *Journal of Political Economy,* vol. 83, April, pp. 241–54.

Sargent, T. and Wallace, N. (1976) 'Rational Expectations and the Theory of Economic Policy', *Journal of Monetary Economics,* vol. 2, April, pp. 168–83.

Sargent, T. and Wallace, N. (1981) 'Some Unpleasant Monetarist Arithmetic', *Federal Reserve Bank of Minneapolis Quarterly Review*, Fall, pp. 1–17.

Savage, D. (1978) 'The Channels of Money Influence: A Survey of the Empirical Evidence', *National Institute Economic Review,* vol. 83, February, pp. 73–89.

Savage, D. (1982) 'Fiscal Policy 1974/5–1980/1: description and measurement', *National Institute Economic Review,* vol. 87, February, pp. 85–95.

Scarth, W.M. (1975) 'Fiscal Policy and the Government Budget Constraint Under Alternative Exchange Rate Regimes', *Oxford Economic Papers,* vol. 27, March, pp. 10–20.

Schumpeter, J.A. (1952) *History of Economic Analysis* (London: Allen & Unwin).

Seater, J.J. (1993) 'Ricardian Equivalence', *Journal of Economic Literature,* vol. 31, March, pp. 142–90.

Shapiro, C. and Stiglitz, J.E. (1984) 'Equilibrium Unemployment as a Worker Discipline Device', *American Economic Review,* vol. 74, June, pp. 433–44.

Shapiro, N. (1977) 'The Revolutionary Character of Post-Keynesian Economics', *Journal of Economic Issues,* vol. 11 (3), pp. 541–60.

Shaw, G.K. (1988) *Keynesian Economics: The Permanent Revolution* (Aldershot: Edward Elgar).

Siebert, H. (1997) 'Labour Market Rigidities: At the Root of Unemployment in Europe', *Journal of Economic Perspectives,* vol. 11, Summer, pp. 37–54.

Silber, W.L (1970) 'Fiscal Policy in IS–LM Analysis: A Correction', *Journal of Money Credit and Banking,* vol. 2, pp. 461–71.

Smith, A. (1961)[1776] *An Inquiry into the Nature and Causes of the Wealth of Nations* (London: Methuen).

Smith, W.L. (1956) 'A Graphical Exposition of the Complete Keynesian System', *Southern Economic Journal,* vol. 23, pp. 115–25.

Solow, R.M. (1956) 'A Contribution to the Theory of Economic Growth', *Quarterly Journal of Economics,* vol. 70, February, pp. 65–94.

Solow, R.M. (1957) 'Technical Change and the Aggregate Production Function', *The Review of Economics and Statistics,* vol. 39, August, pp. 312–20.

Solow, R.M. (1985) 'Insiders and Outsiders in Wage Determination,' *The Scandinavian Journal of Economics,* vol. 87, pp. 411–28.

Spiethoff, A. (1925) 'Krisen' in *Handworterbuch der Staatswissenschaften*, vol. 4, 4th edn.

Stadler, G.W. (1994) 'Real Business Cycles', *Journal of Economic Literature,* vol. 32, pp. 1750–83.

Steuart, J. (1966)[1767] *An Inquiry into the Principles of Political Economy* (Edinburgh: Oliver & Boyd).

Stiglitz, J.E. (1979) 'Equilibrium in Product Markets with Imperfect Information', *American Economic Review,* vol. 69, May, pp. 339–45.

Stiglitz, J.E. (1992) 'Methodological Issues and the New Keynesian Economics', in A. Vercelli and N. Dimitri (eds), *Macroeconomics: A Survey of Research Strategies* (Oxford: Oxford University Press), Chapter 3, pp. 38–86.

Stone, R. and Stone, G. (1977) *National Income and Expenditure*, 10th edn (London: Bowes & Bowes).

Stoneman, P. (1979) 'A Simple Diagrammatic Apparatus for the Investigation of a Macroeconomic Model of Temporary Equilibrium', *Economica,* no. 46, March, pp. 23–27.

Summers, L.H. (1981) 'Taxation and Corporate Investment: a q-Theory Approach', *Brookings Papers on Economic Activity,* vol. 1, pp. 67–127.

Summers, L.H. (1986) 'Why is the Unemployment Rate so very High near full Employment', *Brookings Papers on Economic Activity,* no. 2, pp. 339–83.

Sumner, M.T. (1984) 'The History and Significance of the Phillips Curve', in D. Demery, N.W. Duck, M.T. Sumner, R.L. Thomas, and W.N. Thompson, *Macroeconomics* (Harlow: Longman), pp. 169–225.

Surrey, M.J.C. (1989) 'Aggregate Consumption and Saving', in D. Greenaway (ed.), *Current Issues in Macroeconomics* (Basingstoke: Macmillan), pp. 132–62.

Swan, T.W. (1955) 'Longer Run Problems of the Balance of Payments', in H.W. Arndt and M.W. Corden (eds), *The Australian Economy: A Volume of Readings* (Melbourne: Cheshire Press), vol. 1963, pp. 384–95.

Swan, T.W. (1956) 'Economic Growth and Capital Accumulation', *Economic Record* 32, November, pp. 334–61.

Swoboda, A.K. (1977) 'Monetary Approach to Worldwide Inflation', in L.B. Krause and W.S. Salant (eds), *Worldwide Inflation* (Washington DC: Brookings Institute), pp. 9–62.

Taylor, J.B. (1979) 'Staggered Wage Setting in a Macro Model', *American Economic Review,* vol. 69, pp. 108–13.

Taylor, M.P. (1990) *The Balance of Payments: New Perspectives on Open Economy Macroeconomics* (Aldershot: Edward Elgar).

Temple, J. (1999) 'The New Growth Evidence', *Jour-nal of Economic Literature,* vol. 37, March, pp. 112–56.

Tew, J.B.H. (1999) 'Kalecki's "Essays in the Theory of Economic Fluctuations"', *Review of Political Economy,* vol. 11, pp. 273–82.

Theil, H. (1961) *Economic Forecasts and Policy* (Amsterdam: North Holland).

Theil, H. (1964) *Optimal Decision Rules for Government and Industry* (Amsterdam: North Holland).

Thomas, R.L. (1984) 'The Consumption Function', in D. Demery, N.W. Duck, M.T. Sumner, R.L. Thomas, and W.N. Thompson, *Macroeconomics* (Harlow: Longman), pp. 53–99.

Thomas, R.L. (1991) *Using Mathematics in Economics* (Harlow: Longman).

Timbrell, M. (1989) 'Contracts and Market Clearing in the Labour Market', in D. Greenaway (ed.), *Current Issues in Macroeconomics* (Basingstoke: Macmillan), pp. 68–90.

Tinbergen, J. (1952) *On the Theory of Economic Policy* (Amsterdam: North Holland).

Tobin, J. (1956) 'The Interest Elasticity of the Transactions Demand for Cash', *Review of Economics and Statistics,* vol. 38, August, pp. 241–47.

Tobin, J. (1958) ' Liquidity Preference as Behaviour towards Risk', *Review of Economic Studies,* vol. 25, pp. 65–86.

Tobin, J. (1969) 'The General Equilibrium Approach to Monetary Theory', *Journal of Money, Credit and Banking,* vol. 1, pp. 15–29.

Tobin, J. (1972a) 'Inflation and Unemployment', *American Economic Review,* vol. 62, March, pp. 1–18.

Tobin, J. (1972b) 'Friedman's Theoretical Framework', *Journal of Political Economy,* vol. 80, September/ October, 852–63.

Tobin, J. (1975) 'Keyneisian Models of Recession and Depression,' *American Economic Review,* vol. 65, May, pp. 195–202.,

Tobin, J. and Buiter, W.H. (1976) 'Long-Run Effects of Fiscal and Monetary Policy on Aggregate Demand', in J.L. Stein (ed.), *Monetarism* (Amsterdam: North Holland), pp. 273–309.

Townend, J.C. (1976) 'The Personal Saving Ratio', *Bank of England Quarterly Bulletin,* vol. 16, March, pp. 53–73.

Tugan-Baranowsky, M.I. (1894) *Industrial Crises in England* (in Russian), German translation 1901; French translation 1913.

Wisniewski, M. (1991) *Introducing Mathematical Methods in Economics* (London: McGraw Hill).

Yellen, J.L. (1984) 'Efficiency Wage Models of Unemployment', *American Economic Review,* vol. 74, May, pp. 200–5.

Young, A. (1995) 'The Tyranny of Numbers: Confronting the Statistical Realities of the East Asian Growth Experience', *Quarterly Journal of Economics,* vol. 110, August, pp. 641–80.

Author Index

Subject Index